VISUAL QUICKPRO GUIDE

MACROMEDIA
DREAMWEAVER MX
ADVANCED

FOR WINDOWS AND MACINTOSH

J. Tarin Towers, Sasha Magee, and Abie Hadjitarkhani

◯ Peachpit Press

Visual QuickPro Guide
Macromedia Dreamweaver MX Advanced for Windows and Macintosh
J. Tarin Towers, Sasha Magee, and Abie Hadjitarkhani

Peachpit Press

1249 Eighth Street
Berkeley, CA 94710
510/524-2178
800/283-9444
510/524-2221 (fax)
Find us on the World Wide Web at: http://www.peachpit.com
To report errors, please send a note to errata@peachpit.com
Published by Peachpit Press in association with Macromedia Press
Peachpit Press is a division of Pearson Education

Macromedia Press Editor: Wendy Sharp
Project Editor: Cary Norsworthy
Editor: Jill Marts Lodwig
Technical Editor: Angela Drury at Macromedia Press
Production Coordinator: David Van Ness
Copyeditor: Dave Awl
Compositors: Maureen Forys, Kate Kaminski
Indexer: Emily Glossbrenner
Cover Design: The Visual Group, Maureen Forys
Cover Production: Nathalie Valette

ISBN 0-321-15946-2

9 8 7 6 5 4 3 2 1
Printed and bound in the United States of America

Acknowledgments

We'd like to thank everyone who helped us with this book: Jill Lodwig, who shepherded the book through with a combination of heroic patience and an eye for Lilliputian detail; Dave Awl, for copyediting, jokes, and random advice on historical astrology and the Mac; Cary Norsworthy, as always, for helping us across the river; Eunice Holland, who contributed research and art to Chapter 18; Alexander Hearnz, for his contribution to Chapter 16; Paul Toney, for various wise counsels; Marjorie Baer and Nancy Ruenzel for their diligence and patience; David Van Ness, for coordinating the pages and art and making a good-looking book; Wendy Sharp, Peachpit's Macromedia Press contact; Eric Ott, Scott Unterberg, and the whole Dreamweaver/Kojak team at Macromedia for helping us get the stuff we needed; Angela Drury, Macromedia's thorough tech reviewer; the good folks behind the scenes at Macromedia, for writing an even better product; and many, many faithful readers who sent in comments, suggestions, compliments, questions, and encouragement.

The following sites gave us generous permission to reproduce their designs: MySQL.org; Adrian Scott of Ryze (`www.ryze.org`); Marc Liyanage (`www.entropy.ch`); and XMethods (`www.xmethods.net`).

We'd also like to thank everyone who saw us through, including Adrian Chan, Karen Whitehouse, Richard Marshall, Kelleigh Trowbridge, Brett Bowman, Mike Williams, Kenne MacKillop, and Peter Grandmaison.

Dedication

For Matthew and Katy Towers, and Amos Magee

CONTENTS AT A GLANCE

TABLE OF CONTENTS

INTRODUCTION

Welcome to the *Dreamweaver MX Advanced for Windows and Macintosh: Visual QuickPro Guide!* Dreamweaver (**Figures 1** and **2**) offers an incredibly robust combination of features. It's simple to use and it's one of the very best WYSIWYG (What You See Is What You Get) Web-page editing tools ever to come down the pike.

Dreamweaver offers speed and capability when constructing page essentials such as links, images, forms, frames, layers, and cascading style sheets.

But Dreamweaver doesn't just make pages. Dreamweaver MX now offers full integration with your database application server to help you get text, images, and more from your database and onto your pages. Using Live Data view and Dreamweaver's server behaviors, you can display your dynamically generated pages right in the document window as if they were static HTML.

Dreamweaver also offers a vast array of tools for editing your code, whether it's HTML, JavaScript, XHTML, XML, CSS, or any kind of page on a dynamic server platform.

And Dreamweaver's tools take your pages from your desktop to your live site. In the Site window, you can view your files on your computer, your live production server, and your testing server, all without batting an eye. You can upload and download your files using Dreamweaver's checkout tools or in combination with many popular content management tools.

Who Should Use This Book?

This book assumes some familiarity with Dreamweaver and HTML, although we try not to make assumptions or skip any steps. We wrote this book for people who may already have a Web site or a database but would like to take the interactivity and productivity of their sites to a new level.

We intended this book to introduce the basic concepts of databases and application servers both to those who have never used them before and those with a little experience who want to take full advantage of Dreamweaver's time-saving data management tools. If you're a seasoned pro, you may be excited to learn Dreamweaver can help you automate simple or repetitive tasks, or help you and your colleagues integrate Dreamweaver into your collaborative workspace.

You should use this book if you're:

♦ A database beginner who wants to manage an interactive site without learning how to write application code by hand.

♦ Someone who has a dynamic site up and running with someone else's help and wants to learn how to do it on your own.

♦ A graphic designer who's used to working with Web media, and who wants to design dynamic sites and increase the interactivity level.

♦ A Web expert who likes to hand code but wants to streamline your workspace.

♦ Someone who knows that clean code is important, but who doesn't want to hand code everything.

♦ Someone who needs to learn Dreamweaver MX quickly.

QuickPro Conventions

If you've read any other Visual QuickStart or QuickPro Guides, you know that this book is made up of two main components: numbered lists that take you step by step through the things you want to learn, and illustrations that show you exactly what we're doing, anyway.

We explain what needs to be explained, but we don't waste your time reminiscing about the bygone days of ANSI terminals and hand coding entire sites using VI.

✔ Tips

- In every chapter, you'll find tips like these that point out extra information, short-cuts, and alternate methods of completing a task.

- Sometimes you can find extra tidbits of info in the figure captions, too.

- Code in the book is set off in `code font`.

- When we refer to the menu bar, it's the main Document window menu bar unless we specify otherwise.

Our technology

This book was written and researched on several computers: PCs running Windows XP, NT, and 98; and Macintosh computers running OS 9.1 and OS X. When showing Windows XP, we used the Windows Classic Style Appearance Settings in the screen shots to try to represent what the average Windows user would see when using Dreamweaver MX.

Tough Characters: Wrapping Code onto Extra Lines

The pages of this book are obviously narrower than most computer monitors. Because of that, in the code throughout this book, we often had to continue a long single line of code onto a second line. When this happened, we indented the wrapped lines onto additional lines and inserted an → at the beginning of those lines. For example:

```
This is the first part of the long
→ line of code and the line continues
→ down here.
```

You don't have to type these characters. In a few chapters, we do indicate tabs or line breaks as special characters, but those instances are clearly marked.

What's In this Book?

Here's a quick rundown of what we cover in this book.

Diving in to databases and dynamic content

In the first four chapters we introduce you to databases and the Dreamweaver interface (**Figure 1**). We help you get your files set up, both locally and on your testing server. We review basic database and data management concepts, and show you how to poke around the back end of your application server using SQL.

Serving dynamic pages and dynamic content

Chapters 5 through 8 show you how to create recordsets and introduce live data on your pages. Using Live Data view (**Figure 2**), you can display text and images from your database in the Document window as if your page were live and being served to a Web browser. You'll be able to include active forms on your pages, as well as dynamically served text, images, CSS, and HTML attributes. You'll be able to create pages that query results from a search tool or a catalog. And you'll be able to update, edit, and delete records using a Web form.

Interactive tools

Web services and ColdFusion components, covered in Chapter 9, are two ways of including on your pages interactive tools that update regularly. In both cases, you can either use shared resources from other sites to display information; or share information from your own database with other Web sites. We use Dreamweaver's server behaviors throughout the book, but in Chapter 10 we dig a little deeper into editing and creating custom server behaviors.

Figure 1 Here's Dreamweaver MX, including the Document window, where you edit your pages. Below that is the Property inspector, for editing all sorts of attributes. To the right are some of Dreamweaver's panels, including the Layers panel, for positioning and modifying DHTML layers; and the Site window docked as a panel on the PC, which lets you manage your files locally and remotely.

Live Data view button

Dynamic text displayed in Live Data view and formatted in Document window

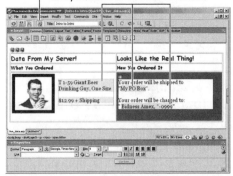

Figure 2 When you work with dynamic pages in the Document window, you can view and format your pages using live data from your testing server.

More Stuff!

The Web site for this book includes links to all the reference URLs we mention; text files for many of the code blocks in this book; and some sample database files you can experiment with if you're unwilling or unable to muck around with your own, real data. You'll find us at
www.peachpit.com/vqp/dreamweaverMX.

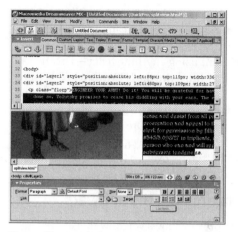

Figure 3 You can view your code and your design at the same time with Split view. Of course, you can also view one or the other.

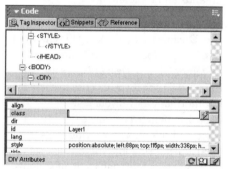

Figure 4 In the Tag Inspector panel, you can set the attributes of a tag either by hand or dynamically.

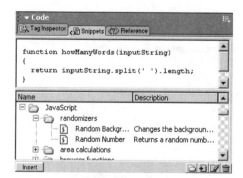

Figure 5 The Snippets panel contains starter code for a lot of useful JavaScript functions and HTML layouts and widgets. You can add your own code to the panel.

Editing and writing code

Chapter 11 dissects Dreamweaver's code editing tools, which you can use to write plain HTML, as well as XHTML, XML, CSS, JavaScript, and all kinds of text and code. You don't have to worry about Dreamweaver chewing up your code, but you can use Dreamweaver's safeguards for all kinds of code checkups: site reports, link checking, spelling checks, code cleanup, and XHTML compliance. If you never want to look at any HTML when you use Dreamweaver, you don't have to; on the other hand, if you want to both work visually and hand code some of the time, Dreamweaver has lots of time-saving tools built in to help you. In this chapter we explain the wide variety of code-editing tools that Dreamweaver presents, all offering variations on hand coding: the Code inspector, Code view and Split view (**Figure 3**), the Snippets panel, the Tag selector and Tag Inspector panel, the Edit Tag command, the Quick Tag editor, and the Tag Chooser.

In Chapter 12 we look at editing custom tag libraries, which you might use in conjunction with XML applications. You can create and define your own custom HTML tags, or you can import custom XML libraries. You can also use the Tag Inspector panel to set the attributes of any of these dynamically (**Figure 4**).

Chapter 13 shows some in-depth serving suggestions for Dreamweaver's JavaScript Behaviors, which are little interactive widgets you can create without having to write and debug JavaScript. However, if you *do* want to write and debug JavaScript, we'll show you some handy shortcuts, including some useful code included in the Snippets panel (**Figure 5**).

continues on next page

Dreamweaver templates, covered in Chapter 14, are accident-resistant, easily updatable HTML documents. New in Dreamweaver MX, you can also use optional regions and repeating regions with template documents, so that pages based on your templates can contain variable information from a catalog or a search request. These templates use XML tags, and you can easily import or export the contents of the tags.

Chapter 15 shows you the ins and outs of head tags, which you can use to improve your chances with the search engines without succumbing to shady spam-unleashing software. You can also control other aspects of your page using head tags, including automatic page refreshes, custom indexing information, and Internet Explorer extensions.

The front end

Chapters 16–19 show you how to create useful, friendly Web interfaces. Chapter 16 discusses accessibility considerations—some sites are required to present information in a manner that's readable by many different kinds of devices, including text-to-speech, large print, Braille, and mobile browsers. Find out what the guidelines are and how to use Dreamweaver to check your pages for cross-device compatibility.

Chapter 17 explores Timelines (**Figure 6**), a fun animation tool you can use to move layers and images across your pages like little movies, without using anything fancy—Dreamweaver will write the HTML layer code and the JavaScript, and you can bring your plain old text and images. Chapter 18 shows how you can work with Dreamweaver to produce different kinds of navigation schemes, including button rollovers, navigation bars, and forms that interact with frames.

Maximizing the software

Chapter 19 shows you how to use the Dreamweaver Document Object Model (DOM) to add your own features to the Dreamweaver interface, including custom commands and toolbars.

Chapter 20 shows you the collaborative features of Dreamweaver, including file checkout names, Design Notes (**Figure 7**), and content management setup. Design Notes are tiny XML-based files that you can use to share file status information with your colleagues. You can also use them to customize the Site window and add columns for viewing and sorting Design Note information. You can also set up many popular content management systems, such as RDS and WebDAV, to work with and track your remote files in the Site window.

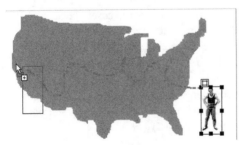

Figure 6 Timelines let you create animated layers without using Flash or writing your own JavaScript.

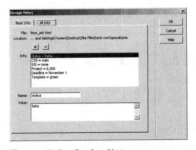

Figure 7 Using Design Notes, you can leave yourself or your colleagues updates and status reports about particular files

Browser Wars

FYI, this is a sidebar. You'll often find advanced, technical, or interesting additions to the how-to lists in sidebars like these throughout the book.

Netscape Navigator and Microsoft Internet Explorer (IE) have a few display differences that may affect your pages subtly. The best way to design for both browsers is to test your pages on both browsers and to compromise where you see differences. Fonts may appear slightly larger in IE. Margins may appear off in IE (or off in Netscape, if you prefer Explorer's way). Table and layer placement are mostly the same, but they're based on slightly different browser margins, so you need to check your work. And there are some differences in how style sheets are processed.

While we were writing this book, the Mozilla project released the first shipping version of the open-source Mozilla browser, which may yet democratize the browser experience. We like Mozilla because it's stable and you can turn off the bells and whistles that other browsers push you around with.

In this book, we show pages in a combination of Netscape and Microsoft browsers.

HTML is HTML

Like the song, HTML remains the same, whether you construct it on a Mac or PC.

No matter how you produce a Web page, it can transport from computer to computer—there's really no such thing as "Mac HTML" or even "Dreamweaver HTML." This is true even for the various flavors of dynamic pages, such as ASP or PHP. The servers may vary in how they process the pages, but your local copies should be the same regardless of platform.

Even better, Dreamweaver's Roundtrip HTML feature ensures that HTML you create outside the program will retain its formatting—although you can ask that Dreamweaver fix some obvious errors for you, such as unclosed tags.

Chapter 11 goes over the various tools and fixes you can use in maintaining, formatting, and checking your code.

WHAT'S IN THIS BOOK

Special to Mac Users

We made the screen captures in this book on both PC and Macintosh computers.

The largest difference between the PC version and the Mac version is in the Site window, which in Windows is alternately docked as a panel (**Figure 8**) or expanded to overtake the entire Dreamweaver interface (**Figure 9**). On the Macintosh (**Figure 10**), the Site window always exists as a separate window from the Document window.

Just as with previous versions of Dreamweaver, Macromedia wrote the program with a code base entirely specific to each platform. Much of the software is itself written in cross-platform languages like JavaScript, XML, and HTML, and the Mac version of Dreamweaver was written for the Mac, not written for Windows and ported over.

The differences between the Mac and Windows versions are negligible, as you can see in **Figure 8** and **Figure 11**.

There are some basic platform differences that will cause the screen shots to look slightly different. Windows windows (ha ha) have a menu bar affixed to each and every window; the Mac menu bar is always at the top of the screen, and it changes based on the program you choose from the Apple menu (the one in the upper right of the Mac screen, next to the clock).

Expander button

Figure 8 On Windows machines, you can dock the Site window as a panel for easy file management access...

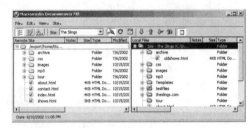

Figure 9 ...or, you can expand it to take up the whole window, so you can view your local files at the same time as your remote or testing server files.

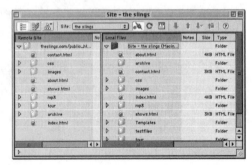

Figure 10 On the Macintosh, the Site window, like the cheese, stands alone.

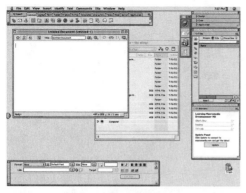

Figure 11 On the Macintosh, everything works pretty much the same as in Windows, although the floating windows float wherever you put them rather than everything acting as self-contained as it does in Figure 8.

Figure 12 For full comparison's sake, this is OS X.

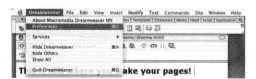

Figure 13 In OS X, the user preferences are under the Application menu.

Windows windows close by clicking on the close box on the upper right, whereas close boxes on the Mac are on the upper left. Occasionally, buttons will have different names. For instance, in some dialog boxes, the button says Browse in Windows and Choose on the Mac. They're always close enough.

There is also the occasional menu difference. In Windows, the Site window includes a Site menu bar. On the Mac, those same commands are included under the Site menu, but occasionally they're under different submenus . We point these differences out where they occur by printing the Windows menu command first and the Macintosh command second, like so: Site > Reports (Site > Site Files View > Reports).

Also, in Mac OS X (**Figure 12**), the Preferences dialog box appears not under the Edit menu but under the Dreamweaver Application menu (**Figure 13**), as do all Preferences dialog boxes in OS X Carbon applications.

Keyboard conventions

When we refer to key commands, we print the Windows command first and the Mac command in parentheses, like this: Press Ctrl+L (Command+L)

Running MX

Dreamweaver MX runs on OS 9.1 or later and OS X. If your Mac won't run a current system, you'll need to stick with Dreamweaver 3 or 4. That's not the end of the world; you'll still be able to make great Web sites, but the newer features in MX won't be available to you. If you want dynamic application capabilities, you can run UltraDev 4, but again, many of MX's features are newer and not included in UltraDev.

Mouse conventions

Some Mac mice have more than one button; some don't. For that matter, some folks don't really use mice at all, they have those touch-pad and stylus thingies. That said, we do refer to right-clicking a lot. On a Windows machine, when you click the right rather than the left mouse button, a context menu appears (**Figure 14**).

Pop-up menus, or context menus, are available on all Mac systems that can run Dreamweaver MX. To make a pop-up menu appear on a Mac, Ctrl+click on the object. Options available from pop-up menus are always available as menu bar options, too, so you'll never miss functionality in Dreamweaver even if you don't right-click.

Figure 14 If you're a Windows user, right-click on an object to pop up a context menu. If you're a Mac user, just click on the object while holding down the Ctrl key. The pop-up menu will appear in a second or two.

What About the Other Book?

Occasionally throughout this book we refer to the book's older sister, *The Dreamweaver MX Visual QuickStart Guide*. Note the word "Start" there—that book is intended as a book for beginning to intermediate users. You can use it as a quick flip reference or to begin learning about making Web pages and using Dreamweaver.

In the book you have in your hands, we assume you're familiar with Dreamweaver and with the basic concepts of HTML and the Web, such as placing images and working with tables. If you need more help with HTML, especially with the nitty-gritty details, here's some of what you'll find there:

◆ How to make links

◆ How HTML links work

◆ How to place images

◆ How to include multimedia files

◆ How to use color on the Web

◆ Designing with tables

◆ Designing with frames

◆ Designing with layers

◆ Creating and updating CSS

◆ JavaScript behavior basics

◆ Basic templates and library items

◆ The ins and outs of FTP and site management

◆ Basic Customization: rearranging menus, using the History panel to repeat tasks, and modifying keyboard shortcuts

We don't skip any steps in this book, but we don't define all the options in, say, the Layers panel. Instead, for topics covered in the other book, we show you just what you need for the task at hand.

And now... on to this book!

About Dynamic Content

HTML is a perfectly good way to create *static* Web pages—pages with content that doesn't change very often. But static pages aren't flexible or easily updated. Dreamweaver MX allows you to create pages that are *dynamic*—their content can vary based on information the user provides, on criteria that you specify ahead of time, or even on the time of day. Examples of dynamic pages in action include search result pages, online shopping carts, and daily publications like online newspapers.

To create pages with dynamic content, Dreamweaver MX generates pages containing HTML, plus additional *server-side* code—commands that the server needs to process before sending the page to the browser. That server-side code often gets its information from a *database* and uses the requested information to fill in the details of the page that users ultimately see in their browsers. A database is a piece of software that stores and sorts pieces of information—and those data can be as simple as a list of names or as complex as a collection of sound and movie files.

In this chapter, we provide an overview of what you can do with dynamic content, what software you'll need to generate it, and how to choose that software.

What Is Dynamic Content?

Dynamic content is all about saving you, the Web developer, time and effort. Suppose you're creating a site for an online store with 1,200 products. You might create 1,200 static pages, with each page detailing a different product. That in itself is very time consuming, but what happens when you decide you need to change the prices? You end up also having to update all 1,200 pages by hand.

Instead, you can create a single dynamic page that displays information about any of the 1,200 products. Then when you need to change the design, price, address, or what have you, you only have to update one page, not all 1,200.

Dynamic content relies on two things: *server-side* code and dynamic data. To process server-side code, you need an *application server*, and to store and retrieve dynamic data, you need a *database*.

Dynamic Content vs. Dynamic HTML

Despite the similar-sounding name, Dynamic HTML (or DHTML) has nothing to do with the dynamic content we describe in the first half of this book.

The term DHTML refers to the combined use of HTML, Cascading Style Sheets (CSS), and JavaScript. DHTML can be used to create simple animations and *visually* dynamic pages (with elements that appear and disappear, follow the cursor around, or move in response to being dragged or clicked on).

In this book, the term *dynamic* refers to a single page with *content* that changes, depending on what information it receives from your database and how you script your application server. Chapters 13, 17, and 18 in this book describe some uses of DHTML to provide interactivity and animation on your page.

For more information about DHTML, refer to Chapter 12 of *JavaScript for the World Wide Web: Visual QuickStart Guide* by Tom Negrino and Dori Smith, or *DHTML and CSS for the World Wide Web: Visual QuickStart Guide* by Jason Cranford Teague, both available from Peachpit Press.

So in the online store example we just discussed, product information is stored in a database, and the dynamic page contains server-side code instead of specific product data. The dynamic page also contains HTML describing the layout for the page, plus any static information that appears on every page, such as the store name, navigation buttons, and copyright information. When a site visitor requests information on a specific product, the server processes the code on the page, retrieves the appropriate data from the database, combines the data with the static elements on the page, and presents the user with the results.

✔ Tips

- Because dynamic pages contain code that needs to be processed by the server, they can't be previewed directly in the browser in the same way plain HTML files can. We discuss how you can configure Dreamweaver MX so that you can preview pages through your server in Chapter 2.

- If you need to change a page design over many pages, you can use Dreamweaver template files, covered in Chapter 14, or Cascading Style Sheets (CSS), which we touch on throughout this book. These are two different technologies that provide the same basic function: When you update a central document that defines what a page should look like, all pages based on that document can be updated.

WHAT IS DYNAMIC CONTENT?

About Database Integration

You can think of a database as a virtual filing cabinet filled with information. That information is usually organized in some structured way, such as by customer address information, product details, and ordering histories. The simplest kind of database, called a *flat-file database*, stores data like a big stack of index cards. Each index card, or *record*, stands on its own, and no information is shared between records.

Working with dynamic content on the Web, you'll come across databases with a slightly more complex structure known as *relational databases*.

In a relational database, you can have several different stacks of index cards, each for a different kind of record (say, customers and orders). In one pile, the customer pile, you might have a record for a customer that contains references to all the orders they've placed, which would be pointers to records in the orders pile. Each order might have a reference to the customer record for the customer who placed the order. For a detailed introduction to database terminology and concepts, see Chapter 3, *A Basic Database Primer*.

Choosing a database application

You'll need a database application to use the Dynamic Content features of Dreamweaver MX. You can use any database that understands the standard database query language known as SQL.

Structured Query Language (SQL) is as close to a universal database language as it gets. In Dreamweaver, you use SQL to write *queries*, which extract the information you want from your databases. You can also use SQL to create interfaces to your databases so that you can add, change, and delete information, all from the Web, without ever having to open the database application directly.

Dreamweaver generates the SQL for many of the basic tasks for you, but for advanced queries, you will want to write some custom SQL yourself. For information about learning to write your own SQL queries, see Chapter 4, *Using SQL*.

Almost any database you're likely to use will understand SQL. Some examples include MySQL, Microsoft Access, SQL Server, and Oracle. For all but the most demanding of applications, you can select a database based on cost and convenience. MySQL, for example, is available as a free download; whereas Microsoft Access is expensive, but easier for the novice to administer.

For Mac OS X and Windows (as well as Linux and Unix) operating systems, MySQL is a revered favorite. It's well suited for everything from storing recipes to driving mission-critical enterprise-level applications. We chose to work with MySQL for most of the examples in this book because it's fast, powerful, and relatively easy to administer. Lots of other people use it too, so good documentation and plenty of tutorials are easy to find. Best of all, MySQL is free for noncommercial uses.

For more information about MySQL or to download the application, visit the official MySQL site at http://www.mysql.org (**Figure 1.1**).

For Windows users, another option is Microsoft Access. This basic database is an acceptable choice if you've got a simple site that gets low-to-medium traffic. A more robust database from Microsoft is SQL Server, which is better equipped to handle larger quantities of data and heavier traffic.

Figure 1.1 You can download the MySQL database application and read the complete documentation at http://www.mysql.org/.

A home for your database

In many cases, your database will be installed on the same machine as your Web server. But at high-traffic sites, where server load balancing is an issue, the database can also be installed on a separate server.

For details on configuring Dreamweaver to access your database—whether it's on the same server as your main production server or a separate machine—see Chapter 2, *Setting Up Dreamweaver MX*.

I Say Sequel, You Say S-Q-L

The correct pronunciation of SQL is "ess queue ell," according to the American National Standards Institute (ANSI), but in practice lots of perfectly respectable people just say "sequel" (which we like because it has the advantage of being one syllable shorter). So you're fine either way.

ANSI is the standards body that back in 1989 published the first specification of SQL known as SQL-89. Since then, ANSI has issued two minor revisions to the specification, SQL-92 and SQL-99.

ANSI-SQL is the standard or "pure" form of SQL. Almost all database vendors have added a few non-standard features to their own implementation of SQL, so you may come across references to different "flavors" of SQL. However, if you use standard ANSI-SQL, you'll have guaranteed compatibility across database products because all databases understand the core commands described by the ANSI standard.

If you do want to eat a specific flavor of database pie, Dreamweaver MX lets you write customized SQL in any flavor you like (in case you need to access some advanced feature of, say, an Oracle database).

The Role of the Application Server

The term *application server* refers to a Web server that has the ability to run some kind of server-side code.

When you view an ordinary HTML page on a Web server, the server doesn't interpret what's in the file. It just sends the file out to your browser, which in turn translates the HTML into an actual page layout. If there's any JavaScript in the page, your browser handles that as well.

However, dynamic content relies on additional code, which must be interpreted *before* the file is sent to the browser. That additional code tells the application server what to do. The instruction can be as simple as including the current time of day at the bottom of the page, or as complex as retrieving data froma database, sorting it, filtering out certain records, and displaying the results as a list of rows in a table.

✔ Tip

■ Some Web pages use what are called *http-equiv* instructions to mimic Web server instructions. This instruction is one possible attribute of the meta tag in the document head. If you want to include refresh instructions (instructions to fetch the page), a no-cache instruction, or an expiration date on pages that should request fresh data every so often, see Chapter 15, and in particular the section *Inserting a Refresh Tag*.

Words, Words, Words: What's the Difference Between a Waiter and a Server?

Many people are confused by the differences between a Web server and an application server. Much of this confusion stems from the fact that the word *server* can have so many different meanings. It can refer to the computer that hosts a Web site (as in, "The server crashed.") It can also refer to the software that runs on that computer. What follows are descriptions of what we think of when we use the words *server*, *Web server*, and *application server*. (For yet more fascinating nomenclature, see Chapter 2 for a discussion of the difference between a testing server and a production server—the *production server,* called a *remote server* by Dreamweaver, is what we call a Web server here.)

The word *server* by itself refers to the actual hardware, the physical box sitting on your desk or in a closet somewhere. It's a computer that has a specific function: to store and deliver files of some kind.

A *Web server* is an application that serves plain HTML files (which usually end with `.html` or `.htm`, whereas an *application server* is an application that serves dynamic pages (which can end in `.php`, `.cfm`, `.jsp`, `.asp`, or `.aspx`).

The Web server is the front line of interaction with visitors' Web browsers. If a browser connects to the server and requests a simple HTML page, the Web server handles the request itself. It finds the appropriate file on disk and sends the information out to the browser that made the request. When a request comes in for a dynamic page, the Web server passes the request off to the application server. The application server processes the server-side code in the dynamic page (reading in data from a database if necessary) and generates HTML which it passes off to the Web server to be sent to the user.

In some cases, the same application can incorporate the functions of the Web server *and* the application server. Internet Information Server (IIS) and Personal Web Server (PWS) from Microsoft, for example, can serve up HTML as well as process ASP pages. In other cases (ColdFusion and JSP) the application server is a separate application that runs alongside the Web server. And in the case of PHP, the application server is neither built-in to the Web server nor a separate application. Instead it is an add-on module to the Web server.

Dynamic content = interactivity

Using an application server to access your data in a database—whether it's product information, press releases, or cataloging information about your candy wrapper collection—transforms your Web site from an informational brochure into an application that actually *does* things.

Some of the most common (and useful) examples of Web-based applications include:

◆ **Searching.** You can create a search form so that you (or other people) can search your data using any criteria you specify. "Do I have any candy wrappers from the 1950's that were printed in Philadelphia?"

◆ **Storing.** You can create a Web interface to store information by adding it to your database. "Fill out this form to join the discussion group on candy wrapper design trends."

◆ **Interacting.** You can use databases to create a community. Dynamic pages can be used to build a bulletin board site where people can post messages to each other (**Figure 1.2**).

You will need an application server package installed on your server to work with the Dynamic Content features in Dreamweaver MX. You may already have access to one or more application server packages as part of your Web hosting account or your server operating system. Before you decide whether to use one of these or install a new one altogether, it helps to have an understanding of the different types of dynamic content out there.

Figure 1.2 Ryze is an online networking community where users can create personal information pages and post messages on discussion forums. All of this functionality was created using the Dynamic Content features of Dreamweaver UltraDev, the predecessor to Dreamweaver MX.

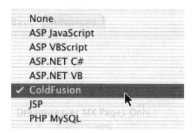

| None |
| ASP JavaScript |
| ASP VBScript |
| ASP.NET C# |
| ASP.NET VB |
| ✓ ColdFusion |
| JSP |
| PHP MySQL |

Figure 1.3 Dreamweaver's Server Model option menu shows the range of server-side scripting languages Dreamweaver can speak.

Dynamic Content Types

Different *application servers* work with different types of *server-side code*. When you configure your site definition, Dreamweaver MX allows you to choose from seven different server models (**Figure 1.3**). The term "server model" is slightly confusing—you're actually choosing from seven different server models that are based on one of five major server scripting languages: PHP, CFML, JSP, ASP, and ASP.NET.

If you plan to manually edit or add to the server-side code generated by Dreamweaver, you may want to consider the relative merits of these languages, and which one best serves your needs:

◆ PHP (PHP: Hypertext Preprocessor) is an object-oriented language with its roots in the open source community. It is powerful, stable, and easy to work with, but initial installation and configuration can be complicated. The application server that runs PHP is not actually a separate application but rather is implemented as an add-on module to your Web server. The add-on can be downloaded for free from www.php.net. PHP is most commonly used with the open-source Apache Web server, which is available for most operating systems including Linux, Mac OS X, and Windows. Modules are also available for Microsoft's PWS and IIS Web servers.

continues on next page

DYNAMIC CONTENT TYPES

◆ CFML (Cold Fusion Markup Language) is a tag-based language, similar to HTML, which was designed to be as easy to use as possible. CFML is the easiest of the four languages for someone new to writing code, but as a result it is not as powerful or as flexible as some of the more complex languages. CFML can only be used with the ColdFusion application server, which runs on Linux, Solaris, HP-UX, and Windows (the Windows Developer Edition of ColdFusion is included in the Macromedia Studio MX bundle). The ColdFusion application server is a stand-alone application that integrates easily and well with most Web servers.

◆ JSP (Java Server Pages) is the most powerful and most complicated server scripting language available in Dreamweaver. Writing JSP code requires a good understanding of Java syntax and concepts. For people who already know Java, it's a great way to apply that skill to server-side scripting. JSP runs on any of a wide variety of Java-based application servers. Enterprise application servers like WebSphere and WebLogic, as well as open-source products like Tomcat, are some of the servers that use JSP.

◆ ASP (Active Server Pages) is a slightly different animal than the other server scripting languages. It's actually not a language at all, but rather a framework designed by Microsoft to integrate well with Windows. Support for ASP is built in to Microsoft's Web servers, Personal Web Server (PWS) or Internet Information Server (IIS). To create ASP code, you use one of several languages: Dreamweaver lets you choose between ASP VBScript or ASP JavaScript. If you anticipate editing any code by hand, make sure you choose the language you're more comfortable with.

◆ ASP.NET is part of Microsoft's newer .NET Framework for defining and accessing Web services. Web services provide a way of accessing the dynamic content of one site from an entirely different site. Using Web services you could, for example, make the product information from your database available to the Web sites of several different sales partners. Dreamweaver gives you the choice of generating ASP.NET code in Microsoft's Visual Basic (VB) or C# languages. For more information about Web services, see Chapter 9, *Web Services and Cold Fusion Components*.

✔ Tip

■ *Open-source* software is software whose source code is not owned by a corporation and therefore can be changed, legally, by anyone. (On the other hand, if you find a bug in your copy of a commercial software product, it would be a violation of your license agreement for you to hack into the source code and fix it yourself.) Linux is an open-source operating system, Apache is an open-source Web server package, and Mozilla is an open-source browser. In the open-source community, many programmers and engineers help to design, build, and fix products that are not only free in the monetary sense but free in the information-sharing sense. Anyone with the know-how can modify, share, sell, or create their own versions of open-source software.

Choosing an Application Server

Setting up and running an application server can be a daunting process. Fortunately, an application server is probably already available to you, so you may not need to start from scratch. Your options depend entirely on whether you're hosting your Web site with a service provider or administering your own server.

Hosting your Web site with an ISP

If you have a Web hosting account with an Internet Service Provider (ISP), you're limited to whatever application server the ISP uses. The majority of ISPs use Apache as a Web server to host their sites, and some of these same ISPs also offer access to the MySQL database as well. One server-scripting language often used with Apache is PHP, so you may have a PHP/Apache or PHP/MySQL setup already in place. (Another common development setup used with Apache is JSP.) It's also possible to find specialty ISPs that run particular application servers, so if you definitely want to use ColdFusion, for instance, you should look for an ISP that hosts ColdFusion-based sites.

Check the Frequently Asked Questions (FAQ) page on your ISP's Web site or contact its technical support to find out more. For details on configuring Dreamweaver to work with a PHP application server and MySQL database, see Chapter 2, *Setting Up Dreamweaver MX*.

Access of Evil

Many small companies just beginning to build a database or bring their data online rely on Microsoft Access as their database application.

Microsoft Access has one clear advantage, and that is that it's easy for the novice user to install and run. It's also got such a similar interface to other Microsoft programs that it's less daunting to start poking around in than an open-source program that you have to compile and install without having a talking paper clip to help you.

Access has some huge security issues, however, and it is not robust or powerful enough to handle large data tables or to serve many simultaneous requests. Access was designed for use in small offices, rather than for serving data over the Internet. That means that once you get the customer base you dream of, your database may not be able to serve the data as fast as your customers are demanding it.

If you want to start out using Access, you're welcome to, for the simple reason that you can learn about databases while you go. But if you're serious about running a speedy, more-secure, data-driven site, you should consider migrating to a platform that was built to serve data over the Internet.

Running your own server

If you're running Mac OS X, then you've already got Apache installed. To add application server functionality, you need to download and install PHP. If you'd rather use MySQL with PHP on Mac OS X, Marc Liyanage's Mac OS X page (http://www.entropy.ch/) is an excellent resource (**Figure 1.4**).

If you're administering your own Apache server, you should be aware that PHP support is handled by a separate module. The PHP module is often, but not always, installed by default. Check your Apache configuration to find out whether you've got the module installed.

If you're administering your own Windows-based server, you may already have Personal Web Server (PWS) or Internet Information Server (IIS) installed. These servers handle both traditional Web-serving tasks and the script-processing tasks of the application server. PWS is designed to work out-of-the-box with very little administration. These products are not as robust as much more expensive software, but they have the advantage of being both free and relatively idiot-proof. You can find information about installing and running both products at http://www.coveryourasp.com.

To use PWS or IIS, you'll need to install a database. Some Windows packages come bundled with Microsoft Access, which, like PWS, is relatively easy to configure.

For details on configuring Dreamweaver to work with ASP-based application servers, see Chapter 2, *Setting Up Dreamweaver MX*.

Figure 1.4 Marc Liyanage's Mac OS X page (http://www.entropy.ch/) is chock full of information about downloading and installing PHP and MySQL for Mac OS X.

SETTING UP DREAMWEAVER MX

2

Some of the most exciting new features in Dreamweaver MX involve the ability to create dynamic pages that do away with much of the tedium involved in maintaining folders full of dozens of static pages that do exactly the same thing. In this chapter we'll look at how to set up and begin using Dreamweaver's dynamic data features (also known as server-side features) to create flexible pages that can display different information each time they're accessed.

Two additional kinds of software you need to know about before you can take advantage of Dynamic Data are database applications and application servers. To find out more about database applications and application servers, and for help in determining whether you already have one or more of these installed, see Chapter 1.

Once you've got the basic setup in place, you'll want to start creating some of these versatile new pages using the data from your database. In the Application panel group, Dreamweaver provides its specialized set of tools, which you'll use to work with Dynamic Data. In this chapter, we'll discuss these four panels: the Database panel, the Bindings panel, the Server Behaviors panel, and the Components panel. You can get more in-depth information about the Bindings panel in *Displaying a Recordset on a Page* in Chapter 5, and more about the Components and Server Behaviors panels in Chapter 10.

Defining a Local Site and a Testing Server

To use dynamic data (data from a database) in your pages, you need to create a site definition that describes the kind of server you're using, where you're keeping your local files, and how you'll be getting those files to the server. Dreamweaver MX includes a new Basic interface with a wizard that steps you through the site definition in three major panels: Editing Files, Testing Files, and Sharing Files. The Advanced interface lets you access your Site Definition settings directly, and gives you a few additional options (see the *Testing Servers and Production Servers* sidebar in this chapter for more on those).

✔ Tip

■ If you are not going to be using a database, you do not need to set up a testing server. You should set up a local site—and if your files are going to the Web via FTP with no database involved, put the Web server information in the Remote Info category, not the Testing Server category, of the Site Definition dialog box. For more information, skip to the end of this chapter and read *Local Site 411* and *Additional Remote Server Setup*.

To define a site:

1. From the menu bar, select Site > New Site (**Figure 2.1**).

   or

   From the Site window's Site drop-down menu, select Edit Sites and, in the Edit Sites dialog box, click on New (**Figure 2.2**).

   (To add dynamic information to an existing site definition, double-click the site name in the Site drop-down menu and skip to the areas you need to fill in.)

Figure 2.1 Select Site > New Site or Site > Edit Sites from the menu bar.

Figure 2.2 In the Edit Sites dialog box, click on New.

Figure 2.3 The Site Definition dialog box opens with the Basic tab selected by default. If you'd rather not use the wizard, click the Advanced tab to see the traditional interface.

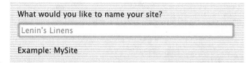

Figure 2.4 When giving your site a name, you're free to use any characters you want, including spaces and punctuation.

Figure 2.5 In the Editing Files, Part 2 panel you'll set up information about your application server.

The Site Definition dialog box will appear. The Basic tab is selected by default. To access the Site Definition settings directly, click on the Advanced tab (**Figure 2.3**).

2. Type a name for your site. This name is purely for your own use, so you're free to use spaces and non-alphanumeric characters like apostrophes and punctuation marks (unlike naming conventions for actual Internet-ready files or folders) (**Figure 2.4**).

3. Click Next. The Editing Files, Part 2 panel will appear (**Figure 2.5**).

or

In the Advanced interface, click Testing Server in the Category List (**Figure 2.6**) and omit the "click on Next" from the following steps.

continues on next page

Figure 2.6 To set up application server information using the Advanced interface, click Testing Server in the Category List.

DEFINING A LOCAL SITE AND A TESTING SERVER

4. In the wizard, click on the Radio button labeled "Yes, I want to use a server technology." From the drop-down menu that appears (the Server Model menu in the Advanced interface), choose the server technology that corresponds to the type of server you're using: ASP JavaScript; ASP VBScript; ASP.NET C#; ASP.NET VB; ColdFusion; JSP; or PHP MySQL. Then click Next (**Figure 2.7**).

These choices are described in more detail in *Dynamic Content Types* in Chapter 1.

5. In the Editing Files, Part 3 panel that appears, specify how you'll access the files you work on, and how you'll transfer them to the testing server (**Figure 2.8**).

In the Advanced interface, skip to Step 6.

6. In the Wizard, after you've chosen one of the above options, click on the Browse button to choose the local directory where you want the copies of your files to be stored locally. When you're done, click Next.

In the Advanced interface, you set up your local site folder in the Local Info panel of the Site Definition dialog box. Click Browse 📁 to choose or create a local folder.

See the sections *Local Site 411* and *Additional Setup* at the end of this chapter for help setting up the local and remote info.

7. In the Testing Files panel that appears (**Figure 2.9**), or from the Access drop-down menu on the Advanced interface, specify how you'll connect to your testing server. You can choose one of the following: FTP, Local/Network, and RDS.

FTP is the most common way to connect to a remote server. See the *Express Transfer* sidebar for information about these three methods of transferring files.

continues on page 18

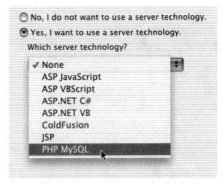

Figure 2.7 You can choose from seven scripting languages associated with different application servers. Once you choose, Dreamweaver handles the hard work of writing the code.

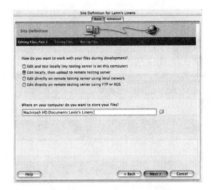

Figure 2.8 Specify where on your own machine you'll store the local copy of your files and how you'll transfer them to the server.

Figure 2.9 In the first Testing Files panel, define how you'll connect to your server.

Testing Servers and Production Servers

You'll see references in Dreamweaver and throughout this book to both testing servers and production servers. What's the difference, and do you need both? The production server is the "live" server, with a full-time connection to the Internet. This is the server that actually hosts your site and makes your pages available to the world. The testing server, on the other hand, is a server that is running the same software your production server is running, but it isn't necessarily live and accessible on the Internet (although it can be). You don't *need* to use a testing server, but there are several advantages to using one:

◆ You can run a testing server on the same machine that you're using to create and edit your site, which means you don't have to connect to your production server every time you want to preview your work.

◆ You can put changed files on a testing server first and then run them through their paces before uploading them to your production server. This is a good idea particularly when there are databases and application servers involved: You'll avoid revealing any unsightly and embarrassing bugs in your pages to world at large.

The Basic tab assumes your production server is the same as your testing server. To set up separate testing and production servers, you'll need to use the Advanced tab in the Site Definition window.

◆ Choose "Edit and test locally" if your testing server is running on the same machine you're working on.

◆ Choose "Edit locally, then upload to remote testing server" if your testing server is on an ISP or somewhere else that isn't on a local network. There will be two copies of the files, your local copies and the remote copies, and you'll be transferring the files to the testing server manually using FTP. This method is probably what you're accustomed to doing if you've used Dreamweaver before. If you choose this option, click on the Browse button to choose or create the local folder where your files will be stored.

◆ Choose "Edit directly on remote testing server using local network" if you can access the testing server on your local network. Click on the Browse 🗂 button to select the folder on your network where your files will be stored. (On Windows, that server will be part of your Windows network. On the Mac, if the server appears on your desktop or in the Shortcuts menu just like a hard drive, then it's on your local network).

◆ "Edit directly on remote testing server using FTP or RDS" is the right choice if your server is not on the local network, and you don't want to have to transfer the files manually. This choice allows to you to work on the remote files *as if* they were right there on your machine.

8. If your testing server is on the same machine you're working on, click on the Browse button to choose a local directory that your Web server can access to serve files.

or

If your testing server is on a remote machine, type the path to the remote directory where you normally upload your files to make them available on the Web.

9. Click Next. The Testing Files, Part 2 panel will appear. (**Figure 2.10**).

10. On this panel, or in the URL prefix text box on the Advanced interface, specify the Web address of the testing server, just as you would type it in a browser.

- If your testing server is connected to the Internet, this will be a typical URL, like `http://www.leninslinens.com/`

- If you're running a testing server on your own machine but it doesn't have a Web address (most machines don't unless you've specifically set this up with a service provider), you can usually access it with the special purpose URL `http://127.0.0.1/` or `http://localhost/`. Note that these URLs work only if the Web server you want to access is running on the same machine you're working on, and that you may need to specify the whole path, including all appropriate directories.

11. You can click on Test URL 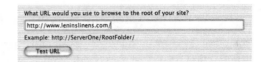 to make sure you've chosen the right path. Click Next to proceed to the Sharing Files panel.

12. If other people will also be using Dreamweaver to work on the same site, you may want to set up file check-in and check-out. Click Yes to set up check-in information, or No to skip it (**Figure 2.11**).

This feature helps keep more than one person from making changes to the same file at the same time. See *Checking In and Checking Out* in Chapter 20 to find out more.

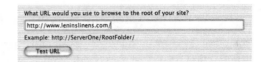

Figure 2.10 In the Testing Files, Part 2 panel, specify the URL of your site.

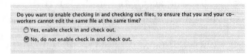

Figure 2.11 Click Yes to set up check-in information, or No to skip it.

Figure 2.12 If there's anything in the Summary that doesn't look right, you can go back and change it now, or you can change it later using the Advanced tab.

13. Click Next to preview a summary of your site settings. If your site settings are accurate, click Done. Otherwise, you can click Back to change any of the settings. (**Figure 2.12**).

✔ **Tip**

■ After you've used the wizard to set up your site information, you can return to the Site Definition window and use either the Basic or the Advanced tabs to change any of the items we've just completed.

Express Transfer

FTP, RDS, and WebDAV are three methods (also called protocols) for transferring files from your machine to a remote machine. FTP is the oldest and most widely used of these protocols (it even predates the Web). You may be familiar with FTP from previous versions of Dreamweaver.

With **FTP**, you have relatively limited control over the files on the server: You can copy them to and from the server, rename them, and delete them from the server—but that's about it.

WebDAV (Web-based Distributed Authoring and Versioning), on the other hand, is a collaboration tool built on the HTTP protocol. Using WebDAV, you can access a directory on the server as if it were a drive attached directly to your machine. This allows much greater control over the manipulation of files on the server, including version control mechanisms, searchable metadata, and advanced scripting capabilities. WebDAV resources and setup are described in Chapter 20.

RDS (Remote Development Services) is a file management and remote access system for use with a ColdFusion application server. Like WebDAV, RDS allows you to access files and databases on the server using the HTTP protocol, but in addition, RDS allows the server administrator to control which resources are accessible to different users based on their access privileges. RDS is described further in Chapters 9 and 20.

Which of these protocols you use depends on what you have access to; you won't be using RDS unless you're using ColdFusion, and you or your server admin need to install WebDAV in order to able to use it. You can set both WebDAV and RDS settings in the Remote Info panel of the Site Definition dialog box.

Adding a Database Connection

To access data from a database in Dreamweaver, you'll also need to set up a connection that tells Dreamweaver where the database is and how to access it.

If your database is Microsoft Access, SQL Server, or another database running on a Windows-based server, you'll need to set up a System DSN (Data Source Name) first. If your database is MySQL or another database running on an OS X, Linux, or Unix server, you do not need to set up a DSN. You can proceed directly to *To add a database connection*.

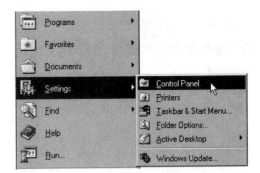

Figure 2.13 From the Start Menu, open Settings › Control Panel.

✔ Tips

- If you're using SQL Server, you probably won't be using a System DSN.

- The following steps may differ slightly for databases such as Oracle—if you get stumped by a dialog box choice, ask your database administrator for help setting up your DSN.

To define a System DSN (for Windows-based databases):

1. From the Windows Start Menu, choose Settings > Control Panel (**Figure 2.13**). On XP, that's Start > Control Panel; then double-click Administrative Tools.

2. Open the ODBC Data Sources Control Panel—on 2000 or XP, that's Data Sources (ODBC). The ODBC Data Source Administrator window will open.

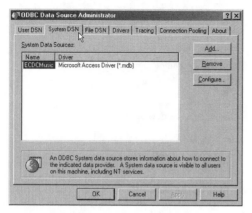

Figure 2.14 Setting up a System DSN (Data Source Name) allows applications like Dreamweaver to connect to databases like Access, SQL Server, Oracle, and many others.

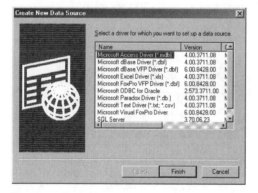

Figure 2.15 Choose the driver that corresponds to the type of database you're using.

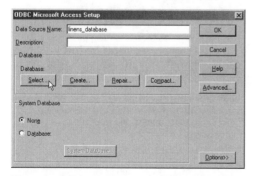

Figure 2.16 Give your System DSN a name (which you'll use to create a Connection in Dreamweaver) and choose the database file you want to use for your site.

3. At the top of the ODBC Data Source Administrator window, click the System DSN tab, and then click Add (**Figure 2.14**). The Create New Data Source window will appear.

Note: The ODBC Data Source Administrator window will open with the User DSN tab selected by default. Be sure to switch to the System DSN tab. If you create a User DSN, Dreamweaver won't be able to access it.

4. From the list box, choose the driver for the type of database you will be using. Windows includes drivers for Access, dBase, SQL Server, Oracle, and many other popular database formats (**Figure 2.15**).

Note: You can choose only those drivers your machine is set up to use; for example, if you have not installed Oracle components, you cannot set up a DSN for Oracle.

5. Click Finish.

A Setup/Create New Data Source window specific to your database will appear (**Figure 2.16**).

6. In the Data Source Name text box (or its equivalent), type a name for the DSN you wish to create. You may choose any name you like.

7. Click Select. In the Select Database dialog box, choose the database on your local file system or network that you want to use in Dreamweaver.

8. Click OK.

continues on next page

ADDING A DATABASE CONNECTION

To add a database connection:

1. In the Document window, open or create a page of the appropriate file type for your server model. (**Figure 2.17**).

   If you're using MySQL, choose MySQL Connection from the New Connection menu under the + (plus) button (**Figure 2.18**).

   or

   If you're using a Windows-based database like Access or SQL Server, choose Data Source Name (DSN) from the New Connection menu under the + (plus) button (**Figure 2.19**).

+ (plus) button

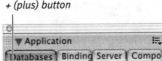

Figure 2.17 To add a connection, in the Databases panel, click the + (plus) button.

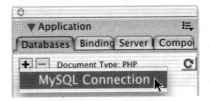

Figure 2.18 If you've selected PHP as your application server model, MySQL Connection will be the only choice available.

✔ Tips

- You won't be able to click the + (plus) button on the Databases panel (it'll be grayed out) until you have a dynamic-type page open in the Document window.

- On ColdFusion environments running on Windows machines, you don't get a + button in Step 2. Instead, you need to set up your data source within the ColdFusion Administrator. You can either supply an RDS password within the CF Administrator, or you can "turn off" RDS from there.

- For a more-detailed description of the steps specific to setting up a ColdFusion connection, see Chapter 9, *Web Services and ColdFusion Components*.

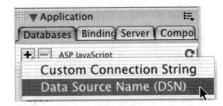

Figure 2.19 If you've selected JSP or ASP as your application server model you'll see two choices: Custom Connection String and Data Source Name.

Connection Name: leninslinens_db

Figure 2.20 The name you give your Connection will be the name you see in the Databases panel and in Dreamweaver dialog boxes whenever you have the option of specifying a database to use.

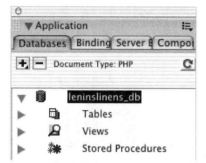

Figure 2.21 The Databases panel shows you a list of database connections you've made and lets you browse column names, views, and stored procedures.

- You cannot change the connection name; it will appear grayed out. If you need to change this name, you'll need to create a new connection.

- Double-clicking a ColdFusion connection opens the list of tables, not the Configuration Settings dialog box.

2. In the Connection dialog box that appears, give your connection a name. This is how you'll see the connection referred to in Dreamweaver menus later on (**Figure 2.20**).

3. If you chose MySQL Connection in Step 2, specify the name of the server where your database application is running. If it's the same machine you're working on, you can leave this blank for now.

4. If your database is password protected, you'll need to enter a valid username and password. Otherwise, you can leave these fields blank.

5. If you chose MySQL Connection, click Select. Dreamweaver will connect to your database server and the Select Database dialog box will appear, listing the databases on your server. Choose the database you want to use from the list box and click OK.

   or

   If you chose Data Source Name (DSN), click the DSN button **DSN...** and in the Select DSN dialog box, select from the list the DSN that identifies your database.

6. Click OK one more time to close the Connection dialog box.

   The connection you just defined will now appear in the Databases panel (**Figure 2.21**).

✔ Tips

- Once you've selected a database, you can click Test in the Connection dialog box to confirm that Dreamweaver can successfully connect to the database server and open the database you chose. This test does not check the username or password; it merely pings the server to make sure it exists.

- To change any settings for a database connection, double-click on its name in the Databases panel to re-open the Connection dialog box.

ADDING A DATABASE CONNECTION

Using the Site Window

Dreamweaver's Site window (**Figure 2.22**) is both a file-management tool and a full-fledged FTP client that helps you put your site online. In Windows, the Site window is a part of the Files panel group, but you can also undock it by clicking on the Expander button. On the Macintosh, the Site window is always a stand-alone window, but it functions pretty much the same.

To view the Site window:

◆ From the Document window menu bar, select Window > Site Files.

or

Press F8.

or

Open the Files panel group and click on the Site tab.

Regardless which way you choose, the Site window will appear (**Figure 2.22**). If you view the Site window before creating any site definitions, the window will be empty.

✔ Tips

■ Click the Expander button ⬜ (Windows only) to display both areas, local and remote. On the Macintosh, both areas are always visible.

■ All the column headings are also buttons; click on any one of them to sort the directory contents by that criterion.

■ You can drag the borders between the column buttons to adjust the column width.

■ See Chapter 20 for more information about such Site window features as File Check-in, Design Notes, and Site Reporting.

Expander button

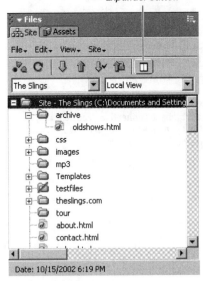

Figure 2.22 Use the Site window to upload and download files to and from the production server. The top view is the Macintosh Site window. The bottom window is the Site panel docked on a Windows machine. Click the Expander button to show a two-pane view like the one on the Macintosh. When you do this, the Site window will take over the Dreamweaver workspace.

Figure 2.23 To edit a connection, double-click on the connection name.

Figure 2.24 Every setting in the Connection dialog box is editable except the name itself.

Using the Databases Panel

In addition to adding database connections, the Databases panel also lets you edit and delete existing connections, as well as browse any database for which you've defined a connection.

To edit a database connection:

1. In the Databases panel, double-click the name of the connection you want to edit (**Figure 2.23**).

   In ColdFusion, you need to edit your connection using the CF Administrator. Double-clicking the connection will instead expand the list of data tables.

2. In the Connection dialog box that appears, you can modify any of the fields except the Connection Name, which is grayed out (**Figure 2.24**).

3. Click OK to close the Connection dialog box.

continues on next page

To delete a database connection:

1. In the Databases panel, click on the name of the connection you want to delete.

2. Click the – (minus) button in the upper left (**Figure 2.25**).

3. Click OK in response to the warning dialog box (**Figure 2.26**).

To browse a database connection:

1. In the Databases panel, click on the expander arrow to the left of the connection you want to browse.

2. Click the expand triangle to the left of the elements you want to browse (**Figure 2.27**).

   For more information about tables, views, and stored procedures, see *Databases and the Dreamweaver Interface* in Chapter 3.

Click to delete connection

Figure 2.25 To delete a connection, click the – (minus) button.

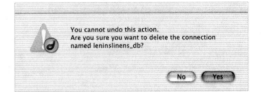

Figure 2.26 Deleting a connection can have a serious impact on your document if any behaviors rely on it, so make sure you really mean what you say when you're deleting.

Figure 2.27 The contents of your database are listed hierarchically in the Database panel.

Figure 2.28 To add a recordset, click the menu control button in the upper left of the Bindings panel.

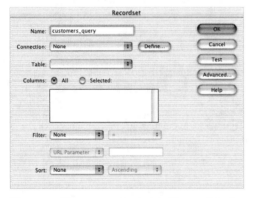

Figure 2.29 Name your recordset, but be careful not to use spaces or non-alphanumeric characters.

Figure 2.30 In the Connections drop-down menu, you'll find a list of connections you've defined for this site.

Using the Bindings Panel

A database can contain lots of different kinds of information, but you generally only want a small part of that information on a particular page. To identify only the data you need and grab it from your database, you need to create a recordset (also called a query). You can find more detailed information about database concepts and terminology in Chapter 3.

To add a recordset to a page:

1. In the Bindings panel, click on the Options menu button and choose Recordset (Query) from the menu (**Figure 2.28**).

2. Give your recordset a descriptive name (don't use spaces or non-alphanumeric characters) (**Figure 2.29**).

3. Choose a database connection from the Connection drop-down menu (**Figure 2.30**).

continues on next page

USING THE BINDINGS PANEL

4. Choose a table from the Table drop-down menu (**Figure 2.31**).

The default query is to select all columns for all records. To restrict your query, refer to *Talking to a Database* in Chapter 3.

5. Click Test to verify that your query is valid.

If your query is valid you will see a simple spreadsheet-like view of the data in your recordset result (**Figure 2.32**). Note that you can have a valid query that returns no records.

6. Click OK.

✔ Tips

- If you need to define a new connection to a database, you can do that right from the Recordset dialog box by clicking Define  .

- The Test button is also a handy way to look at the data in your table without having to open your database application separately. In Chapter 5, we'll look at using Live Data view to see data from your database inline in pages in the Document window.

In addition to recordsets, the Bindings panel lets you add several different server variables to the page. For more information about how to work with server variables, see *Built-in Server Behaviors* in Chapter 10.

To delete a recordset from a page:

1. In the Bindings panel, click on the name of the recordset you want to delete.

2. Click the – (minus) button (**Figure 2.33**).

Figure 2.31 In the Table drop-down menu you'll find a list of the tables in the database you've chosen to connect to.

Figure 2.32 When you click the Test button you can see the results of your query laid out in a spreadsheet format.

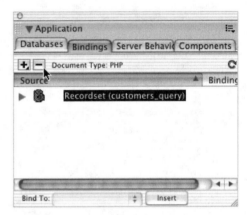

Figure 2.33 To delete a recordset, simply click the – (minus) button.

Figure 2.34 The Server Behaviors panel lists many of the server-based actions you can add to your page with Dreamweaver, all without typing a single line of code.

About the Server Behaviors Panel

Server Behaviors are customizable blocks of server code (written in ColdFusion, PHP, JSP, ASP, or ASP.NET) which, when used in conjunction with data from a database, add dynamic functionality to your page.

The Server Behaviors panel provides a menu from which you can choose behaviors you want to use, including displaying a recordset on a page, creating recordset navigation controls to allow users to view previous or next records, and creating forms for updating information in a database (**Figure 2.34**).

The Server Behaviors panel also lists all behaviors that you've inserted into your page so you can manage your behaviors, keep track of what you've done, and easily delete behaviors or add new ones. The specifics of working with Server Behaviors are covered in detail in Chapters 6, 8, and 10.

Local Site 411

The *local site folder* is the folder on your machine that holds the "not ready for prime time" copies of your pages. You may also hear this folder referred to as a *local root folder;* on the remote site, the equivalent folder is called the *site root folder.*

Setting up a local site is one of the big points of confusion for beginning Dreamweaver users—hence the new wizard in Dreamweaver MX. You don't need a testing server if you don't have a database, but you should set up a local site folder regardless.

Telling Dreamweaver where your local site root folder is lets you use many tools you wouldn't be able to access otherwise, such as the Site window and its FTP and file management tools; the Assets panel; the Library; Templates; HTML Styles; the Link Checker; and Site Reporting.

Keeping your files in a local site root folder is also a good way to keep other detritus out of your Web project folders—and to make sure you know where those files are so that you can link them together properly.

✔ Tip

- One of the benefits of working with a local site is that your work is done on development files that are stored on your local machine, rather than on the live Web site files. This way, you're less likely to break something that people are currently looking at on your live site. This is what's known as a development/production environment: Your local files are the development files, and they don't go live until you upload them to your remote site.

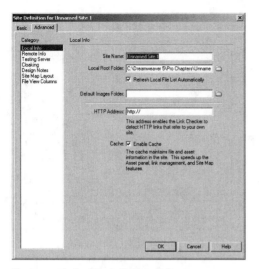

Figure 2.35 In the Site Definition dialog box, you can set up information for a local folder and a remote production server as well as for a testing server.

Figure 2.36 Type a name for your site and then tell Dreamweaver what folder it lives in. You can also specify where your default images folder for that site is so the program will look there first for images.

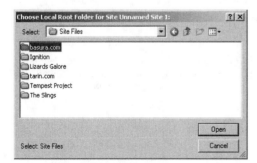

Figure 2.37 In the Choose Local Root Folder dialog box, select the folder your files reside in. You can also create a new folder if you don't have files yet for the site you're about to create.

To set up only a local site:

1. From the Site window menu bar, select Site > New Site. The Site definition dialog box will appear. If it doesn't look like **Figure 2.35**, click the Advanced tab, and in the Category list, click on Local Info.

2. Type a distinctive name (not "My Site") for your site in the Site Name text box (**Figure 2.36**).

3. Click the Browse button 📁 next to Local Root Folder. The Choose Local Root Folder dialog box will appear (**Figure 2.37**).

4. Select or create a folder in which to store your files. You can choose any existing folder, but Dreamweaver prefers you don't store one site root folder inside another.

5. That's all there is to it. Click on OK to save your site information, or continue to the next section to set up your remote information.

Additional Remote Server Setup

In the Site window, you can view the files and folders on your local, remote, and testing servers. At the beginning of this chapter, we set up a local site in the section *Defining a Local Site and a Testing Server.*

If you'll be transferring files from your local machine or testing server to a *production server* or *remote server*, you'll also want to set up Remote Info. The remote server is the server that actually delivers your pages to the public when they connect using a Web browser.

To set up remote site info (FTP):

1. From the Site drop-down menu, Site > Edit Sites. The Edit Sites dialog box will appear (**Figure 2.38**).

2. Select the local site you want to set up, and click on Edit. The Site Definition dialog box will appear (Figure 2.35). Click on the Advanced tab if it's not selected.

3. In the Category box at the left, click on Remote Info. That panel of the dialog box will come to the front (**Figure 2.39**).

Figure 2.38 In the Edit Sites dialog box, you can create, edit, remove, and make a copy of any site.

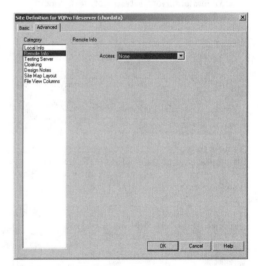

Figure 2.39 In order to send your files to a Web server (a production server rather than a testing server), you need to specify remote site information.

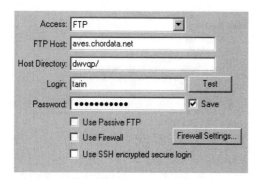

Figure 2.40 Fill out your FTP information—check with your ISP or Web site admin if you're not sure about any of these settings.

4. From the Access drop-down menu, select FTP. The dialog box will display FTP information (**Figure 2.40**).

5. In the FTP Host text box, type the alphanumeric address for the Web server (for example, `ftp.site.com` or `www.site.com`). Do not include folders.

6. In the Host Directory text box, type the name of the initial root directory for the site (e.g., `public_html` or `html/public/personal`).

7. In the Login text box, type the username for the ftp or www account. In the Password text box, type the password for the ftp or www account.

8. To save the username and password, place a checkmark in the Save checkbox.

9. To test your connection, click on the Test button. If the test is not successful, be sure your Internet connection is active, and double-check your entries in Steps 5 through 7.

   When both the local and remote site information are filled out, click on OK. You'll now be able to use the Site window to Get and Put your files.

continues on next page

ADDITIONAL REMOTE SERVER SETUP

✔ Tips

- If you use a local network connection to see and transfer files on a Web server, select Local/Network from the Access drop-down menu in Step 4 (**Figure 2.41**). Type the name of your server or click the Browse button (the little folder) to select your remote server from your network or, on the Mac, the Options menu or the Desktop.

- If you use a content management system to interface with a Web server, select RDS, WebDAV, or SourceSafe Database from the Access drop-down menu in Step 4 (Figure 2.41). Then, click on Settings. A configuration dialog box will appear; specify the URL of the host, your username and password, and other pertinent information such as the port (RDS, **Figure 2.42**); your e-mail address (WebDAV, **Figure 2.43**); or the project name (SourceSafe, **Figure 2.44**). Each of these types of content management systems is discussed in greater detail in Chapter 20.

- If you use the same remote host for several different sites, you can avoid having to repeat these steps again and again. In the Edit Sites dialog box, you can select a site with remote information already set up, and then click on Duplicate to make a copy of it. Then, rename the site and edit the local root folder information.

- You can export site definition information to share it between computers. In the Edit Sites dialog box (Figure 2.38), click on Export, and choose whether or not to save login information. The file you save will be an XML file with the extension .STE, which you can import using the Edit Sites dialog box on the other machine.

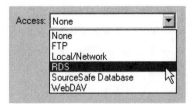

Figure 2.41 You can use any of these types of connections to connect to a production server. These are discussed in more detail in Chapter 20

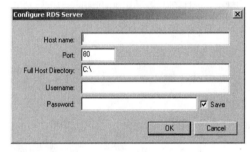

Figure 2.42 To connect using RDS, specify the host name, the host directory, the port, and your username and password.

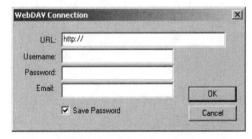

Figure 2.43 If you use WebDAV in conjunction with your production server, specify the host URL, your username and password, and your e-mail address.

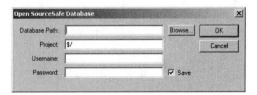

Figure 2.44 To work with a SourceSafe database, specify the path for the database, the project name, and your username and password.

A BASIC
DATABASE PRIMER

Databases are an extremely powerful, but often misunderstood, tool for building Web-based applications. Although the primary purpose of a database, as the name might suggest, is to provide a container for data, it's a common misconception to assume that the data is just numbers, or names and addresses, or really anything specific.

Databases can contain everything from a price list, to video files, to an entire magazine article. In fact, one of the most common uses for a database on the Web is to provide a content management system, which serves up articles, ads, and whatnot automatically, without having to create a separate page for each item. Other common uses for databases on the Web include facilitating online stores, where all the product information is maintained in a database; tracking user information including usernames and passwords; and managing internal company information.

Although you can design an HTML Web site without knowing any HTML, it's not really possible to design a database-driven Web application without knowing at least the basics of how databases work. This chapter will introduce you to the basic structure of databases, and then take you through the process of creating a sample database.

Database Structure

Before you actually create a working database, it's important to understand the structure that databases have. A useful way to think about the database server is as a series of containers: The server contains a number of *databases*; each of those databases contains a number of *tables*; each of those tables contains a number of *records*; and each of those records contains a number of *fields* (**Figure 3.1**). The field is what contains the piece of data.

Tables and records

Most of the database manipulation you do will be executed at the table level. A table is essentially a spreadsheet, with a number of records (often called rows), each of which has a number of fields (occasionally called columns) (**Figure 3.2**).

For example, to collect information about visitors to your site, you might want to have them enter their name, e-mail, and ZIP code. After four people have signed up, your visitors table might look like **Figure 3.3**.

Looks quite a bit like a spreadsheet, doesn't it? Each row across is a record, which has values for each field, or column. Although your final Web site will rarely display a table in this format, it's useful to keep in mind that this is the way the server sees your data.

Tables usually contain a number of records. A basic rule for organizing separate databases is to put all records of any one kind in their own table. This way you'll always be able to make an educated guess as to which table a given record may be found in. So all customers, for example, should go in a `customers` table, while all products would go in a `products` table.

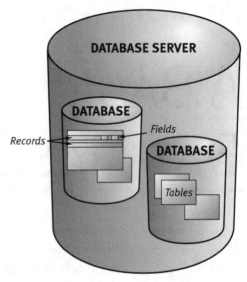

Figure 3.1 A database server is a series of containers that house tables.

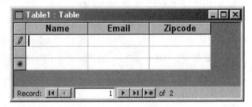

Figure 3.2 A database table looks just like a spreadsheet.

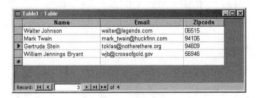

Figure 3.3 A guestbook table with four entries.

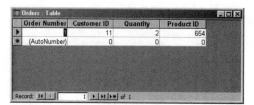

Figure 3.4 Records often represent a physical object, but not always.

✔ Tip

- You might be tempted to break up data of the same type, for example, by creating separate tables for good_customers and bad_customers. But that can get you into trouble rather quickly. What happens if your customer misses a payment? You would then have to move him from one table to another. It's almost always better to have a good_or_bad field in your customer record, which you can alter much more easily.

Records often represent physical objects (like customers or a product), but not always. **Figure 3.4**, for example, shows a record from an online store that represents a transaction, rather than an actual object.

You can think of *each record in a table* as a single chunk of data containing interrelated information. A customer record, for example, would include a name, an address, a phone number, an e-mail address, and so on—all of which relates to the customer directly.

Good database programming practices dictate that records must contain data that is unique to only that record and is not duplicated anywhere else. So you might include a customer's name in the customer record, but not a list of every order the customer has made. To do it any other way would be extremely inefficient.

continues on next page

For example, if you decided you were going to list every order a customer made in one record, you would first have to estimate how many orders you are going to get when you design your database so that you leave enough room for them. Too much room, and most customers would have a bunch of blank order spaces (and even blank entries take up memory and disk space). Too little room, and you run into problems down the line when someone attempts to order something but your table doesn't have enough space to accommodate it.

✔ Tip

■ When you have a variable (but small) number of possibilities for the data in a set of records, you can include fields for all of those possibilities. This may seem inefficient, but as long as the number is small it's no problem. For example, a customer might provide not only a work number, but also a cell phone number, a home phone number, a fax number, an emergency contact, and so on. So you might have anywhere from one to five phone numbers in your customer record.

Fields

Fields are the columns in the database table that contain data for each record (**Figure 3.5**). It's important to note that *fields hold different types of data*. So a field for a customer's name, for instance, would be a `text` field, while a customer ID# field would be a `number` field. So when you design your table, you should consider carefully the kind of information you'll want in each field.

Another thing to remember about fields is that every record has the same fields as the other records in their respective table. So even if a field is not used for most records in a table, it takes up memory and disk space for every record, even the ones that don't use it.

Figure 3.5 Fields in the database table are like the columns in a spreadsheet.

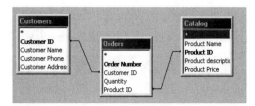

Figure 3.6 When displaying an order, we look up items in other tables by their ID fields.

Databases and Relationships

The most common kind of database in use on the Web is a *relational* database. A relational database is not a list of your relatives or your exes, but rather a collection of tables that have a defined relationship with one another.

An online store, for example, might contain a database with three tables:

◆ A Catalog table, which lists the products, their item ID numbers, their descriptions, and their prices

◆ A Customers table, which lists customer information, including a customer ID number

◆ An Orders table, which includes the customer ID number and some amount of item ID numbers (one for each item ordered)

To display a customer order, the database must look up the customer in the Customer table using the customer ID and the product in the Catalog table using the product ID. Usually the result displayed will include the order number from the Orders table and the products ordered, with their descriptions and prices (**Figure 3.6**).

From these results, you could go on to create a page that prompts the user for an order number and then fills in the customer name and information, providing details about each item in the order. As you can see, the data in these three tables are interrelated—the tables are relational to one another.

Planning table relationships

If you are using a database to do anything more complicated than displaying a list, you need to think carefully about the way you'll want the various tables in the database to interact. This kind of planning is critical to making your application work.

For instance, you would always want to assign a unique number to every order in the orders table; otherwise, the orders wouldn't sync up with the customer table correctly. If you didn't, the shipping clerk would be unable to match the customer name with the products ordered, and someone in Kansas would end up with twelve cases of fishing line instead of a 12-string bass.

So you must carefully plan the way the database will be organized—with painstaking attention given to the way the relationships among the tables are defined. Every database application contains three possible kinds of relationships. They are called *one-to-one;* *one-to-many;* and *many-to-many.* Let's look at each of those types.

One-to-one relationships

When each bit of data is uniquely associated with one other chunk of data, that is called a one-to-one relationship. Each customer, for example, has only one name and one ID number, so the customer ID and the customer name have a one-to-one relationship.

Generally, this kind of relationship is contained within a record, but when one piece of the data is optional, the data can be put in a second table, especially if that optional data is large (**Figure 3.7**). A good example might be if some, but not all, customers have a photo ID associated with them.

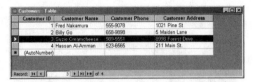

Figure 3.7 One-to-one relationships are usually contained within the same record, like the Customer ID, name, phone number, and address in this table.

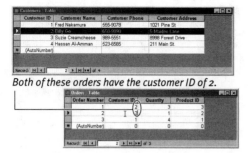

Both of these orders have the customer ID of 2.

Figure 3.8 This customer has made two orders, which is a one-to-many relationship.

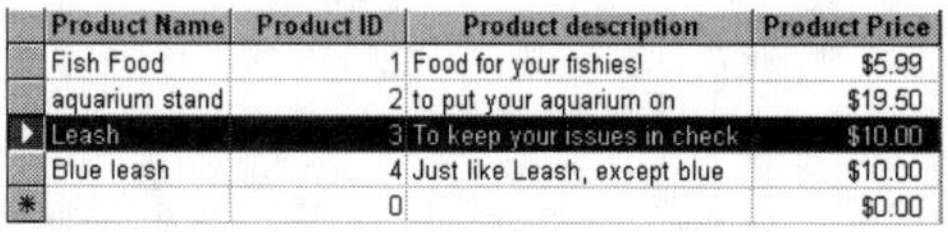

Product Name	Product ID	Product description	Product Price
Fish Food	1	Food for your fishies!	$5.99
aquarium stand	2	to put your aquarium on	$19.50
Leash	3	To keep your issues in check	$10.00
Blue leash	4	Just like Leash, except blue	$10.00
	0		$0.00

Figure 3.9 A many-to-many relationship. Each order had several (many) products, and those products can appear in many orders.

One-to-many relationships

When a record in one table has multiple records in another table that are associated with that record only, this is called a one-to-many relationship.

A customer record in a Customer table, for example, can have many orders in an Orders table associated with it, but each order is related only to that customer record, and not to any other (**Figure 3.8**).

Many-to-many relationships

When one record is associated with multiple other records that are associated with still more records, this is called a many-to-many relationship.

Think about a product detail record, which contains information about that product, including the price and availability. An order record in the Orders table will contain several of these product records (one for each product ordered), and these product records will appear in many orders (**Figure 3.9**).

Addressing these different kinds of table relationships takes some time during the planning phase, but it will definitely be worth it in the long run. Let's take a look at the planning process.

To plan a database:

1. First, determine what kind of data you'll be dealing with.

   All the examples we've cited thus far deal with customers and products, as well as the interaction between these two categories—the customer orders—so we'll continue with that model.

2. Decide which data will have a one-to-one relationship.

   This is the simplest relationship, so it's a good place to start. A customer, for example, has an ID #, a name, an address, and a phone number, so that information should all go in one table. Similarly, a product has a number, a name, a description and a price, all of which go in one table. Order information would be similarly grouped in the Orders table.

3. Now determine which of your data will have one-to-many relationships.

   One-to-many relationships are where the bulk of the work happens. In our model—as we discussed earlier—each customer can have any number of orders, so it makes sense to have separate tables for customers and orders.

4. Address the last possibility—whether any of your data will have many-to-many relationships.

   In our case, we have products, which have a many-to-many relationship with both the customer and order data. So the products should be kept in a separate table as well.

After careful consideration and planning of the model we've been discussing, our database structure would look something like **Figure 3.10**. Each table has information that is not in any other table, and the Orders table links the customers with the products they have ordered.

Catalog : Table			
Product Name	**Product ID**	**Product description**	**Product Price**
Fish Food	1	Food for your fishies!	$5.99
aquarium stand	2	to put your aquarium on	$19.50
Leash	3	To keep your issues in check	$10.00
Blue leash	4	Just like Leash, except blue	$10.00
	0		$0.00

Orders : Table			
Order Number	**Customer ID**	**Quantity**	**Product ID**
1	2	3	3
2	2	1	2
3	1	4	1
4	3	2	3
(AutoNumber)	0	0	0

Product appears multiple times.

Figure 3.10 A simple database structure with three tables.

Unlike the ID, multiple products can have the same price.

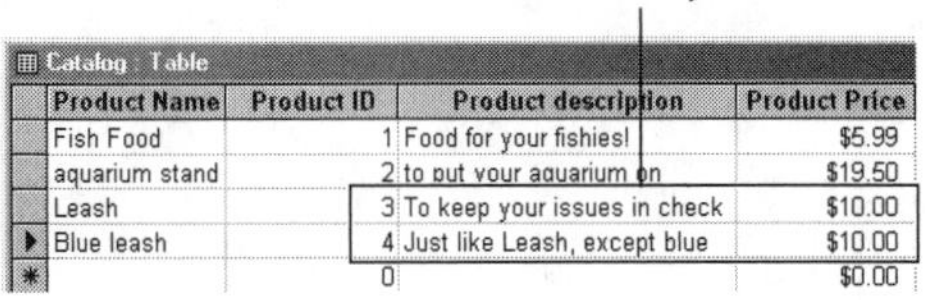

Product Name	Product ID	Product description	Product Price
Fish Food	1	Food for your fishies!	$5.99
aquarium stand	2	to put your aquarium on	$19.50
Leash	3	To keep your issues in check	$10.00
Blue leash	4	Just like Leash, except blue	$10.00
	0		$0.00

Figure 3.11 Every product has a unique ID, which allows it to be identified specifically. (Generally, of course, unique IDs tend to be longer than one digit. Think of telephone numbers or e-mail addresses as unique IDs.)

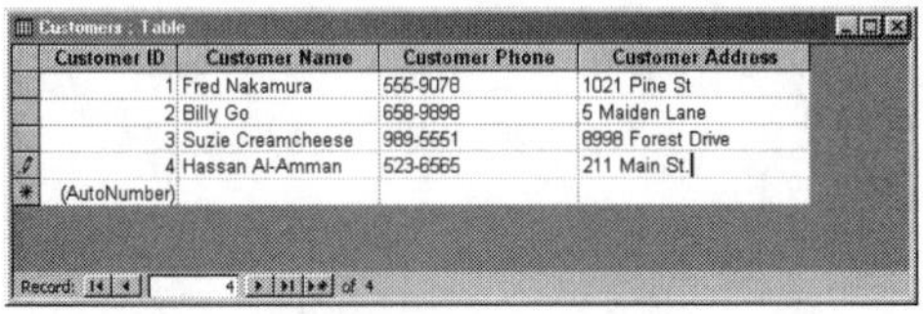

Customer ID	Customer Name	Customer Phone	Customer Address
1	Fred Nakamura	555-9078	1021 Pine St
2	Billy Go	658-9898	5 Maiden Lane
3	Suzie Creamcheese	989-5551	8998 Forest Drive
4	Hassan Al-Amman	523-6565	211 Main St.
(AutoNumber)			

Record: 4 of 4

Figure 3.12 Many databases have an autonumber field type that you can designate as the key.

Keys and indexes

Most database applications that you'll be working with use a system of *keys* to positively identify records in a table. A key is a field that has a unique value for every record in a table. In the product catalog example we've been using, the product ID field could be used as a key, because the product ID is unique to each record. However, the product *price* field could *not* function as a key, because two different products could easily have the same price—thus the data for that field isn't unique to each record (**Figure 3.11**).

Keys are important—if a customer orders a pillowcase, you don't want to add a mattress pad to the order simply because they cost the same. However, the terminology database applications use to refer to keys may vary. Many applications refer to them as *indexes*, while others use both keys and indexes. Regardless, they all use a unique value to identify each record.

The way you assign keys varies from application to application. In Microsoft Access, for example, the application asks you to specify a key when you create a new table, whereas in MySQL, you have to remember on your own to specify a key. Regardless which application you use, however, you can designate any kind of field as a key. Most database applications have an autonumber-like field that is automatically generated, which assigns a new number for each record. This field is often an ideal key, because those numbers will be unique for each record (**Figure 3.12**).

Now that we have an idea of what a database contains, let's create one to work with.

DATABASES AND RELATIONSHIPS

Creating a Database

It should come as no shock that to use Dreamweaver to display content from a database, you must first have a database, and it has to have stuff in it. This section walks you through the steps of creating a small database and populating it with fabricated information.

✔ Tip

- If you are working with a database server that is administered by someone else, you should definitely discuss how to create databases on the server with him or her. Messing around with someone's database is a good way to make enemies, and in most cases your administrator will have to give you appropriate privileges before you can create new databases anyway.

In this section, we deal exclusively with creating a MySQL database. We do this because MySQL is freely available, and many databases use the SQL language. If we were to cover every database out there, it would require a book much bigger than the one you hold in your hand. So if you are using a system that *doesn't* rely on using SQL, make sure you consult the manual for your database application to perform the equivalent operation.

While Dreamweaver is great in that it automates most of the SQL processes, it doesn't allow you to create a database within it. So we need to create a very simple database outside of Dreamweaver using MySQL. This database will help us illustrate how to work with a SQL server in Dreamweaver later on.

We're going to create a small guestbook database, which will necessitate running the MySQL program directly. Again, if you are not working with a database server that you have sole control over, check with whoever manages the server to figure out how to do it.

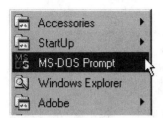

Figure 3.13 Opening an MS-DOS command window.

To work with the SQL server directly, you must have MySQL installed on your local machine. If you don't, you need to do that first. See Chapter 1 for more information about choosing and working with an application server.

Logging into the SQL server

Now, let's walk through the process of logging in to the SQL server. (If you use Mac OS 9, you'll need to visit a Windows machine or an OS X machine to log into the server and perform all commands.)

To log in to the SQL server:

1. In Windows, from the Windows Start Menu, open a DOS window by selecting Program Files > MS-DOS Prompt (**Figure 3.13**).

   or

   In Mac OS X, launch the Terminal application.

2. In Windows, once the DOS window appears, navigate to the \bin\ folder under the folder where you installed MySQL, and then press Enter.

   For example, if you installed MySQL in c:\mysql, you would type:

   cd c:\mysql\bin

   Note: In Mac OS X you can skip this step. Since Mac OS X is Unix-based, you don't need to navigate to any specific directory. MySQL is installed in the /usr/local/ directory by default, and that happens to be one of the standard places the system checks when you launch an application from the command line.

3. At the command prompt, type mysql -u root and press Enter to run the SQL server as the root user.

continues on next page

CREATING A DATABASE

or

If you have already set a password for the root user in MySQL, log in using this password instead.

(A *root user* is the superuser, or someone who has complete control over everything on the server.)

You should now see a `mysql>` prompt.

4. To see what databases are currently running, type `SHOW DATABASES;` and then press Enter (**Figure 3.14**).

The semicolon is a very important part of SQL syntax. If you forget to include it, your command won't be executed. We talk more about SQL syntax in the next chapter.

The results of the `SHOW DATABASES;` command should show two databases running: mysql and test. These are the default databases, and we don't need to do anything with them, other than to verify that they're there.

5. Now it's time to create our new database. In the DOS window at the mysql> prompt, type `CREATE DATABASE quickpro;` and press Enter. Remember that database names are case-sensitive, so we suggest using all lower case for the database name, so that you don't get confused later.

6. Now confirm that you successfully created the database. In the DOS window at the mysql> prompt, type `SHOW DATABASES;` again and press Enter.

What you see should look something like **Figure 3.15**.

7. Now we need to designate the quickpro database as the one we are working with. Type

`USE quickpro;`

You should get a database changed message (**Figure 3.16**).

Now that you're logged in to the SQL server, you can create a table to hold some data.

Figure 3.14 You can see which databases are running. Here it's just the default databases that always run when MySQL is running.

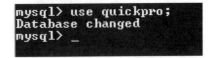

Figure 3.15 We have successfully created a new database, called quickpro.

```
mysql> use quickpro;
Database changed
mysql> _
```

Figure 3.16 MySQL confirms that you've switched databases.

✔ Tip

■ If you see a -> prompt instead of a `mysql>` prompt after typing any of the above commands, the server is unable to execute and is waiting for more information. It's probably because you forgot to include the semicolon at the end of your command. We talk more about the importance of the semicolon in SQL syntax in the next chapter.

Creating and populating the database table

Before we create the table, we want to think about what information it needs to contain. Once we create the table, it's difficult to change the format, so it is important to plan your table before you actually create it.

Because this database is a one-table database with only one-to-one relationships, it's not important to spend a lot of thought on what data to put where. We just need to make sure that the fields are the correct format for the data we want them to hold.

For the purposes of our guestbook database, each record in our table will need fields for a name, an e-mail address, the time the entry was made, and comments.

In SQL, the fields are defined like this:

- `guest_name`   `varchar(24)`
- `guest_email`   `varchar(32)`
- `guest_time`   `timestamp(12)`
- `guest_entry` `text`

We'll see how to use the above definitions to create our table in a moment, but first let's examine them in a bit more detail. The first item in each line is the name of the field. We've prepended `guest_` to each entry. This is not strictly necessary, but is a common practice known as using *reserved words*. Fields like "name" are common to many tables, and it's often less confusing if the table's own name is part of each field's name.

continues on next page

CREATING A DATABASE

The second column is the data type. The types used above are as follows:

◆ *varchar(n)*. Varchar is short for "a variable number of characters up to the number specified." This data type is used a lot because it allows great latitude in input length without huge storage overhead. For example, "Jane Doe" is only 8 characters, (including the space between the first and last names), while "Abie Hadjitarkhani" is 18 characters. Using the varchar data type, the field can accommodate both names without taking up 18 characters worth of storage for every name. For the guestbook database we're creating here, storage isn't much of an issue, but in an application like voter rolls or a user database on a busy site, using a data type like varchar can make a big difference. Varchar can be any length up to 255 characters.

◆ *timestamp(n)*. Timestamp is a year/date/time value that is automatically set every time a record is altered. The number corresponds to the amount of detail displayed in the table. In this case (12), we are showing year, month, day, hours, minutes and seconds.

◆ *text*. Text is an arbitrarily large field of characters, or text. The maximum length of this data type is 2^{16} characters, or roughly 65,536 characters.

Now that you have the information you need to understand how tables are created, it's finally time to make one.

✔ Tip

■ Actions aren't executed until and unless you include the semicolon (;) at the end of the line where specified. For more on SQL syntax, see Chapter 4.

Other Common Data Types

SQL includes a number of fields we're not using in our example. Here are some other common data types. Check the documentation for your database application to find out how your application defines field types.

● *char(n)*. A fixed number of characters. For example, you would use char(1) for people to specify "m", "f" or "o" in a gender entry.

● *int(n)*. An integer, or whole number. The number in parentheses governs how many digits are displayed in the table.

● *float(m, n)*. A floating-point, or decimal number. The first number in parentheses specifies the total number of digits displayed, and the second specifies how many of those are after the decimal point.

There are a number of other data types that we don't have the space to detail here, but they can be found in the MySQL documentation at http://www.mysql.com.

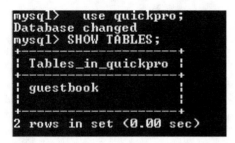

```
mysql>    use quickpro;
Database changed
mysql> SHOW TABLES;
+--------------------+
! Tables_in_quickpro !
+--------------------+
! guestbook          !
!                    !
+--------------------+
2 rows in set (0.00 sec)
```

Figure 3.17 The tables in our new database.

```
mysql> DESCRIBE guestbook;
+------------+--------------+------+-----+---------+-------+
! Field      ! Type         ! Null ! Key ! Default ! Extra !
+------------+--------------+------+-----+---------+-------+
! guest_name ! varchar(24)  ! YES  !     ! NULL    !       !
! guest_email! varchar(32)  ! YES  !     ! NULL    !       !
! guest_time ! timestamp(12)! YES  !     ! NULL    !       !
! guest_entry! text         ! YES  !     ! NULL    !       !
+------------+--------------+------+-----+---------+-------+
4 rows in set (0.17 sec)
```

Figure 3.18 MySQL can show you what the format of your table is.

To create a database table:

1. If you aren't logged in to the SQL database and already working with the "quickpro" database, follow Steps 1 through 3 and Step 7 of the previous task, *To log in to the SQL server.*

2. At the mysql> command line prompt, type the following:
   CREATE TABLE guestbook (guest_name →varchar(24), guest_email var →char(32), guest_time time- →stamp(12), guest_entry text);
   Now press Enter (Return). A "Query OK" message should appear. If you get an error message, check your typing carefully.

3. Type SHOW TABLES; to confirm that your table was created successfully (**Figure 3.17**).

4. Type DESCRIBE guestbook; to see the format of your table. It should look something like **Figure 3.18**.

Now that we have a table, we need to put some actual information in it. There are several ways to do this, but because we're starting with an empty table, we'll do it the fast way and read information in from a text file. To see how to add records using the INSERT statement, see Chapter 4, *SQL Syntax.*

To fill the table with information:

1. First, we need to create a text file. Open your text editor and create a new file.

2. Type the following script, with the exception that in the instances where you see \<tab> in the script, you must press the Tab key, and in the instances where you see \<Return>, you must press the Enter (Return) key.

```
Fred Jones
→<tab>fred@homemaker.org<tab>\n<tab>
→I love this site!<Return>
Samantha Jones<tab>s_jones@company.
→com<tab>\n<tab>My husband Fred
→told me about this site, and I'm
→glad he did<Return>
Suzy
→Jones<tab>suzy@middleschool.edu
→<tab>\n<tab>My parents don't do
→anything but surf this site!
→Help!!!<Return>
Fred
→Jones<tab>fred@homemaker.org<tab>\n
→<tab>I still love this site!
→<Return>
```

The \n character value in this script tells MySQL that there is a NULL, or blank, field in the record. We have decided that we don't want a timestamp for entries not actually made by guests, so this will set the values to 00000000000000. We could set the timestamp to some arbitrary time, but there are many cases in which you would want to have a blank field in a record, so we'll let it stand.

3. In Windows, navigate to the `c:\mysql\data` directory and save the file as a text-only file called `dummy.txt`.

   or

   In Mac OS X, navigate to the `/usr/local/mysql/data` directory and save the file as a text-only file called `dummy.txt`.

Pasting Code vs. Typing Code

You can find many of the code blocks like the ones we print in this chapter on the companion Web site for this book (www.peachpit.com/vqp/dreamweaver MX). That way, you won't have to type everything over again if you don't want to.

Figure 3.19 The MS-DOS prompt window limits the display, which makes it wrap awkwardly.

4. Now we want to load this data directly into the SQL database. At the `mysql>` prompt, type

   `LOAD DATA INFILE "./dummy.txt" INTO ⇥TABLE guestbook;`

   It may seem redundant to specify the filename as `./dummy.txt` instead of just `dummy.txt`. But if you use `dummy.txt`, MySQL will look for the file in the wrong place. By specifying the current (or `./`) folder, we are telling MySQL to look for the filename in the data directory, which is, conveniently, where we placed it.

5. To verify that the data loaded correctly, type

   `SELECT * FROM guestbook;`

   The purpose of the `SELECT` statement may not be making a lot of sense to you right now. `SELECT` is the SQL keyword for retrieving records from a table. By telling MySQL to `SELECT *`, we are telling it to get everything from the table. We delve deeper into the SELECT keyword and how to use it in the next chapter, *Using SQL*.

   You should see the data in a columnar format, although the limited text display may wrap the rows in a strange way (**Figure 3.19**).

Tidying the database

Before we leave the command-line MySQL interface and move on to Dreamweaver, we need to do some maintenance to make the database more secure.

You may have noticed that you didn't need a password to log in to the SQL server as the root user in Step 3 of *Logging into the SQL server*. Because the root is the superuser, or someone who has complete control over everything on the server, it's obviously not a good idea to let just anyone log in this way. Let's add a password.

To add a password for root user:

1. While logged into the database, type
   `SET PASSWORD=PASSWORD('<psswd>');`
   where <psswd> is the password you want to use.

   You need to include the single quotes, but not the angle brackets. So if you wanted your password to be "dreamweaver" you would type
   `SET PASSWORD=PASSWORD('dreamweaver');`.

2. Log out of the database by typing `exit` and press Enter (Return).

3. Log into the database by typing
   `mysql -u root -p`.

4. Type your password at the password: prompt (**Figure 3.20**).

✔ Tip

- For all passwords in the real world, as you probably know, you want to use a non-guessable password that is not a word found in the dictionary, such as ch33R or FR89unkle.

Figure 3.20 MySQL hides your password when you enter it.

To set up a Web user name and password:

Because it's not a good idea to let just any Web user connect to your database as the root user, let's create a user name and password specifically for the people connecting to your Web site.

1. If you are not already logged into the database as the root user, do so by following Steps 3 and 4 in the previous task.

2. Type
```
GRANT ALL ON quickpro.* TO webber
→IDENTIFIED BY 'dreamweaver';
```
and press Enter (Return).

This creates a user called 'webber' who has the password 'dreamweaver' and has rights to any table in the quickpro database. For testing purposes, you'll also need to add an identical user on the local machine.

3. To add user 'webber' to a local machine, type
```
GRANT ALL ON quickpro.* TO
→webber@localhost IDENTIFIED BY
→'dreamweaver';
```
and press Enter (Return).

That's it for the command-line SQL interface! Quit out of the database by typing **exit** and pressing Enter (Return). Then close the DOS window by typing **exit** and pressing Enter (Return).

CREATING A DATABASE

Connecting to a Database

Now that you know how to set up a database, let's look at what happens when you want to talk to it.

To talk to a database, you first need to tell it who you are and what information you want from it. In Dreamweaver MX, those steps break down into creating a database connection, creating a recordset, and then displaying the results of that recordset on your page.

The basics of creating a database connection and a recordset are covered in the *Databases Panel* and *Data Bindings Panel* sections of Chapter 2. How to display the results of a recordset is covered in Chapter 5, *Adding Dynamic Text and Using Recordsets*. Here, we're going to focus a bit more on the details of connecting to your database.

Regardless of which database you use, you still tell Dreamweaver to connect to the database the way we explained in Chapter 2. However, there are different types of database drivers you use depending on the kind of database you have, as you can see by looking at **Table 3.1**.

For several years, the database world has been showered with various competing database drivers: ODBC, OLE DB, JDBC, and so on. We'll tell you what all those inscrutable acronyms stand for, but it's not really important that you memorize them. What is important is that you understand what these drivers do.

✔ Tip

■ Dreamweaver only supports using a MySQL database connection with the PHP protocol. You'll likely be using PHP as the file type for your dynamic pages if you want to interact directly with MySQL.

Table 3.1

Kinds of Database Connections	
DATABASE TYPE	CONNECTION
ASP.NET	OLE DB connection
ASP	ODBC (DSN) connection (see *Setting up a DSN* later in this chapter)
Cold Fusion	Cold Fusion Data Source
JSP	JDBC or ODBC connection
PHP	Basic connection (see the *Databases Panel* section in Chapter 2)

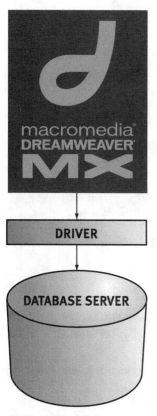

Figure 3.21 Database drivers translate for Dreamweaver and HTML.

Database drivers essentially take what you're telling the database and translate it into the appropriate format for the database to understand (**Figure 3.21**). This is useful because it means that the fine folks who created Dreamweaver can spend their time making the program do cool things, instead of spending their time building data dictionaries for every database on the market. It's also useful because it means that you can create your application using a small database like Microsoft Access and then transfer it to an industrial-weight product like Oracle Server without having to rewrite everything.

There are far too many server/driver combinations to cover in this book, but we've included a discussion of some of the major ones here, along with stepped instructions for how to implement them. If your particular combination is not covered here, you can probably find it in the Dreamweaver Help documentation, under the heading *Connecting to a Database*.

✔ Tips

- To do any of the tasks that follow, you must have a database and the appropriate application server already set up.

- Although Dreamweaver MX can be used with a wide variety of databases and drivers, it has been tested only with Access, SQL Server, MySQL and Oracle 9i. For a list of drivers that have been tested with MX, see the Dreamweaver Dynamic FAQ at

  `http://www.macromedia.com/support/`
  `dreamweaver/ts/documents/`
  `dwmx_dynamic_faq.htm`

OLE DB connections

OLE DB (Object Linking and Embedding Database) connections use Microsoft's OLE layer to connect to a database.

OLE DB connections are most often used in ASP.NET applications. When you connect with an OLE DB driver, Dreamweaver looks for what's called a *connection string*, which contains the path to the database, the user and password information, and so on. Here's a sample connection string:

```
Provider=SQLOLEDB;Server=dataland;Data
base=infomatic;UID=jdoe;PWD=lemmein
```

Fortunately, Dreamweaver provides you with tools to make generating this string a little easier.

To create an OLE DB connection:

1. Open an ASP.NET page in Dreamweaver, and then open the Databases panel.

2. Click the + (plus) button on the panel and select OLE DB Connection from the pop-up menu.

   The OLE DB connection dialog box will appear (**Figure 3.22**).

3. Enter a name for the connection in the Name text box.

4. Click the Templates button to open the Connection String Template dialog box, and select the appropriate template for your database (**Figure 3.23**).

5. Replace the placeholders in the string with the appropriate information for your database.

   This usually includes the server name, database name, and occasionally the user name and password (**Figure 3.24**).

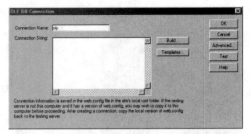

Figure 3.22 The OLE DB connection dialog, where you start building a connection string.

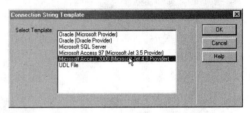

Figure 3.23 Most common databases have a connection string template included with Dreamweaver.

Figure 3.24 You replace the placeholder with the actual information for your database.

Figure 3.25 The Custom Connection String dialog box doesn't give you much of a hint as to its purpose, but you use it to request information from a database.

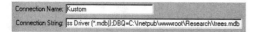

Figure 3.26 Connection strings can look pretty obscure, as you can see in the Connection String text box.

ODBC connections

There are two ways to connect to a database using the ODBC drivers. The first is to use a custom connection string; the second is to use a DSN, or Data Source Name. We'll deal with the latter in the *Setting up a DSN* section later in this chapter, but first let's look at how to set up a custom connection string for an OBDC connection.

To create a custom connection string:

1. Open an ASP page in Dreamweaver, and then open the Databases Panel.

2. Click the + (plus) button on the panel and select Custom Connection String from the pop-up menu.

    The Custom Connection String dialog box appears (**Figure 3.25**).

3. Fill out the dialog box with the information that corresponds to your database (**Figure 3.26**).

It's that easy.

ColdFusion

A ColdFusion server uses what's called a *data source* to connect databases to Web pages. You use this type of connection in the same way as any other connection, but the procedure for creating it is a bit different. You need to create the data source right in the ColdFusion program, and then you need to instruct Dreamweaver to use that data source. (Data source is a term used for many different functions, such as the location of a record in a database. In ColdFusion, however, it's also what the connection method is called.)

ColdFusion is very complex—worthy of a QuickPro guide all on its own—so we won't even try to do it justice here, other than to say the procedure for connecting to a data source is similar to the general procedure for connecting to a database in the *Databases Panel* section of Chapter 2.

To connect to a ColdFusion data source:

What follows is a general description of how you'd connect to a ColdFusion data source. For more specific information, you should consult a book on ColdFusion or the product documentation.

1. Create a data source in the ColdFusion Administrator.

2. From Dreamweaver, open a ColdFusion file.

3. In the Databases panel, click the Modify Data Sources button (**Figure 3.27**).

   This will open the ColdFusion Administrator. You must have an admin login to choose your data source from within the CF Administrator. If you don't have this kind of access, see your human database administrator to get set up.

   Once you choose your data source from within the administrator, your database will appear in Dreamweaver's Databases panel with your tables arranged hierarchically in the panel.

Modify Data Sources button

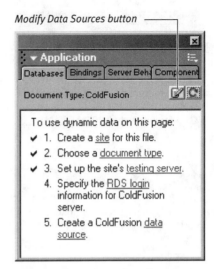

Figure 3.27 You'll start here in the Databases panel to set up your ColdFusion connection, but you'll do the actual choosing of your data source from within the CF Administrator.

Figure 3.28 You need to know the URL and database names to use a JDBC driver. Click the + (plus) button to select the driver you want to use.

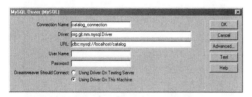

Figure 3.29 The dialog box for your driver. Your URL and Driver will appear; correct the placeholders in brackets with actual URL information.

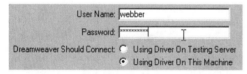

Figure 3.30 Type your username and password, and specify whether to use a local driver or one on your testing server. (If your testing server is *on* your local machine, you may still want to specify to use the non-local option.)

JDBC Connections

If you're already aware that the J in JSP stands for Java, it will come as no surprise that the J in JDBC also stands for Java. JDBC is the Java equivalent of ODBC. There are two ways to connect to a database using a JDBC driver. One way is to use a JDBC-ODBC Bridge driver. This lets you create a DSN (see the DSN section that follows), and only works on Windows.

The second way to connect through a JDBC driver is to create a JDBC connection.

To create a JDBC connection:

1. Open a JSP page in Dreamweaver.

2. In the Databases Panel, click the + (plus) button and select the appropriate driver for your database (**Figure 3.28**).
   The MySQL Driver dialog box will appear.

3. In the Connection Name field of this dialog box, enter a name for the connection. Then in the URL field, replace the placeholders (the text in square brackets) with the actual information for your server (**Figure 3.29**).

4. Now fill in the user name and password below the URL field. Choose Using Driver On This Machine if you are running the database on your current machine, or Using Driver On Testing Server if your database is running on another computer (**Figure 3.30**).

5. Click OK to close the dialog box.

We have covered only a small slice of the possible database/driver combinations. Again, consult your Dreamweaver Help documentation, under the heading *Connecting to a Database*, if you want to learn more about the other possibilities.

Now let's focus on the other method for setting up an ODBC driver—using a Data Source Name.

Setting up a DSN

A DSN, or Data Source Name, comprises all
the information about a database connection
in a tidy little package. DSNs are not a Dreamweaver component, but rather a function of
Microsoft's ODBC drivers. Unfortunately, they
work only on Windows machines.

To create a DSN:

1. Open an ASP file in Dreamweaver. In
   the Databases panel, click on the + (plus)
   button, and select Data Source Name
   (DSN) from the pop-up menu.

   The DSN dialog box appears.

2. Click on the Define button (**Figure 3.31**).

   The ODBC Data Source Administrator
   appears.

3. Click on the System DSN tab of the ODBC
   Data Source Administrator dialog box
   (**Figure 3.32**).

   The dialog box displays the list of DSNs
   currently on your system.

4. Click on the Add button on the right to
   add a new DSN to the list.

   The Create New Data Source dialog box
   appears, listing all the drivers currently
   loaded on your system (**Figure 3.33**).

5. Select a driver from the list, and then click
   Finish.

   The dialog box that appears depends on the
   driver you just selected. In our case, because
   we've selected the Microsoft Access Driver,
   the ODBC Microsoft Access Setup dialog
   box appears.

   If a driver for your database application
   does not appear in the list, you'll have to
   download the driver from the vendor's
   Web site and install it.

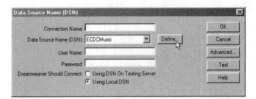

Figure 3.31 You create a System DSN to use with
Dreamweaver.

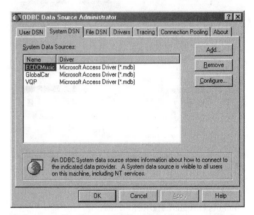

Figure 3.32 The System DSN panel provides a list of
the DSNs already on your system.

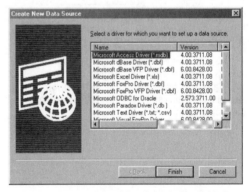

Figure 3.33 Choose your driver from the available list.

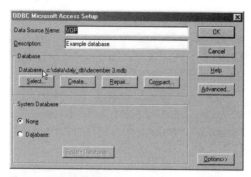

Figure 3.34 Specify your connection parameters in the ODBC Setup dialog box.

6. Enter a name for the DSN in the first field of the ODBC Setup dialog box and specify the connection parameters (**Figure 3.34**).

The way you specify the parameters will vary, depending on the dialog box that appeared. In the ODBC Microsoft Access Setup dialog box, for example, you enter a name, click Select, locate the database file on the hard disk, and click OK.

7. Click OK to close the dialog box.

The new DSN will be added to your list of system DSNs. You can now connect to the database using the DSN by selecting it in the Database window in Dreamweaver.

✔ Tip

■ If you need to open the ODBC administrator, navigate from the Start menu to your Control Panel, and double-click on Administrative Tools. Then, double-click Data Sources (ODBC).

Databases and the Dreamweaver Interface

So far, we've spent this chapter looking at databases and the way they connect to Dreamweaver and not much time looking at what to do with them once they're connected. Don't worry, we'll get into those specifics in the next chapter, and continue through most of the rest of this book. First, though we need to address some of the common concerns about how databases work in a Web context.

Making it easier for you

Dreamweaver's interface has two main functions when it comes to databases.

The first is that it insulates you from having to spend a huge amount of time writing code to access the database. When you create a recordset (see the *Bindings Panel* section in Chapter 2), for example, what's going on behind the scenes is that you are actually creating a command in a scripting language, such as PHP or JSP, which then creates a command that tells the database what information to give back to you (**Figure 3.35**).

The other main function of the Dreamweaver interface is to provide a handier way of displaying the information that comes back from the database. So when you display dynamic text on a page (see *Adding a Recordset to a Page* in Chapter 5), for instance, you are getting information from your database and using Dreamweaver's interface to display that information (**Figure 3.36**).

Figure 3.35 Creating a recordset creates PHP code.

Figure 3.36 Displaying a recordset creates yet more PHP code.

How you can make it easier, too

It is a common misconception that you need to create different copies of your data if you want to permit different levels of access to a database. However, by using the Dreamweaver interface intelligently, you can provide different views of the data, and different levels of access to it, while maintaining only one copy of the data.

Let's return to our online store example. A customer, a marketing rep, and a shipping clerk are all going to need different things from the database:

Although each of these users needs different information, they are getting the data from the same database. Dreamweaver provides convenient ways to create interfaces for each of these users, as you'll discover through the rest of this book.

Table 3.2

Different Users, Different Needs	
USER	WHAT THE USER NEEDS
Customer	Customers need to be able to change their own records, create new orders, and browse the product catalog.
Marketing rep	Marketing reps need to be able to find customers who have bought a certain product, get a list of products that are overstocked, and be able to create orders.
Shipping clerk	Shipping clerks need to get a list of the day's orders, including addresses and customer names; and update the inventory of a particular product to reflect the day's shipments.

DATABASES AND THE DREAMWEAVER INTERFACE

How the database and Dreamweaver interact

What actually happens when a Web application talks to a database may still be a little obscure, but it's actually not that hard to understand.

In a traditional Web interaction, the user makes a request of the Web server, saying "Give me this page." The server then sends the HTML code for the page to the user, and the user's browser converts the HTML into a page on-screen (**Figure 3.37**).

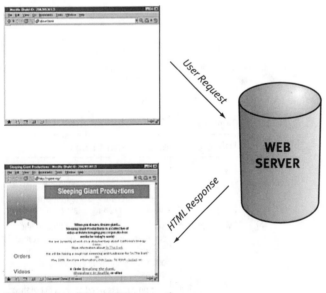

Figure 3.37 A traditional HTML transaction.

When you add a database to the equation, one more step is added as well. The user makes a request of the Web server, saying "Give me this page, which includes some requests for data." The Web server then extracts the database request and forwards it on to the database server. From there, the database server finds the requested information and sends it back to the Web server. Finally, the Web server takes that information, packages it as HTML and sends it back to the browser. The browser recognizes the HTML and displays the information in the usual way, even though this time it's displaying data (**Figure 3.38**). All this happens in less time than it took you to read this paragraph.

In the next chapter, we'll delve more deeply into MySQL—one of the most commonly-used database applications.

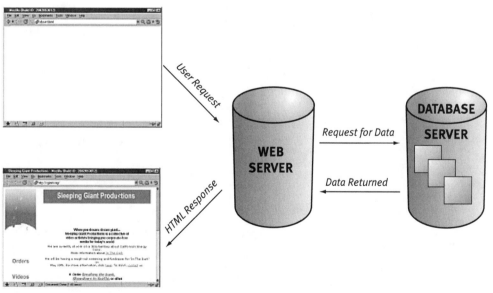

Figure 3.38 A database transaction includes an extra step.

Using SQL

Structured Query Language, or SQL (usually pronounced "sequel"), is a very common language used in many database applications that provides a relatively simple, yet powerful, way to access a database. Because it's an open standard, it's used in a variety of database products, from freeware to those costing tens of thousands of dollars. Because SQL is so common and there's a likelihood you'll use it at some point, we'll spend this chapter delving into the details of this language.

Using SQL, HTML, and a scripting language (such as PHP), you can create dynamic Web sites that integrate up-to-the-minute information with optimized design and content. Some of the most common ways to use SQL are tracking visitors to a Web site, providing an interface to a larger pool of information, or allowing site visitors to enter changes directly in a database. Tracking visitors can be as simple as remembering user names and passwords, or as comprehensive as remembering which menus the visitor wants to see when they return. Creating an interface to a larger pool of information can also be a relatively compact task, like looking up a co-worker's phone number, or it can be significantly more involved, like requesting a reverse-threaded screw that's one inch long with a rounded head. And letting visitors make changes directly to a database makes it easier to house up-to-date information, such as new mailing addresses or credit card numbers.

Although there are other database languages you can use with HTML and a scripting language to accomplish the same things, in this chapter we'll focus on SQL for several reasons. For one, SQL is practically ubiquitous, and MySQL, one of the more popular SQL databases, is available without charge on a number of platforms, including Windows. Second, the combination of MySQL and PHP is one of the default configurations included in Dreamweaver MX. Because both components are available free of charge, you get maximum bang for your database/scripting buck when you use SQL. And finally, using PHP and SQL with Dreamweaver MX can be a great way to provide dynamic content on your Web site without mucking about with a large amount of scripting.

Even if Dreamweaver lets you off easy when it comes to scripting, it still makes sense to have at least a rudimentary knowledge of what's going on behind the scenes when you're working with something as complicated as a SQL database. You may not know all the details, but understanding what happens when the user clicks on the Submit button, for example, can help you design your applications most efficiently. If you don't know what's possible with SQL, you'll miss an opportunity to add sophisticated features that could make the difference between someone returning to your site or visiting your competitors'.

This chapter provides an overview of SQL, shows you how to connect to a SQL server, and explains how to use it to embed dynamic content in your Web site.

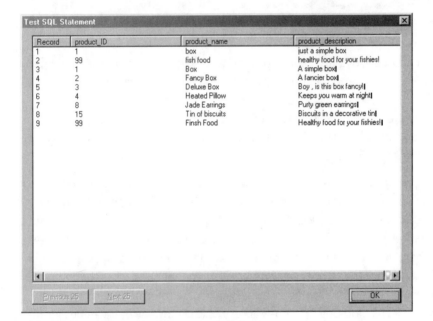

Figure 4.1
A recordset is a snapshot of some of the data in your table.

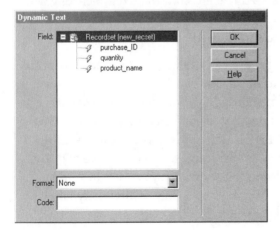

Figure 4.2 You can display a recordset using the Dynamic Text dialog box.

Getting by Without Learning SQL

In many cases, it's possible to work with a SQL database in Dreamweaver without much of a clue as to what is actually happening when your application talks to the database. You do this by using Dreamweaver dialog boxes to define a recordset, which is a snapshot of some portion of the data in your table (**Figure 4.1**). To find out what the basic procedure is for defining a recordset, see the *Using the Data Bindings Panel* section in Chapter 2.

You can also use Dreamweaver to display the data you selected in the recordset using text or tables, by way of the Dynamic Text or Dynamic Tables dialog boxes (**Figure 4.2**). These are covered in detail in Chapter 5 under *Adding Dynamic Text to a Page*.

And you can also click your way around to make changes to existing records or add new records, which are covered in Chapter 8, *Editing Records from Web Interfaces* (**Figure 4.3**).

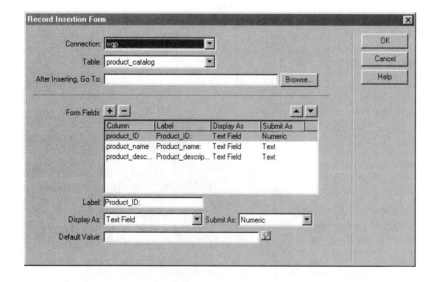

Figure 4.3 You can use Dreamweaver to change or add a record.

69

SQL Syntax

Although Dreamweaver insulates you from having to know a lot about SQL syntax, it's useful to have an idea of what's going on behind the scenes, and it's necessary to know the very basics to create a database.

It's possible to access and manipulate your database by opening a terminal window and sending commands directly to the server (**Figure 4.4**). But usually that's not necessary, because you can use Dreamweaver dialog boxes to perform the most common tasks. You can, however, type some SQL commands directly into Dreamweaver's Recordset definition window. We cover how to do that in the *SELECT Statement* section below.

As we mentioned in the Chapter 3 section *Creating a Database*, SQL commands are terminated with a semicolon. The semicolon tells the server that a command is finished. So SHOW DATABASES; will show you a list of databases, whereas SHOW DATABASES will not.

Another important thing to remember is that SQL syntax uses an unfortunate mix of case sensitivity and case insensitivity that can get very confusing. In general, SQL command words are case insensitive. So select, Select, and SELECT are all the same. But database names, table names, and field names *are* case sensitive, so customer, Customer, and CUSTOMER signify three different things. Traditionally, SQL commands are typed in upper case, but you can use any mix of upper and lower case you prefer for table, database, and field names (although the code tends to be more readable if you use at least some lowercase).

✔ Tip

- Depending on the type of operating system you're running, some SQL elements may not be case sensitive, but don't count on it. To be on the safe side, treat all table names, field names, and aliases as case sensitive.

If you're working with an existing database, you'll be spending most of your time with three basic SQL commands: SELECT, INSERT, and UPDATE. The latter two deal primarily with adding and changing data in your database. They're covered more extensively in Chapter 8. The first command, SELECT, constitutes the meat of this chapter.

The SELECT Statement

The SELECT statement is something like a Swiss Army knife, at least for getting information *out* of a database. It has all sorts of attachments you can use to get the exact results you want.

In this chapter we focus on some of the more basic ways to use this powerful tool, but advanced uses include averages, maximum and minimum values, and all kinds of grouping and aggregating functions that are beyond the scope of this book.

✔ Tip

- If you want to learn more about using SQL and using its more powerful functions, take a look at the *SQL Visual QuickStart Guide,* by Chris Fehily.

Figure 4.4 You can type commands directly to a SQL database in a terminal window.

Figure 4.5 Use the WHERE clause to get a specific record...

Basic Select statements

First, let's look at the basic form of the SELECT statement:

```
SELECT some_stuff
FROM a_table
WHERE conditions_are_met;
```

For readability, we're showing each part of the SQL command on a separate line. You could also write the entire command on one line. It doesn't matter which you do, because SQL won't execute a command until it sees a semicolon.

Let's look at the statement in more detail. What we call "some_stuff" above would be replaced by the names of one or more fields from a table. As we discussed in Chapter 3, *Database Structure*, fields are the columns in the database. So if we had been specifying actual field names, we could have selected, say, the customer name and address while leaving out the phone number, even though the phone number is a field in the database as well. In other words, you can select "some_stuff" without having to select all of it.

The entry "a_table" specifies the table you're using for that particular information. The "conditions_are_met" entry is where you specify which records you're looking for. For example, to show the name and description of a product with the ID number 4, you would type:

```
SELECT product_name,
product_description
FROM product_catalog
WHERE product_ID = 4;
```

This statement will return just the name and description of that one product (**Figure 4.5**).

✔ Tip

- The WHERE clause is actually optional. If you omit it, you will get every record in the table. You will rarely want to do this, however, because most databases are fairly large.

Requesting multiple records

You can also select multiple records with the SELECT statement. To get the names and descriptions of the first 10 products in the catalog, you'd type the following:

```
SELECT product_ID, product_name,
product_description
FROM product_catalog
WHERE product_ID <=10;
```

This command returns the first 10 products in the catalog, and includes the product ID number, for reference (**Figure 4.6**).

✔ Tip

- You can display every field from a record by substituting an asterisk (*) for the list of field names. You'll see this wildcard in action later in this chapter.

The result of a SELECT statement is called a *recordset*. It is the basic building block Dreamweaver uses to display data from a database. We'll examine the recordset more closely later in this chapter.

If you want to type your SELECT statements directly in Dreamweaver instead of building them graphically, Dreamweaver lets you do that.

To write SELECT statements in Dreamweaver:

1. Open a PHP page.

2. Create a new recordset (see Chapter 2, *Using the Data Bindings Panel*).

3. In the Recordset dialog box, click the Advanced button.

4. Type your SELECT statement into the SQL window (**Figure 4.7**).

5. Click on OK to close the dialog box and add the statement to your page.

Figure 4.6 ...or a group of records.

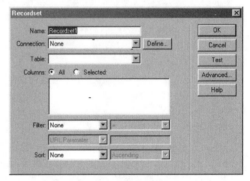

Figure 4.7 To test out a SELECT statement you can type it in the Recordset dialog box.

Sample Data Files

You can find sample database files like the ones we use in this chapter on the companion Web site for this book at www.peachpit.com/vqp/dreamweaverMX.

The INSERT Statement

You use the INSERT statement to add a new record to your table. To alter an existing record, you use the UPDATE statement (see below).

Unfortunately, it's not possible to actually type an INSERT or UPDATE statement directly into Dreamweaver. But when you insert or alter a record using Dreamweaver's Record Insertion Form (see *Adding Database Records* in Chapter 8), Dreamweaver is generating these statements behind the scenes. So it's a good idea to make sure you're familiar with them and how they function.

The basic format for the INSERT statement is:

```
INSERT into table_name
(column1, column2,…columnN)
values (value1, value2, …valueN);
```

We've specified the table into which we want to insert a record. Then we specified the columns for which we want to add data. Finally, we specified the data we want to put into those columns *in the same order we specified the names.*

You can list the columns you want to add in any order, but you must list the values in the same order, or they will end up in the wrong place. (This can also cause errors when the browser requests the data.) If any of your values is a string, you must to enclose it in single quotes.

To add a new product to our catalog, the statement would look a bit different:

```
INSERT into product_catalog
(product_ID, product_name,
product_description)
values (99, 'Fish Food', 'Healthy food
for your little fishies!');
```

Here, we are adding a record to the table "product_catalog." For the new record, the product_ID is 99, the product_name is "Fish Food," and the contents of the description field are "Healthy food for your fishies!"

The UPDATE Statement

The UPDATE statement is used to change a record that is already in the database. Because you are actually altering the data in your table with this command, you should be careful. If you get careless, you can end up with seriously mangled data.

The generic form of the UPDATE statement looks like this:

```
UPDATE table_name
SET column_name = new_value
WHERE condition_is_true;
```

This statement works a little differently. We specify the table name just like in the previous examples, but then we specify the field (also called a column) that we want to change, and tell it the new value. Finally, we use the WHERE clause we saw when we used a SELECT statement to specify which records we want to change.

Suppose, for example, the marketing department wants to capitalize on the health benefits of your new-formula fish food. They ask you to change the name of your Fish Food product to Healthy Fish Food. You can do this with the following UPDATE statement:

```
UPDATE product_catalog
SET product_name = 'Healthy Fish Food'
WHERE product_name = 'Fish Food';
```

✔ Tips

- The WHERE clause doesn't handle just numbers—it can also handle strings, as you can see from the previous example.

- Because the UPDATE statement has the potential to thoroughly swizzle your data, it's usually best to perform a SELECT statement with the same WHERE clause first to make sure you are changing only those records you want to change.

Updating multiple records

You can also change multiple columns of a
record at once, instead of just one at a time.
What if, for example, the FDA decides that
your fish food is not actually healthy and
requires you to remove the word *healthy* from
both the name and description? You can do
that, too, with the UPDATE statement:

```
UPDATE product_catalog
SET product_name = 'Fish Food',
product_description = 'Food for your
little fishies!'
WHERE product_ID = 99;
```

Other SQL Statements

There are several other SQL statements that we don't have the space to address here. They
include DROP, which deletes a table from a database; USE, which sets the current database;
and IMPORT, which reads a chunk of text into your table.

Generally, these commands are most useful for database administration and initial database
setup. Your database administrator is most likely the person who deals with this kind of thing.
If you are your own database administrator, you should pick up a good SQL reference, or check
the many tutorial sites on the Web. Some good sites are:

◆ http://www.sqlcourse.com/

◆ http://www.baycongroup.com/tocsql.htm

◆ http://www.geocities.com/SiliconValley/Vista/2207/sql1.html

THE UPDATE STATEMENT

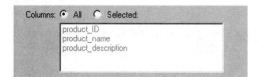

Figure 4.8 All the columns in your table are selected by default.

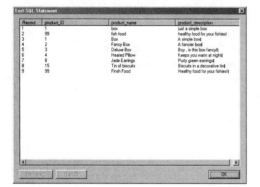

Figure 4.9 After you click the Test button (Figure 4.7), a preview of your recordset will appear in this dialog box.

Defining Your Records

Now that we've touched on the basics of the most common SQL commands, let's look at how you can use SQL in Dreamweaver.

When you display information from a database, you might not want to show every field in a record. Your internal product catalog, for example, might contain your cost, in addition to the price you are charging consumers. You probably wouldn't want to display that information to just anyone shopping online.

You can control the fields you display by generating a recordset containing only those fields you want to include (For more on recordsets, see *The Data Bindings Panel* section in Chapter 2). As you might have guessed, behind the scenes, Dreamweaver uses our old friend the SELECT statement to generate the recordset.

Creating a recordset

You were introduced to the recordset dialog box in Chapter 2. Here, we'll be using the same dialog box, but we'll be delving a little deeper into it. First, let's create a recordset that contains an entire table.

To create a recordset that contains the entire table:

1. Create a recordset by following the steps in *To create a recordset*, in the *Data Bindings Panel* section of Chapter 2.

2. In the Recordset dialog box, select your database connection from the Connection drop-down menu.

3. In the Table drop-down menu, a list of the tables in the active database will appear. By default, the All Columns radio button will be selected (**Figure 4.8**).

4. Click the Test button to see a preview of your recordset (which in this case is equivalent to the whole table) (**Figure 4.9**).

continues on next page

This may seem pretty straightforward, and only tangentially related to SQL, but we're about to show you the man behind the curtain. What Dreamweaver is doing behind the scenes as a result of the information you plugged in is to create a SQL command. Fortunately, Dreamweaver lets you see the SQL it generates.

To see the SQL behind creating a recordset:

1. Follow Steps 1-3 on the previous page to create a recordset, choose your database connection, and specify a table.

2. In the Recordset dialog, box, click the Advanced button.

   The dialog box will switch to advanced mode (**Figure 4.10**).

   In the SQL text box, you can see the SQL command that shows the whole database (**Figure 4.11**).

Selecting the appropriate fields

You often want to display only some of the fields in a record, or in a group of records. You already know how to do that with SQL (at least if you read the beginning of this chapter); now we'll see how that fits in with Dreamweaver.

To create a recordset without all the fields:

1. Follow Steps 1-3, on the previous page under *To create a recordset that contains the entire table,* to create a recordset, choose your database connection, and specify a table.

2. In the Recordset dialog box, click the Selected Columns radio button.

   The list of fields will not be grayed out any more (**Figure 4.12**).

Simple button to return to regular mode

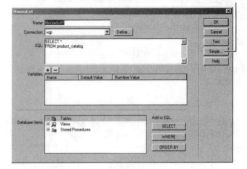

Figure 4.10 The Recordset dialog box has an Advanced mode setting...

Figure 4.11 ...which shows the SQL statement behind your query.

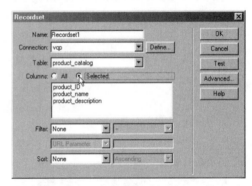

Figure 4.12 Clicking the Selected Columns radio button activates the field list.

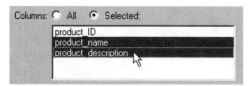

Figure 4.13 You can Shift+click (Command+click on the Mac) to select multiple fields.

Figure 4.14 The Advanced mode shows the SQL for selecting only some fields.

3. Click on the fields in the list box to select the fields that you want the recordset to include.

You can Shift+click to select a range or Ctrl+click (Command+click on the Mac) to select multiple fields (**Figure 4.13**).

4. Click the Test button to show your recordset.

Again, all well and good, but where's the SQL?

To see the SQL:

1. Follow steps 1-3 in the previous exercise to select the fields you want to include.

2. Click the Advanced button in the Recordset dialog box to switch to Advanced mode.

You'll see the SELECT statement with the appropriate fields specified (**Figure 4.14**).

✔ Tip

- You can type a SQL statement directly into the SQL box in Advanced mode. If you do, you don't have to include the semicolon at the end of the statement.

DEFINING YOUR RECORDS

Limiting the Number of Records in a Set

A database can contain millions of records but you rarely, if ever, want to display them all on a Web page. You can limit the records you retrieve from a database by using the SQL WHERE clause.

To create a recordset with only specific records:

1. In the Application panel group, click on the Data Bindings panel.

2. Click the + (plus) button. Select Recordset (Query) from the menu.

3. In the Recordset dialog box, type a name for your recordset, select your connection from the Connection drop-down menu, and select the appropriate table from the Table drop-down menu.

4. Select a field name from the first Filter drop-down menu.
   This is the field name in the WHERE clause.

5. From the second Filter drop-down menu (just to the right of the first one), select the operator (=, >, < etc.) that describes how you want to limit your data (**Figure 4.15**).

6. In the third Filter drop-down menu (just below the first drop-down), select Entered Value.

7. Finally, in the text box to the right, type the value you want to test against.

Of course, if you click on the Advanced button, you will see the SQL behind the scenes, with the WHERE clause included (**Figure 4.16**).

Figure 4.15 You can use the Filter drop-down menus to limit the records you get.

Figure 4.16 Using the Filter drop-down menus creates a SQL WHERE clause.

✔ Tips

■ You can request an exact match, a range of values (such as greater than 10 or less than 10,000), or a "like" match. One example of a "like" match would be phone numbers starting with 415, in which case you'd type 415% as your value.

■ The % (percent sign) is a variable in SQL that allows for partial searches rather than exact matches. If you use a "like" match and type a partial search string followed by a %, the database will return all matches that start with that phrase. So requesting "White%" would return "Whitening," "Whitehouse," and "White Castle". Requesting "Whiteh" would return "Whitehouse," but not the others just mentioned.

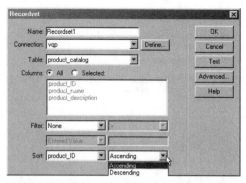

Figure 4.17 You can sort in either direction.

Figure 4.18 Sorting, like all recordset operations, is previewable.

Figure 4.19 Sorting adds an ORDER BY clause to your SQL.

Sorting Records

It's often not enough to limit the quantity of data you're working with, especially when dealing with larger databases. Unless that data is in some useful order, even a hundred records can quickly become unwieldy. Fortunately, SQL provides a way to wrangle your data into an order that makes sense to you. SQL's solution for ordering data is the ORDER BY clause. This clause lets you sort your recordset by one of the fields (such as name, price, or whether it's on sale) and allows you to specify ascending or descending order.

To create a sorted recordset:

1. In the Application panel group, click on the Data Bindings panel.

2. Click the + (plus) button. Select Recordset (Query) from the menu.

3. In the Recordset dialog box, name the recordset, select your connection, and specify the appropriate table.

4. In the first Sort drop-down menu, select the field by which you wish to sort.

5. In the second Sort drop-down, select Ascending or Descending (**Figure 4.17**).

6. Click Test to see the sorted records (**Figure 4.18**).

It should come as no surprise that you can click the Advanced button to see the SQL command (**Figure 4.19**).

✔ Tip

■ By default, SQL sorts in ascending order. Although Dreamweaver always adds the keyword ASC, when you're writing your own SQL, you can leave it out.

Retrieving Data From Multiple Tables

So far in this chapter, we've dealt only with recordsets that get their data from a single table. Because most database applications need to use data from more than one table, the procedures outlined earlier are only the beginning.

Using the Database Items tree

Dreamweaver provides a tool to create recordsets from more than one table, called the Database Items tree. This allows you to pick fields from all the tables in your database without having to type too much.

To create a recordset using the Database Items tree:

1. In the Application panel group, click on the Data Bindings panel.

2. Click the + (plus) button. Select Recordset (Query) from the menu.

3. In the Recordset dialog box, name the recordset and select your connection.

   You can ignore the table drop-down menu for the time being.

4. Click the Advanced button to switch to the advanced mode.

5. Select all the text in the SQL text box and delete it.

   No, really, do this. You'll be generating all-new text using the Database Items tree.

6. In the bottom panel of the dialog box, which is the Database Items tree, click on the Expand button (+) next to the word Tables to show all the tables in your database (**Figure 4.20**).

7. Expand one of the tables to show a list of the fields in that table (**Figure 4.21**).

Figure 4.20 The Database Items tree includes a list of all the tables in your database.

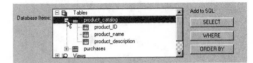

Figure 4.21 Expanding a table shows all of its fields.

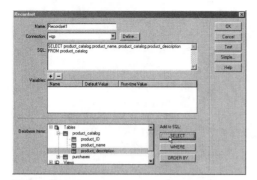

Figure 4.22 Clicking the SELECT button adds the highlighted field to the SQL command.

Figure 4.23 You need to type the WHERE condition manually.

Figure 4.24 To sort the results by a particular field, we can add an ORDER BY statement.

8. Select the first field you want in your recordset and click the SELECT button.

The field will appear as part of the SELECT statement in the SQL window, and the table name will appear in the FROM clause.

9. Repeat Step 8 for each field you wish to show (**Figure 4.22**).

10. Select the field you want to use for the WHERE clause. Click the WHERE button to add that clause to the SQL window.

11. In the SQL window, after the field name, type the condition the WHERE clause requires (**Figure 4.23**).

12. If you want to sort by a field, select it and click the ORDER BY button.

Your statement is now complete (**Figure 4.24**).

13. Finally, click TEST to show the results of the statement you've built.

Some New SQL Details

When you click on a field name, you've probably already noticed it appears in the SQL window with the name of the table and a period before it. This is SQL's way of making sure it knows exactly which field you are specifying. Several tables can have a field called ID, for example, so you need to specify customer.ID for the customer name and product.ID for the product name.

Additionally, you probably want to stay away from using the word "name" as a fieldname, because it's a reserved word in Access databases. In Access, you can use fname, lname, or prod_name, or you'll get a complicated error message when the page loads in the browser.

Selecting data from multiple tables

We could have executed all the previous tasks much more simply—you don't always need to check to see how the SQL is working. But now that you have an idea of what's happening behind the scenes, we can get to the real meat of working with SQL: joining data from more than one table.

In most cases, when you're working with multiple tables, one field in a table corresponds to a field in another table. Let's return to the product catalog example we used at the beginning of this chapter. There might be a second table, called purchases, which has a list of purchases with a product ID and the quantity purchased. (If this were an actual online store, we'd probably need to know when the purchase was made and by whom, but for our purposes, that's unnecessary.) In this case, the product ID would be the field that combines the two tables.

To create a recordset from multiple tables:

1. Follow steps 1-6 from the previous task, *To create a recordset using the Database Items tree.*

2. Expand all the tables that have data you want to include (**Figure 4.25**).

3. Select all the fields you want to display by clicking on the field name and clicking the SELECT button.

4. Select the field in one table that corresponds to the field in the other table (**Figure 4.26**).

   In our example, the fields are both named product_ID. First we'll select this field in the product_catalog table.

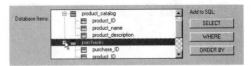

Figure 4.25 You can expand more than one table.

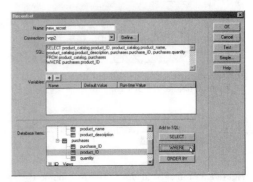

Figure 4.26 The product_ID field is the link between tables in our example.

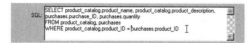

Figure 4.27 A WHERE clause can include fields from more than one table.

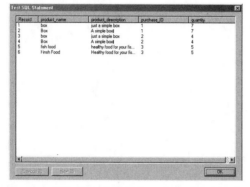

Figure 4.28 The test window shows two tables joined.

5. Click the WHERE button.

6. In the SQL window, type the equal sign (=) after the field name.

7. Select the corresponding field in the other table **(Figure 4.27)** and click the WHERE button.

In Step 4, we selected the field product_ID in the product_catalog table. Now we're selecting the product_ID field in the purchases table.

8. Click Test to see the results of your query **(Figure 4.28)**.

✔ Tip

■ Generally, once you've done anything in the Advanced mode of the Recordset window, Dreamweaver will not let you switch back to the Simple panel. If you need to go back, you can delete everything from the SQL text box, and click the Simple button.

This chapter has shown you some of the basics of SQL and how to use Dreamweaver to get data out of a SQL database. In the next chapter, we will look at how you can use your data now that you have it.

DYNAMIC TEXT AND RECORDSETS 5

So far, our discussion of creating database-driven Web applications has centered mostly on the back end of the process. We've talked extensively about databases and how to use them, as well as how to connect them to Dreamweaver. None of this information does you any good, of course, if you don't know how to use the information from the database once you get it.

Dreamweaver MX includes a wide array of tools for displaying information from a database. Now that you're comfortable with what's happening behind the scenes, we can raise the curtain and delve into these tools.

In this chapter, we'll take a close look at some of the simple ways you can make your Web site dynamic using a database, including Dreamweaver's dynamic text, images, and attributes. We'll also look at how you can use Dreamweaver's Live Data view to preview your pages with the actual data. Finally, we'll introduce some of the ways you can make your data look pretty, just like you would with static text.

One aspect of this topic we won't cover in this chapter is displaying large lists of data. We've saved the really heavy lifting for Chapter 7, *Displaying Query Results on Web Pages.*

Displaying a Recordset on a Page

Occasionally, you just want to dump the contents of a recordset onto a page, perhaps to see what the results look like, or to prepare formatting. There's no magic button you can press to do this, but Dreamweaver's features come pretty close.

To display a recordset on a page:

1. Create a recordset. (If you're not sure how to do this, review the *Bindings Panel* section in Chapter 2.)

2. On the Application tab of the Insert toolbar, click on the Dynamic Table button (**Figure 5.1**).

   The Dynamic Table dialog box will appear (**Figure 5.2**).

3. Select the recordset you just created from the recordset drop-down menu, and click OK.

   The table will appear on the page (**Figure 5.3**). It won't look like much and won't yet display any data.

4. Preview the page by uploading it to your server (Site > Put) and previewing it in a browser (press F12 or use File > Preview in Browser > [Browser Name]). (If you need to set up server information, see the sections *Defining a Local Site...* and *Additional Remote Server Setup* in Chapter 2.)

   You'll see the table on the page, badly formatted, with the data from your database (**Figure 5.4**). We cover how to improve the formatting in the next section.

✔ Tips

- If you get an error that begins, "Failed opening Connections/", and you are using PHP, you have not yet uploaded the Connections folder.

Dynamic Table

Figure 5.1 You can display a recordset with a dynamic table.

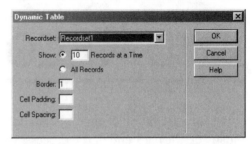

Figure 5.2 Specify the source for the table in the Dynamic Table dialog box—it's full of placeholders.

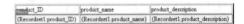

Figure 5.3 In Design view, the table doesn't look like much.

Figure 5.4 Previewed in a browser, the table displays the recordset data.

- Because Dreamweaver has no idea how many lines of data the recordset holds, the program uses a *repeating region*, which basically just repeats a command (in this case a table row) as long as there is more data. Repeating regions will be covered more extensively in Chapters 7 and 14.

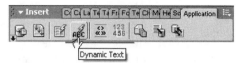

Figure 5.5 You insert dynamic text using the Dynamic Text button.

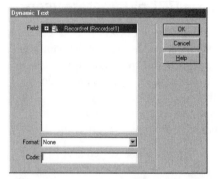

Figure 5.6 This kind of dialog box quickly becomes familiar as you work with dynamic content.

Figure 5.7 You choose only one field to display using dynamic text.

Figure 5.8 In Design view, the text is simply a placeholder.

Figure 5.9 The dynamic text entry, previewed here in a browser, displays only the first record of the recordset.

Adding Dynamic Text to a Page

Just dumping your recordset onto a page is rarely very useful. Usually, you want to format the data so that it doesn't look like you're madly spewing stuff from a database onto a page.

Dreamweaver's dynamic text feature lets you insert data from your database onto a page and make it look just like regular HTML.

To insert dynamic text onto a page:

1. If you haven't already done so, create a recordset.

2. On the Application tab of the Insert toolbar, click on the Dynamic Text button (**Figure 5.5**).

   The Dynamic Text dialog box will appear (**Figure 5.6**).

3. Click on the table name in the list box, and select the one field that you wish to display (**Figure 5.7**).

4. Click on OK.

   A placeholder for the dynamic text will appear on the page (**Figure 5.8**).

5. Save and upload the file to your server, and then press F12 to preview the file.

   The file will display the first record of the selected field in your recordset (**Figure 5.9**).

It may seem a little strange that the page shows the selected field of only the very first record in the recordset. We'll look at how you can specify which record it draws from in the next section.

Filtering Recordsets

Usually, when you want to retrieve something from a database, you want to retrieve either a specific record or a group of records. In the case of the Dynamic Text feature, as we discovered in the previous section, it's only going to display one record anyway, so we should probably figure out how to display the right one.

Dreamweaver lets you filter your recordset results in a number of ways, and the Recordset dialog box works pretty much the same way, regardless of which method you use. In this section, we'll be looking at one of those methods—using URL parameters—because it's available to you regardless of which database you're using.

What is a URL parameter?

A URL parameter is text that is appended to the URL when your browser links to a Web page. The usual form is something like:

```
http://www.company.com/catalog.
php?product_id=668
```

The parameter includes everything after the question mark. Your browser looks at the URL only up to the question mark when determining which page to request and display. Once the browser loads the page, it puts the text after the question mark into memory, making it available for any scripts that might need that information. In general, the URL parameter is in the format parameter=value. In the example above, the parameter is product_id and the value is 668.

How are URL parameters used?

There are a number of ways you can generate URL parameters. One of the most common is to use forms, but URL parameters also can be coded into the HTML of a link or generated from a script, among other things. You can even type the parameter into the location bar of your browser, if you want.

For testing purposes, it's often best to use a form to type the value for the parameter, so let's create a simple one. For the purposes of this example, we'll be looking up a product name from a catalog using the product_ID field. We'll be using PHP in this example, but the process should work exactly the same regardless of which database you're using.

✔ Tip

- Of course, when we say it will work the same no matter what database you're using, we mean that the commands are the same. Your field and table names are your own business—we're using common placeholder names; we're not legislating what you name fields and tables in your own databases.

Sample Data Files

You can find sample database files like the ones we use in this chapter on the companion Web site for this book at www.peachpit.com/vqp/dreamweaverMX.

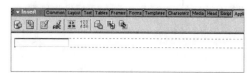

Figure 5.10 You can use a text field on your dynamic page to specify the value of a parameter using a Web form.

Figure 5.11 The name of the field is the name of the parameter.

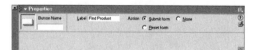

Figure 5.12 Label the button so it's obvious what it does.

Creating a form for a URL parameter

For our purposes, we'll want the URL parameter to be generated by user input from a form on a Web page. We'll first create the form, similar to any form your visitors might fill out. We'll then add a text field that will, when a visitor to the page fills out the form, specify the value of the URL parameter. You'll name your text field the same thing as the parameter name.

To create a form to generate a URL parameter:

1. Open or create a new HTML page. From the Insert menu, select Form.

   An empty form will appear on the page—the red dashed line outlines the form (and represents the <form></form> tags).

2. From the menu bar, select Form > Form Objects > Text Field; *or*, click the Text Field button on the Forms tab of the Insert toolbar.

   A text field will appear in the form on the page (**Figure 5.10**).

3. In the Property inspector, type a name for the text field in the TextField text box; let's call our field product_number (**Figure 5.11**).

4. From the menu bar, select Form > Form Objects > Button; *or*, click the Button button on the Forms tab of the Insert toolbar.

   A button will appear on the page.

5. In the Property inspector, delete the Button Name, and change the Label to "Find Product" (**Figure 5.12**).

continues on next page

FILTERING RECORDSETS

6. Select the form itself in the document window (either by clicking on the red dashed line or by clicking on the `<form>` tag in the Tag selector), and in the Property inspector, type `show.php` in the Action text box (**Figure 5.13**).

    This will tell the form to open the file `show.php`. (If you aren't using PHP, type the appropriate extension for your environment.)

7. From the Method drop-down menu on the Property inspector, select GET (**Figure 5.14**).

    Selecting GET is not strictly necessary, but it makes it easier to see what's going on.

8. Save the File as `get.html`. (This page, as it exists right now, is static, so it uses the `.html` extension.)

The form is now ready to go.

If you upload the file and test it, you'll get an error (the browser will look for a file that doesn't yet exist). You can work around this by typing "4", for example, in the text box, and the URL of the page that the browser is trying to locate will look something like `http://localhost/show.php?product_number=4`. That tells you the form is working.

✔ Tip

- You can find out more about the GET and POST methods of submitting forms in Chapter 8.

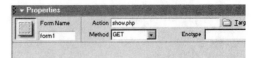

Figure 5.13 The Action text box in the Property inspector is where you tell the form what to do.

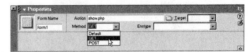

Figure 5.14 Choosing GET makes parameters easier to read by visibly appending them to the URL.

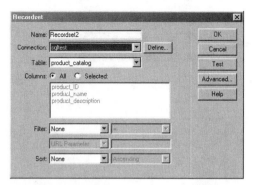

Figure 5.15 As always, you need to specify your table and your data source.

Figure 5.16 The name of the parameter is the same as the name of the field we created a minute ago.

Now let's see how to use this information by creating a page that uses the URL parameter.

To create a product lookup page:

1. Open a new PHP (or whatever's appropriate) file.

2. If you haven't created a database connection, do so. (For more information, see *Adding a Database Connection* in Chapter 2.)

3. Go to the Bindings panel. Click the + (plus) button, and from the menu that appears, select Recordset.

   The Recordset dialog box will appear.

4. In this dialog box, type a name for the recordset, select the database connection from the Connection drop-down menu, and select the appropriate table from the Table drop-down menu (**Figure 5.15**).

5. At the bottom of the dialog box, select the field name you wish to search by from the first Filter drop-down menu. Then leave the equal sign in the second Filter drop-down menu and select URL Parameter from the third Filter drop-down menu. Type `product_number` in the final Filter text box (**Figure 5.16**).

   (If we were designing the form on this dialog box, we'd label the second row of fields "Parameter.")

   Please note that the spelling and case of your Filter name must match exactly the name you used for your text field in the form we created a couple pages ago. In our case, it's `product_number`, but please make sure you double-check your form field names.

6. Click OK to close the dialog box.

7. On the Application tab of the Insert toolbar, click on the Dynamic Text button.

   The Dynamic Text dialog box will appear.

continues on next page

FILTERING RECORDSETS

8. Expand the table in this window to see a list of the fields in the table. Select any field other than the search field you specified in Step 5 (**Figure 5.17**).

9. From the Format drop-down menu at the bottom of the same dialog box, select AlphaCase-Upper (**Figure 5.18**).

   The format drop-down menu lets you format the data, regardless of the way it was originally typed into the database. In this instance, we're making it all upper case.

10. Click OK to close the dialog box.

    The dynamic text placeholder will appear on the page.

11. Save the file as show.php (using whatever the appropriate extension is).

12. Upload both this and the get.html file to your server.

13. Open the get.html file, type a value into the text box, and click the "Find Products" button.

    The page should display the selected field from the appropriate record.

✔ Tips

■ If you leave the text box blank in the last step, you'll get a syntax error on the show.php page. That's because the database is looking for a value that doesn't exist. In a production environment, you'd want to validate the form using JavaScript or something similar before actually sending it to the database.

■ You can use Dreamweaver's Validate Form behavior to perform some simple form validations. See Chapter 13 for more about behaviors, and apply the Validate Form behavior to a text field in your form.

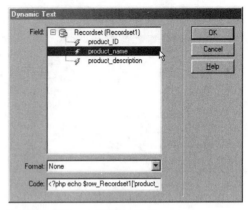

Figure 5.17 Choose a field to display.

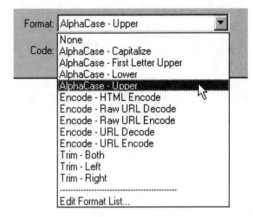

Figure 5.18 We're making the data appear in all upper case.

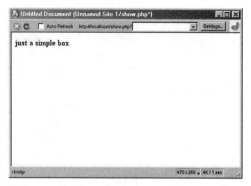

Figure 5.19 Live Data view lets you preview your file with actual data plugged in.

Using Live Data View

Up until now, if we wanted to see the results of the dynamic content on the Web pages we created, we've had to upload the pages to a server and preview them in a browser. This may seem like taking two steps back, given that Dreamweaver is supposed to be a WYSIWIG ("What you see is what you get") editor. Fortunately, Dreamweaver includes a tool that lets you display your pages and include actual data from the server, without uploading and previewing from a browser.

Live Data view allows you to talk to the server continuously, without the browser as an intermediary. Unfortunately, you should only use Live Data view if your server is on your local machine or local network, or if you have a very fast connection, because your system will slow drastically if you have a slow connection to the server. (Forget about it on dial-up connections.)

To use Live Data view:

1. Open a file that contains dynamic content.

2. From the menu bar, select View > Live Data, or click the Live Data View button ▓ on the Document toolbar. The content from the server will appear on the page (**Figure 5.19**).

In addition to letting you display the data from the server on your page in Dreamweaver, Live Data view also lets you specify the parameters for filtering which records are retrieved from a database.

You can specify the value for a URL parameter, so that you can filter records as we did in the previous section.

To filter records using Live Data view:

1. Open a page that uses a URL parameter to filter a recordset (see the previous section, *Filtering Recordsets*, for more information).

2. From the menu bar, select View > Live Data Settings.

   The Live Data dialog box will appear (**Figure 5.20**).

3. Click the + (plus) button at the top of the window to add a variable.

4. Type the name of the URL parameter in the left-hand column and the value to use for testing on the right (**Figure 5.21**).

5. Click OK to close the dialog box.

   The page will treat the value you entered as if it came from the URL and will filter your data appropriately (**Figure 5.22**).

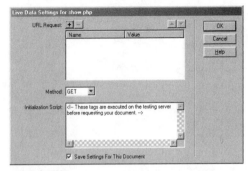

Figure 5.20 You can specify parameters in the Live Data dialog box.

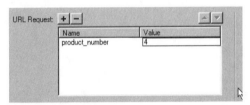

Figure 5.21 The parameter name is exactly the same as the one we used to name our text field in Figure 5.11.

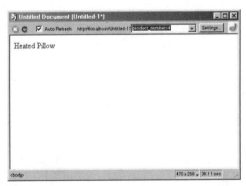

Figure 5.22 The data will now be filtered, even in Live Data view.

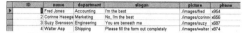

Figure 5.23 An example employee database.

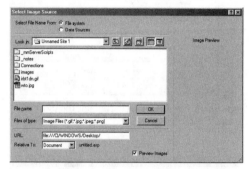

Figure 5.24 The Select Image Source dialog box lets you specify a data source for the file name.

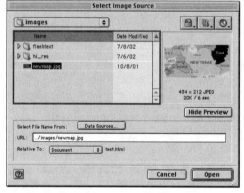

Figure 5.25 You can do this using the Macintosh OS as well, although it works a little differently.

Inserting Images and Media Dynamically

Just as you can insert text dynamically, you can also choose which images or other media to display dynamically on a page.

Although some databases can contain images or media, Dreamweaver can't handle getting them directly from a database. So the way to do this is to retrieve the URL of the image or media from the database.

In this example, we'll be using the database in **Figure 5.23**, which is a simple employee-information database populated with imaginary people. You can use any database to insert an image—as long as your database has a field populated by images.

To dynamically insert an image:

1. From the menu bar, select Insert > Image.

   or

   On the Common tab of the Insert toolbar, click the Image button [img].

   Either way, the Select Image Source dialog box will appear, which is laid out differently on Windows (**Figure 5.24**) and Macintosh (**Figure 5.25**).

2. On Windows, select the Data Sources radio button

   or

   On Macintosh, click the Data Sources button.

   continues on next page

3. Select the field from the recordset that contains the image URL (**Figure 5.26**).

4. Click OK to close the dialog box.

A dynamic image placeholder will appear on the page (**Figure 5.27**). You can preview the file in your browser or switch to Live Data view to see the actual image (**Figure 5.28**).

Inserting dynamic media works almost exactly the same way, except that you're looking for a different kind of file.

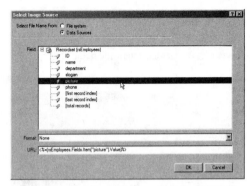

Figure 5.26 The selected field contains the URL for the image.

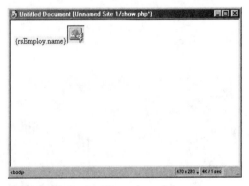

Figure 5.27 In Design view, a dynamic image placeholder appears.

Figure 5.28 Previewing shows the file retrieved from the database.

The Magic Folder

The general procedure outlined in this section for dynamically inserting objects is useful not only for images and Flash movies, but also in any dialog box where you see a Browse button, which often appears as a little folder icon 📁 .

You can have the destination for any clickable link, for example, generated from a database. You can also specify that the background image of a table be loaded from a database.

You can choose a dynamic external style sheet, a dynamic image, a dynamic Flash movie—you can serve pretty much anything from a database, not just pieces of text.

Unfortunately, this doesn't seem to work with frames. You can't dynamically set the source file of a frame from a database within Dreamweaver. You can, however, add dynamic content to pages within a frameset, so call it a draw.

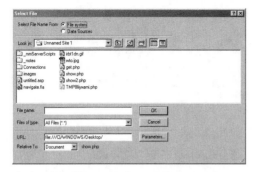

Figure 5.29 You'll get very familiar with this dialog box...

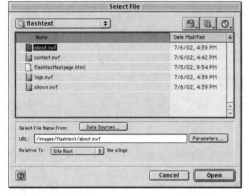

Figure 5.30 ...unless you're using the Macintosh OS— then this dialog box will be your friend.

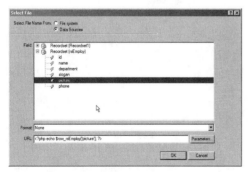

Figure 5.31 The selected field contains the URL for the Flash movie.

To dynamically insert a media (Flash) file:

1. From the menu bar, select Insert >Media > Flash, or click on the Flash button ● on the Common tab of the Insert toolbar.

   The Select File dialog box will appear, which looks somewhat different on Windows (**Figure 5.29**) and Macintosh (**Figure 5.30**).

2. On Windows, select the Data Sources radio button

   or

   On Macintosh, click the Data Sources button.

3. Select the field from the recordset that contains the URL for the Flash movie (**Figure 5.31**).

4. Click OK to close the dialog box.

   A Flash movie placeholder will appear on the page (**Figure 5.32**). You can preview the file in your browser to see the actual movie (**Figure 5.33**).

Figure 5.32 Again, the dynamic movie is represented by a placeholder.

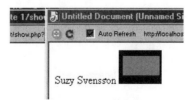

Figure 5.33 You can preview to see if your movie is retrieved correctly.

Setting Tag Attributes Dynamically

In addition to dynamically loading images and inserting text, you can also adjust the attributes of certain tags dynamically.

Unfortunately, the Dreamweaver interface is somewhat particular about the tags it allows you to adjust in this way. So you'll need to figure out by trial and error what tags you can work with.

Image tags are one of the tags Dreamweaver will allow you to link with a database. You can set any attribute of the image tag to be generated dynamically. In the following set of instructions, we show you how to set the Alt text attribute dynamically. You can apply these steps to many other attributes of many tags, but as we've said, your mileage may vary.

To set the Alt attribute of an image automatically:

1. Create or open a dynamic page.

2. From the menu bar, choose Insert > Image.

   or

   On the Common tab of the Insert toolbar, click the Image button ![Image button].

   Either way, the Select Image Source dialog box will appear.

3. Select any image from this dialog box.

   The image will appear on the page in the Document window.

4. Define a recordset for the page (see the *Bindings Panel* section in Chapter 2 for more information).

5. In the Document window, select the image you have inserted. A drop-down menu at the bottom of the Bindings panel will activate; it contains a list of the image tag attributes (**Figure 5.34**).

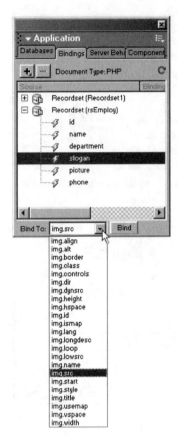

Figure 5.34 You can set image attributes dynamically.

Figure 5.35 This field can be the source for your Alt text.

Figure 5.36 In this case we've set the Alt text of the image from the database.

6. In the Bindings panel, click on the field in the recordset that will be the source for your Alt tag (**Figure 5.35**).

7. Select img.alt from the drop-down menu at the bottom of the Bindings panel.

8. Click the Bind button located to the right of the drop-down menu to bind the data field and the tag attribute together.

The Alt tag now reflects the contents of the field you have selected (**Figure 5.36**).

The tags that Dreamweaver allows you to link in this way seem somewhat arbitrary, so feel free to experiment to see which ones you can use.

✔ Tips

■ In Figure 5.36, the code we're looking at is the code in the browser's View Source mode, after the page has been processed by the browser. The code as Dreamweaver will insert it on the page looks like this:

```
<img src="./images/fred.jpg"
→ alt="<?php echo
→ $row_Recordset1['slogan']; ?>">
```

■ You can also set attributes dynamically by using the Tag Inspector panel. See Chapters 11 and 12 for information about using this panel.

SETTING TAG ATTRIBUTES DYNAMICALLY

Styling Dynamic Content

One of the most powerful features of Dreamweaver is that it allows you to format dynamic content in the same way you format static content. This means you can apply HTML formatting or CSS (Cascading Style Sheets) to dynamic content.

To apply a CSS style to dynamic text:

1. Create a new dynamic page by selecting File > New in the Site window.

2. Add a recordset to the page (see the *Bindings Panel* section of Chapter 2 for more information).

3. On the Application tab of the Insert toolbar, click on the Dynamic Text button to insert a dynamic text element.
   The Dynamic Text dialog box will appear (**Figure 5.37**).

4. In the Dynamic Text dialog box, select the field you want to use as the source for the dynamic text.

5. Click OK to close the dialog box.
   A placeholder for the Dynamic Text will appear on the page.

6. From the menu bar, select Text > CSS Styles > New CSS Style.
   The New CSS Style dialog box will appear.

7. In the New CSS Style dialog box, name the style ".dynamic," select Make Custom Style (Class), and click on the radio button beside This Document Only (**Figure 5.38**).

8. Click on OK to open the CSS Style Definition dialog box.

9. Change the text size to 36, and color it red (**Figure 5.39**).

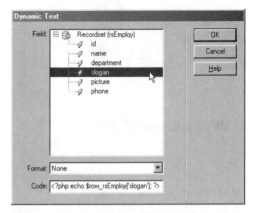

Figure 5.37 The Dynamic Text dialog box allows you to select only one field.

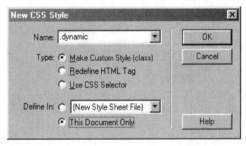

Figure 5.38 A new style we'll apply to dynamic text.

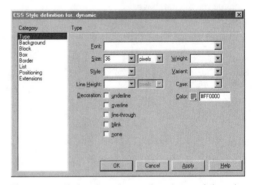

Figure 5.39 Obviously, we're not choosing a subtle style.

Figure 5.40 Assign styles to text using the CSS Styles panel.

Figure 5.41 The style is applied to the dynamic text we selected in Step 11.

10. Click OK to close the dialog box.

11. In the Document window, select the dynamic text you inserted earlier.

12. In the CSS Styles panel, located in the Design panel group (**Figure 5.40**, Window > CSS styles), click on the .dynamic style.

The dynamic text placeholder will change size and color.

13. From the View menu, select Live Data to see your dynamic text in all its styled glory (**Figure 5.41**).

✔ Tip

■ Remember that you can also serve style sheets dynamically, so that you can apply different external CSS files to pages depending on other parameters. See the sidebar *The Magic Folder* and the sections on inserting images and media dynamically.

This chapter has been an introduction to presenting dynamic information. In the next chapter we'll delve into using the information to present forms dynamically.

STYLING DYNAMIC CONTENT

Dynamic Forms

In the finite world of Web interfaces, forms are the only way to gather any kind of data from your users. Any input that's more complicated than a mouse click and less infinite than a personal e-mail, such as customer feedback or information required to join a mailing list or place an order, is going to come from a form.

Dreamweaver MX gives you a level of control over sophisticated behind-the-scenes form processing without requiring you to have advanced programming skills. Using an ordinary Web server, for example, you'd need to write a separate CGI script (usually in Perl) to process information from a form. But using an application server instead of an ordinary Web server, you can use Dreamweaver's built-in server behaviors to easily execute many common form-processing tasks such as searching a database or updating or modifying a database. You can even use forms to design a complete interface that lets you administer your database directly from your browser, and even remotely over the Web, as you'll learn in Chapter 8, *Editing Records From Web Interfaces*.

In this chapter, we'll set up a form so that you and your users can communicate with a database. Our interface will also be able to be populated by a database—that is, on the dynamic page on which the form appears, each form field can itself be a field in a database. That will allow you to provide different forms based on the type of site, type of customer—or time of day, for that matter.

Setting Up a Form

For a form to function properly, you need to provide two key pieces of information: the *action*, or *where* the information in the form should be sent; and the *method*, or *how* the information in the form should be sent. A third piece of information you may need is the *form name*, which mainly helps distinguish between forms when more than one form will be presented on the same page.

You specify the action, method, and form name in Dreamweaver's Property inspector (with the `<form>` tag selected).

✔ Tips

■ You can insert a form by selecting Insert > Form from the menu bar or by clicking the Form button on the Forms tab of the Insert toolbar. You can insert any form field using the Forms tab of the Insert toolbar.

■ You can select a form by clicking its red border or by clicking on the `<form>` tag in the Tag selector, which appears in the status bar of the Document window. You can select any form field by clicking on the object in the Document window, or by clicking on its tag in the Tag selector.

About form actions

The action (*where*) usually refers to another file on your server. This may be a CGI script, but because we're using an application server, it could also be an ordinary PHP, JSP, CFML, or ASP document. To process form input, the file has to have at least one server behavior designed. For more information on using server behaviors to process forms, see Chapter 8, *Editing Records from Web Interfaces* and Chapter 10, *Server Behaviors*.

About form methods

The method (*how*) for transferring data from the browser to the server generally falls into one of two categories: GET and POST. These terms are confusing—GET implies it might be used for receiving data, and POST implies it might be used for sending data. But they're actually quite similar: Both methods provide instruction for sending information from the browser to the server.

Search engines often use GET to pass a search query from the search form to the script that processes and returns the search results. GET tacks form information onto the end of the URL, making it easy to see what's going on (**Figure 6.1**).

However, two drawbacks to this method make it a little less desirable than POST. With GET, users can easily edit the URL and send information to the server that is different from the information your form is designed to send. So if you're sending information that needs either to be secure or in a specific format, the GET method is a problem. The other disadvantage is that the information you send is limited to 255 characters. So if you've got the potential for a lot of data, like a comment box, GET won't work.

Of course, you should *never* use GET where passwords or credit card numbers are involved, because anyone sniffing through Web traffic could "see" the information appended to the end of the URL.

The POST method is less problematic. It sends form information as a separate transaction with the server. Because the information isn't easily accessible to users, it's more secure than GET. And POST doesn't place an upper limit on the number of characters you can send. But POST isn't perfect—because form information is sent as a separate transaction, it places an additional load on the server. However, the load is relatively small, so the drawback is minor.

Setting form properties

Now that we've got the theoreticals mastered, let's modify a form to work with our application server. If you haven't yet inserted a form on your page, you can do so by selecting Insert > Form from the menu bar.

To define Form Properties:

1. Select the form whose properties you want to define by clicking on the form's red, dashed border

   or

   Click anywhere within the form and then click on <form> in the Tag selector (at the left of the Document window status bar (**Figure 6.2**).

   Dreamweaver's Property inspector will display the fields for defining form properties (**Figure 6.3**). If the Property inspector is closed, open it by choosing Properties from the Window menu or by pressing Ctrl+F3 (Command+F3).

2. To specify a form name, type a name in the Form Name field. Don't use spaces or non-alphanumeric characters.

3. To specify an Action, click on the Browse button to the right of the Action field. In the Select File dialog box, specify the file that will be receiving and processing the information from the form, and then click OK (Choose).

✔ Tips

- For each different form field discussed in this chapter, we tell you how to insert the field from scratch and then make it dynamic. You can also select any existing form field on a dynamic page, or save an existing HTML page as a dynamic page, and then make the form fields dynamic.

- You can select any form field and then make it dynamic by clicking on the lightning bolt in either the Property inspector or the Tag Inspector panel. For more on the Tag Inspector panel, see the relevant sections in Chapters 11 and 12.

- See *The Tag Selector* section in Chapter 11 to find out neat tricks when using this tool, such as deleting or modifying a selected tag.

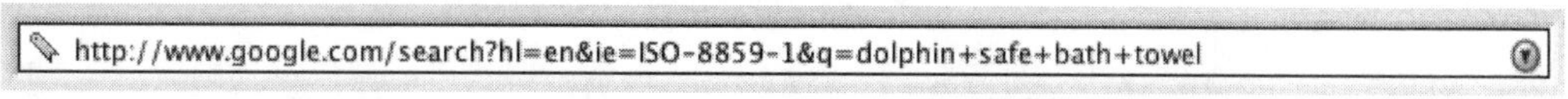

SETTING UP A FORM

---

http://www.google.com/search?hl=en&ie=ISO-8859-1&q=dolphin+safe+bath+towel

Figure 6.1 Search engines often use GET (which appends the form data to the end of the URL) to pass your search query from the search form to the script that processes and returns the results of your search.

```
<body> <form> <p>
```

Figure 6.2 The Tag selector in the status bar of the Document window allows you to select any tag by clicking on its name.

Figure 6.3 The Property inspector, displaying form properties, lets you specify a Name, Action, and Method for your form.

Using Dynamic Text Fields

Text fields allow users to type input directly into a text box. The basic building block of any form, text fields are an absolute must when you need data that only your user can provide, such as his or her name, address, and telephone number.

Unlike ordinary text fields that are blank when users first view a form, Dynamic Text Fields can be pre-filled with data from a database that users can either modify or leave as is. This comes in handy when you're providing an update page, for instance, in which the user will be modifying the contents of an existing database record. (Creating update pages is covered in more detail in Chapter 8, *Editing Records from Web Interfaces*.)

Before you can create a Dynamic Text Field, you'll need to have a recordset already defined. If you need help creating a recordset, see the section *Using the Bindings Panel*, in Chapter 2.

To insert a Dynamic Text Field:

1. Click to place your insertion point inside the form where you'd like to insert a dynamic text field.

2. From the menu bar, select Insert > Form Objects > Text Field

   or

   Click on the Text field button [⬚] on the Form tab of the Insert toolbar.

   Either way, a text field will appear, and the Property inspector will show Text Field properties (**Figure 6.4**).

3. In the Property inspector, type a name for your text field in the Name text box.

4. On the Server Behaviors panel, click the + (plus) button and choose Dynamic Form Elements > Dynamic Text Field (**Figure 6.5**).

   The Dynamic Text Field dialog box will appear (**Figure 6.6**).

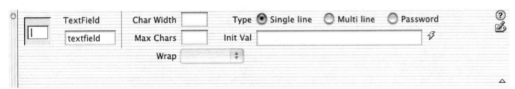

Figure 6.4 The Text Field Property inspector lets you specify a name for your text field.

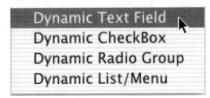

Figure 6.5 On the Server Behaviors panel, click the + (plus) button, and from the menu that appears, choose Dynamic Form Elements › Dynamic Text Field.

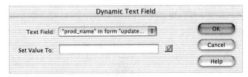

Figure 6.6 In the Dynamic Text Field dialog box, choose the text field you want to make dynamic.

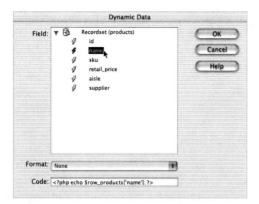

Figure 6.7 Choose the column that you want to link with your Dynamic Text Field.

Figure 6.8 The new Dynamic Text behavior you just created will appear in the Server Behaviors panel.

5. In this dialog box, select the text field you want to make dynamic from the Text Field drop-down menu. (If you have only one text field it will be selected by default.)

6. Click the Dynamic Data button ![icon] to the right of the Set Value To field.

The Dynamic Data dialog box will appear, showing a list of recordsets you've defined (**Figure 6.7**).

7. To fill in the Dynamic Text Field, click the plus sign (on the Mac, it's an arrow) to the left of the recordset you want to use to expand the list of column names, and then select the column you want to use.

A preview of the relevant server-side code will appear in the Code field. You don't have to do anything with this code, but if you know the language being used, you can edit the code directly in this field.

8. Click OK to close the Dynamic Data dialog box.

9. Click OK to close the Dynamic Text Field dialog box.

On the Server Behaviors panel, you should now see an entry in the list of server behaviors that corresponds to the Dynamic Text Field behavior you just added (**Figure 6.8**).

✔ Tips

- If you select the Text Field and display its properties in the Property inspector in Step 3, you can click on the Dynamic Data button ![icon] to jump directly to the Dynamic Data dialog in Step 9.

- You can set a character limit for any text field in the Property inspector. This is useful for items such as phone numbers or credit card numbers, or for items to be stored in a 256-character field in your database.

USING DYNAMIC TEXT FIELDS

Using multi-line text fields

You can use a multi-line, guestbook-type text field, too. To change any text field into a multi-line text field, select the field and click the Multi-line radio button in the Property inspector. You can also insert a multi-line text field directly from the Insert menu or the Forms tab of the Insert toolbar. A multi-line text field looks like this:

Once you insert a multi-line text field, you can use the Property inspector to set the number of lines high it appears and the type of wrapping to use (*virtual*, which doesn't insert hard line breaks, or *physical*, which does).

Using password fields

Password fields are simply text fields that replace what users type with bullets or asterisks instead of displaying their keystrokes for all to see. To employ password fields, you can apply the Dynamic Text Field behavior to password fields exactly the same way you would with a regular text field. You can change any text field into a password field by selecting it and then clicking the Password radio button on the Property inspector.

Figure 6.9 In the Radio Group dialog box, you can type labels and values for all the radio buttons in the group.

Using Dynamic Radio Buttons

Radio buttons are perfect when you want to limit users to a preset number of choices. Radio buttons traditionally come in groups— if you think you need only one radio button, use a checkbox instead.

All buttons in the same group will have the same name, but different values. Choosing any radio button in a group automatically deselects any previous selection, so only one button can be selected at any given time. These buttons are called radio buttons because on old-fashioned radios, you could program in five different stations, but pushing in one button caused the last-selected button to pop out. (This is in contrast to checkboxes, which allow you to select more than one box at a time. Checkboxes are discussed in the next section, *Using Dynamic Checkboxes.*)

An item in a Dynamic Radio Group can be pre-selected based on a value from a database.

To insert a Dynamic Radio Button Group, you will need to have a recordset already defined. If you need help creating a recordset, see the section, *Using the Bindings Panel*, in Chapter 2.

To insert a dynamic radio button group:

1. Click to place your insertion point inside the form where you'd like to insert the dynamic radio button group.

2. From the menu bar, choose Insert > Form Objects > Radio Group.

   or

   On the Forms tab of the Insert toolbar, click on the Radio Group button ▦ . Either way, the Radio Group dialog box will appear (**Figure 6.9**).

continues on next page

USING DYNAMIC RADIO BUTTONS

3. Give your radio group a name by typing a name in the Name text box.

4. In the Radio Buttons list box, you'll see two buttons listed by default. For each button you'd like to create, click and type a Label (the text that you want to see on the Web page, like "Back Ordered") and a Value (the value that you want to store in your database, such as "BACK").

If you need to add more buttons, click on the + (plus) button ⊕.

To delete an item, click the – (minus) button ⊖.

To re-order the buttons, highlight the item you want to move and click on the up or down arrow button ▲ ▼.

5. To lay out your table, click the Line Breaks radio button if you want each radio button on its own line, or Table if you want your buttons laid out in a table. In either case, or if you want the buttons all on one line or in one cell, you can edit the layout by hand later.

6. Click on OK to insert your radio group.

7. Now, on the Server Behaviors panel, click the Options menu button, and then select Dynamic Form Elements > Dynamic Radio Group (**Figure 6.10**).

The Dynamic Radio Group dialog box will appear (**Figure 6.11**).

8. In this dialog box, select the radio group you want to make dynamic from the Radio Group drop-down menu. (If you have only one radio group, its name will be selected by default.)

9. Click the Dynamic Data button ⚡ to the right of the Set Value Equal To field.

The Dynamic Data dialog box will appear, showing a list of recordsets you've defined.

Figure 6.10 Choose Dynamic Form Elements › Dynamic Radio Group from the Server Behaviors panel's Options menu. You can also get this menu by right-clicking (Ctrl+clicking) on the title bar of the Server Behaviors panel.

Figure 6.11 In the Dynamic Radio Group dialog box, choose the radio group you want to make dynamic.

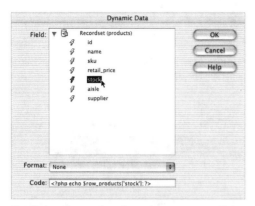

Figure 6.12 Choose the column that you want to link with your Dynamic Radio Group.

Figure 6.13 The new Dynamic Radio Group behavior you just created will appear in the Server Behaviors panel.

10. To select an item in the Dynamic Radio Group, expand the list of column names by clicking the + (arrow, on the Mac) to the left of the recordset you want to use. Then select the column you want to use (**Figure 6.12**).

A preview of the relevant server-side code will appear in the Code field. You don't have to do anything with this code, but if you know the language being used, you can edit the code directly in the field.

11. Click OK to close the Dynamic Data dialog box.

12. Click OK to close the Dynamic Radio Group dialog box.

On the Server Behaviors panel, you should now see an entry in the list of server behaviors that corresponds to the Dynamic Radio Group behavior you just added (**Figure 6.13**).

✔ Tip

- There's a faster way to call up the Dynamic Radio Group dialog box in Step 7, without first going to the Server Behaviors panel. Immediately after clicking OK in the Radio Group dialog box in Step 6, you can click on one of the new radio buttons you just created to display radio button properties in the Property inspector for that Radio Button. From there you can click on the Dynamic Data button 〔 ✔ Dynamic... 〕 to jump directly to the Dynamic Radio Group dialog box.

Using Dynamic Checkboxes

A checkbox is a great way to represent a value that is either true or false. Dynamic checkboxes can be pre-checked, based on a value from a database.

To insert dynamic checkboxes, you'll need to have a recordset already defined. If you need help creating a recordset, see the section *Using the Bindings Panel* in Chapter 2.

To insert a dynamic checkbox:

1. Place your insertion point inside the form where you'd like to insert a dynamic checkbox.

2. From the menu bar, choose Insert > Form Objects > Check Box

    or

    On the Forms tab of the Insert toolbar, click on the Checkbox button .

    Either way, a checkbox will appear, and the Property inspector will show CheckBox properties (**Figure 6.14**).

3. Type a name for your checkbox in the Name text box.

4. On the Server Behaviors panel, click the + (plus) button in the upper left, and then choose Dynamic Form Elements > Dynamic CheckBox (**Figure 6.15**).

    The Dynamic CheckBox dialog box will appear (**Figure 6.16**).

5. In this dialog box, select the checkbox you want to make dynamic from the Check Box drop-down menu. (If you have only one checkbox, it will be selected by default.)

Figure 6.14 The Property inspector lets you specify a name for your checkbox.

Figure 6.15 In the Server Behaviors panel, click the + (plus) button and then choose Dynamic Form Elements > Dynamic CheckBox.

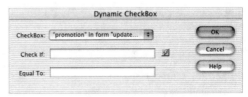

Figure 6.16 In the Dynamic CheckBox dialog box, choose the checkbox you want to make dynamic.

USING DYNAMIC CHECKBOXES

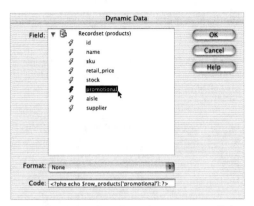

Figure 6.17 Choose the column that you want to link with your dynamic checkbox.

Figure 6.18 The new Dynamic CheckBox behavior you just created will appear in the Server Behaviors panel.

6. Click the Dynamic Data button  to the right of the Check If field.

   The Dynamic Data dialog box will appear, showing a list of recordsets you've defined (**Figure 6.17**).

7. To fill in the dynamic checkbox, click the + (arrow, on the Mac) to the left of the recordset you want to use to expand the list of column names. Then choose the column you want to use.

   A preview of the relevant server-side code will appear in the Code field. You don't have to do anything with this code, but if you know the language being used, you can edit the code directly in this field.

8. Click OK to close the Dynamic Data dialog box.

9. In the Equal To field on the Dynamic CheckBox dialog box, type the value that corresponds to the checkbox being selected.

   For example, if you have a column in your table called "Promotional" that has a value of either Yes or No, then type Yes in the Equal To field.

10. Click OK to close the Dynamic CheckBox dialog box.

    On the Server Behaviors panel, you should now see an entry in the list of server behaviors that corresponds to the Dynamic CheckBox behavior you just added (**Figure 6.18**).

✔ Tips

- From the CheckBox Property inspector in Step 3, you can click on the Dynamic Data button to jump directly to the Dynamic CheckBox dialog box in Step 4.

- In Step 9, you can use a value other than "Yes" for your checkbox, such as Owns_Car or Send_News.

Using Dynamic Lists and Menus

Like dynamic radio button groups, dynamic list boxes and drop-down menus are a great way to let users choose from a predefined set of possibilities. Lists and menus look quite different, but they're lumped together because they use the same HTML tag, the <select> tag. A *list* lets users see and select more than one item at a time; whereas a *menu* is a drop-down menu that lets users select only one item.

Before you can create a dynamic list or menu, you'll need to have a recordset already defined. If you need help creating a recordset, see the section *Using the Bindings Panel*, in Chapter 2.

To insert a list or menu:

1. Place your insertion point inside the form where you'd like to insert the Dynamic List/Menu.

2. From the menu bar, select Insert > Form Objects > List/Menu.

   or

   On the Forms tab of the Insert toolbar, click on the List/Menu button ▦.

   A tiny menu will appear, and the Property inspector will show List/Menu properties (**Figure 6.19**).

3. Type a name in the Name text box.

4. Click on the List Values button
   ⌐List Values...⌐ to define the items in the list.
   The List Values dialog box will appear
   (**Figure 6.20**).

Figure 6.19 The Property inspector lets you specify whether your form field will be a list or a menu; you also name the field here.

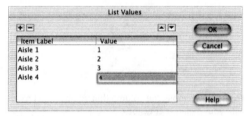

Figure 6.20 In the List Values dialog box you can enter Labels that the user will see and Values that will be sent to the server for each list/menu item.

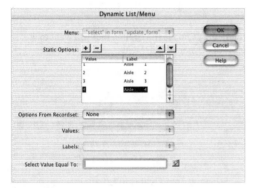

Figure 6.21 On the Server Behaviors panel, click the + (plus) button and select Dynamic Form Elements > Dynamic List/Menu.

Figure 6.22 In the Dynamic List/Menu dialog box, choose the list or menu you want to make dynamic.

5. For each List/Menu item that you'd like to create, enter a Label (the text that you want to see on the Web page, like "Aisle 4") and a Value (the value that you want to store in your database, like "4"). For many items, the name and value may be the same, such as "Maryland" and "Maryland".

To add more items, click on the + (plus) button ◼. You can also press the Tab key when you're in the Value column to automatically add a new item.

To delete an item, click the – (minus) button ◼.

To re-order the items, highlight the item you want to move and click the up or down arrow buttons ◼ ▼.

6. When you're done entering items, click OK. Now your list or menu will be inserted.

7. To make the selection a list, click the List radio button in the Property inspector (Figure 6.19). You can then specify a line height and check the Allow Multiple checkbox.

To make the selection a menu, click the Menu radio button.

In either case, you can specify the initially selected item by selecting it in the Initially Selected list box. Now that we've got the list or menu, let's make it dynamic.

To make a list or menu dynamic:

1. Select the list or menu.

2. On the Server Behaviors panel, click the + (plus) button, and then choose Dynamic Form Elements > Dynamic List/Menu (**Figure 6.21**).

The Dynamic List/Menu dialog box will appear (**Figure 6.22**).

continues on next page

USING DYNAMIC LISTS AND MENUS

3. In this dialog box, select the list or menu you want to make dynamic from the Menu drop-down menu. (If you only have one list or menu, it will be selected by default.)

4. Click the Dynamic Data button 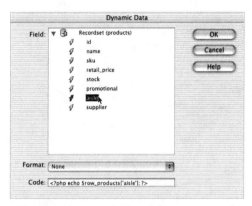 to the right of the Set Value Equal To field.

The Dynamic Data dialog box will appear, showing a list of recordsets you've defined (**Figure 6.23**).

5. Click the + (arrow, on the Mac) to the left of the recordset you want to use to expand the list of column names, and choose the column you want to use to select an item in the Dynamic List/Menu.

A preview of the relevant server-side code will appear in the Code field. You don't have to do anything with this code, but if you know the language being used, you can edit the code directly in the field.

6. Click OK to close the Dynamic Data dialog box.

7. Click OK to close the Dynamic List/Menu dialog box.

On the Server Behaviors panel, you should now see an entry in the list of server behaviors that corresponds to the Dynamic List/Menu behavior you just added (**Figure 6.24**).

✔ Tips

■ After Step 7 under *To insert a list or menu*, you can click on the Dynamic Data button to jump directly to the Dynamic List/Menu dialog box in Step 2 under *To make a list or menu dynamic*.

■ If you want to include a moot menu item, such as "Select One," you can add the `disabled` attribute to the `option` tag for the relevant menu or list item. If you're using XHTML, you need to insert this attribute as `disabled="disabled"`.

Figure 6.23 Choose the column that you want to link with your Dynamic List/Menu.

Figure 6.24 The new Dynamic List/Menu behavior you just created will appear in the Server Behaviors panel.

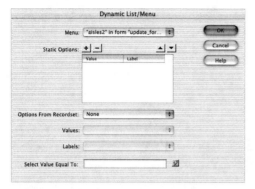

Figure 6.25 If you're creating a dynamically generated dynamic list or menu, you won't see any entries in the Static Options list.

Dynamically Generated Menus

Like the other dynamic form elements, the Dynamic List/Menu lets you pre-select an option based on a value in your main record-set. But it also offers an additional dynamic feature: It lets you get the *list items themselves* from a second recordset!

So, for example, in the menu we just created, if we have a separate table with a list of aisle names in it, we can grab that list of names from this second table instead of manually creating the list of aisles in our menu.

Before you can create a Dynamic List/Menu, you will need to have *two* recordsets already defined. If you need help creating a recordset, see the section *Using the Bindings Panel*, in Chapter 2.

To insert a dynamically generated list or menu:

1. Place your insertion point inside the form where you'd like to insert the dynamic list or menu.

2. From the Insert menu, choose Form Objects > List/Menu.
   A List/Menu will appear, and the Property inspector will show List/Menu properties.

3. Give your List/Menu a name by typing one in the Name text box.

4. On the Server Behaviors panel, click the + (plus) button, and then choose Dynamic Form Elements > Dynamic List/Menu.
   The Dynamic List/Menu dialog box will appear (**Figure 6.25**).

5. In this dialog box, select the list/menu you want to make dynamic from the Menu drop-down menu. (If you have only one list/menu it will be selected by default.)

   continues on next page

6. Click the Dynamic Data button  to the right of the Set Value Equal To field.

The Dynamic Data dialog box will appear showing a list of recordsets you've defined.

7. To select an item in the Dynamic List/Menu, click the + (arrow, on the Mac) to the left of the recordset you want to use to expand the list of column names. Then choose the column you want to use.

Note: You have two recordsets. In our example, we have a **products** recordset and an **aisles** recordset. Here you're choosing the *aisle column* from the *products recordset*.

A preview of the relevant server-side code will appear in the Code field. You don't have to do anything with this code, but if you know the language being used, you can edit the code directly in this field.

8. Click OK to close the Dynamic Data dialog box.

9. From the Options From Recordset dropdown menu, choose the recordset from which you want to get the menu items.

Note: In our example, this is the *aisles recordset*.

10. From the Values drop-down menu choose the column that you want to use for the Values in your List/Menu.

11. From the Labels drop-down menu choose the column that you want to use for Labels in your List/Menu.

Note: You won't see anything listed in the Static Options list because your list/menu items are generated dynamically from your second recordset (**Figure 6.26**).

Figure 6.26 Choose a second recordset to use to dynamically generate the values and labels in the list or menu.

12. Click OK to close the Dynamic List/ Menu dialog box.

You should now see an entry in the list of server behaviors that corresponds to the Dynamic List/Menu behavior you just added.

That's pretty much all you need to know about creating dynamic form fields.

✔ Tips

■ There are no dynamic behaviors associated with submit or push buttons or with hidden fields. You can insert either of these buttons from the Insert > Form Object menu or from the Forms tab of the Insert toolbar.

■ You can set the source of an image field dynamically. See Chapter 5.

■ Remember to test your forms energetically before you unleash them on your visiting public.

DISPLAYING QUERY RESULTS

Almost every dynamic page you create will involve displaying the results of database queries, or recordsets, as they're called in Dreamweaver MX. The results of a query can be as simple as a single field from a single record, or as extensive as 50 records, each with 15 fields. In Chapter 5 we covered simple methods for displaying a single record from a recordset.

Query results can be any request for a record or for several records from a database. In Web terms, the user's query will be the equivalent of "Give me the ZIP Code for Peculiar, Missouri" or "Show me red T-shirts" or "List all the classes in the art department offered on Wednesdays."

Query results can be one record or several records (a recordset). In the case of a search engine, search results may include hundreds of records. Here, we'll find out about how to display such results. Search engines such as Google and shopping sites such as Amazon.com are good examples of how to display complex results, combining many data fields, in a readable, clickable format.

If the user is requesting information based on limited, specific data such as an order number or a ZIP Code, only one record may be included in the results.

In this chapter we'll cover several methods you can use to display query results, including specialized behaviors and custom objects to help you organize and navigate multiple pages' worth of results. After all, if you or another user asked for a list of data that ended up being 500 records long (such as people living in Livingston with the last name Smith), you wouldn't want to view these 500 entries one at a time; nor would you patiently wait for a gigantic page to load that contained all 500 records.

Default Query Results

When you create a recordset, you are requesting a set of records (hence the name *recordset*) from your database. The results take the form of one or more records, each containing one or more columns. For more information about fine-tuning your query to get exactly the results you want, see Chapter 4, *Using SQL*.

In the sample **Table 7.1**, each entry (name, job, and pay) is a record. Each row is, well, a row, and the user, given the right form, could select just one record (pay for one individual), a column (pay for all individuals), a row (all data in the row for one name, such as Django), multiple rows, or some of each (pay for all names that start with Z).

The Bindings panel contains a list of recordsets you have defined, each showing a list of columns that were included in the query (**Figure 7.1**). If you imagine your recordset in the form of a spreadsheet, the list of columns in the Bindings panel represents the top row of the spreadsheet where the column names are listed. Though there's no visual representation for this in the Bindings panel, you can imagine each record as a row in the spreadsheet.

When you use Dreamweaver's dynamic text feature to display your results (as shown in Chapter 5, *Adding Dynamic Text and Using Recordsets*), by default you are displaying only the values for the first row, regardless of how many records are actually in your recordset. To see more than the first row, you'll need to use the Repeat Region behavior to define an area on your page to be repeated for each record.

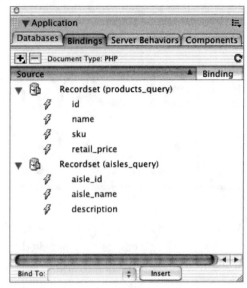

Figure 7.1 The Bindings panel lists all the recordsets you have defined in relation to the current document. Each recordset contains a list of data columns returned as part of your query.

Table 7.1

A Simple Data Table

NAME	JOB	PAY
Ariel	Server	$12
Benny	Cook	$15
Carla	Hostess	$10
Django	Server	$12
Ephraim	Cook	$15
Fargie	Server	$12
Gretchen	Server	$12

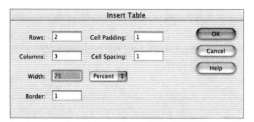

Figure 7.2 Use the Insert Table command to create a table that you can use to neatly display multiple results from your recordset. You can insert a table using the Table button on the Common or Layout tab of the Insert toolbar.

About Repeating Regions

When you want to display several rows of data, you can repeat the request for data and display those results sequentially. Think of a search engine: When you search for "picnic baskets" you may get hundreds of results, and each result is either a record, a few records, or an entire row of data in your table. That row includes data such as the title of the matching page, that page's URL, its keywords, the date the search engine last visited it, and a summary of the page.

Using the Repeat Region behavior, you can show the values from multiple records, and from multiple data rows, on a single page. In other words, each row may contain a name, an address, and a phone number, and to display several of those rows, you can use a repeating region to display the requested data.

Although you can define any area to be a repeating region, a clean, organized way to display multiple records is to repeat a table row or even an entire small table. In this example we'll create a simple, functional table.

To use the Repeat Region behavior:

1. On a page that already has a recordset defined, create a region to be repeated by defining a table with two rows and as many columns as you wish to display from your recordset (**Figure 7.2**). (You can insert a table by selecting Insert > Table from the menu bar, and you can modify a table and its rows and cells using the Property inspector.)

2. Click on OK to close the Insert Table dialog box and add a table to the page.

3. In the first row of your table, create labels for your display by typing the names of the columns you wish to display.

continues on next page

ABOUT REPEATING REGIONS

4. In the second row, use dynamic text to insert values for each of the columns you wish to display (**Figure 7.3**). For a refresher, see *Adding Dynamic Text to a Page* in Chapter 5.

5. When selecting a region to repeat, like a table row, it's important to include the opening and closing tags in the selection. Place your insertion point anywhere in the second table row, then click on the <tr> tag in the Tag selector to select the row and its contents (**Figure 7.4**).

6. On the Server Behaviors panel, click the + (plus) button in the upper left, and select Repeat Region (**Figure 7.5**).

7. In the Repeat Region dialog box, select the recordset you used to create the Dynamic Text items (**Figure 7.6**).

8. The Show option defaults to 10 records at a time. If you wish, you can enter a different number of records to show on one page, or click All to show all records on a single page.

9. Click on OK.

The table row you selected should now show a small tab labeled "Repeat" on its left side ▐Repeat▌.

If you want to preview your data, click the Live Data View button 🖳 on the Document toolbar.

✔ Tips

■ Unless you know your recordset will only contain a few records, you shouldn't choose All in the Repeat Region dialog box. Unless you limit the number of records on a page, the Web page might become too cumbersome to easily navigate, and it could make the page load slowly.

■ To find out about using repeating regions with Dreamweaver Templates, see Chapter 14.

■ To insert the table itself dynamically, see Chapter 5.

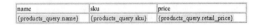

Figure 7.3 Use dynamic text to insert columns from your recordset into a table row that you can repeat.

Figure 7.4 To select the entire row, click on the <tr> tag in the Tag selector (in the Document window's status bar).

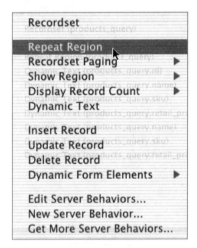

Figure 7.5 Choose the Repeat Region behavior from the Server Behaviors panel.

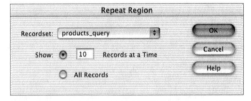

Figure 7.6 In the Repeat Region dialog box, specify the recordset from which you're displaying multiple records.

ABOUT REPEATING REGIONS

Figure 7.7 Click the Dynamic Table button on the Applications tab of the Insert toolbar.

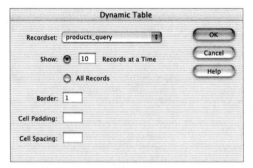

Figure 7.8 In the Dynamic Table dialog box, specify the recordset and number of records you want to display per page.

Figure 7.9 The Dynamic Table button creates the table, inserts the Dynamic Text objects, and applies the Repeat Region behavior. Until you preview the page or use Live Data view, these placeholders will appear, showing which records from the set will be displayed in these columns.

Using Dynamic Tables to Format Results

If you want to reuse the repeating region idea across an entire table, the easiest way to do so is to use a repeating table. If you like the idea of using a table row as a repeating region and plan to do it often, Dreamweaver MX provides an Application object to automate the process.

To insert a repeating region using the Dynamic Table object:

1. On the Application tab of the Insert toolbar, click on the Dynamic Table button (**Figure 7.7**).

   The Dynamic Table dialog box will appear (**Figure 7.8**).

2. Select the recordset you want to use from the recordset drop-down menu, and click on OK.

   The table will appear on the page (**Figure 7.9**), complete with the Repeat Region behavior already applied.

✔ Tip

- The Dynamic Table object will automatically create a table that includes every column listed in your query. If you want to omit any columns, you must either create your table and repeating region by hand (as in the previous example) or delete those table columns you don't want.

The Recordset Navbar

If you have more than a handful of results to display, you'll want to limit the amount of data you see on a single page. To create a navigation bar that pages through the result list, you can use the Recordset Navigation Bar object. This list might look something like this:

Top << This Page >> Last

or this:

< Prev 1 Next >

✔ Tip

- When you insert a recordset navbar, it will appear at the insertion point, but it will be centered on the page. You'll need to adjust how your results are inserted if you'd like the navigation text to appear left-aligned or right-aligned. Just select the text, the table, or some of the table cells, and re-align them using the Property inspector.

Figure 7.10 Click the Recordset Navigation Bar button on the Applications tab of the Insert panel.

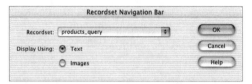

Figure 7.11 In the Recordset Navigation Bar dialog box, specify the recordset and your choice of text or images for the navigation bar.

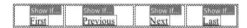

Figure 7.12 A navigation bar appears with buttons for navigating forwards and backwards through your list of results.

To create a Recordset Navigation Bar:

1. In the Document window, click to place your insertion point where you'd like the navigation bar to be inserted.

2. On the Application tab of the Insert toolbar, click on the Recordset Navigation Bar button (**Figure 7.10**).

   The Recordset Navigation Bar dialog box will appear (**Figure 7.11**).

3. Select the recordset you want to use from the recordset drop-down menu.

4. Click the Text radio button to create text labels for the navigation bar, or click the Images radio button to use Dreamweaver's built-in images for the navigation buttons.

5. Click on OK.

   A table containing a navigation bar will appear in your document at the insertion point (**Figure 7.12**).

   You can format this text to fit your own conventions; for example, instead of the words Previous and Next, you could use brackets like this: $\leq$ This Page $\geq$

✔ Tips

- Another kind of navigation bar can be used to present buttons that let the user navigate through various sections of a site. This navigation bar is inserted using the command Insert > Interactive Images > Navigation Bar. See Chapter 18 for more on navigational schemes.

- You can use recordset navigation links to navigate through only one recordset per page.

- To display the status of the navigation, that is, how many total records there are and which of those are being displayed on a page ("Records 11-20 of 50"), see the next section.

Showing Search Navigation Status

Figure 7.13 Click the Recordset Navigation Status object on the Applications tab of the Insert toolbar.

If you've got multiple records on multiple pages, it's handy to know exactly how many records and how many pages you're dealing with. Suppose you're searching Amazon.com for CDs with the word "Rock" in the title. There may be hundreds of results, displayed on 50 pages, and you may like to know whether you're near the beginning or the end of the search. The Recordset Navigation Status object creates a status display that provides precisely that information.

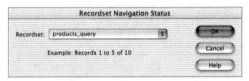

Figure 7.14 In the Recordset Navigation Status dialog box, specify the recordset.

Creating a Recordset Navigation Status display:

1. In the Document window, click to place the insertion point where you'd like the status display to be inserted.

2. On the Application tab of the Insert panel, click on the Recordset Navigation Status button (**Figure 7.13**).

3. Select the recordset you want to use from the recordset drop-down menu (**Figure 7.14**).

4. Click on OK.

   A navigation status display will appear in your document at the insertion point.

You can use this information to tell a coworker or a user how many records were fetched, which record you're on, and how many were displayed.

Editing Records from Web Interfaces

Most Web applications that rely on database content require that changes be made to the database at some point. For instance, a new entry must be added to a database whenever a customer submits an online order. And a database must be updated whenever a customer changes billing information, such as a change of address or a new credit card number.

Fortunately, Dreamweaver provides tools to make adding new records or updating existing ones easy. *Master detail page sets,* for example, make it easier to locate records that you want to change or examine in more detail. A *master page* lists a summary of groups of records, each of which includes a link. That link goes to the *detail page*, which lists a more complete summary of a single record. (You've seen information organized in this way on Web directories and catalog pages.) On both master and detail pages, you can decide which fields in a record and which records in a set will be displayed on the actual page. In this chapter, we show you how to get the most out of master detail page sets and look at the mechanics of adding, deleting and changing records, paying particular attention to Dreamweaver's built-in tools for those tasks. We also look into some basic ways to manage permissions and user privileges—that is, how to allow users to create user names and passwords for logging in to your site.

In previous chapters, we've used PHP as our scripting language, but as this book covers Dreamweaver MX rather than a particular application platform, we're using ASP in this chapter for our examples. Some of the built-in server behaviors used in this chapter, such as Go to Detail Page, are available only to users of ASP and JSP platforms. If you're working with ColdFusion or JSP, you can manually create links that will open dynamically created related pages.

Master Detail Page Sets

Master detail page sets (what a clunky phrase, no?) organize data so that it's easier to read and work with. When users search your site, they're requesting information from your database. You don't want to make them (or let them) look at *all* the fields in your database, so you give them a subset.

A *master page* summarizes the requested records and provides a link to a *detail page* for each record. For example, someone searching a database of users may look for "Jones." The search results page that lists the names of all users named Jones is the master page. The master page would then include a link to Fred Jones. Click that link, and you'd get a detail page for Fred Jones that would include not only his name but his department, extension, and photo.

So in essence, a master page typically displays a number of records, but provides only limited information (usually just a few fields) on each one (**Figure 8.1**). A detail page usually displays only one record, but shows most, if not all of the record (**Figure 8.2**). The most common way to use this combination of master and detail pages is to present the user with a list of records on a master page, then have her select one record from the list, which then brings up a detail page with the selected record.

There are two ways to create master detail page sets. The first method is to use the Master/Detail Page Set live object, which is a quick and easy way to build them. However, this live object is not available in PHP or ASP.NET, so for developers using those systems, we'll also show how to build a master detail page set by hand.

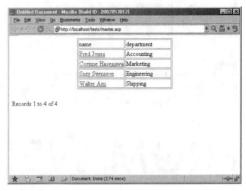

Figure 8.1 A master page usually contains only summary information.

Figure 8.2 A detail page provides (surprise!) more detail about a single record.

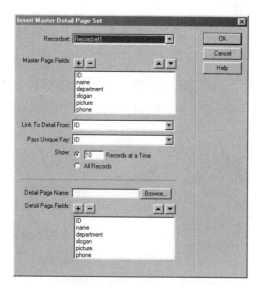

Figure 8.3 The Insert Master/Detail Page Set dialog box is a handy way to get started. You can also open this dialog box by clicking the Master Detail Page Set button on the Application Tab of the Insert toolbar.

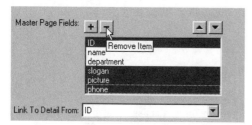

Figure 8.4 Select the fields you don't want to be displayed and remove them by clicking on the – (minus) button.

Creating a master page

First, let's create a master page—the summary of retrieved records—using live objects. You can limit the number of records displayed at one time here, in which case the user will be able to click a link to display the next chunk of records in a set.

To create a Master/Detail Page Set live object:

1. Create a new ASP, JSP or ColdFusion page.

2. Define a recordset (see the *Bindings Panel* section in Chapter 2 if you need help).

3. From the menu bar, select Insert > Application Objects > Master Detail Page Set.

   The Insert Master Detail Page Set dialog box will appear (**Figure 8.3**).

4. From the Recordset drop-down menu, select the recordset you created.

5. In the Master Page Fields list box, select the fields you don't want displayed on the master page and click the – (minus) button (**Figure 8.4**).

   On the master page, the columns will be displayed in a horizontal row. If you want to change the order in which they appear, you can select a field name and click the up or down arrow buttons to move the field in the display.

6. From the Link to Detail From drop-down menu, select the field that you want to be the link to the detail page. This is the field that will be clickable.

7. From the Pass Unique Key drop-down menu, select the field that provides the key for the database. (For more information on keys, see *Keys and Indexes* in the *Databases and Relationships* section of Chapter 3).

continues on next page

131

8. Either type the number of records you want to display at a time on the master page (remember, the user will be able to click a link to display the next chunk of records in the set), or select the All Records radio button (**Figure 8.5**).

Now we have a master page, but it won't do us much good unless we create a detail page to go with it.

Creating a detail page

You only need to create one detail page for each master page, regardless of how many records are on the master page.

To create a detail page:

1. With the Insert Master Detail Page Set dialog box still open (see Figure 8.3 and Step 3 in the previous list), you can choose either a brand new page by typing its name in the Detail Page Name text box; or you can select a page that already exists by clicking on Browse. Either way, Dreamweaver will add the record detail summary information to the page you specify.

2. Now select any fields you don't want to appear on the detail page and click the – (minus) button (**Figure 8.6**).

3. Click OK to close the dialog box.

The master (**Figure 8.7**) and detail (**Figure 8.8**) pages will appear in the Document window.

4. Upload the pages and preview them in your browser to see the set in action.

Clicking on a record on the master page (**Figure 8.9**) will open that record in the detail page (**Figure 8.10**).

Figure 8.5 You can limit the number of records that are displayed at any time.

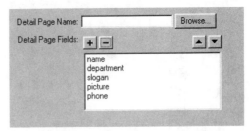

Figure 8.6 By default, all fields are displayed.

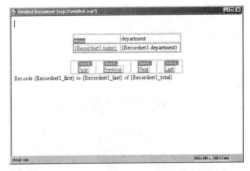

Figure 8.7 The master page created by the dialog box is not overwhelmingly well-formatted.

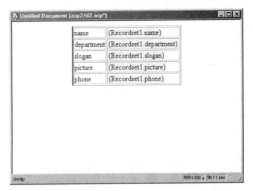

Figure 8.8 Neither is the detail page. (You can, of course, format the tables and text on either page.)

Figure 8.9 A master page such as the one shown here provides a link for each record, and each link is to that record's detail page. So if you click on Fred Jones, you'll get a detail page with more information about Fred (see Figure 8.10).

Figure 8.10 The detail page shows the record you clicked. This is the placeholder information for the Fred Jones detail page.

✔ Tips

- You can certainly optimize the formatting of the master and detail pages. Just make sure that you don't alter the placeholders for the data.

- You may be tempted to use Dreamweaver's Live Data view to preview your master and detail pages, but because links don't work in this view, you can't. You'll need to upload the set and test it in a browser to see it in action. (For more information on Live Data view, see the section *Using Live Data View* in Chapter 5.)

Sample Data Files

You can find sample database files like the ones we use in this chapter on the companion Web site for this book at www.peachpit.com/vqp/dreamweaverMX.

MASTER DETAIL PAGE SETS

Manually creating a master page

The above procedure was very easy. But what if you're running PHP or ASP.NET? Or what if (like us) you are masochistic and don't want to use the live object? In that case, you need to define a master detail page set manually.

To define a master page manually:

1. Create a new PHP (or ASP.NET) page. This will be your master page.

2. Add a recordset to the page (see the *Bindings Panel* section in Chapter 2).

3. On the master page, insert a two-row HTML table with a column for each field you want to display. (To refresh your memory: You can use Insert > Table to pop up a dialog box that lets you specify the number of columns and rows in your table; click on OK to insert the table.)

4. In the first row of the table, type column heads to clarify what kind of data appears below them.

5. In the Bindings panel, expand the recordset to show individual fields, and then select those fields you want to display on the master page (**Figure 8.11**).

6. Drag the fields you selected into the second row of the table, one in each column, on the master page (**Figure 8.12**).

7. Select the second row of the table.

8. In the Server Behaviors panel, click the + (plus) button and choose Repeat Region (**Figure 8.13**).
   The Repeat Region dialog box will appear.

9. Type the number of records you want to display on the master page or select All Records.

Figure 8.11 Expanding a recordset in the Bindings panel lists that recordset's individual fields.

Figure 8.12 You can drag fields from the Bindings panel directly onto the page.

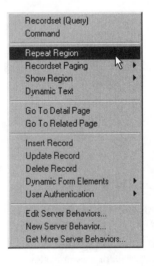

Figure 8.13 The Repeat Region server behavior repeats the selected text once for each record in the recordset.

MASTER DETAIL PAGE SETS

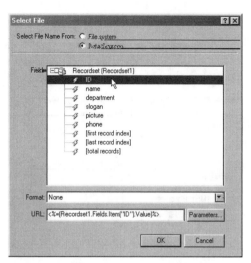

Figure 8.14 The link to the detail page uses the key field from your database.

Figure 8.15 If you build your master detail page set manually, you need to do some typing in the Property inspector.

✔ Tips

■ In Step 1, you can select the text, table, or table cells you like by clicking and dragging or by selecting specific tags in the Tag selector, which appears in the left of the Document window status bar.

■ See the section *Using Dynamic Tables to Format Results,* in Chapter 7, to format your master pages and detail pages using tables that are created and formatted based on the result of the query.

■ For more information on filtering recordsets, see *Filtering Recordsets* in Chapter 5.

If you want to show only a few records at a time and also provide a way to let the user navigate through the entire set, you'll need to add a recordset navigation gizmo (see the section *The Recordset Navbar* in Chapter 7). Now we need to add the links to the records on the master page so that the user can get to the detail page. (When you use the live object to create your page set, Dreamweaver adds the links for you.)

To add links to the records on the master page:

1. On the master page, select the text placeholder that you want to make clickable. (You can select more than one field.)

2. In the Property inspector, click the Browse button 📁 next to the Link text box. The Select File dialog box will appear.

3. Click on the Data Sources button.

4. In the Fields list box, select the key field for your database (**Figure 8.14**). For more information on keys, see *Keys and Indexes* in the *Databases and Relationships* section of Chapter 3.

5. Click OK to close the Select File dialog box.

6. Now here's the tricky part: In the Property inspector's Link text box, click to place the insertion point at the very beginning, and type the name of your detail page, followed by a question mark (?), followed by the name of your key field, followed by an equal sign (=).

   For example, we used `detail.asp?ID=` (**Figure 8.15**), where `detail.asp` is the detail page and `ID` is the name of the key field.

   Specifying this data string at the end of the URL in the Link text box tells the server to treat the field as a URL parameter. As we'll see below, that allows us to link to the correct detail record.

Creating a detail page manually

Now that we've created our master page, we need to create the detail page.

To create a detail page by hand:

1. Create a new page. Save it as the same name you assigned it in Step 6 under the previous list, *To add links to the records on the master page.*

2. In the Bindings panel, click on the + (plus) button and choose Recordset from the menu that appears.

   The Recordset dialog box will appear. If the dialog box opens in advanced mode, click on simple to switch modes.

3. In the Recordset dialog box, select the fields you want to display on the page (**Figure 8.16**).

4. In the first Filter text box, select the key field for your database (the one you specified in Step 4 in the previous list).

5. In the drop-down menu directly below that, select URL Parameter (**Figure 8.17**).

6. In the final Filter text box, enter the name of the parameter you chose in Step 6 in the previous list (the name of your key field, if you followed our instructions) (**Figure 8.18**).

7. Click OK to close the dialog box.

8. You can now display the fields on the page by simply dragging them from the Bindings panel onto the page (**Figure 8.19**).

You'll find the master detail page set a useful tool for helping you locate the appropriate record to change or delete, as we shall see in the rest of this chapter.

Figure 8.16 Include only those fields you want to display in the recordset. (Here, we're omitting the ID field.)

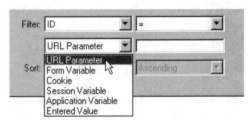

Figure 8.17 The detail page looks for the URL parameter we created earlier.

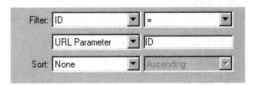

Figure 8.18 The parameter is the one we added to the link on the master page.

Figure 8.19 You can format your detail page more attractively than we have. See Chapter 7 for more on formatting your query results as repeating regions or dynamic tables.

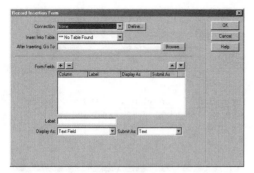

Figure 8.20 The Record Insertion Form dialog box allows you to specify how the form information gets added to the database.

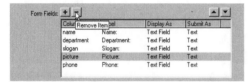

Figure 8.21 You can remove fields from the form. Here, we're removing the picture field from the update page because we don't want to deal with haphazardly submitted photos.

Adding Database Records

Adding, editing and deleting database records work somewhat similarly, in that they all involve linking a form (or at very least a button) to a database, and adding a server behavior to actually make the changes to the database.

In this section, we first look at how to add a record to a database. This procedure doesn't actually involve using a master detail page set, because no detail is available for a non-existent record.

Dreamweaver provides a Record Insertion Form live object, which does most of the complicated work for you. Unlike the live object for the master detail page set, this live object works on all database platforms.

To add a record to a database:

1. Create a new dynamic page.

2. From the menu bar, select Insert > Application Objects > Record Insertion Form.

   The Record Insertion Form dialog box will appear (**Figure 8.20**).

3. From the Connection drop-down menu, choose the connection to the database.

4. From the Insert Into Table drop-down menu, select the table to which you wish to add the record.

5. In the After Inserting, Go To text box, type the page you want users to see after they submit the form.

6. The Form Fields list box displays all the fields in your table. If there are fields you don't want the user to fill in (if there is an automatic key field in your database, for example), select those fields and click the – (minus) button (**Figure 8.21**).

continues on next page

137

7. You can set the way each field displays in the form—that is, you can use text boxes, menus, and so on to display the fields on the page.

8. In the Form Fields list box, click the first field.

9. In the Label text box, type a display name for the form element.

10. In the Display As drop-down menu, select the format for the field (**Figure 8.22**).

If there are only a few values that can be entered, for example, you might want to make the field a menu instead of a text box.

11. In the Submit As drop-down menu, select the format your database expects for that field.

12. For text fields, you can specify a default value that will appear in the field before the user edits it. Type this value in the Default Value text box.

13. Repeat Steps 9-12 for each field in the form.

14. Click OK to close the dialog box.

The form will appear on your page (**Figure 8.23**).

✔ Tips

- To edit the server behavior that drives the record insertion form, in the Server Behaviors panel, double-click on the Insert Record (form) entry (**Figure 8.24**).

- Once the form has been added to a page, you can fine-tune the layout and the properties of the form elements as you would with any other form.

- For more on editing forms, see Chapter 6. To make the field a menu as in Step 10, see the section *Using Dynamic Lists and Menus*.

Next we'll look at editing a record using the Record Update Form.

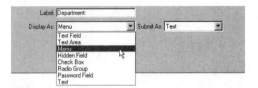

Figure 8.22 You can set the way the user enters data. Here, we're selecting a menu to limit the choices for the department field.

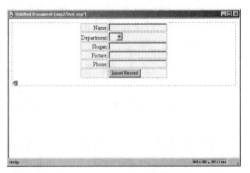

Figure 8.23 This record insertion form could use some prettying up.

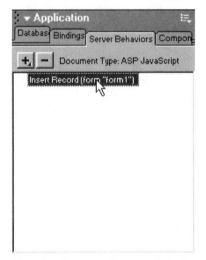

Figure 8.24 You can edit a server behavior by double-clicking its name in the Server Behaviors panel.

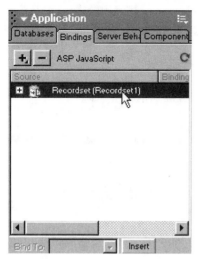

Figure 8.25 You can copy recordsets from the Bindings panel.

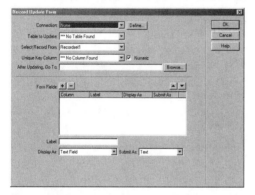

Figure 8.26 The Record Update Form dialog box looks quite a bit like the Record Insertion dialog box. In Step 7, you can also open this dialog box by clicking the Record Update Form button on the Application tab of the Insert toolbar.

Editing Database Records

You can edit database records most easily with the Record Update Form live object. This tool works almost exactly like the live object for the Record Insertion Form, with two exceptions: you need to first tell Dreamweaver which record you want to edit; and each field will have a default value (the one that's already there).

The easiest way to specify the record you want to edit is to replace the detail page you created in the *Master Detail Page Sets* section earlier in this chapter.

To create a record update page:

1. Create a new dynamic page.

2. Save the page as update.asp (or whatever the appropriate extension is).

3. Open the detail page you created above, in *To create a detail page* or *To create a detail page by hand*.

4. In the Bindings panel, select the recordset linked to the page (**Figure 8.25**).

5. Copy that recordset by pressing Ctrl+C (Command+C).

6. Switch back to the new update page and paste the recordset into the Bindings panel.

   (We also could have simply created a new recordset, but because we went through all the trouble to build one earlier, we might as well use it.)

7. With the update page in front in the Document window, select from the menu bar Insert > Application Objects > Record Update Form.

   The Record Update Form dialog box will appear (**Figure 8.26**). Looks a lot like the Record Insertion dialog box, doesn't it?

continues on next page

EDITING DATABASE RECORDS

8. Select the connection to your database and select the recordset you've pasted into the page (**Figure 8.27**).

9. In the Unique Key Column menu, select the key for your database.

10. In the After Updating, Go To text box, enter the name of the page you want to go to after the user updates the record.

11. Select the fields you don't want to display in the update form and click the – (minus) button to remove them from the form.

12. Repeat Steps 9-11 in the previous list, *To add a record to a database*, for each field remaining.

Don't mess with the default value, which is the current value of the field in the database. (Otherwise, you won't be able to edit the data, because the server will look for a field that doesn't exist.)

13. Click OK to close the dialog box.

The form will appear on the page (**Figure 8.28**). If you want to add some formatting, you can do that now. (You can leave the page as ugly as you want, but you'll probably want to format it a bit.)

14. Save and close the detail `update.asp` file. Close the detail page (`detail.asp`) we used from the previous section, if you haven't done so already. Don't save your changes, however, because we'll be using the detail page again and want to preserve its original state. (If you want, you can do a Save As to save a copy of your current work, but it's not necessary.)

We've now created and saved an update page. In order to make it go, we'll duplicate the master page and add linking information to activate the update page.

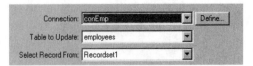

Figure 8.27 The recordset tells the form (and by proxy, your database) which record to change.

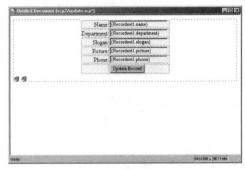

Figure 8.28 Like all of the example in this chapter, this one is perfectly functional, and you can feel free to redesign it in the Document window.

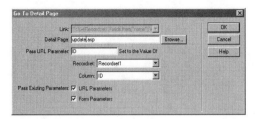

Figure 8.29 We need to go to the update page, rather than the detail page.

To add a link to the update page on a copy of the master page (ASP and JSP only):

1. In the Site window, duplicate the master page you created in the *Master Detail Page Sets* section of this chapter by right-clicking on the file (Ctrl+clicking on the Macintosh) and selecting Duplicate from the pop-up menu. Type a name for your new file; let's call it `master_update.asp`. (You can also open the master page in the Document window and then do a File > Save As to duplicate the page.)

2. Open the duplicate you just created.

    (At some point you probably want to add some interface information to this page, such as changing the link names to "Update File." You can do this now or later on.)

3. In the Server Behaviors panel, double-click on the Go to Detail Page behavior.

    The Go To Detail Page dialog box will open (**Figure 8.29**).

4. In the Detail Page text box, type the name of the file you just created (in our example, `update.asp`).

5. Click OK to close the dialog box.

6. Save and close the duplicate master page file.

7. Upload the files to your server and open the duplicate master page in your browser.

8. Click on a record to go to the update page.

    The update page will appear. You can now use this form to make changes to records in the database.

The next thing we'll do is add an interface to delete a record from the database.

Deleting a Database Record

Creating an interface for deleting a record is actually a lot less work than either adding or editing one. Since the important thing about deleting a record is making sure that you're deleting the correct record, we'll use the detail page we created at the beginning of the chapter, in *Master Detail Page Sets*, to show the record, and then simply add a button to delete the record that gets shown on the detail page.

To add a button to delete a record:

1. Open the detail page you created in the first section of this chapter.

2. From the menu bar, select Insert > Form to insert a blank form with its gaily dashed red line.

3. From the menu bar, select Insert > Form Objects > Button to insert the button that will request the deletion.

4. Select the form by clicking on that dashed line, and in the Property inspector's Form Name text box, change the form's name to delete.

5. Select the button, and in the Property inspector, change its label to "Delete Record."

6. In the Server Behaviors panel, click the + (plus) button and select Delete Record from the menu that appears.

   The Delete Record dialog box will appear (**Figure 8.30**).

Figure 8.30 The Delete Record dialog box is much simpler than the others.

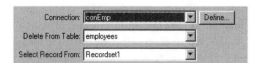

Figure 8.31 Make sure you're deleting the correct record!

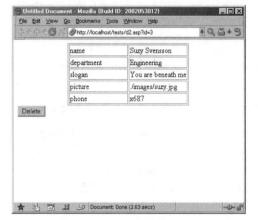

Figure 8.32 Now you can punch holes in your database to your heart's content.

7. Choose the connection to your database, and choose the appropriate data table. The recordset should be selected by default (**Figure 8.31**).

8. In the Unique Key Column, select the key field for your table.

9. The Delete By Submitting menu should already be set to `delete` (the form we created and renamed in Steps 3 and 4).

10. In the After Deleting Go To text box, type the name of the file you want to appear after the deletion is submitted.

11. Save the file and upload it to your server.

12. Open the Master page you created at the beginning of this chapter in your browser (not the duplicate you created in the most recent section) and click on a record.

    The detail page will appear, complete with a delete record button (**Figure 8.32**).

We've looked at the easiest ways to modify records in your database. Next we'll look at ways to control who gets to make changes to the database.

Managing Permissions

One of the trickier parts of managing a database-based Web site is managing user permissions. Obviously, you want to allow public access to your site, but you also may need parts of the site to be accessible only to people in your organization.

✔ Tip

■ First, the bad news: Dreamweaver's user management doesn't work for PHP or ASP.NET sites. So if you're using one of those systems, you need to figure out your own way to do user management.

Dreamweaver lets you manage user access in two ways. The first one is simple: logged in versus not logged in. Users who are logged in get access to the site or some specific portion of it. And users who are not logged in are limited to visiting purely public portions of the site (which can be as small as a single log-in page).

The second method is to assign access levels to users. For example, you might have three privilege levels: guest, user, and administrator. That way, guests can have access to teaser pages, registered members can have access to all of the "official" or "private" content on the site, and administrators can have access to the *entire* site, plus statistics and other information.

It's important to note that these user permissions differ from the database application's user/permissions setup, but it does use the database, as we shall see. In other words, Web users are not precisely the same as database users, so even if you've created a guest user profile for your database, you can manage Web user permissions separately. What happens is that Dreamweaver creates a *session variable*, which stays valid until the user logs out or doesn't access the site for a while.

Simple user management

Let's first take a look at managing users without separate access levels. You need four things:

◆ A registration page (`register.asp`)

◆ A log-in page for registered users (`login.asp`)

◆ A way to limit access to your pages

◆ A way for users to log out (`test.asp`)

The filenames listed above are the ones we'll create in the upcoming sections. If you're using a platform other than ASP, you'll also be using different file extensions.

User management may seem like a daunting administrative task, but the one component that you need is a simple database table. This table needs to have just two columns (at least for now): user name and password. (You saw earlier in this chapter how to create a form that allows users to add records to a database, and these records can include user name and user password.)

In addition to the `username` and `password` columns, We'll add a third column, user number or `userid`, in our example, which will be a unique key for the table, in case we need it later on. A simple example would be something like **Figure 8.33**.

At its heart, a user registration page is simply a record insertion form. Let's see how it works with a database of users.

username	userpass	userid
▶ billy	salad	1
suzyq	fate	2
walter_johnson	fastball	3
marktwain	calaveras	4

Figure 8.33 A simple user database.

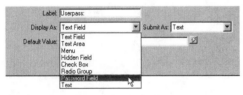

Figure 8.34 Usually, you want users to be able to log in after they register.

Figure 8.35 Select Password Field to hide what the user types in the form in the browser window.

Figure 8.36 You can check to make sure the username doesn't already exist.

To create a registration page:

1. Create a Users table in your database of choice, with two columns: username and userpass.

2. Open a new dynamic page.

3. On the Application tab of the insert toolbar, click Record Insertion Form. The Record Insertion Form dialog box will appear.

4. From the Connections drop-down menu, select the connection to the database that contains your Users table.

5. From the Insert Into Table drop-down menu, select the Users table.

6. In the text box named After Inserting Go To:, type login.asp (or whatever the appropriate extension is) (**Figure 8.34**).

7. In the Form Fields list box, select the userpass field.

8. From the Display As drop-down menu, select Password Field (**Figure 8.35**).

9. Click OK to close the dialog box.

10. In the Server Behaviors panel, click the + (plus) button and from the User Authentication submenu, select Check New Username.

    The Check New Username dialog box will open (**Figure 8.36**).

11. From the Username Field drop-down menu, specify the column in your table that contains your user names.

12. In the text box named If Already Exists, Go To, type the page you want users to see if the username they picked is already taken and already exists in the database.

13. Click OK to close the dialog box.

14. Save the file as register.asp (or your appropriate extension).

Now that you've created a registration page, we'll look at how to create a log-in page.

To create a log-in page:

1. Create a new dynamic page.

2. Insert a blank form by selecting Insert > Form from the menu bar.

3. On the Forms tab of the Insert toolbar, click on Text Field to insert a text box where the user will type a login name.

4. In the Property inspector, change the name of the text field to "username" (**Figure 8.37**).

5. From the Insert menu, choose Form Objects > Text Field again to insert the password text box.

6. In the Property inspector, change the name of the field to "pass" and click the Password radio button (**Figure 8.38**).

7. From the menu bar, choose Insert > Form Objects > Button to add the log-in button.

8. In the Property inspector, change the label of the button to "Log In" (**Figure 8.39**).

9. Go ahead and add labels to the form so that users can tell one field from another.

   You can also re-format the form so that it looks better, or you can do that later.

10. In the Server Behaviors panel, click on the + (plus) button, and from the User Authentication submenu of the drop-down menu, choose Log In User.

    The Log In User dialog box will appear (**Figure 8.40**). The Get Input from Form drop-down menu should read Form1 (unless you renamed the form).

11. Make sure the Username Field drop-down menu has "Username" selected.

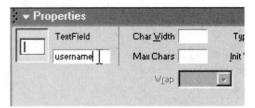

Figure 8.37 You can change the form field names in the Property inspector for easier reference.

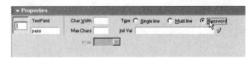

Figure 8.38 Again, you want to hide what the user actually types.

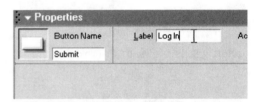

Figure 8.39 You can also change the button label, so it's obvious what the button does.

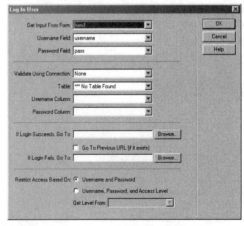

Figure 8.40 You can specify where the Login behavior looks for users.

Figure 8.41 The form fields correspond to fields in the database. To make things tidy, name the form fields to correspond with the database fields.

Figure 8.42 Make sure the database fields that are specified are the right ones.

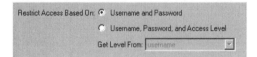

Figure 8.43 Right now, when we let a user log in, we're just checking for username and password.

12. Make sure the Password field drop-down has "pass" selected (**Figure 8.41**).

13. From the Validate Using Connection drop-down menu, select the connection to the database that has your user database in it.

14. From the Table drop-down menu, select the users table.

15. Make sure that the appropriate columns are selected in the Username Column and Password Column drop-down menus (**Figure 8.42**).

16. In the text box named If Login Succeeds, Go To, specify the page to which you want users redirected if they log in successfully.

17. If you want users redirected to the page that directed them to the log-in page in the first place, check the Go To Previous URL checkbox.

Redirecting users to the previous URL is useful in situations where a page automatically sends the user to the log-in page (more on that in the next section).

18. In the If Login Fails text box, specify the page to go to if the log-in fails (often the current page, so the user has a chance to try to log in again).

19. For the Restrict Access Based On option, leave the Username and Password radio button checked for the moment (**Figure 8.43**).

20. Click OK to close the dialog box.

21. Save the file as `login.asp` (or whatever your appropriate extension is).

Now that you've added a log-in page to the list of requirements for managing your users, it's time to create the penultimate piece of the puzzle: a page that restricts access so that only logged-in users can visit it.

MANAGING PERMISSIONS

To restrict a page to logged-in users:

1. Create a new dynamic page, or open an existing one.

This page will be the page we use to test our access level functionality. When the user logs in, they'll go to this page. In the next section, we'll add a "log out" link to this page.

2. In the Server Behaviors panel, click on the + (plus) button and then choose Restrict Access to Page from the User Authentication submenu.

The Restrict Access to Page dialog box will appear (**Figure 8.44**).

3. Leave the Restrict Based On option the way it is.

4. In the If Access Denied, Go To text box, enter your log-in page.

5. Click OK to close the dialog box.

6. Save the file as `test.asp` (or appropriate extension), but don't close it yet.

Finally, we need to add a way for the user to log out.

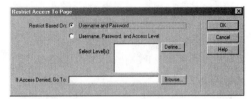

Figure 8.44 You can control who gets to see a page.

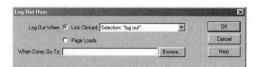

Figure 8.45 You can specify a button or link that the user can click to log out.

To create a log-out link:

1. On the test page we created in the previous stepped list (`test.asp`), add the text "log out."

2. Select the text.

3. In the Server Behaviors panel, click the + (plus) button and then select Log Out User from the User Authentication submenu.

   The Log Out User dialog box will appear (**Figure 8.45**).

4. If the Log Out When drop-down menu doesn't say "selection: "log out"," cancel the dialog box, select the text, and repeat Step 3.

5. In the When Done, Go To text box, enter the location of the page to which you want users redirected after they log out. In our case, we're just going to send the user back to the log-in page to avoid having to create yet another page.

6. Click OK to close the dialog box.

7. Save the file.

You can now test the system by going to the register page and creating a new user, and then logging in and going to the test page.

Now that we have the basic procedure for tracking users, we'll look briefly at ways to distinguish between various access levels for users.

MANAGING PERMISSIONS

Managing multiple access levels

Access levels are essentially just another column in the user database . You'll notice by looking at **Figure 8.46** that there are only two types of users in our database: members and administrators. There is actually a third level however, called "Guest," which is for users who are not logged in.

Because Dreamweaver provides an interface only for checking access levels, not for setting them, you manage multiple access levels almost the same way you deal with logged-in users.

You'll need to decide what works best for you in terms of managing changing access levels, but defining user levels and restricting pages to various user levels is quite easy in Dreamweaver.

To define an access level for a user:

1. Add a column in your user database for access levels, and include two or more kinds of user levels in that column.

2. Open the log-in file (`login.asp`, in our example) you created in the earlier list, *To create a log-in page.*

3. In the Server Behaviors panel, double-click the Log In User behavior to edit it. The Log In User dialog box will appear.

4. For the Restrict Access Based On option, check the Username, Password, and Access Level radio button.

5. From the Get Level From drop-down menu, select the column of your table that contains the user levels (**Figure 8.47**).

That's all there is to assigning a level to a user. Now let's look at how to use those levels.

username	userpass	userid	usertype
billy	salad	1	Member
suzyq	fate	2	Administrator
walter_johnson	fastball	3	Member
marktwain	calaveras	4	Member
		(AutoNumber)	Member

Figure 8.46 You can store access levels for each user in the user database.

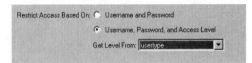

Figure 8.47 Tell the Login server behavior which column holds the access levels.

Figure 8.48 We need to tell Dreamweaver we're getting a little fancy here.

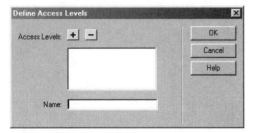

Figure 8.49 You can define access levels, but make sure the ones you type here are the same as they appear in your user database.

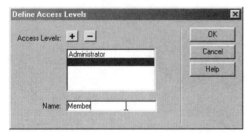

Figure 8.50 You need to list all of the access levels you created.

To restrict a page to certain user levels:

1. Create a new dynamic page.

2. In the Server Behaviors panel, click on the plus button and then choose Restrict Access to Page from the User Authentication submenu.

   The Restrict Access to Page dialog box will appear.

3. For the Restrict Based On: option, click on the Username, Password and Access Level radio button (**Figure 8.48**).

4. Click on the Define button next to the Select Levels list box.

   The Define Access Levels dialog box will appear (**Figure 8.49**).

5. Click the + (plus) button, and type in one of the access levels you have defined in your user database.

   Make sure you type the access level exactly as it is in the database.

6. Repeat Step 5 for each of the levels you have defined (**Figure 8.50**).

   You only need to do this for the levels you actually have defined in your user database. Additionally, you only have to do this once for each site. Dreamweaver will remember the list.

7. Click OK to close the dialog box.

8. Now that we've listed all the access levels within the Dreamweaver environment, we'll define which of these levels actually has access to this page.

   In the Select Levels list box on the Restrict Access to Page dialog box, select the user levels you want to have access to the page.

   You can Shift+click (Ctrl+click) to select multiple levels.

continues on next page

MANAGING PERMISSIONS

151

9. In the If Access Denied text box, select the page you want users to see if they don't have access privileges.

10. Click OK to close the dialog box.

Your page is now restricted to users who have the access levels you have selected.

This chapter has been an introduction to some of the ways Dreamweaver allows you to change information in a database. In the next chapter, we'll look at some more specialized types of data interaction.

WEB SERVICES AND COLDFUSION COMPONENTS

Web services and ColdFusion components are two ways of putting useful or fun widgets on your pages. In both cases, you use Dreamweaver to insert some simple code on your page. Then when your page is live on the Internet, it requests live data from a remote database application to present interactive content, such as search tools, personalized text and graphics, or even mini-applications like weather and traffic forecasts, headlines, daily specials, horoscopes, or other content that may change frequently.

Web services are a way of making application server functions accessible remotely—and seamlessly—by other application servers and Web sites anywhere on the Internet. Dreamweaver's Components panel lets you quickly find and easily use Web services created by others.

If you're using Macromedia's ColdFusion application server, Dreamweaver can help you to create your own Web services (using ColdFusion components) for others to use. In this chapter, we explain the terminology involved in using Web services and ColdFusion components, and then walk you through the process of creating and using these objects in your pages.

Defining Web Services and ColdFusion Components

A Web service is simply a nugget of application server functionality that is accessible over the Web using a standardized XML-based messaging system. For example, you may have created a dynamic page where visitors to your site can get current listings of the items you have in stock. You could package that same dynamic information as a Web service, allowing other Web sites (perhaps your many franchise outlets, or members of affiliate and frequent shopper programs) to provide their visitors with that same current information from your site. A few examples of popular Web services currently available include currency conversion tools, weather information, and traffic updates.

✔ Tip

■ Popular sites such as Amazon.com are beginning to offer Web services to developers—that's a good place to start learning about practical applications of Web services if you're not sure what use to put them to on your own site.

ColdFusion components are a new feature in ColdFusion MX. They provide a way to create self-contained blocks of code that can be easily compiled (and reused) to build applications. Because of their object-oriented design, ColdFusion components are well suited for interfacing with media elements and entities *outside* ColdFusion, such as Flash movies or other Web sites. That makes them perfect for creating and publishing Web services, because they can interact with any application server or data type. They are not

platform dependent, and once they're running on your live Web site, their users on other sites don't need to be running their own ColdFusion server in order to use the Web service.

There are four important acronyms you'll come across when dealing with Web services: XML Remote Procedure Calls (XML-RPC), Simple Open Access Protocol (SOAP), Universal Description, Discovery, and Integration (UDDI), and Web Service Description Language (WSDL).

XML-RPC and SOAP are two different protocols for exchanging the XML messages that make Web services happen. XML-RPC is slightly simpler to work with and SOAP offers slightly more automation of the Web services. Both are platform independent. Unless you're going to code your Web services by hand, you don't need to worry about the specifics of syntax and grammar that make up these protocols.

UDDI is a way for people to find Web services that interest them. You can manually register or find a Web service using a public UDDI registry (see *To add a Web Service component* in the next section for more information about UDDI).

A WSDL document is an XML file that describes a Web service's purpose, where it is located, and how to access it. To use a Web service somebody else has created, you access the service's WSDL file to find out how it is designed to work. If you create a Web service for others to use, ColdFusion can generate a WSDL document for you. You can then publish that WSDL file at a URL and make it available to potential clients of the service.

Consuming a Web Service

A Web service comprises a chunk of server-side code that is packaged so that it can be used by another server. Anyone who maintains an application server can *publish* a Web service for other people (like you) to use. Just as in book publishing, distribution is essential. Web service publishers need to publicize the availability of their services, and Web service consumers need to find out about the Web services that are out there. That's where the UDDI (Universal Description, Discovery, and Integration) registries come in. These registries are search engines devoted to Web services. When you create a Web service, you register it with one or more UDDI registries, and when you're looking for a Web service, you search these registries.

Three of the largest UDDI registries are maintained by xMethods, IBM, and Microsoft. Dreamweaver lets you quickly and easily search these and other sites to find Web services you can use.

Let's take a look at how to add a Web Service component from someone else's site to the Components panel, so that we can then add it to a page in our site. It helps to start with a URL, but Dreamweaver even lets you browse for available services. Later in this chapter, we'll create our own Web services that can be used on our pages and on other sites.

✔ Tips

- Although Web services can be used with any application server, the Components panel is only active when you specify JSP, ColdFusion, or ASP.NET as the server model.

- In order to use ColdFusion components, you must create a ColdFusion site (see Chapter 2) and work with ColdFusion pages in that site.

To add a Web Service component:

1. In the Components panel, select Web
   Services from the drop-down menu
   (**Figure 9.1**).

2. Click the Options menu button. The
   Add Using WSDL dialog box will open
   (**Figure 9.2**).

3. If you know the URL of the WSDL file for
   the Web service you want to use, type it
   in the text box and skip to Step 7.

   Otherwise, click on the UDDI browser
   menu to see a list of UDDI registries
   (**Figure 9.3**).

4. Choose one of the registries listed in the
   menu. Dreamweaver will launch your
   default browser and load the home page
   for that registry (**Figure 9.4**).

5. Browse or search the registry to find the
   URL of the WSDL file for the Web service
   you want to use (**Figure 9.5**).

6. Copy or type the URL ending in `.wsdl`
   into the text box in Dreamweaver's Add
   Using WSDL dialog box (**Figure 9.6**).

   To make sure you're copying the correct,
   full URL, you should open the link to the
   Web service from the directory page,
   and then click the WSDL link to view the
   code and make the full URL appear in the
   browser's location bar. You can also copy
   the URL from the WSDL line highlighted
   at the top of the page.

7. Click OK.

   Dreamweaver will use ColdFusion's Proxy
   Generator to create a proxy object that
   will make the necessary calls to the server
   on which the Web service resides. The
   new Web service will then appear in the
   list of Web services in the Components
   panel (**Figure 9.7**).

   We'll actually add the Web service to our
   page in the next section.

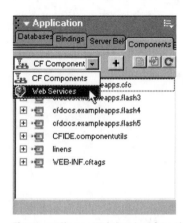

Figure 9.1 Choose Web Services from the drop-down menu in the Components panel.

Figure 9.2 In the Add Using WSDL dialog box, you can enter the URL of the WSDL file for the Web service you want to use.

Figure 9.3 You can choose one of several UDDI registries to search for Web services.

Figure 9.4 The XMethods UDDI registry (at www.xmethods.com) has a wide selection of useful and well-documented Web services.

CONSUMING A WEB SERVICE

156

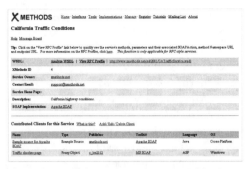

Figure 9.5 For our example we chose the California Traffic Conditions Web service from XMethods.

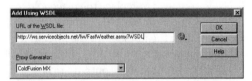

Figure 9.6 Once you've found a Web service you want to use, come back to the Add Using WSDL dialog box and enter the URL, which ends in .wsdl (or better yet, copy it from your browser location bar and paste it into the Add Using WSDL dialog box).

Figure 9.7 The Components panel shows a list of available Web services.

Coaxing ColdFusion to Run on Mac OS X

The ColdFusion server is not officially available for Mac OS X. However, because Mac OS X is based on FreeBSD, a Unix-like operating system, the Linux version of the ColdFusion server can, with very little effort, be coaxed into running on Mac OS X.

You'll need to download and install the Linux version of the ColdFusion server onto a machine that is running Linux. Then you can pack the ColdFusion directory (using an encoding system such as tar) and transfer the files to your computer running Mac OS X.

Dick Applebaum's three-part article for the O'Reilly Network, "ColdFusion MX on Mac OS X" explains the process in detail and includes step-by-step instructions. Go to www.oreillynet.com and search for "ColdFusion MX" to find the most recent articles, including this one.

Dropping Components onto the Page

Using Web service components and ColdFusion components is a simple matter of dropping the component onto a page. For some components, you may need to define the variables that correspond to the inputs that the component may be expecting from a user.

In most cases the component will generate some output that will be included on the Web page, for which you'll also need to define one or more variables. In the following exercise, we're going to use a Web service called CATrafficService that takes one or more California interstate numbers as user input and then returns current information about highway conditions.

✔ Tip

- You will need to have added at least one Web Service component before you can drop one onto the page. If you haven't added one yet, take a look at *To add a Web Service component* earlier in this chapter. The Web service we're using in this example can be found at `http://www.xmethods.net` – for the full URL, look under "Demo Services."

To drop a Web Service component onto the page:

1. In the Components panel, select Web Services from the drop-down menu.

2. In the Document window, click on the Code View icon ⟨⟩.

3. In the Components panel, click on the name of the Web Service component you want to use and drag it into the Document window.

   A `<cfinvoke>` code block will appear in your page code.

4. Review the code for the component; in our example, the CATrafficService code should look something like this:

```
<cfinvoke webservice=
→ "http://www.xmethods.net/sd/2001/
→ CATrafficService.wsdl"
→ method="getTraffic"
→ returnvariable="aString">
    <cfinvokeargument
    → name="hwynums"
    → value="enter_value_here" />
</cfinvoke>
```

5. Now you need to replace the placeholder value "enter_value_here" in the code above with the number for the interstate highway you want to check, for example, 280. The input and the output are both variables, as their content will vary based on the user's request.

   These kinds of input parameters will usually be listed in the `<cfinvokeargument>` tag and can often be identified by the descriptive placeholder value. In this case, the input parameter is `value`.

6. Note the value of the output parameter. You'll need it later in this exercise. This value usually can be found in the opening `<cfinvoke>` tag with the name `returnvariable`. In this case, the value of the `returnvariable` variable is "aString".

7. Click the Bindings panel tab to bring that panel to the front. We're going to add a Cold Fusion parameter to make the input easier to work with.

8. On the Bindings panel, click the Options menu button and choose CFParam from the menu that appears (**Figure 9.8**).

   The CFParam dialog box will appear (**Figure 9.9**).

9. Type the name of the output parameter you noted in Step 6, `aString`, and click OK.

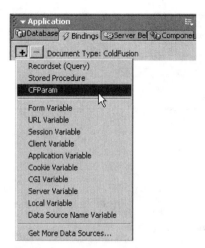

Figure 9.8 Add a CFParam to make working with the input parameter easier.

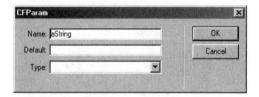

Figure 9.9 Enter the name of the CFParam exactly as it appears in the code.

10. Insert the variable you created, which will be designated **"String"**, onto the page either by dragging and dropping the variable name from the Bindings panel or by selecting the variable and clicking the Insert button in the Bindings panel.

You can do this in Design view to bind the variable to a specific page element, or you can do this in Code view to insert code between specific tags.

11. Format the page as you like, and save it.

12. Upload the page to your Web server, and preview it in the browser. It should be ready to go as a functioning Web service.

✔ Tips

- In Step 1, if you want to see both what the page will look like and the code that comprises the Web service, you can click on the combined Code and Design View button to see the page in split view in the Document window. You cannot drop a Web Service component onto the page in Design view; you need to drag it into the code in Code or Split view.

- Some Web services are quite complex and contain multiple component elements. In such cases, you'll need to drag and drop each component of the Web service separately in Step 2. The specifics of how to use these complex Web services vary from service to service. For more information on using a specific Web service on your own pages, review the documentation available at the UDDI registry where you found the service.

- To find out about using forms to receive user input, see Chapter 6.

DROPPING COMPONENTS ONTO THE PAGE

159

Publishing a Web Service Using a ColdFusion Component

If you want to create modular reusable code units in ColdFusion, the traditional methods have always been to use custom tags and user-defined functions. With ColdFusion MX, there's another way to create reusable code, using ColdFusion components.

There are both advantages and limitations to this method—once you get it up and running, ColdFusion components are quite flexible and portable. On the other hand, you may not want to deal with learning yet another kind of syntax just to put a widget on your page.

The function we're primarily interested in with ColdFusion components is using them to create publishable Web services. We'll create a simple ColdFusion component that takes a name as input and outputs a greeting. On a real Web page, you could use such a component to personalize pages that users log in to. Similar components could return information requested by the user that corresponds to the request contextually. For example, users who specify that they live in a certain area code could be shown specific daily specials, weather, or headlines.

To create a ColdFusion component:

1. The first thing we're going to do is create and name a ColdFusion file. In the Components panel, select CF Components from the drop-down menu (**Figure 9.10**).

2. Click the Options menu button. The Create Component dialog box will open (**Figure 9.11**).

Figure 9.10 Choose CF Component from the Components panel drop-down menu.

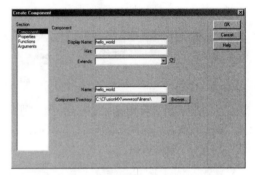

Figure 9.11 Specify a name and display name for your component in the Components section of the Create Component dialog box.

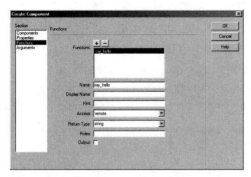

Figure 9.12 Add functions in the Functions section of the Create Component dialog box.

3. Type a name for the component in the Name text box, just above the Component Directory text box. Use only letters, numbers, or the underscore character, because this name will also serve as the filename of the component file. ColdFusion components are saved as separate files with a `.cfc` extension, but don't add `.cfc` to the end of the filename—Dreamweaver will do that for you. For our example, we'll name the component `hello_world`.

4. In the Component Directory text box, type the pathname, or click on Browse and choose the folder where Dreamweaver should save the new `.cfc` file. If you want to make the component available as a Web service, be sure to choose a directory that is accessible to your Web server.

5. Now that we've created the file, you'll need to add at least one function to your component so that it actually does something. Click on Functions in the Section list on the left (**Figure 9.12**), and click on the + (plus) button to add a function.

6. In the Name box, type a name for your new function. For this example, type `say_hello`.

7. To make your ColdFusion component available as a Web service, select remote from the Access drop-down menu.

8. In nearly all cases, you'll want your function to return a value that will be printed on the Web page. Select the type of value you want to return from the Return Type drop-down menu. For this example, choose *string*, which could encompass any string of characters.

9. Check the Output checkbox to include `output="true"` in the code.

continues on next page

10. If you want your function to take any input from the user (for example, if the user will be submitting a form), you must add an argument for each input. Click on Arguments in the Section list on the right to do this (**Figure 9.13**).

11. From the Available Functions drop-down menu, select the function to which you want to add an argument. In this case, you'll only have one choice: the say_hello function we created in Step 6.

12. Click on the + (plus) button to add an argument. The grayed out text boxes will become available.

13. In the Name text box, type a name for the argument. Because our function will be taking the user's name and then saying hello to that user by name, call this argument name.

14. From the Type drop-down menu, choose the type of argument you want. In this case, choose string.

15. Check the Required checkbox to include the cfinvokeargument tag.

16. Click OK.

A new Document window will open containing the code generated by the Create Component process. The code will look something like this:

```
<cfcomponent
→ displayName="hello_world">
    <cffunction name="say_hello"
    → access="remote"
    → returnType="string"
    → output="true">
      <cfargument name="name"
      → type="string">
<!--- sayHello body --->
    <cfreturn>
  </cffunction>
</cfcomponent>
```

Now we'll need to make one change to the component in order to make it generate the output.

17. Add an attribute, "Hello, #name#" to the <cfreturn> tag:

```
<cfreturn "Hello, #name#">
```

18. Save this file (in our example it's called hello_world.cfc).

✔ Tips

■ In Step 3, the name you type in the Name text box will be the filename for your component. If you want to see a descriptive name in the <cfcomponent> tag as well, then type a name in the Display Name text box at the top of the screen. Often it makes sense to use the same name you used for the filename.

■ Of course, you need to upload your files before they'll be accessible to any site, yours or someone else's.

Now that you've created a ColdFusion component, you can add it to one of your own pages. You can also publish it as a Web service so that other people (running any kind of application servers) can also use it on their pages.

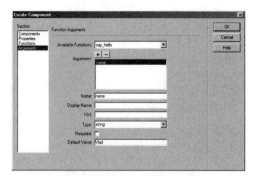

Figure 9.13 Add arguments to your functions in the Arguments section of the Create Component dialog box.

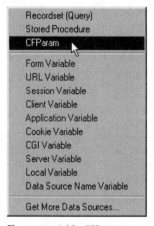

Figure 9.14 Add a CFParam to simplify working with the output parameter of your ColdFusion component.

To add a ColdFusion component to your page:

1. In the Components panel, select CF Components from the drop-down menu.

2. On the Document toolbar, click on the Code View button <>.

3. In the Components panel, expand the name of the ColdFusion component you want to use. (Ours will be nested under the name of our site, linens, and called hello_world.)

4. Drag the string beneath the name of your component into the Document window. (CF components work slightly differently than Web services in that you insert the actual string rather than the entire component.)

   A `<cfinvoke>` code block will appear in your page code.

5. Review the code that you should see for the hello_world component; it should look something like this:

   ```
   <cfinvoke
    → component="linens.hello_world"
    → method="say_hello"
    → returnvariable="say_helloRet">
   <cfinvokeargument name="name"
    → value="Vlad" />
   </cfinvoke>
   ```

6. Replace the placeholder value "Vlad" with your name.

   You'll find the input parameters listed in the `<cfinvokeargument>` tag. In our case, the input parameter is name.

7. Now you'll want to note the value of the `returnvariable` variable because you'll need to type it in later in this exercise.

   The output parameter can be found in the opening `<cfinvoke>` tag with the name `returnvariable`. In our case, the value is "say_helloRet".

   continues on next page

8. Click the Bindings panel tab.

9. Click the Options menu button and choose CFParam (**Figure 9.14**). The CF Param dialog box will appear.

10. Type the name of the output parameter you noted in Step 6, say_helloRet, and click OK.

11. Insert the variable you just created onto the page either by dragging and dropping the variable name from the Bindings panel or by selecting the variable and clicking the Insert button in the Bindings panel. You will see: <cfoutput>#say_helloRet#</cfoutput>.

12. If your ColdFusion server is configured correctly and running, you should be able to preview this file and see the friendly greeting from your application server.

✔ Tips

■ As in the previous exercise, you can also click on the combined Code and Design View button 🔲 in Step 2. You cannot, however, drop a Web service component onto the page in Design view; you need to drop it into the code instead.

■ In Step 3, you may find that Web services components, like ColdFusion components, can be quite complex and contain multiple component elements. So each component may have to be dragged and dropped separately.

Figure 9.15 Opening the .cfc file in the browser gives you a schematic view of the component's contents.

To publish a ColdFusion component as a Web service:

Publicize the URL of the `.cfc` file you just created. You can do this simply by submitting the URL to one or more of the UDDI registries. Techniques differ slightly from registry to registry.

✔ Tip

■ To see how the world will interface with your new Web service, simply open the .cfc file in your browser and ColdFusion will provide an informational display (**Figure 9.15**).

For a more in-depth look at the nuts and bolts of the ColdFusion Markup Language (CFML) and programming ColdFusion components, take a look at Peachpit's *ColdFusion MX Development with Dreamweaver MX: Visual QuickPro Guide* by Susan Hove and Mark Garrett.

PUBLISHING A WEB SERVICE

165

SERVER BEHAVIORS

One of the trickier parts of Web development is figuring out how to combine the HTML content on a Web page—that is, the front end your users see—with the application code that makes that page dynamic and lets your users interact with your application sever. In most cases, just pasting in a bunch of PHP or other server scripts is not going to make your page magically become database aware.

Fortunately, Dreamweaver's server behaviors streamline and simplify the process of interweaving server code with HTML for you. As you may remember from Chapter 2, server behaviors are customizable blocks of server code (written in ColdFusion, PHP, JSP, or ASP) which, when used in conjunction with data from a database, add dynamic functionality to your page. Using Dreamweaver's built-in tools, you don't need to write complex code blocks in order for your pages to communicate with your application server. Instead, you simply fill out the appropriate dialog box with the names and locations of the relevant data, and Dreamweaver writes the code for you. In this chapter, we look at the built-in Server behaviors supplied with Dreamweaver that let you do things like register users and update database records.

If you yourself are an advanced user who writes server scripting code and wants to build your own code into Dreamweaver MX, we show you how to create your own server behaviors.

The Server Behaviors Panel

The Server Behaviors panel provides a menu from which you can create, insert, edit or delete behaviors (**Figure 10.1**). It also lists all the behaviors you've inserted into your page so that you can manage your behaviors and keep track of what you've done.

You may have noticed that we have been using server behaviors fairly extensively throughout this book. Dynamic Text (covered in Chapter 5) is a server behavior, as are the Application Objects we dealt with in Chapters 8 and 9. The latter can be especially useful, in that many of them, such as Update Record and Insert Record, combine a Server Behavior with an automatically created HTML form.

Previous chapters in the book have addressed adding server behaviors to your document. Let's review the behaviors supported by Dreamweaver and then review the process for inserting one of these on your page. (This will give you an idea of the range of capabilities of server behaviors and may inspire you to create your own.)

Figure 10.1 You manage server behaviors in the Server Behaviors panel.

Built-in Server Behaviors

Dreamweaver includes many built-in server behaviors that we've used throughout this book so far to perform common tasks, such as presenting search results, modifying database records, and registering users. Let's take a look at these built-in server behaviors, as well as a few others that you'll use only if you're handy with writing your own JSP or SQL.

Adding a recordset to a page

The most common server behavior, Recordset (Query), is used throughout this book and is covered in great detail in Chapter 2, under the *Bindings Panel* section. You must add a recordset to a page in order to use most other server behaviors.

Behaviors for displaying and navigating recordsets

Most of the time that you display data on a page, you'll be displaying multiple records in a specific format. Controlling how these records are shown is covered in Chapter 7. This process includes the server behaviors Repeat Region (for defining the display of multiple records in a table); the Show Region server behaviors (which write conditional statements that define under what conditions a record is included on a page); and Recordset Paging (for defining how many records will appear on a Web page if the set includes more than 20 records). These server behaviors can also be used in conjunction with XML and Dreamweaver templates, as discussed in Chapter 14.

Modifying database records from Web interfaces

To allow coworkers or users to add, edit, and delete recordsets, you'll use the Insert Record, Update Record, and Delete Record server behaviors, which are covered in the instructions in Chapter 8.

Using master detail pages and defining related pages

A master detail page set is another way to control the display of records. The master page shows a summary of several records returned by a user query; for example, a search of an online catalog. The detail page is a more-complete display of a single record. You click on a link on a master page to view the detail page. Using these tools, which include the Go to Detail Page and the Show Related Page server behaviors, is covered in Chapter 8.

Creating users, passwords, and access levels

The server behaviors under the User Authentication group allow you to let users create login names and passwords and log into and out of your site. You can also set access levels such as "Guest," "Member," and "Administrator" for different sections of your site. These tools are covered in Chapter 8.

Presenting dynamic content

Aside from simply displaying the contents of a recordset on your page, you can also serve formatted content, forms, and media from your application server. The Dynamic Text server behavior is discussed in Chapter 5, which also instructs you on using dynamic HTML tag attributes, dynamic images and media, and working with CSS on an application server. Chapter 6 discusses the behaviors under Dynamic Form Elements, which allow you to serve the form fields themselves dynamically based on the interaction with the user.

Using JavaBeans with JSP

JavaBeans are little applets that are used in conjunction with dynamic JSP pages. A JavaBean acts as a go-between so that the instructions that interact with the server are stored in the JavaBean rather on the JSP page.

If you're using JavaBeans, you can use one of these server behaviors (Java Bean or Java Bean Collection) to attach the bean to your page and display it in the Bindings panel, from whence you can use the JavaBean to display database records on your page.

When you use the JavaBean dialog box, you need to specify the name of the bean; its scope (this page, this request, this user session, or an entire application); and its class name and location (similar to a Java class, you can browse for ZIP or JAR files), expressed like so: `package.class`. You can also specify default values for specific bean properties, either by presetting them or by setting them dynamically. You add a JavaBean Collection in the same way, and you also specify an indexed property for the beans to use as part of their logic for communicating with the server.

Advanced database maintenance using SQL

Two of the server behaviors, Callable (Stored Procedure), and Prepared (Insert, Update, Delete), are used when you want to work with SQL code to modify the contents or structure of a database. The Prepared server behavior allows you to use SQL statements to modify records. SQL is introduced in Chapter 4, and editing database records using Web interfaces is covered in Chapter 8. The Callable server behavior is used to run operations on a database using SQL—that is, an operation such as a routine addition, deletion, or other record cleanup, or even the deletion of columns or data tables. You store the contents of the procedure on the database itself as an SQL statement and insert it as JSP code on a JSP page. Microsoft Access and mySQL do not support stored procedures, and you should have a firm grasp of SQL yourself in order to use them.

Figure 10.2 The menu under the + (plus) button in the Server Behaviors panel lists all the server behaviors available on your current platform.

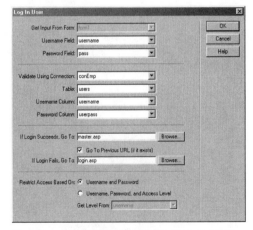

Figure 10.3 Each server behavior has its own dialog box. This one is especially complicated.

Adding a Server Behavior to a Page

What follows is a review, if you've used any built-in server behaviors. These are generic instructions for adding a server behavior; see the previous section if you want to know in which chapter a specific, built-in server behavior is covered. When you create your own server behaviors in Dreamweaver, you'll actually add them to individual pages or templates in the same way you add any other, as follows.

To add a server behavior to a page:

1. Create a new dynamic page.

2. Add a recordset to the page (for more information on how to do this, see the *Bindings Panel* section of Chapter 2).

3. In the Server Behaviors panel, click the + (plus) button.

   From the menu that appears (**Figure 10.2**), select the server behavior you want to add to the page.

   The dialog box for the server behavior you selected will appear (**Figure 10.3**).

4. Fill out the dialog box appropriately.

5. Click OK to close the dialog box.

The server behaviors that are available in the drop-down menu vary depending on which application platform you're running, but they're generally grouped according to function.

You can also change the parameters of a server behavior after you add it to the page by double-clicking on it in the Server Behaviors panel.

Modifying a server behavior on your page is different from selecting Edit Server Behavior from the drop-down menu—in that case, you're adding code to the Dreamweaver interface itself rather than modifying the code on a given page. See the sidebar *Editing Server Behaviors*.

The last basic operation that you can do in the Server Behaviors panel is, of course, to remove server behaviors from the page.

To remove a server behavior from the page:

1. In the Server Behaviors panel, select the server behavior you want to remove (**Figure 10.4**).

2. Click the minus (-) button to remove it.

We'll look next at downloading server behaviors created by other Web developers and adding them to the Server Behaviors panel using Macromedia Exchange.

Figure 10.4 You can remove a server behavior from the page by using the Server Behaviors panel.

Server Behaviors vs. Behaviors

In addition to server behaviors, Dreamweaver also includes client-side behaviors, which are called, simply, behaviors.

The main difference between these two kinds of behaviors is that server behaviors, as the name suggests, call on the server to do something, possibly in a language other than JavaScript; whereas behaviors work solely with the client, or browser, and are all written in JavaScript. These latter behaviors are usually triggered by a user event such as a click or a mouseover.

A server behavior generally requests a record from a database or submits a record to a database, and then does something with the data—displays it, updates it, and so on. A client-side behavior interacts with the user in the browser, doing something like popping up a message, changing the content of a layer, or activating an image rollover.

We cover Behaviors in Chapter 13, *JavaScript and Dreamweaver Behaviors*.

Editing Server Behaviors

You may notice that the drop-down menu in the Server Behaviors panel includes an Edit Server Behavior item. This menu item does what you'd expect: It allows you to edit server behaviors. There is one important caveat, however: You can edit only those server behaviors that you create with the Server Behavior Builder (see the upcoming section, *Creating Custom Server Behaviors*).

You can also edit server behaviors that you download from Macromedia Exchange, because these are also generally created using the Server Behavior Builder. See Chapter 19 to find out about customizing Dreamweaver by adding code that your fellow developers have submitted to Macromedia Exchange.

Of course, if you were expecting to edit a server behavior that's been inserted on your page, you simply need to double-click it in the Components panel to reopen its dialog box and reset its parameters.

Unfortunately, the built-in server behaviors were not themselves built with the Server Behavior Builder. So you can't edit them, and not only that—you also can't create a new behavior based on them. This is an annoying limitation, but it's not the end of the world.

ADDING A SERVER BEHAVIOR TO A PAGE

Creating Custom Server Behaviors

There may be a time when you need a server behavior that isn't included in Dreamweaver and is not available on the Macromedia Exchange site. In such a traumatic event, you can create your own, if you are proficient in the scripting language your server uses.

Fortunately, Macromedia has provided a tool to streamline the process of creating a new server behavior, called the Server Behavior Builder (**Figure 10.5**). However, it's not particularly easy to use, and the documentation provided with Dreamweaver is not too helpful. But luckily, you bought this fine volume, which will walk you through the process.

Getting new server behaviors from Macromedia Exchange

One way to begin writing server behaviors is to look at the code written by developers like you. Macromedia Exchange, at **www.macromedia.com/exchange/**, is a repository of code that other people have written and shared. The site includes server behaviors, application code, specific widgets for JSP and ColdFusion, and other useful tools for both front-end and back-end development.

The server behaviors available on the site include such tools as user session management, random record serving, and PHP "show-if" scripts that let you serve data based on a user's form submissions. To find out more about using Macromedia Exchange, see Chapter 19. To search the Exchange site specifically for server behavior code, click on Advanced Search and then search for "Dreamweaver MX" and "Server Behaviors."

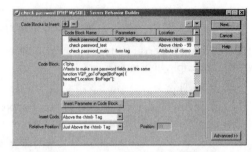

Figure 10.5 Dreamweaver's Server Behavior Builder can streamline the creation of server behaviors.

Figure 10.6 Server behavior code is interspersed with HTML.

About Server Behaviors

A server behavior comprises one or more blocks of server code interspersed with the HTML on a page (**Figure 10.6**). As we mentioned earlier, this combination of server code and HTML has a number of advantages. For example, you can add the code to confirm a password and automatically attach the behavior to a form. Or you can add user parameters to let other Web application developers in your workgoup specify to which form the behavior should be attached.

To get a better idea of how this works, let's create a PHP server behavior, which will confirm that users consistently enter the same password. The principles for coding server behaviors are the same regardless of which language you're using. However, we're using PHP in our example because it illustrates some particulars for this very common language.

The server behavior we will create is called Check Password. It simply verifies that the contents of both password fields match one another, and if they do, it directs the browser to another page. You might find this server behavior useful despite its simplicity, but regardless, it should give you the basic idea of how to use the Server Behavior Builder.

In this example, we'll create two password fields, named **pass1** and **pass2**. When creating real server behaviors for a real-world production environment, you and your developers can name form fields whatever you want, but if you're following along, keep in mind that you must keep form field names consistent in order for the code to work. That is, once you create the server behavior, don't go renaming your form fields.

Throughout the next few stepped lists, we work extensively in the Server Behavior Builder dialog box and with the same code, so don't close that dialog box until we instruct you to do so.

To create a server behavior:

1. In the Server Behaviors panel, click on the + (plus) button and select New Server Behavior from the menu that appears.

   The New Server Behavior dialog box will appear (**Figure 10.7**).

2. From the Document Type drop-down menu, select PHP/MySQL.

3. In the Name text box, type Check Password.

4. Leave the checkbox for Copy existing server behavior unchecked and click OK to close the New Server Behavior dialog box.

   The Server Behavior Builder dialog box will appear (**Figure 10.8**).

5. Click the + (plus) button to add a new code block.

   The Create a New Code Block dialog box will appear (**Figure 10.9**).

6. In the Name text box, type Check Password_main.

7. Click OK to close the Create a New Code Block dialog box.

   The code block will now be listed in the Server Behavior Builder dialog box (**Figure 10.10**).

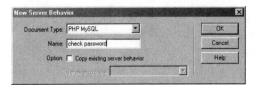

Figure 10.7 You name your server behavior in the New Server Behavior dialog box.

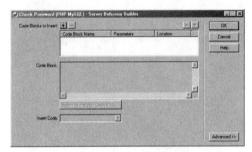

Figure 10.8 You'll be seeing a lot of this dialog box.

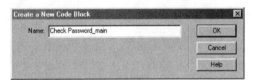

Figure 10.9 You should name your code block descriptively.

Figure 10.10 The dialog box contains a list of code blocks.

```php
<?php
//tests to make sure password fields
→ are the samefunction
→ VQP_goToPage($toPage)
{
header("Location: $toPage");
}
if (count($HTTP_POST_VARS)>0)
{
if ($HTTP_POST_VARS[pass1]
→ ==$HTTP_POST_VARS[pass2])
{       VQP_goToPage ("");
} else
{       VQP_goToPage("");
}
}
?>
```

8. In the Code Block text box, type the code on the left.

Note that you can't actually indent the code in the text field, although we've done it here to make it easier to read.

Let's take a close look at what this code accomplishes. First we defined a function called VQP_goToPage, which treats a URL as an argument and directs the browser to the specified page. We called the function VQP_goToPage (as opposed to just goToPage) because Macromedia recommends you pre-fix all of your function and variable names with initials to avoid conflict with other server behaviors.

Next, the code serves to verify that the page has indeed been called as the result of a sub-mitted form, which in this case means the user has filled out the login dialog box cor-rectly. For details on why we're using the specific functions that we are, specifically the ()header function, see the sidebar *Opening a New Page With PHP*.

After the behavior checks to make sure the page has been called as the result of a sub-mitted form, it checks to see if the contents of the two fields **pass1** and **pass2** are identi-cal. If so, we'll want to send the browser to a successful registration page, and if not, we'll want to send the browser to a warning page or warning message.

If you've closely scrutinized this code, you may have already noticed that it doesn't actually instruct the browser to go to any page. For both success and failure, the script calls for the same thing: VQP_goToPage(""). This is obviously not going to get us anywhere.

We need to add parameters to the code, so that the developer can fill in to which pages the browser should be directed, depending on whether the login was successful or unsuccessful.

Pasting Code vs. Typing Code

You can find many of the code blocks like the ones we print in this chapter on the companion Web site for this book (www.peachpit.com/vqp/dreamweaver MX). That way, you won't have to type every-thing over again if you don't want to.

Opening a New Page With PHP

Using PHP to send instructions to a browser is not a straightforward operation. Unlike, say, JavaScript, where you can directly instruct the browser to open a new page (using the `document.open()` method), in PHP you need to essentially trick the server into sending a different file from the one your code appears in, because the page itself needs to request something, rather than the user doing so. Your application server is basically pretending to be an HTTP server, by either sending the browser to a page or by dynamically creating a page to display in the browser. You can do this by using the PHP `header()` function. The `header()` function is intended to be used as a way to set the HTTP header information for a document (remember that HTTP controls what gets sent from the server to your browser, whereas HTML just controls how your browser interprets what gets sent). By using the special `header ("Location:")` variation of the function, you can get the server to send whatever page you specify.

There's a trick to this, however. Unlike JavaScript, where you can tell the browser to open a new document at any time, you can only use PHP to set header information before the document actually starts to display in your browser. In other words, any use of the `header()` function must come before the <html> tag in a document.

It is for this reason that you'll often see PHP pages calling themselves rather than calling specific documents. When a page calls itself, it essentially reloads itself with updated information from the database, rather than having either to request a static page that doesn't include the new data, or to create a brand-new document.

Figure 10.11 You can insert design-time parameters in your code block. These allow a Web Page designer to specify to what objects on the page a server behavior will apply.

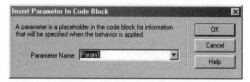

Figure 10.12 Naming your parameter Param1 won't really remind you later on what the parameter does. Additionally, Macromedia suggests you prepend your initials to parameter names. A better name here would be VQP_GoodPage, which we're using.

Figure 10.13 The @@ symbols tell Dreamweaver what the parameters are.

To add a parameter to the code:

1. In the Code Block text field of the Server Behavior Builder dialog box, click in between the quotes in the first VQP_goToPage("") call (**Figure 10.11**).

2. Directly below this text field, click the Insert Parameter in Code Block button.

   The Insert Parameter in Code Block dialog box will appear (**Figure 10.12**).

3. Name the parameter VQP_goodPage.

4. Click OK to close the dialog box.

   The parameter will be inserted into the code (**Figure 10.13**).

5. Click between the quotes in the second VQP_goToPage("") call.

6. Click the Insert Parameter in Code Block button.

7. Name the parameter VQP_badPage.

8. Click OK to close the dialog box.

Now that we've created the function that is responsible for the real work in this server behavior, we need to make sure we place the function in the right place on the page.

Because we want the script to be called first, before anything else, we need to put it at the very top of the file, before any HTML on the page.

To put the script at the top of the file:

1. From the Insert Code drop-down menu, located at the bottom of the dialog box, select Above the <html> Tag (**Figure 10.14**).

2. From the Relative Position drop-down menu below it, select The Beginning of the File.

We're now finished with the first code block. Because we want the code to be triggered by a form, we need to make sure the form actually calls the code. To do this, we need the form itself to call the page, and we'll accomplish that by having the form action, when the submit button is pushed, call the script. We'll be using the POST action in this case.

✔ Tip

■ By having the form call its own page, we can keep all the code for the server behavior on one page. This makes using it much easier for the developer, because one page will contain all the password verification code, making the whole deal much easier to manage.

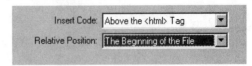

Figure 10.14 You can specify where each code block goes on the page.

Figure 10.15 This code tells the form to call the same page the form code appears on; that is, it calls itself.

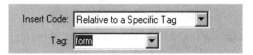

Figure 10.16 You can get more specific about where the code block appears, whether in relation to the HTML tag, the form tag, or another tag.

Figure 10.17 We want this code to be the form tag's action attribute.

To specify an action for the form:

1. In the Server Behavior Builder dialog box, click the + (plus) button to add a new code block.

2. In the Create a New Code Block dialog box, name the block Check Password_action.

3. Click OK to go back to the Server Behavior Builder dialog box.

4. In the Code Block text field, type the following code:
   ```php
   <?php echo
   $HTTP_SERVER_VARS['PHP_SELF']; ?>
   ```
   (**Figure 10.15**).

5. From the Insert Code drop-down menu, select Relative to a Specific Tag.

6. From the Tag drop-down menu, select form (**Figure 10.16**).

7. From the Relative Position drop-down menu, select As the Value of an Attribute.

8. From the Attribute drop-down menu, select action (**Figure 10.17**).

What we've done here is added a new (and very short) code block, which simply specifies that the action of the form is to call the page that it's on.

Now, because we're checking the page for POST variables in the first code block we created, we need to make sure the form is making an HTTP POST request, rather than an HTTP GET. This is set in the method attribute of the <form> tag. (These two form submission methods, POST and GET, are discussed in terms of their advantages and disadvantages in Chapter 6.)

As you might have guessed, we'll add a third code block to force the form to use the post method, regardless of how the developer initially set up the form.

CREATING CUSTOM SERVER BEHAVIORS

To specify the form's method:

1. In the Server Behavior Builder dialog box, click the + (plus) button to add a new code block.

2. In the Create a New Code Block dialog box, name the block Check Password_method.

3. Click OK to go back to the Server Behavior Builder dialog box.

4. In the Code Block text field, enter the following code:
```
<? php echo "post"; ?>
```
(**Figure 10.18**).

5. From the Insert Code drop-down menu, select Relative to a Specific Tag.

6. From the Tag drop-down menu, select form.

7. From the Relative Position drop-down menu, select As the Value of an Attribute.

8. From the Attribute drop-down menu, select method (**Figure 10.19**).

We have now created all the code blocks for our server behavior. Now we need to specify the settings for the dialog box that your developers will see when they add the server behavior to a page.

Figure 10.18 We force the form to use the POST method to keep the code simple.

Figure 10.19 This code block should be the method attribute of the form tag.

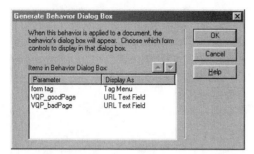

Figure 10.20 The Generate Behavior Dialog Box dialog box shows the parameters you added to the code.

To specify the dialog box settings:

1. In the Server Behavior Builder dialog box, click the Next button to move on to the dialog box editor.

   The Generate Behavior Dialog Box dialog box (say *that* five times fast) will open. You should see the same three entries in the Items in Behavior list box as shown in **Figure 10.20**.

2. Click on the VQP_goodPage variable to highlight it.

3. Click the down arrow to the right of the variable, and from the Display As drop-down menu, select URL Text Field.

   Because we want the developer to be able to select an HTML page to go to, we use this style of control, which provides a Browse button.

4. Repeat Steps 2 and 3 for the VQP_badPage variable.

   The form tag entry is there so that the developer can specify to which form the server behavior should be attached. It's a Tag Menu, and you can'tcontrol the format and use a different type of field instead.

5. Click OK to close the dialog box.

   You've now created a server behavior. Now we can go ahead and test it on a page. This is the part where we actually create the password fields on a test page, and then pose as a user who's typing the password that our server behavior will validate.

CREATING CUSTOM SERVER BEHAVIORS

To test the server behavior:

1. Open a new PHP page.

2. From the menu bar, select Insert > Form to insert a blank form onto the page.

3. From the menu bar, select Insert > Form Objects > Text Field to insert a text field within the form.

4. Repeat Step 3 to insert another text field.

5. From the menu bar, select Insert > Form Objects > Button.

   Your page should look something like **Figure 10.21**.

6. Select the first text field on your page. In the Property inspector, name the field **pass1** and click the Password radio button (**Figure 10.22**)

7. Select the second text field on your page. In the Property inspector, name the field **pass2** and click the Password radio button.

8. In the Server Behaviors panel, click the + (plus) button and select Check Password from the menu that appears.

   The Check Password dialog box—the one we made ourselves—will appear (**Figure 10.23**).

9. Specify the pages to go to in case of success or failure, and click OK to close the dialog box.

10. Upload the file to a PHP server and test it out.

We'll close this chapter by exploring how to customize the dialog box attached to your server behavior.

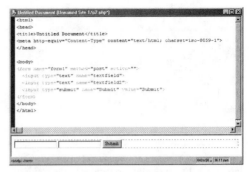

Figure 10.21 We first create a form to which we will add the server behavior.

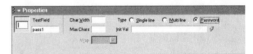

Figure 10.22 Because our server behavior is not extremely robust, we need to name the fields specific things to remind ourselves of their purpose.

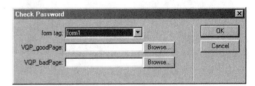

Figure 10.23 This is the dialog we automatically generated earlier. Not overly helpful, is it? Even though we ourselves created the parameters, some indication of what we should do next would help us the next time we tried to use this behavior.

Figure 10.24 Here's the HTML representation of the dialog box we created earlier.

Customizing the Server Behavior Builder

One limitation of Macromedia's Server Behavior Builder is that the dialog boxes it generates are not at all self-explanatory. The only labels it adds for the controls are the variable names you've used in the code. And if you've followed Macromedia's guidelines and prefixed the variable names with your initials, the dialog box is even harder to read.

Fortunately, there's a way to tidy up the dialog box a little. The dialog box is actually an HTML page that's automatically generated by the Server Behavior Builder, and you can edit it within Dreamweaver.

To edit a Server Behavior dialog box.

1. From the menu bar, select File > Open. The Open dialog box will appear.

2. Navigate to your Dreamweaver application folder, which should be something like `C:\Program Files\Macromedia\Dreamweaver MX` on Windows and `Macintosh HD:Applications:Macromedia Dreamweaver MX` on the Macintosh.

3. From there, open the `Configuration` folder, then `ServerBehaviors`, and finally, open the folder for your platform (in the example above, the `PHP_MySQL` folder).

4. The dialog box file for your behavior will be named the same as your server behavior with a .htm or .html extension. So select the Check Password.htm file and click Open to open the file.

   An HTML file for the dialog box will open, presenting the dialog box as an HTML form (**Figure 10.24**).

continues on next page

5. Edit the file as you would any HTML file, but be careful not to disturb any of the code that the Server Behavior Builder has added to the page. Also be careful not to change the names of any of the form's fields.

We've changed the labels on the form (**Figure 10.25**) so that the dialog box is more understandable (**Figure 10.26**).

✔ Tip

■ Be sure, if you're going to cut and paste any form fields, that Dreamweaver's safeguards don't rename the fields. In the Preferences dialog box (Edit > Preferences), go to the Code Rewriting category and make sure the Rename Form Items when Pasting checkbox is unchecked.

This chapter has been a basic introduction to server behaviors. In the next chapter, we'll look at some of the tools Macromedia provides to make editing code easier.

Figure 10.25 We've cleaned up the form...

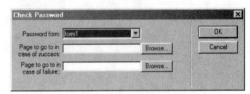

Figure 10.26 ...so the dialog box is more self-explanatory.

Testing Server Behaviors

No custom Web site is complete until you've tested any code you've written, and server behaviors are no exception.

The Dreamweaver online help files offer a number of good suggestions about how to test your server behaviors. Many of their suggestions are good ideas for testing any code that you write or that you use a tool to automatically generate.

CODE EDITING TOOLS

Dreamweaver MX is a full-fledged text and code editor. It works with you, whether you like to code by hand or whether you prefer mostly sticking to the WYSIWYG environment and tweaking your code every once in a while.

You can open and edit not only HTML and XML in Dreamweaver MX, but XHTML, plain text, JavaScript, CSS, and nearly any other kind of text file, including the server document types described in Chapter 1 and the rest of the first half of the book.

In this chapter, we first look at Dreamweaver's Document window, where you have a number of options for viewing your pages. You can view them in Design view, which is how the browser sees it; Code view, which displays the code; or Split view, which lets you see both views at once. You can also float a Code inspector window. Selections in any of these views show you the code in one place and the objects in another.

In Design view, you can use the Insert toolbar, the Property inspector, and the Quick Tag editor to modify your page.

In Code view, you have available many, many tools for inserting tags while also browsing lists of them and using reference information about them. The Reference panel provides descriptions of code and attributes for many languages. This reference information is also available in the Tag Editor, which lets you use a dialog box to choose and set tag attributes, and in the Tag Chooser, which lists and describes tags by category and lets you edit and insert them from there.

In either view, you can also insert prefab code from the Snippets panel, and you can add your own frequently used widgets or text blocks to the panel.

Later in the chapter we take a look at some of the many safeguards and validation tools that Dreamweaver provides for cleaning up your page. We'll show you in particular how to use XHTML, browser profiles, and tag validation. And you can set preferences for nearly anything you could have an opinion about here—such as whether certain features (tag rewriting, Code Hints, Syntax Coloring, and CSS shorthand) take effect, and when.

So let's take a look at the ins and outs of coding with Dreamweaver.

The Dreamweaver Code Environment

Dreamweaver's Document window shows you, in Design view (**Figure 11.1**), the WYSIWYG version of your page—that is, the page that your visitors will see when they open it using a Web browser.

In Design view, elements such as comments, scripts, and named anchors are marked with little icons. Click on any of these to see its properties in the Property inspector. To toggle invisible element icons on and off, select View > Visual Aids > Invisible Elements from the menu bar. You can set preferences for which of these to show, too: Edit > Preferences > Invisible Elements. (In Mac OS X, that's Dreamweaver > Preferences > Invisible Elements.) In the Preferences dialog box, select or deselect the items for which you want to see markers.

Code view and Split view

You can also view your code in the Document window in Code view (**Figure 11.2**), or you can view both Code and Design views at once—what we like to call Split view (**Figure 11.3**).

You open Code, Split, or Design view by clicking the appropriate button on the Document toolbar (**Figure 11.4**).

Layer marker   Script marker

Named anchor marker

Comment marker

Figure 11.1 Dreamweaver's WYSIWYG view is called Design view. You can turn off invisible element viewing to hide the markers.

Figure 11.2 You can also view code in the Document window—this is the same page in Code view.

Figure 11.3 You can also view both code and design.

Code view

Design view

Split view (Code and Design views)

Figure 11.4 Select your view using the Document toolbar.

Figure 11.5 The Code inspector lets you view your code and page side-by-side, if you prefer. You can also float the Code inspector to another part of the desktop—very handy if you have a big screen or two monitors.

The Code inspector

To show the code for the page you're working on in a separate, floating window, press F10 to open the Code inspector (**Figure 11.5**). The menu command is Window > Others > Code inspector.

The Code inspector is technically part of Design view; many commands not available in Code view *are* available when using the Code inspector. These include adding items to the library and using the Quick Tag editor.

On the other hand, some tools that are available only in Code view, such as context-sensitive buttons, are not available in the Code inspector. And the context menus that appear in the Code inspector when you right-click (Ctrl+click) an object are the menus for Design view, which differ slightly from those for Code view.

About selections

No matter what view you're in, if you select something in Design view, the code will also be selected in Code view or the Code inspector (Figure 11.5), and vice-versa—select code, and the objects will appear selected in Design view.

Bear in mind that dragging to select text in Design view doesn't always select all the relevant tags—it's often a good idea to double-check your selections in Code or Split view before making changes (**Figure 11.6**).

✔ Tips

- To select a line of code, you can click on its line number in either Code view or the Code inspector.

- See the upcoming section *The Tag Selector* for how to select specific tags in Design view.

Opening <b> tag not selected

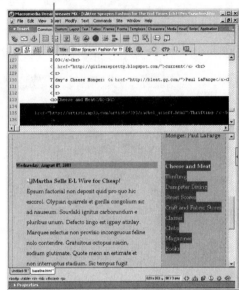

Figure 11.6 When we dragged to select the links in the Document window, everything looked kosher, but you can see in Split view that the opening B tag for our first selected line wasn't selected.

Figure 11.7 Properties for a selected image.

Figure 11.8 Properties for a selected table.

Click to toggle between text and CSS properties

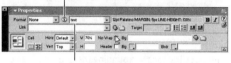

Select the CSS class from this menu

Figure 11.9 New in Dreamweaver MX, you can apply CSS to text and some objects using the Property inspector.

Figure 11.10 The various tabs of the Insert toolbar include buttons that allow you to insert objects—such as tables, comments, and horizontal rules—or access tools, such as Layout Mode on the Layout tab.

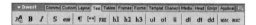

Figure 11.11 For many buttons, such as those on the Text tab, you can make a selection in any view and then wrap the button's code around it.

Contextual buttons

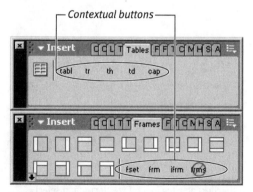

Figure 11.12 These buttons on the Frames and Tables tabs of the Insert toolbar only work when the insertion point is in Code view.

Editing Code in the Document Window

Whether you're in Code view or Design view, you're basically editing code. Some tools work only in one view or another; we mention this when it's relevant.

The Property inspector

No doubt you're already familiar with editing selections using the Property inspector (Window > Properties). Just click on an object or select some text or a tag, and then make changes to properties using the Property inspector, which changes appearance based on your selections (**Figures 11.7** and **11.8**).

You can also apply CSS using the Property inspector (**Figure 11.9**).

The Insert toolbar

Unlike the Property inspector, the buttons on the Insert toolbar don't let you know what's already been applied to your selection—these buttons just insert code (**Figure 11.10**).

There are two ways to use these buttons: to insert objects, or to apply code to a selection. To insert an object, click on a button. (A dialog box may open asking for more information before the object is inserted, such as the Insert Table dialog box for tables).

You can also wrap a tag around a selection. For example, use the Text tab on the Insert toolbar to wrap tags such as `<strong>` or `<h1>` around selected text or code in any view (**Figure 11.11**).

Contextual buttons

Some buttons work only when Code or Split view is open. They will be grayed out if the Code inspector is open and you are in Design view. These buttons appear on the Tables and Frames tabs of the Insert toolbar (**Figure 11.12**).

The Tag Selector

No matter what view you're in, the tags surrounding your current selection appear in the Tag selector on the status bar (**Figure 11.13**). Click anywhere to display all tags surrounding your selection.

Then, you can click any tag to select that tag and everything inside it.

✔ Tips

- On Windows machines, the Tag selector will appear at the bottom of each window if the Document window is minimized, or below the file tabs if the Document window is maximized (**Figure 11.14**).

- If the current selection is a whole tag, that tag will appear in bold (Figure 11.14).

- In Dreamweaver, CSS instances are depicted in the Tag selector as being appended to their tags, like this: `<p.class>` (Figure 11.14).

Removing a tag

Right-click (Ctrl+click) on any tag in the Tag selector and, from the menu that appears, select Remove Tag (**Figure 11.15**). You cannot remove some tags, such as `table` and `body`.

Setting the class or ID of a tag

When you're working with CSS, you can apply classes or IDs directly to tags using the Tag selector. Right-click (Ctrl+click) on any tag in the Tag selector and, from the menu that appears, select Set Class (**Figure 11.16**) or Set ID. Any classes or IDs available to your page, including through external style sheets, will become available through a sub-menu.

Editing a tag

Right-click (Ctrl+click) on a tag in the Tag selector and select Edit Tag to open the tag in the Quick Tag editor. See the next section, *Editing Code in Design View (the Quick Tag Editor)*.

Tag selector

Figure 11.13 The tags surrounding the current insertion point or selection will appear in the Tag selector.

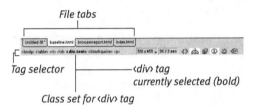

File tabs

Tag selector — — *<div> tag currently selected (bold)*

Class set for <div> tag

Figure 11.14 When your Document window is maximized (Windows machines only), the Tag selector appears below the file tabs.

Figure 11.15 To get rid of a tag, right-click (Ctrl+click) on a tag in the Tag selector and select Remove tag.

Figure 11.16 To set a CSS class or ID, right-click (Ctrl+click) on a tag in the Tag selector and select Set Class or Set ID, then make your selection.

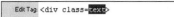

Figure 11.17 The Quick Tag editor lets you edit a single tag, wrap a single tag around your selection, or insert small chunks of HTML.

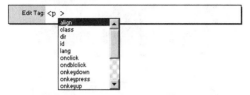

Figure 11.18 When you type in the Quick Tag editor, a hints menu will appear.

Dragging editor

Quick Tag editor button

Figure 11.19 Here we've selected an image and we're going to edit its code with the QT editor. We've also dragged the editor away from its default position right next to its button on the Property inspector.

Figure 11.20 Right-click (Ctrl+click) on an object in the document window, and select Edit Tag Code to open the Quick Tag editor. (Selecting just Edit Tag opens the Tag Editor dialog box, described later in this chapter.)

Editing Code in Design View (the Quick Tag Editor)

The Quick Tag editor, or QT editor for short, (**Figure 11.17**) lets you insert or edit code while you're working in Design view. The editor has three modes: Wrap Tag, Edit Tag, and Insert HTML. Which mode you work in depends on what item(s) you select (text, tag, object, and so on) when you open the editor.

Wrap Tag mode wraps a tag around the selection. *Edit Tag mode* opens the selected tag and its attributes. *Insert HTML mode* appears when you've selected no tag, and inserts the tags you type at the insertion point in the code.

✔ Tip

- For information on using the Tag Hints menu (**Figure 11.18**) with the QT Editor or when hand coding, see *Built-in Tag Writing Shortcuts,* later in this chapter.

To open the QT editor:

◆ Click on the QT editor button on the Property inspector (**Figure 11.19**)

 or

 Design View Only: Right-click (Ctrl+click) on an object or text in the Document window, and select Edit Tag Code (**Figure 11.20**) from the context menu

 or

 Press Ctrl+T (Command+T).

You'll see a typing area, and the name of the mode the QT editor is in.

EDITING CODE IN DESIGN VIEW

To close the QT editor:

◆ Simply press Enter (Return).

To move the QT editor:

◆ Click on its selection handle; that's the gray part of the editor (Figure 11.19), and drag it.

To switch modes:

◆ Press Ctrl+T (Command+T) again until the preferred mode appears.

Selecting parent and child tags

You may want to edit a tag other than the one you see in the QT editor. In Design view, you can use these commands by selecting the tag in the Tag selector or by opening the tag in the QT editor. The code will be selected in both Code and Design view after you use the command in Design view.

For example, if you have the <tr> tag selected, selecting its parent tag will select <table> and selecting its child tag will select its first <td>.

To select the current tag's parent tag:

◆ Press Ctrl+[(left bracket); on the Mac, it's Command+[.

or

From the menu bar, select Edit > Select Parent Tag. The parent tag's contents will be selected in the Document window, and if the QT editor is open, the parent tag will appear there (**Figure 11.21**).

To select the child tag:

◆ With the QT editor open and in Edit Tag mode, press Ctrl+] (right bracket); for Mac, it's Command+Shift+].

or

From the menu bar, select Edit > Select Child. The child tag's contents will be selected in the Document window, and if the QT editor is open, the child tag will appear there (**Figure 11.22**).

Tag code selected   *Tag appears in editor*

Tag appears selected in Tag selector

Figure 11.21 With the <tr> tag selected in the Tag selector and the QT editor, we've selected the parent tag, <table>.

Tag code selected   *Tag appears in editor*

Tag appears selected in Tag selector

Figure 11.22 With the <tr> tag selected in the Tag selector and the QT editor, we've selected the child tag, <td>.

Figure 11.23 If you type only the opening ‹p› tag in Wrap Tag mode, the closing ‹/p› tag will be added after your selection.

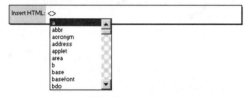

Figure 11.24 If you don't make a selection, the QT Editor will appear in Insert HTML mode, from which you can insert tags, text, and so on. Also pictured is the Hints menu, which offers selections of HTML tags and attributes.

Figure 11.25 Here, we're sloppily typing invalid code. Part of our error is that it's easy to forget that the quasi-helpful opening and closing brackets are provided: <>

Figure 11.26 Dreamweaver did the best it could: It closed the ‹b› tag, re-nested the b and i tags, and it second-guessed our formatting and provided an additional i tag for the brackets that were included. We should remove the extra i tag and the extra brackets.

✔ QT Editor Tips: Wrap Tag mode

- The editor opens in Wrap Tag mode if you select text or an object rather than a tag.

- You need to type only the opening tag. The QT editor will add the closing tag for you (**Figure 11.23**).

- After you type your tag, press Enter (Return) to wrap it around your selection.

- In Wrap Tag mode, you can enter only one tag at a time.

✔ QT Editor Tips: Insert HTML mode

- Insert HTML mode (**Figure 11.24**) is the default Quick Tag editor mode if you haven't selected a specific object or tag. You can insert as much code as you want, and it will be popped in at the insertion point.

- If you insert only an opening tag with Insert HTML mode, the closing tags will be inserted for you if they're required. You can move them afterward, if you like. If the tags are not 100-percent required, Dreamweaver may not close them, so check your code to see if there are any elements—particularly in table code— that need closing.

- If you insert invalid HTML (**Figures 11.25** and **11.26**), Dreamweaver will do one of the following: close your tags; mark improperly wrapped tags; change incorrect closing tags into the correct tag; omit extra closing tags; or display a dialog box letting you know you inserted invalid code. Dreamweaver will not remove or alter non-standard tags.

✔ QT Editor Tips: Edit Tag mode

■ The easiest way to select a specific tag is by using the Tag selector (**Figure 11.27**). You can also right-click (Ctrl+click) on a tag in the Tag selector and select Edit Tag (Figure 11.20). The QT editor will open in Edit Tag mode.

■ If you select the contents of a tag, but not an entire tag, the QT editor will second-guess you and select the whole thing.

■ You can edit the tag itself, or any attribute of the tag. To scroll through the attributes of the tag, press Tab (**Figure 11.28**); to move backward, press Shift+Tab.

✔ More QT Editor Tips

■ The hints menu will appear (Figure 11.24) when you open the QT editor, or if you pause while typing or selecting an attribute, or if you type a space after a tag name or attribute. See *Built-in Tag Writing Shortcuts*, later in this chapter.

■ If you Tab or Shift+Tab after you've edited an attribute, your changes will be applied. You can pause changes until you close the QT editor. To set preferences, see *Quick Tag editor and Tag Hints preferences,* later in this chapter.

Figure 11.27 To select one of the many tags surrounding the word coalesce, we'll click on the appropriate choice in the Tag selector.

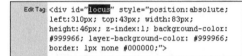

Figure 11.28 In this layer, which has many attributes and values, you can hop from one to the next by pressing Tab (or Shift+Tab to go backwards).

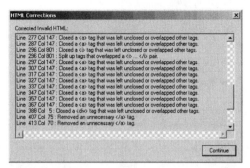

Figure 11.29 We found a page online whose code we wanted to study. However, the page was coded sloppily, with many tags improperly wrapped and closed in funny places. Dreamweaver to the rescue—when we opened the page, the errors were fixed. You can discard the fixes by closing the page without saving.

View Options menu button

→ *Invalidly wrapped or unclosed tags*

Figure 11.30 On the same page, we discarded the changes and looked at them—double links with no closing </a> tags, lots of improper wrapping. We turned on Invalid HTML Highlighting (under the View Options menu button) to see the tags highlighted in yellow in the Document window and the Code inspector. Select the invalid markup marker to read a description in the Property inspector.

Roundtrip HTML

When developers at Macromedia designed Dreamweaver, they were well-aware that the biggest gripe among coders about HTML editing tools is that the editor makes unnecessary changes to the code, introducing mistakes that can be difficult to isolate.

With that in mind, Dreamweaver does not rewrite code unless you ask it to. There are three circumstances where you can ask for help:

◆ If you turn on Code Rewriting preferences, Dreamweaver will fix code when you open a page that's been sloppily coded—including if it's been coded by FrontPage or coded sloppily by a human (**Figure 11.29**). See *Code Rewriting preferences,* later in this chapter.

◆ For individual pages, you can turn on Invalid HTML Highlighting in both the Document window and Code inspector. Select Highlight Invalid HTML from the View Options menu on the Document toolbar in any view (**Figure 11.30**).

◆ For individual pages, you can use the Clean Up HTML command. See *Cleaning Up HTML,* later in this chapter.

In any of these instances, you can instruct Dreamweaver to rewrite the big three mistakes: unclosed brackets, quotes, and tags; improperly nested tags; and extra closing tags.

Dreamweaver will not remove proprietary tag markup, which may be valid XML or server code. (When performing a cleanup, you can have Dreamweaver remove a specific proprietary tag.)

One place where you may see Dreamweaver appear to chew up a page is on hand-coded tables, which may employ unclosed <td> or <tr> tags and still display properly in the browser window. If Dreamweaver seems to be changing your tables, turn off the tag rewriting features and turn on tag highlighting to see where the unclosed tags are.

Using the Tag Reference

Dreamweaver includes a built-in tag reference for looking up the properties of different languages. The HTML guide is provided by O'Reilly, the technical reference publisher that puts furry animals on its covers (and good technical information inside).

The Reference panel (**Figures 11.31** and **11.32**) is part of the Code panel group and includes entries for HTML, CSS, Accessibility, JavaScript, ASP, JSP, CFML, and SiteSpring. Wherever you see the Reference button <?>, including on the Property inspector, click on it to get info about the current tag. Or just browse the panel.

Figure 11.31 The Reference panel for CSS.

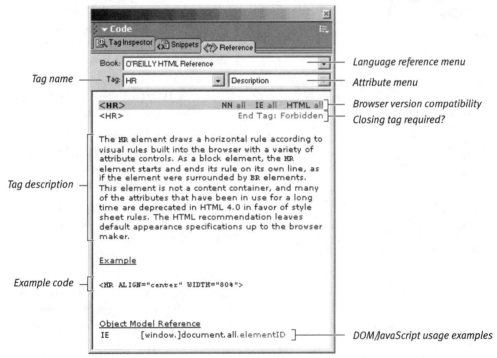

Figure 11.32 The Reference panel provides handy information for most HTML tags and attributes, as well as a few other languages.

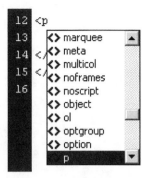

Figure 11.33 When you type code, a hints menu will appear for HTML tags and attributes and some JavaScript and server-side entities.

Figure 11.34 Type a space after a tag, and a menu of attributes will appear.

Built-in Tag Writing Shortcuts

Besides Dreamweaver's myriad tools for coding in Design view, the program includes many other panels, shortcuts, and dialog boxes to help you manage your code.

When you hand code in Code view or the Code inspector, tag hints menus appear, and your tags will be closed automatically. (You can turn these features off.) Additionally, the Tag Inspector panel, the Tag Editor dialog box, the Tag Chooser, and the Snippets panel provide tag-editing shortcuts.

Tag completion

When you're hand coding, Dreamweaver's code engine will complete any open tags after you type a space after them, like so:

<p> becomes

<p></p>

Which is fine, except you may have wanted to type this instead:

<p>my content, lots of it </p>

This is Dreamweaver's way of locking the barn door before there are any horses in it—it makes sure those tags get closed! You can always type your content, select it, and then use the Property inspector and the Insert toolbar to apply formatting, but that's not exactly hand coding. You can also turn off tag completion. See *Quick Tag editor and Tag Hints preferences*, later in this chapter.

Tag Hints

When you type any HTML code in Code view, the Code inspector, or the Quick Tag editor, a menu of hints will appear, listing all the tags or attributes available (**Figures 11.33** and **11.34**). You can select a tag, you can ignore the menu, or you can turn the menu off. See *Quick Tag editor and Tag Hints preferences*, later in this chapter.

The Tag inspector (Tree view)

The Tag Inspector panel (**Figure 11.35**, part of the Code panel group, **Window > Tag Inspector**, offers a hierarchical view of every tag on the current page. You can expand and collapse tags to view or hide their contents, and you can edit tags and attributes. (If you want to set a dynamic attribute, click next to the attribute name and then click on the Lightning Bolt button to select the recordset (See *Setting Tag Attributes Dynamically*, in Chapter 5).

You can also edit tag libraries from this panel; see Chapter 12 for more about this.

BUILT-IN TAG WRITING SHORTCUTS

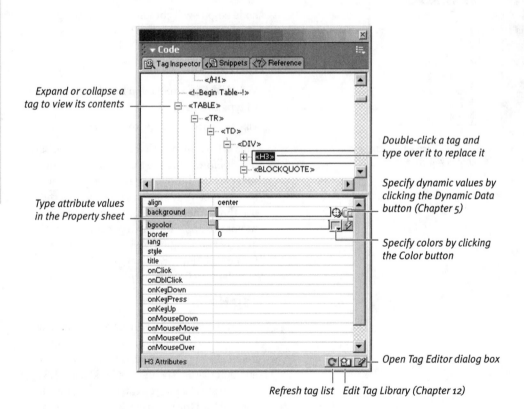

Expand or collapse a tag to view its contents

Double-click a tag and type over it to replace it

Specify dynamic values by clicking the Dynamic Data button (Chapter 5)

Type attribute values in the Property sheet

Specify colors by clicking the Color button

Open Tag Editor dialog box

Refresh tag list   Edit Tag Library (Chapter 12)

Figure 11.35 Use the Tag Inspector panel to browse the structure of your page by expanding and collapsing parent tags. You can also change any tag or modify any attribute by selecting it in the Property Sheet and typing over it.

200

Legacy tags (with brackets) will be inserted

Tags without brackets will open in the Tag Editor before insertion

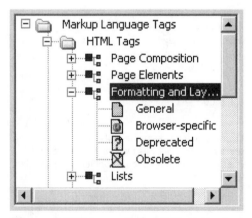

Reference panel button

Insert tag

Show or hide Reference info

Reference info

Figure 11.36 The Tag Chooser lets you browse a list of available tags for different code languages.

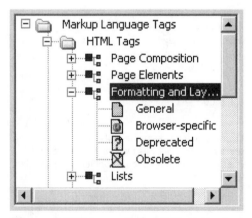

Figure 11.37 HTML tags are further divided into sub-categories.

The Tag Chooser

The Tag Chooser is a peculiar dialog box that most hand-coders probably won't have much use for. Who would use this tool? Perhaps people learning one of the languages, such as WML, or people who want to browse the tags considered accessible.

Anyway, to open the Tag Chooser, right-click (Ctrl+click) on some space in Code view and select Insert Tag from the context menu. The Tag Chooser will appear (**Figure 11.36**). From there, you can browse through the various listed languages: HTML, CFML, ASP.NET, JSP, Jrun Custom Library, ASP, PHP, WML, and SiteSpring.

For most of the languages, including HTML, the tags are grouped by categories such as Page Composition, Lists, Forms, and Tables, and are further divided into General, Browser-Specific, Deprecated (HTML 4.0 transitional tags slated for deletion), and Obsolete (**Figure 11.37**).

For each tag, you can read reference information in the tag chooser, or click the Reference button to open the same information in the Reference panel.

To insert a tag, select it and click on Insert. Tags listed without brackets and closing tags will open in the Tag Editor dialog box, which is further described in the following section.

BUILT-IN TAG WRITING SHORTCUTS

The Tag Editor

Yet another dialog-box view of tags and tag code in Dreamweaver is the Tag Editor dialog box. Right-click (Ctrl+click) on any tag or object in Code view, Design view or the Code inspector and select Edit Tag [tag name] from the context menu. The Tag Editor dialog box will appear (**Figure 11.38**). (You may first have to select a tag in the Tag selector to open this dialog box from Design view.)

Or you can just press Ctrl+F5 with a tag selected.

For most tags, the Tag Editor includes categories for General, Style Sheet/Accessibility, and Language. For some tags, you'll also see Content, Events, and Browser Specific categories.

The **General** category (Figure 11.38) lists common attributes normally associated with a tag, such as color, size, and face for the font tag, or bgcolor, width, and so on for the table tag.

The **Style Sheet/Accessibility** category (**Figure 11.39**) includes the following: Class and ID are style sheet class settings; both are required for XHTML. The Style setting allows you to apply a style attribute directly to a tag; this is a CSS-2 specification not supported by all browsers. The Title attribute is an accessibility attribute; see Chapter 16.

Language (**Figure 11.40**) allows you to set the lang="nn" attribute. This attribute's theoretical uses include indexing by specific language search engines and displaying characters available only in the set language. This attribute is not yet used commonly.

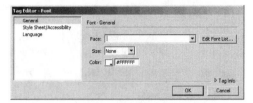

Figure 11.38 The Tag Editor dialog box allows you to edit many tag attributes at once, presented in commonsensical categories. The version shown here is the General category for the FONT tag. To edit a category for a given tag, select it from the list box at left.

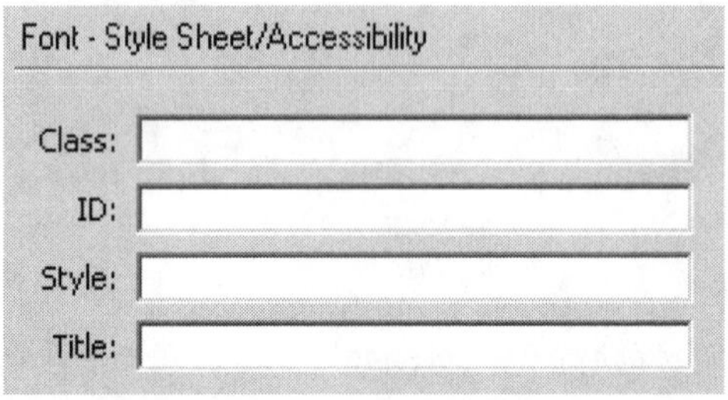

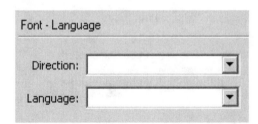

Figure 11.39 A close-up of the Style Sheet/Accessibility category for the FONT tag.

Figure 11.40 In the Language category, you can specify a language by its two-letter code and specify whether the language should print left to right or right to left.

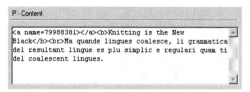

Figure 11.41 The Content category for this P tag includes several child tags as well as text. We can edit any of this right here.

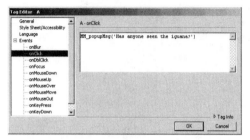

Figure 11.42 The Events category of the Tag Editor dialog box includes available user events that can be used with JavaScript. Here, for the event OnClick, we've got a Dreamweaver behavior specified for Popup Message. See Chapter 13 for more on behaviors.

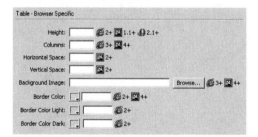

Figure 11.43 The Browser Specific category lists both proprietary attributes and attributes not supported until a late-model version of a popular browser. An icon appears only if a browser supports an attribute, and indicates the earliest version that does so.

Content (**Figure 11.41**), for block and block-type elements such as P, DIV, SPAN, TD, CODE, and PRE, lets you view and edit the content of the tag, which may include child tags. For some tags, such as TABLE and the H tags, the Content textbox appears in the General or Style Sheet/Accessibility category.

Events (**Figure 11.42**) lets you see and edit user events for JavaScript (see Table 13.1, a list of common user events, in Chapter 13). Use the Behaviors panel to limit the list to events available in a particular set of browsers.

Browser Specific (**Figure 11.43**) shows the earliest browser version for post-HTML 1.0 tags. Internet Explorer, Netscape Navigator, and Opera are all listed when they support a given attribute. For example, only Netscape supports vspace and hspace for tables; Opera supports table height settings after version 2.1; only Internet Explorer supports light and dark border colors.

Using the Snippets Panel

The Snippets panel (**Figure 11.44**) is used to store reusable chunks of code. It comes preloaded with handy widgets—things like footers, breadcrumbs and other navigation tools, and little JavaScript widgets such as a random image generator, a cookie setting script, and a script to disable right-clicking or Ctrl+clicking a link (so that the user can't open a link in a new window, for example).

Using snippets

You can use any snippet by dragging it onto your page or double-clicking its name to drop it in at the insertion point.

Of course, you'll probably want to edit the text and links of most snippets after you insert them, unless your site is IpsemLorem.com and none of your links go anywhere. For details on some of the handiest JavaScript snippets, see Chapter 13.

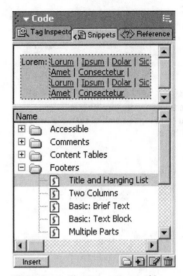

Figure 11.44 The Snippets panel is stocked with some useful chunks of code.

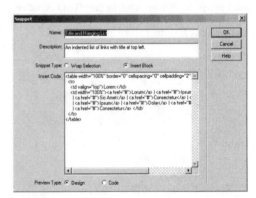

Figure 11.45 Create or edit a snippet in the Snippet dialog box.

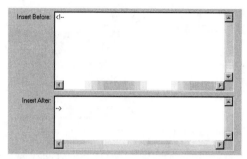

Figure 11.46 For snippets that will wrap around a selection, such as this simple comment, you'll see two text boxes—a before and an after.

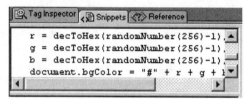

Figure 11.47 You can use Design view to preview a snippet as in Figure 11.44, or Code view, as pictured here.

Editing snippets

You can edit any snippet by selecting it in the Snippets panel and clicking the Edit button. The Snippet dialog box will appear; see below.

To save your own snippet:

1. Select the code in the Document window (in any view) and click the New Snippet button. The Snippet dialog box will appear (**Figure 11.45**), where you can edit your code.

2. A snippet can wrap around a selection, in which case you'll have two text boxes (**Figure 11.46**); or you can insert one chunk. Click on Wrap Selection or Insert Block.

3. Snippets are previewed in the Snippets panel either as code (**Figure 11.47**) or as the browser would see it (Figure 11.44); click either the Code or Design radio button.

4. Type a name for your snippet, and a description, if you like.

5. Click on OK.

Your snippet will appear in the panel; you can drag it into any folder; and you can click the New Snippet Folder radio button to create your own.

Setting Code View Options

The Document toolbar and the Code inspector toolbar both include a View Options menu (**Figure 11.48**) that includes options for Word Wrap (soft text wrapping), Line Numbering, Syntax Coloring, and Auto Indent. You can toggle any of these on and off by selecting it from the menu.

About Word Wrap

When you turn on Word Wrap, the text will wrap to the window width. This is soft wrapping—no line breaks are inserted. You can toggle wrapping on and off by selecting Word Wrap from the View Options menu. Unwrapped code is shown in **Figure 11.49**, and Word Wrap is turned on in **Figure 11.50**. To set hard wrapping preferences, see *Code Format preferences*, later in this chapter.

About Line Numbering

When you turn on Line Numbering, each line of code is numbered. When Word Wrap is also turned on, lines of code may wrap over onto unnumbered lines (Figure 11.50). Line numbers—sans wrapping—should be the same in Dreamweaver as in line editors such as vi.

Figure 11.48 To use Word Wrap, Line Numbering, Syntax Coloring, and Auto Indent, use the View Options menu on the Document toolbar in Code view or the Code inspector.

Figure 11.49 Unwrapped code stretches offscreen.

Link and Comment tags use Syntax Coloring

Table tags use
Syntax Coloring

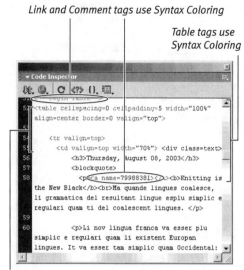

Table code indented below table tag

Figure 11.50 Here in the Code inspector, we have Word Wrap, Syntax Coloring, and Auto Indent turned on. The wrapped lines are numbered individually— line 58 wraps over onto unnumbered lines.

About Syntax Coloring

Syntax Coloring marks specific tags with particular colors as soon as you insert an object or close a tag (Figure 11.50). You must turn on Syntax Coloring in order for Dreamweaver's Reference feature to work properly (see *Using the Tag Reference*, later in this chapter). To select colors for a tag or family of tags, see *Customizing Syntax Coloring*, later in this chapter.

About Auto Indent

Dreamweaver can automatically indent blocks of code, such as indenting table rows and cells (Figure 11.50). See *Code Format preferences* later in this chapter to turn this on or off globally. See Chapter 12 for information about setting indent preferences for specific tags by editing the tag library.

SETTING CODE VIEW OPTIONS

Checking Your Pages

Dreamweaver offers several safeguards for code written in the program or in files written in other programs.

Earlier in this chapter, we saw automatic tag completion (see *Built-in Tag Writing Shortcuts*) and the HTML-checking features in *Roundtrip HTML*.

You can also check for common errors by using the Clean Up HTML/XHTML command and the Clean Up Word HTML command. Additionally, you can check your pages against browser profiles to see if you've used proprietary or obscure tags that won't work in some browsers. All these features are covered in this chapter.

✔ Tips

- To spell-check your page, select Text > Check Spelling from the menu bar. The Check Spelling dialog box will appear (**Figure 11.51**).

- To perform find-and-replace for text, code, tags, and regular expressions, select Edit > Find and Replace from the menu bar. The Find and Replace window will appear (**Figure 11.52**). You can search the current page, the entire site, or selected folders. You can also save your search results.

- To check local links in your site, select Check Links Sitewide from the Site window menu bar. The Link Checker panel of the Results panel group will appear and begin checking links (**Figure 11.53**). This link checker will list as broken any links to files that are not located in your local site, even if these pages exist on the testing or production server. The link checker also provides lists of external links and orphaned files.

- To find out how to check your page for accessibility compliance, see Chapter 16.

- For details on how to debug JavaScript, see *Debugging Your JavaScript* in Chapter 13.

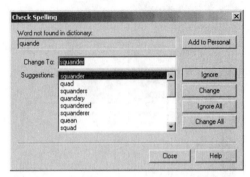

Figure 11.51 You can check your spelling and add words to your personal dictionary.

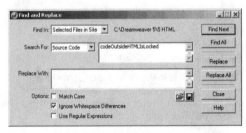

Figure 11.52 You can find and replace words, code, or specific tags over a page, a folder, or a site.

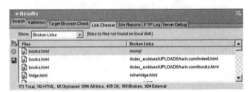

Figure 11.53 Use the link checker to sniff out and fix broken relative links over your local site. The link checker does not check external links but does provide a list of them.

Cleaning Up HTML

For the most part, Dreamweaver writes passable, clean code. If you modify the code, Dreamweaver usually avoids changing it back. On the other hand, you may be working with code that isn't clean enough to eat off, which may be your fault, the original page author's fault, or a problem created by a weaker page editing tool.

Dreamweaver does make some errors that are easily fixed; it'll throw in the occasional duplicate font tag or empty formatting tag.

Cleaning up when opening a file

Dreamweaver can make certain revisions to a page when it's first opened—in Dreamweaver MX, these preferences are not on automatically, so if you're upgrading and expect your old pages to be fixed in MX, see *Code Rewriting preferences* to turn on these features. See *Roundtrip HTML*, earlier in this chapter, for additional details.

Highlighting sloppy code

You can have Dreamweaver point out common errors such as unclosed tags, bad tag nesting, unclosed quotation marks, and so on. From the View Options menu on the Document window in Code view or the Code inspector, select Highlight Invalid HTML. You'll see yellow tags marked in the Document window in Design view; the highlighting works intermittently in Code view. See *Roundtrip HTML*, earlier in this chapter, for details.

Performing clean-up

You can ask Dreamweaver to look for and fix common errors in HTML or XHTML files.

To clean up HTML code:

1. From the Document window menu bar, select Commands > Clean Up HTML. The Clean Up HTML dialog box will appear (**Figure 11.54**).

   For XHTML files, the command will read Clean Up XHTML. Read *About XHTML compliance*, later in this chapter, for more on what will be fixed in XHTML files.

2. Dreamweaver lets you remove the following boo-boos (**Figure 11.55**):

   ◆ Empty Tags (Lines 8 and 9)

   ◆ Redundant Nested Tags (Line 11)

   ◆ Non-Dreamweaver HTML Comments (regular comments not inserted by the program; Line 13)

   ◆ Dreamweaver HTML Comments (This option removes comments Dreamweaver inserts with scripts and the like).

   ◆ Specific Tags (any specified tag; Line 15). You must type the tag in the text box. Type tags without brackets, and separate multiple tags with commas. For example: `blink, u, tt`).

   Check the box beside the garbage you want to be removed (Figure 11.54).

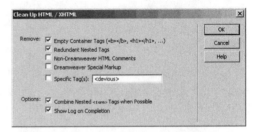

Figure 11.54 You can clean up HTML and XHTML—this dialog box can check for improperly wrapped and unclosed tags, as well as specific tags, comments, and redundant font tags.

Figure 11.55 These are the kinds of errors Dreamweaver can fix.

```
9  <font color="#00CC33"><font face="Arial, Helvetica,
   sans-serif"><font size="+1">
10 modified text
11 </font></font></font>
```

Figure 11.56 Who knows how many extra font tags are lurking on your pages—clean up your code and combine them.

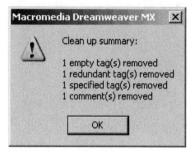

Figure 11.57 All clean!

3. Multiple font tags aren't necessary when modifying text; it's more efficient to put all the attributes in a single font tag, when possible. (**Figure 11.56**). To combine redundant font tags, check the Combine Nested <font> Tags When Possible checkbox.

4. To see a list after cleanup of the errors Dreamweaver caught and fixed, check the Show Log on Completion checkbox.

5. Click on OK. Dreamweaver will scan the page for the errors you asked it to, and if you chose to display a log, it will return a list of what it fixed (**Figure 11.57**).

Cleaning Up Word HTML

You can save Microsoft Word documents as HTML and then clean them up using the Dreamweaver command Commands > Clean Up Word HTML. In the Clean Up Word HTML dialog box, select the version of Word that saved the file (For Word X or XP, choose Word 2000). You may want to experiment with different settings for things like converting Word's funny font sizes to actual font tag settings and removing Word's bizarre XML and CSS formatting.

CLEANING UP HTML

Tag validation (HTML, XML)

You can, besides cleaning up a page, validate its tags. (You can clean up HTML and XHTML, and you can validate both of these as well, but you can also validate XML, ColdFusion, SMIL, WML, and JSP, as well as browser-specific tags for some versions of Netscape and Internet Explorer.

To set which languages you're validating against, see *Tag Validator preferences,* later in this chapter.

To validate a page:

1. Open or save the page.

2. From the menu bar, select File > Check Page > Validate Markup. For XML, select File > Check Page > Validate as XML.

The Validation panel will appear as part of the Results panel group, displaying a list of errors (**Figure 11.58**). If there are no errors, it will tell you so.

(For templates and XHTML pages, you may elect to validate both for HTML and XML, one after the other.)

✔ Tips

■ You can double-click any error or warning to highlight it in the document.

■ To perform a validation of multiple pages or an entire site, open the Validation panel (Window > Results > Validation) and then follow the steps in the upcoming section, *Checking an Entire Site,* substituting the Validation panel for the Target Browser Check panel (all the buttons work the same).

■ To save the validation report as an XML or HTML file, follow the steps in the upcoming section *Using Browser Check Results,* substituting the Validation panel for the Target Browser Check panel (all the buttons work the same).

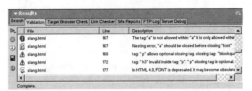

Figure 11.58 When you validate a page using the Validation panel, it will list warnings, errors, and notes on your HTML syntax.

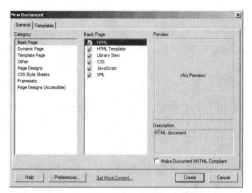

Figure 11.59 You can create many kinds of pages in the New Document dialog box and you can make most of them XHTML compliant.

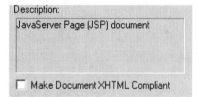

Figure 11.60 Just check the box. Until you uncheck it again, all pages you create will be XHTML pages.

Creating and Complying with XHTML

XHTML is the eXtensible HyperText Markup Language. It's HTML 4.0 re-imagined as an XML application. XHTML uses standard HTML tags, with a few syntax differences.

Developers envision XHTML taking the place of HTML in the not-so-distant future. XHTML is based on both HTML and XML. XHTML differs from HTML in that it is extensible, like XML (which means you can add custom tags for Web applications), and that its syntax is stricter.

To make a new page XHTML compliant:

1. Select File > New from the menu bar. The New Document dialog box will appear (**Figure 11.59**).

2. In the New Document dialog box, select the document type you want to create.

3. Check the Make Document XHTML Compliant checkbox (**Figure 11.60**).

Dreamweaver will use XHTML syntax in the document. You'll see the word XHTML in parentheses in the Document window title bar.

CREATING AND COMPLYING WITH XHTML

To convert an existing page to XHTML:

1. With the file open in the Document window, select File > Convert > XHTML (**Figure 11.61**).

2. No dialog box will appear. The document heading information will be converted to XHTML, and the syntax will be edited so that it complies with XHTML.

   You'll see the word XHTML in parentheses in the Document window title bar.

✔ Tips

- You do not have to change the file extension of XHTML documents; you can still use .html, .asp, or whatever.

- For documents that use frames, you must repeat the above step for each frame as well as for the frameset document itself.

- To use XHTML with templates, you must create the template as an XHTML document. You cannot convert pages based on templates to XHTML if the original template document was in regular old HTML.

- However, you can do the following: First, convert the template document (.dwt) to XHTML. Then, perform Commands > Clean Up XHTML. When you save your changes, an Update dialog box will appear. Click Update, and files based on that template will be converted to XHTML.

- When using CSS with XHTML, be aware that your document may behave differently when read by a Web browser or an XML parser.

- Use lowercase for attribute names.

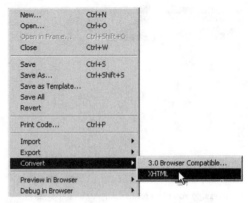

Figure 11.61 Convert your pages to XHTML with a single step.

About XHTML compliance

XHTML is so similar to HTML that it will work on any browser that supports HTML 4.0, whether or not that browser is "designed" to work with XHTML. Dreamweaver changes the following code when converting a document to XHTML:

Document information

Before the document head, several lines of code define the encoding, the document type, and the XHTML namespace (xmlns):

```
<?xml version="1.0" encoding=
→"iso-8859-1"?>
<!DOCTYPE html PUBLIC "-//W3C//
→DTD XHTML 1.0 Transitional//EN"
→"http://www.w3.org/TR/xhtml1/DTD/
→xhtml1-transitional.dtd">
<html xmlns="http://www.w3.org/
→1999/xhtml">
```

Document structure

The document must also include the `<head>` `<title>` and `<body>` tags. These are already included in Dreamweaver's standard HTML documents, but in XHTML, they are strictly required.

Code syntax

- ◆ **Case:** All tags and attributes must be lowercase. Dreamweaver will override your format preferences when converting or cleaning up XHTML. In addition, all attributes that take values from a pre-scribed list (called *enumerated* values) must also be lowercase; `align="LEFT"` is no longer valid; it's now `align="left"`.

- ◆ **Empty tags:** Tags that do or did not take a closing tag in HTML, such as `<img>` and `<br>`, cannot go unclosed in XHTML. These tags are closed as they are in XML, like so:
  ```
  <br />
  ```

with a space before the closing slash. This affects the following tags: `area`, `base`, `basefont`, `br`, `col`, `frame`, `hr`, `img`, `input`, `isindex`, `link`, `meta`, and `param`.

- ◆ **Quotes:** All attribute values must be in quotation marks.

- ◆ **Proper nesting:** Just as in HTML, XHTML requires that tags open and close in the same order, closest to the modified text. XHTML demands it, however, whereas current browsers will forgive sloppy code.

  Proper nesting looks like this:
  ```
  <p><strong>paragraph</strong></p>
  ```
  and not like this:
  ```
  <p><strong>paragraph</p></strong>
  ```

- ◆ **Define all attributes:** In HTML, some attributes are "minimized"—that is, they appear as a tag attribute but do not carry a value. An example is the `disabled` attribute used in form field select elements. You now define such attributes as `minimized="minimized"` or `nowrap="nowrap"`. Dreamweaver makes these changes to the code.

More attribute requirements

- ◆ **Names and IDs:** All tags that take the name attribute must now include an `id` attribute as well. Apparently, the `id` attribute is not required unless the `name` attribute is also being used. The id and name may be the same. For example, a named anchor in HTML looks like this:
  ```
  <a name="TOC">Link to TOC</a>
  ```
  In XHTML, you must add an `id`:
  ```
  <a name="TOC" id="TOC">Link to
  →TOC</a>
  ```

continues on next page

Dreamweaver will add an `id` attribute where required and will set its value to the same as the `name` attribute set with the Property inspector. Tags affected by this rule include `a`, `applet`, `form`, `frame`, `iframe`, `img`, and `map`.

Figure 11.62 Use the Property inspector to add Alt text or empty `alt` attributes to your images.

◆ **Alt attributes:** All images and `area` elements (image maps) require an `alt` attribute. When converting or cleaning up XHTML, Dreamweaver will notify you of how many images are missing this attribute, but it will not fix them for you. You can set an empty `alt` attribute for images that do not represent content, such as spacers, decorative elements, and the like. This code looks like this: `alt=""` This allows non-graphical browsers to skip an image rather than stumbling over it. You can set an empty `alt` attribute for an image in the Property inspector by selecting <empty> from the Alt drop-down menu (**Figure 11.62**).

◆ **Type attributes:** For the tags `style` and `script`, the `type` attribute must be set. In pre 4.0 versions of HTML, the language type had been also acceptable; this is deprecated out of XHTML. Dreamweaver uses the type attribute already in HTML pages, but it will fix it if it isn't there.

With all the strict syntax in place, an image tag will now look like this:

```
<img name="dog" id="dog"
→src="/images/Doggie.gif" alt="" />
```

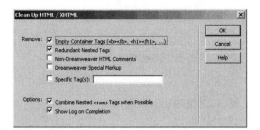

Figure 11.63 You can clean up XHTML just as you do HTML.

Cleaning up XHTML

You can clean up XHTML in a file that you, an application, or Dreamweaver created. We recommend doing these steps before uploading an XHTML page.

To clean up XHTML:

1. With your XHTML page open in the Document window, select from the menu bar Commands > Clean Up XHTML. The Clean Up HTML/XHTML dialog box will appear (**Figure 11.63**).

2. The choices in this dialog box are identical to the ones described in the section *Cleaning Up HTML*. In addition to the options you check here, Dreamweaver will also apply the syntax detailed above in *About XHTML compliance*.

   Click on OK to perform the cleanup.

A prompt will appear detailing what was cleaned up and listing the number of images that do not have alt attributes.

✔ Tips

- You must set an alt attribute for each image used in XHTML. You can set an empty attribute (as in alt="") for non-content images. You can select <empty> from the Property inspector (Figure 11.62) to apply this attribute.

- To find the missing alt attributes, run a site report on the current page. Save the page, and then select Site > Reports from the menu bar. Check the Missing Alt Text checkbox and click on Run. The Site Reports panel of the Results panel group will display a list of all missing alt attributes; double-click any Warning icon to highlight the img tag missing the alt.

Browser Profiles

Most of the time, when you want to figure out what certain browsers do or don't do, you need to memorize a lot of stuff or refer to big, complicated charts that describe compatibility feature by feature, browser by browser.

Dreamweaver makes such things moot by offering automated browser profiles. When you run a target browser check, Dreamweaver compares the code on a page or an entire site with feature sets defined in browser profiles, and then tells you what unsupported features you've used. Depending on the feature and how important it is to the design, you can ignore this information, refine the page using a different tag, or create a lower-end version of the site.

Checking the current page

You can run a check on any open file.

To run a target browser check on the current page:

1. If you haven't done so already, save the current page.

2. From the Document window menu bar, select File > Check Page > Check Target Browsers. The Check Target Browsers dialog box will appear (**Figure 11.64**).

3. This dialog box lists the following browsers: Internet Explorer version 2-6; Netscape Navigator 2-6; and Opera 2-6. Choose the browser(s) you want to check against. To select more than one browser, hold down the Ctrl (Command) key while clicking.

4. Click on Check. The Target Browser Check panel will appear within the Results panel group and display a list of error and warnings, if any were generated by the current page (**Figure 11.65**).

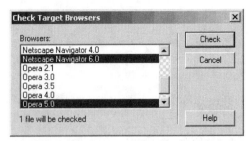

Figure 11.64 Select the browsers to check against. To select nonadjacent items, Ctrl+click (Command+click) to select them.

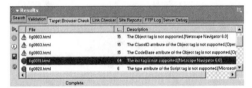

Figure 11.65 The Target Browser Check panel will display the results, including comments, warnings, and errors about particular tags that don't agree with particular browsers.

What If It Ain't Broke?

Well, then don't fix it. Some browser check errors won't really change the look or function of your page significantly, whereas others can be fixed by using alternate tags or attributes. For example, Netscape Navigator uses the attributes `marginheight` and `marginwidth` in the `<body>` tag to set page margins; Internet Explorer uses `topmargin` and `leftmargin` to do the same. To fix this, you'd set all four attributes.

If a tag isn't supported by a browser, you can do some research—use the Reference panel to see what browsers support what tags and attributes. It may be that you can use CSS to accomplish the same thing—but then again CSS isn't supported in the oldest browsers. Test on multiple browsers whenever you can, and you'll learn to see which warning notes are useful and which you can safely ignore.

Figure 11.66
Select the site you want to check from the Site drop-down menu.

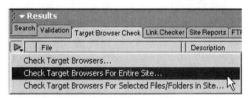

Figure 11.67 From the menu, select whether you want to check the whole site or just selected files.

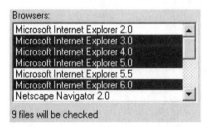

Figure 11.68 The Check Target Browsers dialog box lists how many files are about to be checked.

Description of unsupported tag

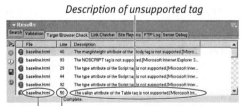

Filename   Line number of questionable tag

Figure 11.69 The results of our check appear in the Target Browser Check panel.

See *Using Browser Check Results* for more about investigating the errors and saving this file or viewing it in a browser.

Checking an entire site

You can also run a target browser check on an entire directory or local site. The commands for this check have changed in Dreamweaver MX.

To run a target browser check on an entire folder or selected files:

1. Open the Sites window and select the site you want to check from the Site drop-down menu (**Figure 11.66**).

   To check only certain files or folders within your site, select them in the Site window.

2. Open the Target Browser Check panel if it's not showing by selecting Window > Results > Target Browser Check from the menu bar.

3. Click and hold the Play button ▶ on the Results panel group, and from the menu that appears, select Check Target Browser For Entire Site or Check Target Browser For Selected Files/Folders in Site (**Figure 11.67**). The Check Target Browsers dialog box will appear.

4. Below the browsers list box, you'll see a count of how many files will be diagnosed (**Figure 11.68**).

5. Select the browser(s) you wish to check your files or site against.

6. Click on Check. After a few moments, the results of the check will appear in the Target Browser Check panel (**Figure 11.69**).

See the next page for information about correcting errors, saving the file, and previewing the results in a browser.

✔ Tips

- Double-click on any error or warning to open the file and highlight the relevant code.

- It's kind of a mystery why some findings are marked as Errors and others as Warnings. Don't worry too much about the semantics.

Using browser check results

You can use these results in a number of ways. Double-click any error icon to open the page and jump to the tag in question. Right-click (Ctrl+click) on an error to see a context menu (**Figure 11.70**).

To get information about an error:

1. In the Target Browser Check panel, click on the More Info button 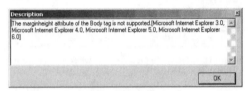 .

2. After several seconds, a Description dialog box will appear (**Figure 11.71**). This dialog box lists the browsers that don't support the given tag or attribute. It may or may not supply more useful information.

To view the report in a browser:

- In the Target Browser Check panel, click on the Browse Report button 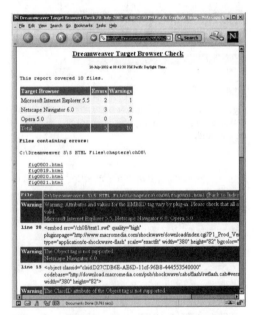 .

The results will be loaded in your default browser, including line numbers and the code itself. For multiple files, results will be displayed per file, with links to each (**Figure 11.72**).

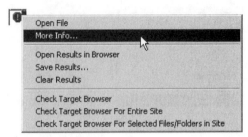

Figure 11.70 Right-click (Ctrl+click) on an error message to see a menu of options such as More Info and Clear Results.

Figure 11.71 A description of the error.

Figure 11.72 The Target Browser Check report page lists the pages checked and their errors, with line numbers. (The Validator Results report uses a similar format to list errors.)

Figure 11.73 The XML file that we saved uses Macromedia tags. You can import this file into a template or a database. See Chapter 14.

Saving the results

The Target Browser Check report shown in the browser window is a temp file. If you'll want to refer to this file later, you can save it (**Figure 11.73**).

To save the report file as XML:

1. In the Target Browser Check panel, click on the Save Report button 💾 . The Save As dialog box will appear.

2. Select the proper folder and type a name for your file.

3. Click on Save.

To save the report file as HTML:

1. View the page in your browser.

2. Select File > Save As from the browser window menu bar, and then follow Steps 2 and 3, above.

Script-Editing Tools

If you hand code JavaScript, and you want to set up your own scripts in Dreamweaver, you're more than welcome to. You can type or paste in a script using the Insert Script object, or you can set up your own actions to use in Dreamweaver behaviors.

You can hand-code JavaScript in Code view or in one of Dreamweaver's dialog boxes.

Using the Script editor

To type in a script:

1. On the Script tab of the Insert toolbar (**Figure 11.74**), click on the Insert Script button . Or, from the Document window menu bar, select Insert > Script Objects > Script. The Insert Script dialog box will appear (**Figure 11.75**).

2. Select the type of script (JavaScript, a specific JavaScript version, or VBScript) from the Language drop-down menu.

3. Type or paste your script in the Content text box, and click on OK. The Insert Script dialog box will close, and the Script icon will appear in the Document window. (If you inserted the script in the document head, you won't see a marker.)

4. For browsers with script-running turned off, use a <noscript> tag. This tag can be empty or can describe the scripts. To insert <noscript> content, type it in the No Script text box.

To insert just a noscript tag:

1. On the Script tab of the Insert toolbar, click the Noscript button . The Tag Editor dialog box will appear (**Figure 11.76**).

2. Type your content, if any, in the Content text box.

3. Click on OK to insert the tag.

Figure 11.74 On the Script tab of the Insert toolbar you'll find buttons for inserting a script, a noscript tag, and a server-side include.

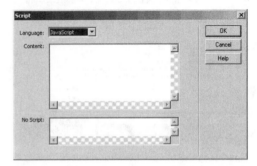

Figure 11.75 Type or paste your script in the Insert Script dialog box. Dreamweaver will insert the <script> tags for you.

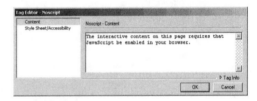

Figure 11.76 You can create or edit a noscript tag using the Tag Editor dialog box.

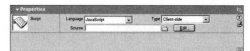

Figure 11.77 Script properties in the Property inspector include Language and URL (if the script is external). You can also set scripts as client-side or server-side.

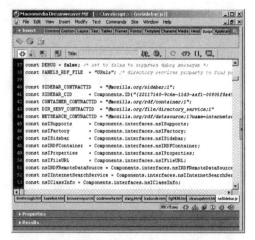

Figure 11.78 External scripts will open in their own Document window in Code view.

Figure 11.79 Type, edit, or paste a script in the Script Properties dialog box.

Importing scripts

You can also insert a script from a file on your hard drive.

To insert a script from a text file:

1. Drag the Script button onto your page and leave the Insert Script dialog box blank.

2. Select the Script icon.

3. In the Property inspector (**Figure 11.77**), type the source of your script in the Source text box, or click on the Browse button 📄 to browse your hard drive for the file.

Script properties

You can type or edit longer scripts in the Script Properties dialog box.

To edit a script:

1. View the script properties in the Property inspector.

2. Most scripts are client-side; that is, they are executed within and by the browser. To set a server-side script, select server-side from the drop-down menu and provide the URL of the script.

3. To edit the script itself, click on Edit. If you are editing a script contained in an external file, it will open in a new Document window in Code view (**Figure 11.78**). Otherwise, the Script Properties dialog box will appear (**Figure 11.79**).

When you're finished typing or editing your script, click on OK to return to the Document window.

✔ Tip

- For help with debugging JavaScript, see *Debugging Your JavaScript* in Chapter 13.

Setting Code Preferences

Dreamweaver allows you to set preferences for many different aspects of code editing, including code format, code rewriting, CSS, the Quick Tag editor and the Code Hints menus, Syntax Coloring, and template and library item highlighting.

Code Format preferences

Code Format preferences allow you to set defaults for indenting, wrapping, line breaks, and tag case, as well as define the settings for the TD tag and a choice of the default centering tag.

To set Code Format preferences:

1. From the Document window menu bar, select Edit > Preferences (Mac OS X: Dreamweaver > Preferences). The Preferences dialog box will appear.

2. In the Category list, click on Code Format. That panel of the dialog box will appear (**Figures 11.80** and **11.81**).

3. **Indenting:** To turn off indenting altogether, uncheck the Indent checkbox.

    To use Spaces or Tabs for indent, select that option from the Use drop-down menu. (Indents in HTML are technically still spaces, but using Tabs allows you to select several spaces as if they were one entity.)

    To set an indent size (the default is two spaces or two tabs), type a number in the Indent text box. To set the tab size (in spaces), type a number in the Tab text box.

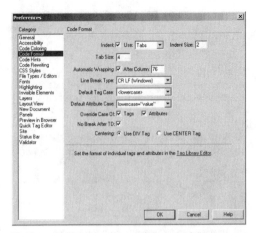

Figure 11.80 The Code Format category of the Preferences dialog box.

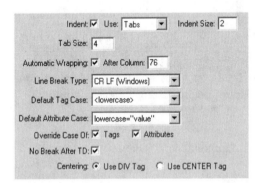

Figure 11.81 A close-up of the Code Format category. You can specify settings for indenting, wrapping, line breaks, tag case, and more.

4. **Wrapping:** You can have Dreamweaver automatically wrap code in your file by checking the Automatic Wrapping checkbox. This adds a hard return after each line, unless the hard return would disrupt the document's appearance.

   To set the column width to wrap after, type a number of characters in the After Column checkbox. (These are monospace characters in most text editors, e-mail programs, and line editors such as Telnet or vi.)

5. **Line Breaks:** Windows, Macintosh, or Unix environments use different characters for hard returns. Select CR LF (Windows), CR (Macintosh), or LF (Unix) from the Line Breaks drop-down menu. Your choice may depend either on the remote server the file will be stored on or any other external text editors you'll be using to work on the file.

   For more on line breaks, see Tips, below.

6. **Tag and Attribute Case:** To set the default case for tags and attributes, select lowercase or UPPERCASE from the Default Tag Case and Default Attribute Case drop-down menus.

   You can have Dreamweaver conform to your case options even when you type your tags and attributes in a different case than the one you specified. To have Dreamweaver override your typing for your preference, check the Tags checkbox or the Attributes checkbox in the Override Case Of area of the dialog box.

   To override tag case, you need to Apply Source Formatting; see the Tips below.

7. **No Break After TD** means that not every table cell is required to stick to its own line of code. Unchecking this option will allow your tables to include more than one cell per line, like so: `<td> </td><td> </td>`.

8. **Centering:** To set the default tag for centering text and objects, click the Use DIV Tag or Use CENTER Tag radio button. To go oldschool, use CENTER. The DIV tag is a block-like tag that's similar to the P tag. Note that regardless of your settings here, paragraphs and headings might or might not use the align attribute, as in `<p align="center">`.

9. When you're all set, click on OK to save your changes and close the Preferences dialog box.

✔ Tips

- Text wrapping using hard returns is saved in the file itself and is different from the soft WordWrap feature you can apply to individual pages by using the Options menu in the Code inspector or Code view.

- When transferring ASCII files using the Site window, your line break choices may be overridden. For downloads, Dreamweaver sets line breaks to the format for your local machine; for uploads, it uses CR LF, the Windows line break character.

- When you change your Code Format preferences, the changes will be applied to all pages you create in Dreamweaver from here on out, but they won't be applied retroactively to pages you've already created.

- To format a page using your new preferences, open the page and select Commands > Apply Source Formatting from the menu bar. Your tag case, indents, and so on, will be applied to the page.

Code Rewriting preferences

Dreamweaver can fix some common errors in your code when you open a file in the Document window. These errors may have been generated by another editor, by hand writing the code, or they may exist in old files you haven't looked at in a while.

Code Rewriting preferences take effect only when you open a file in Dreamweaver and (except for the Rename Form Items When Pasting option) do not affect code you write while the file is open. These options are off by default.

To change Code Rewriting preferences:

1. From the Document window menu bar, select Edit > Preferences (Mac OS X: Dreamweaver > Preferences). The Preferences dialog box will appear.

2. In the Category list at the left, select Code Rewriting. That panel of the dialog box will become visible (**Figure 11.82** through **11.84**).

3. Dreamweaver can fix two kinds of errors (Figure 11.83). The first is Invalidly Nested and Unclosed tags. This re-nests improperly wrapped tags, closes tags that should be closed but aren't, and provides closing quotes and brackets. The other is Extra Closing Tags. Check these check-boxes to turn rewriting on.

4. You can specify exceptions to these rules by excluding some types of files, including scripts, automatically generated documents, database files, and so on (Figure 11.84). These exceptions are for certain file extensions. To add a file type, type it in the list box (no commas separate types). To delete a file type, select it and press Backspace (Delete).

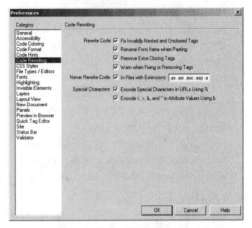

Figure 11.82 The Code Rewriting category of the Preferences dialog box.

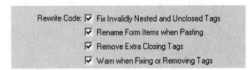

Figure 11.83 By default, all these code rewriting options are off; turn them on to catch common errors.

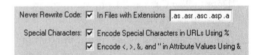

Figure 11.84 You can exclude file-types from being corrected; you can also specify how to code special characters in URLs.

5. If you want to see a dialog box that lists the changes Dreamweaver makes, check the Warn When Fixing or Removing Tags checkbox. Otherwise, you will have no notification that Dreamweaver has fixed anything.

6. To have Dreamweaver code special characters in URLs or attribute values, check the appropriate box (see Figure 11.84 and Tips, below).

7. When you're finished, you can click on OK to close the Preferences dialog box, or you can edit more preferences.

✔ Tips

■ When special characters such as spaces and ampersands appear in URLs, they may need to be coded using Unix escape sequences (which translate these characters into numbers preceded by percentage signs). For example, ampersands are coded as %26 and spaces are coded as %20. To have Dreamweaver convert these for you when they appear in links on your pages, make sure the Encode Special Characters checkbox is checked (Figure 11.84). To turn these off and use actual ampersands and the like, uncheck the box.

■ Similarly, special characters such as < & > " are HTML entities. If you view the source for a page that uses one of these characters, you'll see, for instance, < instead of < in the code. When you type the character in Design view, it will convert to its escape sequence automatically. When these entities appear in a menu or as an attribute value (including in a URL), you may want them either to be themselves or to be printed on the page. Check or uncheck the box depending on what sort of attributes you'll be using these in.

■ If you're redesigning a form and it would be bad if your form fields were renamed, deselect the Rename Form Items When Pasting checkbox.

About Proper Tag Nesting

Improperly unclosed tags look like this:

`<b>bold text`

Dreamweaver will close the tag for you. Some tags, such as `<br>`, don't need to be closed in HTML; in XHTML, these tags are called "empty" and are closed XML-style, like this: `<br />`

Improperly nested tags look like this:

`<b><i>bold italic</b></i>`

Dreamweaver will rearrange them for you:

`<b><i>bold italic</i></b>`

Extra closing tags look like this:

`<b>bold text</b></b>`

Dreamweaver will remove the extra end tag.

Keep in mind that all these errors may occur over much larger chunks of text and probably aren't as easily spotted by the naked eye as these examples.

CSS writing preferences

CSS Styles preferences (oh, redundancy!) allow you to ask Dreamweaver to code cascading style sheet (CSS) instances in shorthand for new definitions and for edited files. For example, the code for a modified h1 tag might look like this:

```
h1
{
color: #FF0000;
text-decoration: none;
font-family: "Courier New",
→Courier, mono;
font-size: 16pt;
font-weight: bold;
}
```

In shorthand, that same code looks like this:

```
h1
{
color: #FF0000;
font: bold 16pt "Courier New",
→ Courier, mono;
text-decoration: none;
}
```

To set CSS Styles preferences:

1. From the Document window menu bar, select Edit > Preferences (Mac OS X: Dreamweaver > Preferences). The Preferences dialog box will appear.

2. In the Category list at the left, select CSS Styles. That panel of the dialog box will become visible (**Figures 11.85** and **11.86**).

3. To turn on shorthand for a type of style, check its checkbox. Your choices are Font, Background, Margin and Padding, Border and Border Width, and List-Style.

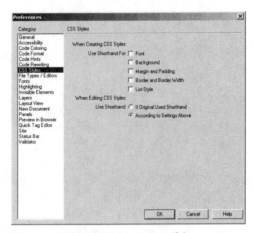

Figure 11.85 The CSS Style category of the Preferences dialog box.

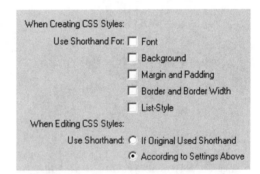

Figure 11.86 A close-up of the CSS Style category. Tell Dreamweaver how to handle and whether to write shorthand CSS.

Figure 11.87 The Quick Tag editor lets you edit code in Design view.

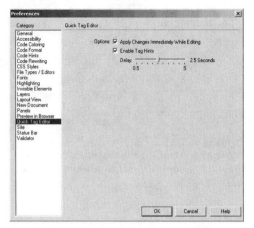

Figure 11.88 Quick Tag Editor preferences.

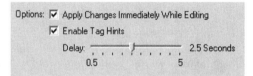

Figure 11.89 You can turn off the instant application of your modifications that happens when you press the Tab key. You can also turn on or off the hints menus in the editor and set the timing for those.

4. For files you open with Dreamweaver, you can elect to use shorthand only if the original file did, or according to your new preferences. Select the appropriate radio button.

5. When you're done, you can continue editing preferences or click on OK to return to the Document window.

Quick Tag editor and Tag Hints preferences

The Quick Tag editor (**Figure 11.87**) is a handy tool that lets you edit tags one at a time or wrap tags around selections. The Hints menus appear while you're typing code in Code view, the Code inspector, or the Quick Tag editor. You can also turn off Tag Completion.

To change Quick Tag editor and Tag Hints preferences:

1. From the Document window menu bar, select Edit > Preferences (Mac OS X: Dreamweaver > Preferences). The Preferences dialog box will appear.

2. In the Category list at the left, select Quick Tag editor. That panel of the dialog box will become visible (**Figures 11.88** and **11.89**).

3. When you're using the QT editor, particularly in Edit Tag mode, your changes become effective when you press Tab to move to an attribute or value. To make changes active only when closing the editor, uncheck the Apply Changes Immediately While Editing checkbox (Figure 11.89).

4. To turn off the Tag Hints menu, deselect the Enable Tag Hints checkbox.

continues on next page

5. To change the time delay for the Tag Hints menu, move the slide bar to the left to decrease the delay or to the right to increase it. The default is 2.5 seconds.

6. To control other hints menus, click on Code Hints in the Category list (**Figure 11.90** and **11.91**). (Menus can also appear when hand coding.)

7. To turn off automatic tag completion, deselect the Enable Tag Completion checkbox (Figure 11.91).

8. To turn off menus for specific kinds of code, deselect the appropriate checkbox.

9. When you're finished, click on OK to save your changes, close the dialog box, and return to the Document window.

Tag Validator preferences

When you use Dreamweaver's tag validator, errors show up based on the information stored in the Tag Validator preferences. You can choose which languages to validate and what kinds of errors you'd like the validator to look for.

To change Tag Validator preferences:

1. From the Document window menu bar, select Edit > Preferences (Mac OS X: Dreamweaver > Preferences). The Preferences dialog box will appear.

2. In the Category list at the left, select Validator. That panel of the dialog box will become visible (**Figures 11.92** and **11.93**).

3. In the Validate Against list box, select or deselect the languages you'd like Dreamweaver to check your pages against.

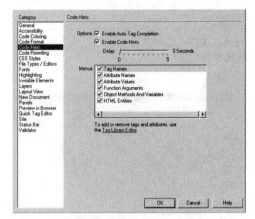

Figure 11.90 Tag Hints preferences. These are different from the menu preferences you can set for the editor—these menus appear while hand coding in Code view.

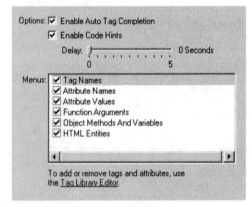

Figure 11.91 Turn tag completion and the various code hints menus on or off. The Tag Library editor, which lets you change the menus themselves, is discussed in Chapter 12.

SETTING CODE PREFERENCES

Figure 11.92 Validator preferences for when you validate HTML, XHTML, XML, or other languages.

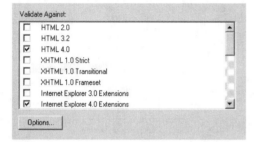

Figure 11.93 Pick your language.

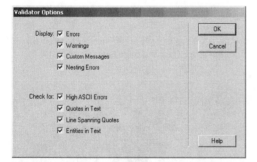

Figure 11.94 The Validator Options dialog box lets you turn off reporting on certain kinds of errors—you'll probably want to run several validation reports before you'll know which of these messages are useful to you.

4. To set options, select a language and click on Options. The Validator Options dialog box will appear (**Figure 11.94**). (This dialog box presents identical options for each language.)

5. The Display options include Errors, Warnings, Custom Messages, and Nesting Errors. Deselect whatever of these you don't need to see on validation.

6. The Check for options include High ASCII Errors (invalid, non-HTML characters); Quotes in Text and Line Spanning Quotes (quotation marks that might inadvertently be orphaned from their tags or attributes); and Entities in Text (angle brackets or ampersands that may need to be part of a tag). Deselect whichever of these you don't need to see on validation.

7. When you're finished, click on OK to save your changes, close the dialog box, and return to the Document window.

✔ Tips

■ Tag validation is performed using tag libraries. See Chapter 12 to find out more about using these.

■ Some tag libraries are based on others. For example, selecting HTML 4.0 will also validate using HTML 3.2 and HTML 2.0, because the definition for HTML 4.0 includes those prior definitions.

■ When you validate both CFML and HTML in the same document, the Validator will not check the pound sign. In CFML, you can use ## but not #; in HTML, you can use # but not ##. All pound signs will be ignored when you validate both at once.

Customizing Syntax Coloring

Syntax Coloring makes it easier to spot certain kinds of tags when you're working in Code view or the Code inspector. You can change the colors used for different types of tags, and you can use different color sets for different types of files.

For example, you could make form tags appear orange on HTML pages but blue on ASP pages.

These tag colors appear only in Dreamweaver; when you open the file in another editor it will not show Dreamweaver's color scheme.

In addition to HTML and various types of server pages, you can edit colors for Library items, CSS, ActionScript, Text, and XML.

To edit Code Coloring preferences:

1. From the Document window menu bar, select Edit > Preferences (Mac OS X: Dreamweaver > Preferences). The Preferences dialog box will appear.

2. In the Category box at the left of the dialog box, click on Code Coloring. That panel of the dialog box will appear (**Figures 11.95** and **11.96**).

3. You can change the background colors of all pages in Code view and the Code inspector.

   To change this color, do one of the following:

   ◆ Type the hex code for the color in the Default Background text box.

   ◆ Click on the Color button, and then click on a color in the Color picker (**Figure 11.97**).

   ◆ Click on the Color button, and then click the eyedropper cursor on a color you like anywhere on your desktop.

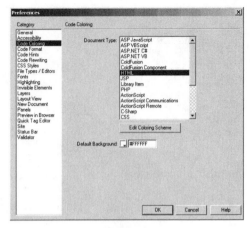

Figure 11.95 Code Coloring Preferences.

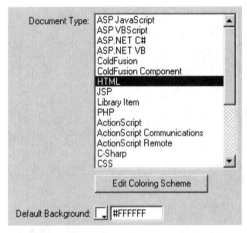

Figure 11.96 You can set preferences separately for different languages and page types.

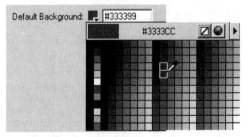

Figure 11.97 Set the default background color for Code view for a particular language.

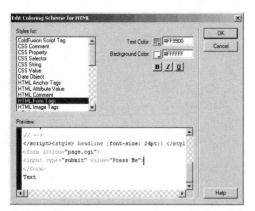

Figure 11.98 Set different colors for different tags or tag types. The Preview area shows samples of many kinds of tags.

Tag highlighting visible in preview area

Figure 11.99 Here we've set a highlight color (background color) as well as a text color for image tags.

4. You can change the text color for kinds of tags, and even apply highlighting to specific tags. You can set separate colors for HTML elements on different kinds of pages.

In the Document Type list box, select the type of page whose colors you want to edit.

5. Click on Edit Coloring Scheme. An Edit Coloring Scheme For [File Type] dialog box will appear (**Figure 11.98**).

6. To set a text or highlight color (**Figure 11.99**) for a specific type of tag, scroll through the Styles for list box until you see the type of tag you want, and then select it. Then, follow Step 3 to set the Text or Background or color for that type of tag.

7. You can also set text as bold, italic, or underline for specific tag types. For example, HTML Comments appear in italics by default. Click on the B, I, or U button for your selection.

8. Click on OK to close the Edit Coloring Scheme dialog box and return to the Preferences dialog box.

9. You can continue editing colors for other document types, you can edit more preferences, or you can click on OK to save your changes and close the Preferences dialog box.

What Color Is Your Highlighter?

You can change the highlight colors for several different entities, including the various Dreamweaver template regions, library items, third-party tags, and live data in Live Data view. In the Preferences dialog box, select the Highlighting category (**Figure 11.100**). To turn off highlighting for an entity, deselect the Show checkbox. To change a highlight color, follow Step 3 under *To edit Code Coloring preferences* in the previous list, using the Color button next to the specific entity whose coloring you want to modify.

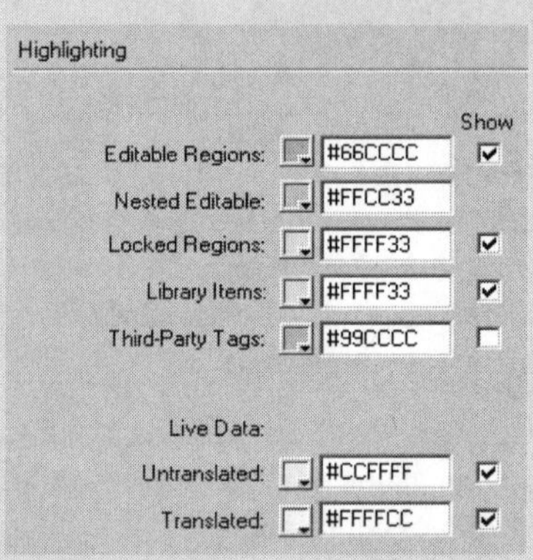

Highlighting

		Show
Editable Regions:	#66CCCC	✓
Nested Editable:	#FFCC33	
Locked Regions:	#FFFF33	✓
Library Items:	#FFFF33	✓
Third-Party Tags:	#99CCCC	☐
Live Data:		
Untranslated:	#CCFFFF	✓
Translated:	#FFFFCC	✓

Figure 11.100 You can set highlight colors for things like template regions, library items, and Live Data view.

EDITING AND USING TAG LIBRARIES

Tag libraries are Dreamweaver's personal dictionary of the tags included in each language it supports. Just like a spell-checker consults a dictionary of acceptable words, Dreamweaver consults its tag libraries to keep track of such things as which tags are known HTML, which of these require a closing tag, and what browsers support each tag. Tag libraries are not well documented within Dreamweaver's help files, and they have some surprising features that aren't immediately apparent.

Many tools discussed in Chapter 11, such as the Tag Chooser, the Tag Inspector panel, the Quick Tag editor, Code Rewriting, HTML/XHTML cleanup, and the Hints menus, all consult Dreamweaver's tag libraries when inserting, formatting, and correcting code.

Dreamweaver's built-in tag libraries include HTML, CFML, ASP, ASP.NET, JSP, JRun, PHP, Dreamweaver template tags, WML, and Sitespring. You can add and remove tags and attributes from each of these libraries, and you can edit the properties of tags and attributes within them.

You can also build your own custom tag library for, say, a particular flavor of XML you've developed for your Web applications. We're going to do this with a made-up protocol called the Evil Markup Language, but there are dozens of real-world applications of custom XML libraries, from the Chemical Markup Language to the RDF protocol used on many personalized sites.

In this chapter we'll try to help you see some of the possibilities inherent in tag libraries and avoid some of the pitfalls that are possible when adding, editing, and removing the tags within the libraries. Tag libraries can act—or not act—in unexpected or confusing ways.

We'll also look at what tag libraries are, what they're good for and how to edit them and create new ones. And we'll look at how to use them with the Tag Inspector panel to sneak dynamic content onto your site through the back door.

With some patience and flexibility, Tag libraries can become a handy tool in your Dreamweaver toolbox.

What Tag Libraries Do

Tag libraries primarily provide backup for various code-writing tools in the Dreamweaver interface. Specifically, you can control what shows up in the Tag Hints menu, the Tag Chooser, and the Tag Inspector panel by editing or adding tag libraries.

Many coders and design houses are picky about the way the code appears on the page, because it makes it easier for humans to read the code. Tag libraries also allow you to specify formatting, such as tag case, indenting, and line breaks, for specific tags. (These tools are all covered in Chapter 11, which describes all of Dreamweaver's helpful tools used to save thought and keystrokes when you're writing code. Start at the section *Built-in Tag Writing Shortcuts*.)

Tag libraries and the Tag Hints menu

Any changes you make to the applicable libraries, as well as any libraries you have added, will show up in the Tag Hints menu. As we learned in Chapter 11, the Tag Hints menu shows up when you're hand-coding (or using the Quick Tag editor) to help you save keystrokes, similar to the autocomplete feature in many e-mail programs that guesses the address you're trying to type in the To: field.

Here, we've added a custom tag called `<evil>`, which shows up in the Tag Hints menu (**Figure 12.1**). If you change tag attributes in a tag library, changes to these will also appear in the Hints menus.

✔ Tip

- Only tags that begin with a letter show up in the Tag Hints menu. So the entries in the PHP and ASP libraries, for example, don't appear in the menu, because they start with a % sign instead of an alphabetic character.

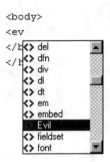

Figure 12.1 Changes you make to the tag libraries show up in the Tag Hints menu.

Figure 12.2 Custom libraries are the only changes that show up in the Tag Chooser—custom tags don't get added to existing libraries for some reason.

Figure 12.3 All custom tags show up in the Tag Inspector panel if you use them on your page.

Tag libraries and the Tag Chooser

The Tag Chooser is a dialog box that contains hierarchical folders of tags in supported languages. This tool is handy for browsing the tags in a language you're beginning to learn or trying to remember, as it contains classifications by category, icons for which browsers support a tag, and easy-to-use links to Reference panel information about the tag. (See *The Tag Chooser* in Chapter 11.)

The Tag Chooser will include any custom tag libraries you add to Dreamweaver (**Figure 12.2**). It does not, however, reflect any changes you make to the built-in libraries. (This is one of the aforementioned confusing aspects of tag libraries—your changes *should* appear in the Tag Chooser, but they don't.) Additionally, you cannot add your own browser information or Reference information for a new tag library.

Tag Libraries and the Tag inspector panel

The Tag Inspector panel is where mucking about with the tag libraries can pay real dividends. Any custom tags you add to a library will show up in the Tag Inspector panel (**Figure 12.3**), where you can view and edit it. Additionally, any attributes you change in a tag library will also be editable in the Tag Inspector.

Using the Tag Inspector to edit tags and attributes is covered in *The Tag Inspector Panel* section of Chapter 11. Later in this chapter, in the *Tag Attributes and the Tag Inspector Panel* section, we'll find out about using the Tag Inspector to set tag attributes dynamically from your application server.

Tag libraries and code formatting

You can specify how you want Dreamweaver to format a tag in Code view by changing the tag's settings in the Tag Library Editor. For example, if you want all italic text to stand out in Code view, you can use the tag library to indent all text that uses the <em> and/or <i> tags (**Figure 12.4**). (The <em> tag, which formats text in italics in most graphical browsers, stands for emphasis, and is the accessible way of presenting italics. The <i> tag is a *physical* tag, and the *logical* version, <em>, can be read with emphasis by text-to-speech browsers.)

Available formatting you can specify includes indenting, requiring line breaks after a tag (as is done with many table tags), and setting the tag case as upper or lower.

```
<body>
<em>
   eye-talic
</em>
```

Figure 12.4 The Tag Library Editor gives you control over formatting tags, such as the automatic indents and line breaks seen here.

WHAT TAG LIBRARIES DO

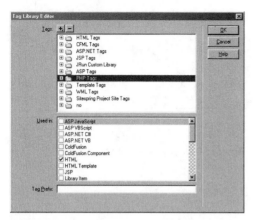

Figure 12.5 Here's where you manage tag libraries.

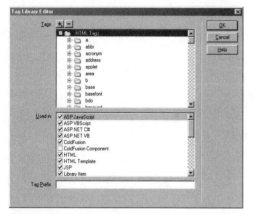

Figure 12.6 When you open the Tag Library Editor, the HTML Tags library will be expanded.

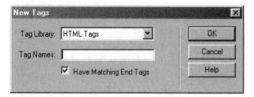

Figure 12.7 You name your new tag in the New Tags dialog box.

Editing and Importing Tags

The main tool for manipulating tag libraries is the Tag Library Editor (**Figure 12.5**). Here you can add tags and libraries, edit tags, and add or remove attributes of those tags. In the following sections we'll look at how to add a tag and how to edit it, and we'll also look at how to import or create whole libraries of tags.

Adding a new tag to a library

Let's start with the basic task of adding a custom tag to an existing library, in this case, our old friend HTML. Perhaps you're in a bad mood one day (or maybe you're just a disturbed person) and you decide that you need a new custom tag called <evil>. You can just keep typing it into your document, but perhaps you want some special formatting so that you can identify it later. Or perhaps you want <evil> to show up in the Tag Hints menus so you have easy access when you're typing, or for Dreamweaver to know whether or not it takes a closing tag so it can work its tag inspection magic.

For these purposes, you can add <evil> (or any other new tag) to the HTML tag library.

To add a custom tag to a library:

1. From the menu bar, select Edit > Tag Libraries.

   The Tag Library Editor will appear (**Figure 12.6**).

2. Click on the + (plus) button, and from the menu that appears, select New Tags.

   The New Tags dialog box will appear (**Figure 12.7**).

3. From the Tag Library drop-down menu, select HTML Tags.

continues on next page

4. In the Tag Names text box, type `evil`.

5. Because our `<evil>` tag requires a closing `</evil>` tag, make sure the checkbox beside Have Matching End Tags is checked.

6. Click OK to close the dialog box.

The new tag will appear in the tag library (**Figure 12.8**).

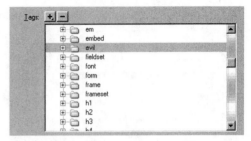

Figure 12.8 We've now added a tag.

✔ Tips

■ You can add more than one tag at a time by typing multiple tags in the Tag Names text box, separated by commas, like this: `evil, good, questionable`.

■ In Step 3, you can add a new tag to any library listed in the drop-down menu. (We listed these languages on the intro page to this chapter.)

■ In Step 5, if your tag is similar to `<br>` or `<img>` in that it requires no closing tag, you can uncheck the checkbox. Many expressions and statements in languages such as JSP and ASP do not take closing tags.

Figure 12.9 The Tag Library Editor dialog box shows formatting options when you select a specific tag. Here, we're going to edit the line breaks option because we want the tag to appear on its own line in Code view.

Specifying code formatting for a new or built-in tag

That's the procedure for adding a custom tag to a library. For this or any tag, however, you might want to adjust the formatting, or how it appears in Code view.

As you might have guessed, the Tag Library Editor provides you with a way to adjust how Dreamweaver formats a tag, whether you insert an object or hand code.

To adjust the formatting of a tag:

1. In the Tag Library Editor, select the tag whose formatting you'd like to adjust (we'll select the <evil> tag we created earlier).

   In the Tag Format area of the Tag Library Editor, the dialog box will change to show the current formatting for the tag you selected (**Figure 12.9**).

2. From the Line Breaks drop-down menu, select one of the following options:

   ◆ No Line Breaks (does not add line breaks unless you type them)

   ◆ Before And After Tag (adds a break before and after the tag itself, like this:
   `<good>[break]`
   `<evil>text</evil>[break]`
   `</good>`

   ◆ Before, Inside, After (adds a break before and after the tag, as well as before and after the content within the tag, like this:
   `<evil>[break]`
   `text[break]`
   `</evil>[break]`

   ◆ After tag only (follows the tag with a line break)

continues on next page

3. From the Contents drop-down menu, select one of the following options:

- ◆ Not Formatted

- ◆ Formatted and Indented (applies formatting and indenting to any text and tags that appear within the tag)

- ◆ Formatted but Not Indented (applies formatting that you have set in the Code Format Preferences. See *Code Format preferences* in Chapter 11 to set these).

4. From the Case drop-down menu, select one of the following options: Default, Uppercase, Lowercase, or Mixed Case (**Figure 12.10**).

If you select Default, it will apply the case you have selected in Dreamweaver's Code Format Preferences. See *Code Format preferences* in Chapter 11 to set these.

If you select Mixed Case, a dialog box will appear asking you to type the name of the tag exactly as you want it to appear. For some server-side or XML tags, for example, you may want parts of them to appear capitalized for special syntax purposes, such as GRR_growl or upStairs.

5. Click OK to close the Tag Library Editor.

6. In Code view, type the tag (and its matching end tag) on your page, with some text in between (**Figure 12.11**).

7. Select the tag, and from the Commands menu, select Apply Source Formatting to Selection.

The formatting you selected will be applied to the tag, or at least some of it will (**Figure 12.12**). That's because Dreamweaver's code-writing preferences may override your choice; do some experimenting with both the tag library formatting choices and the Code Writing Preferences to find out what works for you and your coding style.

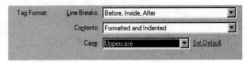

Figure 12.10 We're choosing uppercase so the tag will be easier to see in Code view.

```
<body>
<evil>Here's some evil text</evil>
```

Figure 12.11 The tag prior to formatting.

```
<evil>
  Here's some evil text
</evil>
```

Figure 12.12 The formatting we specified adds the indent, but our Uppercase setting got overridden by our tag writing preferences.

✔ Tips

- ■ When you open a file in Dreamweaver, it applies the appropriate source formatting automatically.

- ■ To have Dreamweaver re-format a page so that it uses your formatting preferences, use the command Commands > Apply Source Formatting. See Setting Code Preferences in Chapter 11.

- ■ If your document is an XHTML document, all non-server tags will appear in lowercase. See *Creating and Complying with XHTML* in Chapter 11.

Importing Tag Libraries

So far, we've just dealt with adding and editing one tag at a time. What if you want to import a whole library of them? Well, it depends on what kinds of tags you are trying to import.

You can import XML, JSP, and JRun tags from a folder on your local machine. Additionally, you can import ASP.NET and JSP tags from a server. There is very little difference in the way you import these different kinds of tags.

We'll show you how to import an XML tag library here. You need to have a copy of the definition file for your flavor of XML in order to do this. This file is commonly called a *DTD* (Document Type Definition) or a *schema*.

To import tags from an XML DTD or schema file:

1. From the Edit menu, select Tag Libraries to open the Tag Library Editor.

2. Click on the + (plus) button, and from the menu that appears, select DTDSchema > Import XML DTD or Schema File.

   The Import XML DTD or Schema File dialog box will appear (**Figure 12.13**).

3. In the File or Remote URL text box, type the location for the file from which you wish to import the tags; or click Browse to locate the file on your local machine or network.

4. In the Tag Prefix text box, specify a prefix to add to all the tags in the library.

Figure 12.13 You can add a Tag Prefix to distinguish custom tags from others that might have similar names.

5. Click OK to close the dialog box and import the tags.

   The tags will appear in the Tag Library Editor (**Figure 12.14**).

The other types of tag libraries work similarly.

✔ Tips

- Many XML DTDs have an opening <DOC-TYPE> declaration. Dreamweaver cannot import DTDs that have this declaration in them. Remove the declaration (and the matching </DOCTYPE>) before importing the DTD into Dreamweaver. If you don't want to mess with this file, make a backup, remove the doctype information from the backup, and then use that file.

- To import tags from an application server, open the Tag Library Editor. Click the + (plus) button, and select one of the following: ASP.NET > Import all ASP.NET Custom Files; ASP.NET > Import Selected ASP.NET Custom Tags; JSP > Import From Server; or JSP > Import JRun Server Tags From Folder. In any case, you'll be prompted to select the location of the tag definitions on the testing server, and you may need to specify other information, such as the URI for a JRun Custom Library.

- You can consult the Dreamweaver Help files (listed in the Index under *importing custom tags*) for special considerations when importing other kinds of tags.

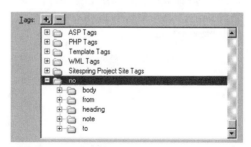

Figure 12.14 Look! A new library.

How to Edit, Add, and Remove Attributes

Attributes are modifiers for tags—they're the adverbs of the tag world. Some tags require one or more attributes—the most obvious example of this is the `src` attribute for an `img` tag (otherwise, how would the browser find the image?). Most attributes are optional, however, like the `alt` attribute that supplies a text equivalent for an image. Other common attributes include `width`, `border`, and `name`, all of which you've seen applied to various tags such as `table`, `img`, `div`, and the frame-set tags.

The Tag Library Editor allows you to add and remove tag attributes for both pre-built and custom tags. It also lets you specify the possible values for those attributes—this can be particularly handy for jogging the memory of those who are coding using your markup language or custom tag. For instance, one attribute of `<evil>` might be `degree`. You might define the possible values of `degree` as numbers, say, from 1 to 7, so that your tag would look like this:

```
<evil degree="5">bad text</evil>
```

Or you might define the possibilities for another attribute, `type`, as `purposeful`, `mercenary`, `ignorant`, and so on, so that the code would look like this:

```
<evil type="lawyer">abogado</evil>
```

See *To add values to an attribute* later in this chapter to specify which values your attribute can take.

Figure 12.15 The dialog box should show the library and tag you've selected.

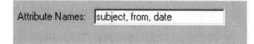

Figure 12.16 You can specify multiple attributes.

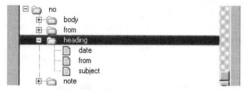

Figure 12.17 The tag now has three new attributes.

Adding an attribute to a tag

Now that we're clear on what attributes are and how one might use them, let's add an attribute to evil.

To add an attribute to a tag:

1. From the Edit menu, select Tag Libraries to open the Tag Library Editor.

2. Select the tag to which you want to add an attribute.

3. Click the + (plus) button, and select New Attributes from the menu that appears.

   The New Attributes dialog box will appear (**Figure 12.15**).

4. From the Tag Library drop-down menu, select the library that contains the tag, if it is not already selected.

5. From the Tag drop-down menu, select the tag if it is not already selected.

   In theory, whatever tag you selected before Step 3 should appear by default in this dialog box, but this doesn't always happen. Just follow Steps 4 and 5 if your tag isn't preselected.

6. In the Attribute Names text box, type the name of the attribute you want to add.

   If you want to add more than one attribute, type all the names, separated by a comma and a space (**Figure 12.16**).

7. Click OK to close the dialog box and add the attributes; or see the following list to add values to your attribute.

   The attribute will now appear as part of the tag (**Figure 12.17**).

If you want the attribute to take a value, you can specify the values and how they're spelled out. See the upcoming list, *To add values to an attribute.*

HOW TO EDIT, ADD, AND REMOVE ATTRIBUTES

Editing tag attributes

Now that you've added an attribute to a tag, let's look at how to edit an attribute. We'll remove the justify option from the H5 tag, just to be obnoxious. (Really, who uses the justify attribute, in the H5 or any other tag? For that matter, who uses the H5 tag? Okay, now we're being *really* obnoxious...)

To edit an attribute:

1. From the menu bar, select Edit > Tag Libraries to open the Tag Library Editor.

2. Click the Expand button next to the HTML Tags library, if it's not already expanded.

   The library display will expand to show all its tags (**Figure 12.18**).

3. Click the expand button next to the H5 tag.

   The tag's attributes will appear in the list (**Figure 12.19**).

4. Click on the align attribute.

   The attribute's info will appear in the bottom part of the Tag Library Editor (**Figure 12.20**).

5. In the Values text box, select justify and the comma before it, and then press Backspace (Delete).

6. Click OK to close the editor.

7. In Code view, type <h5

8. Select align from the Tag Hints menu.

   The possible values for the align attribute will appear (**Figure 12.21**). Note that justify is no longer one of them.

✔ Tip

■ You might notice that in the Property inspector, you can still justify the text. By removing the value from the attribute, you are simply changing the Tag Hints menu and the Tag inspector, not the actual parameters of the tag as defined in the spec.

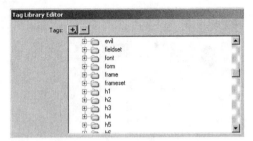

Figure 12.18 The full list of HTML tags is too big to show in the list box all at once.

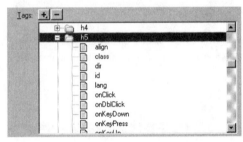

Figure 12.19 You can see the attributes for a specific tag. Dreamweaver includes lots of JavaScript user events as default attributes—even for tags that won't ever use them.

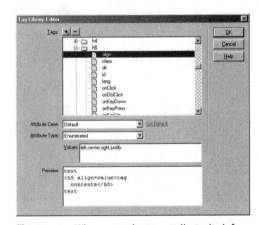

Figure 12.20 When you select an attribute, its info, including values, is displayed in the Tag Library Editor.

Figure 12.21 We've removed the justify value from the align attribute of the <h5> tag.

Adding values to an attribute

When you create or edit an attribute, you may want to add specific attribute values to it. There are many ways of spelling these out. The choices in Step 2, below, do not affect how the code is written, but they do allow you to tell Dreamweaver what the "legal" choices are for attribute values. In return, Dreamweaver can provide handy shortcuts that appear in the Tag Hints menus and the Tag inspector.

To add values to an attribute:

1. Follow Steps 1-3 in the previous list to select a tag and then an attribute. In our example, we'd select the `evil` tag and the `degree` attribute. (Go back to *Adding an attribute to a tag* if the attribute you want to edit doesn't yet exist.)

   The Tag Library Editor will display properties for the attribute, including any existing values (Figure 12.20).

2. If the attribute currently displays some values, you can add values by typing them in the Value list box separated by commas.

   or

   If the attribute currently does not take any values and the Values box is grayed out, select one of the following options from the Attribute Type drop-down menu:

   ◆ **Text** means that the attribute appears within the tag but does not take a value, like the `nowrap` attribute of a table cell.

   ◆ **Enumerated** means that the attribute takes values. Select enumerated and then type the values, such as `1,2,3` or `night,day` in the Values text box, separated by commas.

   ◆ **Color** means that any valid hex or alpha color code is allowable, and Dreamweaver will provide a color picker when you use Tag Hints or the Tag Inspector panel with this attribute.

◆ **Directory**, **File Name**, **File Path**, **and Relative Path** are all ways of allowing URLs, network file paths, folders, and files to be used as values. Dreamweaver will provide a Browse button when you use Tag Hints or the Tag Inspector with these attributes.

◆ **Flag** is a session variable that must be set by the application server. See *Tag Attributes and the Tag Inspector*, later in this chapter, to set this attribute dynamically.

◆ **Font** is similar to the face attribute of the font tag. When you set this type of value, Dreamweaver will provide its font shortcut menu when you're hand coding, for use as a Tag Hints menu.

◆ **Style** is the same as a CSS ID, class, or inline style. Dreamweaver doesn't provide any shortcuts for style.

3. Click on OK to save your changes and close the Tag Library Editor.

You can type the tag, attribute, and value in Code view to test out how Dreamweaver provides tag hints menus.

Removing an attribute from a tag

Now that we've added and edited a tag attribute, all that's left to do is remove one. It's easy.

To remove a tag attribute:

1. From the menu bar, select Edit > Tag Libraries to open the Tag Library Editor.

2. Select the tag attribute you wish to remove.

3. Click the - (minus) button.

Wasn't that easy? Next, we'll look at how attributes work in the Tag inspector.

Tag Attributes and the Tag Inspector

You may have wondered why all the *sturm und drang* about tag attributes. The main reason customizing them is important is that you can set them in the Tag Inspector—that is, they're included in that nifty editing tool that includes all legal attributes for all legal tags. In other words, we've now made our new attributes legal, as far as Dreamweaver is concerned. We covered setting tag attributes with the Tag Inspector panel in the *Tag Inspector (Tree view)* section of Chapter 11.

This may not seem like a big deal, but the combination of the Tag Inspector and Dynamic Data can add some power to your page. By using the Tag Inspector to set a tag attribute dynamically, we can do all sorts of things—reformat tables, supply new or updated class attributes for CSS formatting, change the color of a page, or supply a new location for an image or inline text file.

To dynamically set a tag attribute:

1. Open a dynamic page.

2. Add a recorsdet to the page (see *The Bindings Panel* section in Chapter 2 for more information).

3. Add a tag to your page (we'll use <basefont>).

4. Select the tag.

   The tag's attributes will appear in the Tag Inspector (**Figure 12.22**).

5. Click on the face attribute.

   A Lightning Bolt button will appear next to the attribute name (**Figure 12.23**).

6. Click the lightning bolt. The Dynamic Data dialog box will appear (**Figure 12.24**).

7. Select the field that contains your attribute value.

The attribute's source will now be set from the database.

Figure 12.22
The tag's attributes display as preset options in the Tag inspector.

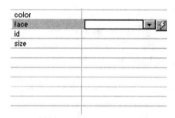

Figure 12.23 The lightning bolt button means you can set this attribute or value dynamically.

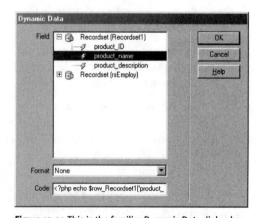

Figure 12.24 This is the familiar Dynamic Data dialog box.

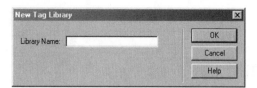

Figure 12.25 When you create a new tag library, adding a tag prefix is optional.

Figure 12.26 You can't change the order in which libraries show up in the editor. Your additions will appear at the bottom of the list.

Creating a Custom Library

You can create entire custom tag libraries from scratch, if you want to. You may be using a special server application, for example, that requires some new tags. Let's say you've written an XML application that has only three tags: evil, good, and neutral. For a customer tracking database, your tags might include name and login.

In most cases, these tags exist in an XML schema or DTD, but what if they don't? In our universe, EML does not have a DTD or schema file yet, because evil is constantly evolving.

We'll look at how to create a custom library for EML, the Evil Markup Language.

To add a new library:

1. From the menu bar, select Edit > Tag Libraries to open the Tag Library Editor.

2. Click the + (plus) button and select New Tag Library from the menu that appears. The New Tag Library dialog box will appear (**Figure 12.25**).

3. Type EML in the Library Name text box.

4. Click on OK to close the dialog box. The library will appear at the end of the library list in the Tag Library Editor's Tags list box (**Figure 12.26**).

continues on next page

CREATING A CUSTOM LIBRARY

5. Now that we're back in the Tag Library Editor, click on the folder for the new language, EML. The dialog box will change to show a list of languages. Check the boxes for PHP and HTML in the list box labeled Used in.

The Evil Server is PHP-based, so we need to make sure the tags we create are available on PHP pages. And because most pages, regardless of their platform, use HTML code to present the front end, we need to have the tags available in HTML documents as well. If your app server is in another platform, of course, you should select the appropriate Used in settings.

6. Select the EML library, click the + (plus) button, and select New Tags from the drop-down menu.

The New Tags dialog box will appear.

7. Make sure the Tag Library drop-down menu specifies EML.

8. In the Tag Names text box, type evil, nefarious, sin, vice (**Figure 12.27**).

9. Check the Have Matching End Tags checkbox.

10. Click OK to close the dialog box.

The tags will now appear as part of the EML library (**Figure 12.28**).

We've now created a custom tag library.

At this point, you should have an idea of some of the power and peculiarity of the Tag Library Editor and custom tag libraries. In the next chapter, we'll look at using JavaScript and Dreamweaver behaviors to provide client-side interactivity in the browser window.

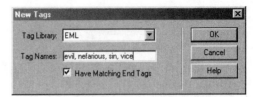

Figure 12.27 This is where you add tags to the library.

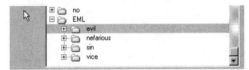

Figure 12.28 The new tags are now part of our custom library.

JavaScript & Dreamweaver Behaviors

One of the interesting side benefits of the rise of the World Wide Web has been the proliferation of JavaScript. JavaScript is a compact, capable language that is relatively easy to learn. Like any programming language, on the other hand, it's not always easy to use well. It's easy enough to get a window to open, but harder to get that window to open in response to an incorrectly filled-out form, for example.

Fortunately, Dreamweaver provides a way to get the most out of JavaScript, with very little programming. Dreamweaver's tools for adding interactive JavaScript to a page are called *behaviors*. Keep in mind that these are not the same thing as the Server Behaviors we discussed in Chapter 10, because they are executed in the browser, rather than by the server.

In this chapter we'll look at how some of the more useful behaviors work, and go into some detail about how they interact with each other and with Fireworks. We'll also look at the JavaScript debugger and how the Snippets panel provides some useful shortcuts for JavaScript widgets.

JavaScript Concepts

Behaviors in Dreamweaver are the combination of an event and an action. The behavior is attached to an object. The object can be a page, a form, a link, a button, or almost anything you can put on a page.

Behaviors in Dreamweaver, as we mentioned in the introduction to this chapter, are written in JavaScript. Specifically, they are *client-side* JavaScript, which means that they are executed by the user's browser, rather than by the server. This is unlike, say, PHP, which is executed by a special program attached to a server.

Unfortunately, JavaScript is not implemented exactly the same way on all browsers. Internet Explorer and Navigator, for example, deal with some objects differently, and even different versions of the same program can have differences. Macromedia claims to have done their darndest to make sure that Dreamweaver's behaviors are compatible with as many browsers as possible, but inevitably, there are exceptions.

Table 13.1 lists the JavaScript events available for behaviors in Dreamweaver and which browsers they are compatible with.

Table 13.1 Events are arranged in logical sets rather than alphabetically. This table does not include all event handlers available to JavaScript, only those that Dreamweaver utilizes for behaviors.

User Events Available in Dreamweaver

Event Handler Name	Description of the User Event *(The event handler may call any number of actions, including dialog boxes.)*	Browsers *(According to Dreamweaver.)*	Associated Tags *(Other tags may be used; these are the most common associated objects.)*
Page Loading Events			
onAbort	When user presses the Stop button or Esc key before successful page or image loading	NN3, NN4, NS6, IE4, IE5	body, img
onLoad	When a page, frameset, or image has finished loading	NN3, NN4, NS6, IE3, IE4, IE5	body, img
onUnload	When the user leaves the page (clicks on a link, or presses the back button)	NN3, NN4, NS6, IE3, IE4, IE5	body
onResize	When the user resizes the browser window	NN3, NN4, NS6, IE4, IE5	body
onError	When a JavaScript error occurs	NN3, NN4, NS6, IE4, IE5	a, body, img

(continues)

User Events available in Dreamweaver *(continued)*

Event Handler Name	Description of the user event *(The event handler may call any number of actions, including dialog boxes.)*	Browsers *(According to Dreamweaver.)*	Associated Tags *(Other tags may be used; these are the most common associated objects.)*
Form and Form Field Events			
onBlur	When a form field "loses the focus" of its intended use	NN3, NN4, NS6, IE3, IE4, IE5	form fields: text, textarea, select
onFocus	When a form field receives the user's focus by being selected by the Tab key	NN3, NN4, NS6, IE3, IE4, IE5	form fields: text, keytextarea, select
onChange	When the user changes the default selection in a form field	NN3, NN4, NS6, IE3, IE4, IE5	most form fields
onSelect	When the user selects text within a form field	NN3, NN4, NS6, IE3, IE4, IE5	form fields: text, textarea
onSubmit	When a user clicks on the form's Submit button	NN3, NN4, NS6, IE3, IE4, IE5	form
onReset	When a user clicks on the form's Reset button	NN3, NN4, NS6, IE3, IE4, IE5	form
Mouse Events			
onClick	When the user clicks on the object (IE3 uses this handler only for form fields)	NN3, NN4, NS6, IE3, IE4, IE5	a; form fields: button, checkbox, radio, reset, submit
onDblClick	When the user double-clicks on the object	NN4, NS6, IE4, IE5	a, img
onMouseMove	When the user moves the mouse	NS6, IE3, IE4, IE5	a, img
onMouseDown	When the mouse button is depressed	NN4, NS6, IE4, IE5	a, img
onMouseUp	When the mouse button is released	NN4, NS6, IE4, IE5	a, img
onMouseOver	When the user points the mouse pointer at an object	NN3, IE3, NN4, NS6, IE4, IE5	a, img
onMouseOut	When the mouse is moved off an object that was moused over	NN3, NN4, NS6, IE4, IE5	a, img
Keyboard Events			
onKeyDown	When a key on the keyboard is depressed	NN3, NN4, NS6, IE3, IE4, IE5	form fields: text, textarea
onKeyPress	When the user presses any key	NN3, NN4, NS6, IE3, IE4, IE5	form fields: text, textarea
onKeyUp	When a key on the keyboard is released	NN3, NN4, NS6, IE3, IE4, IE5	form fields: text, textarea
IE 4+ Events			
onHelp	When the user presses F1 or selects a link labeled "help"	IE4, IE5	a, img
onReadyStateChange	Page is loading	IE4, IE5	img
onAfterUpdate	After the content of a form field changes	IE4, IE5	a, body, img
onBeforeUpdate	After form field item changes, before content loses focus	IE4, IE5	a, body, img
onScroll	When the user uses the page scrollbars	IE4, IE5	body

Note: IE5 in this table should be considered to include IE6 for Windows.

Let's take a look at how to apply behaviors to objects. If you need a broader introduction to behaviors, check out *Macromedia Dreamweaver MX for Windows and Macintosh: Visual QuickStart Guide*, written by our co-author, J. Tarin Towers.

To add a behavior:

1. In the Document window, click on the object you want the behavior to act on, or choose an entire tag (such as <body>), by selecting the tag in the Tag selector in the status bar of the Document window (**Figure 13.1**).

2. If the Behaviors panel isn't visible, select Window > Behaviors from the menu bar, and it will appear as part of the Design panel group.

   On the left side of the Behaviors panel, click on the + (plus) button to pop up a menu that includes both a list of actions that are available and a way to select your target browser. Select the Show Events For submenu and choose your target browser (**Figure 13.2**). If you don't select a browser, the list of events will be limited to those available for both 3.0 and 4.0 browsers.

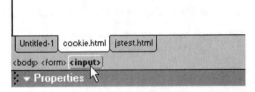

Figure 13.1 Clicking on a tag in the Tag selector selects the entire tag.

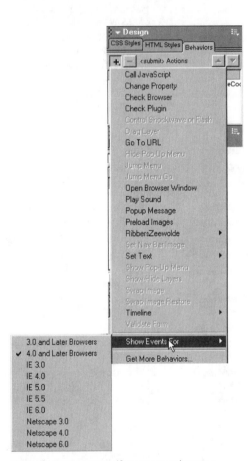

Figure 13.2 You can specify your target browser.

Figure 13.3 The menu adjusts for your browser and the object you have selected.

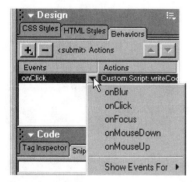

Figure 13.4 You can set the event that triggers the behavior.

3. Click on the plus button again to show a menu of actions that are available for that particular browser/object combination (**Figure 13.3**).

4. Choose your action from the menu. In most cases, a dialog box will appear.

5. Fill out the dialog box and click on OK. The name of the action will appear in the Actions list box.

6. Click on the arrow to the left of the Action name to show a menu of available user events (**Figure 13.4**).

   The available events will depend on the object/browser/action combination you chose. More events are available if you choose 4.0 or later browsers, but remember that only the users with those browsers will be able to use them.

7. Choose your event from the menu (they're described later in this chapter). Its name will appear in the Events list box.

   To see events for a specific browser only, select the browser from the Show Events For submenu.

In the next few sections of this chapter, we'll look at a few of the more useful behaviors, and how to use them to make your Web site more interactive.

✔ Tip

■ Almost anyone who is running a graphical Web browser at all is running version 4.0 or later—for the most part. While those who don't have or can't run a recent Web browser may indeed be technologically challenged, that doesn't mean they're all stubborn Luddites who live in bunkers and use software they compiled themselves on an Amiga toaster. Where do old computers go to die? Sadly, they often go to schools, libraries, and other underfunded public programs—or to secretive nomads whose donkeys have satellite hookups.

Open Window

Dreamweaver lets you take advantage of one of the most misused features of JavaScript, the pop-up window. Now you, too, can barrage your site visitors with endless ads and special offers! (Actually, this *is* how those annoying pop-ups are produced, but there are plenty of viable uses for them, too, particularly if you want to use multiple windows to navigate a site, register a user, or launch a game or movie.)

The basic procedure for opening a new window in JavaScript is pretty easy. Let's run through that quickly, and then we'll show you how to take advantage of some of the advanced features of the JavaScript command.

To make a window open when users click on an image:

1. Create a new HTML page.

2. Add an image to the page.

3. Select the image.

4. In the Behaviors panel, click the + (plus) button and select Open Browser Window from the drop-down menu.

   The Open Browser Window dialog box will appear (**Figure 13.5**).

5. In the URL to Display text box, specify the file you want to open.

6. Specify the size of the window in the height and width text boxes.

7. In the Window Name text box, enter a name for the window.

   We'll ignore all the other options, but you can find out more about them in the Dreamweaver help files.

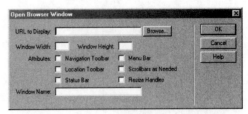

Figure 13.5 The Open Window dialog box allows you to specify the size and style of the window.

Figure 13.6 Now you can pop open a new window—which might actually come in handy for things such as messaging windows, Flash movies, and registration gadgets.

Figure 13.7 Now we get our hands dirty messing with the code manually!

8. Click OK to close the Window.

The behavior will appear in the Behaviors panel.

9. Click on the arrow to the left of the behavior name, and select onClick from the drop-down menu.

You can now preview the file in your browser, and a new window will pop up when you click on the image (**Figure 13.6**).

One thing about this behavior is that the screen location of the pop-up window is based strictly on the location of the last window you opened in your browser. JavaScript allows you to specify the location of the window, but the Dreamweaver behavior doesn't have any way to do that.

Fortunately, we have figured out a way to specify the window location, and it's not hard at all.

To specify the location of a new window:

1. In Code view, find the JavaScript code that calls the `MM_openBRWindow` function (**Figure 13.7**).

2. Right after the height=200 (or whatever height you specified) add the following code: `top=400,left=600`

The `top` and `left` correspond to the number of pixels from the top and left of the *screen*, so expect some variation over different monitors.

Make sure you add the code inside the single quotes, and also make sure you don't add any spaces anywhere. Your code should look something like:
`onClick="MM_openBrWindow('./test.`
`→ html','','width=200,height=200,`
`→ top=400 left=600,3')"`

That's all there is to it. You can now badger users on any part of the screen.

Change Property

Change Property is a flexible but oddly uncharming behavior that allows you to let the user's movements affect attributes of many different kinds of tags, from layers, to text, to forms.

The most skeletal of the dialog boxes that Macromedia includes as a Dreamweaver behavior, the Change Property behavior, is not the most intuitive or user-friendly behavior, in terms of the hints it gives you as to how to use it—but it can be quite powerful in the right hands.

In this section, we'll show you how to use the Change Property behavior to change the background color of a layer, the font size of some text, and we'll also look at how to change arbitrary chunks of text.

In these examples, we'll be triggering the behavior by clicking on an image, but you could use any valid event to trigger the Change Property behavior. Again, consult Tarin's *Macromedia Dreamweaver MX for Windows and Macintosh: Visual QuickStart Guide* for more detail on the possible events.

To change the background color of a layer:

1. Create a new HTML file.

2. Insert an image onto the page.

3. From the menu bar, choose Insert > Layer to add a new layer to the page (**Figure 13.8**).

4. Add some text to the layer.

5. Select the image you inserted earlier.

6. In the Behaviors panel, click on the + (plus) button and select Change Property from the drop-down menu.

   The Change Property dialog box will appear (**Figure 13.9**).

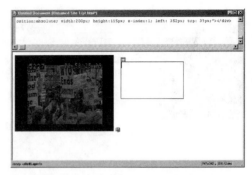

Figure 13.8 The new layer appears at the insertion point.

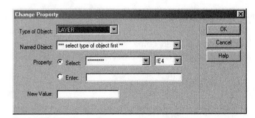

Figure 13.9 The Change Property dialog box is center stage for all work you'll do with the Change Property behavior.

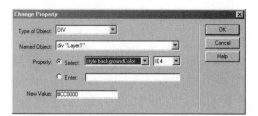

Figure 13.10 Here, we're changing the background color of a layer.

Figure 13.11 Mouse over the image, and the layer's background color changes. (If this book were in color, the new background would be red, not gray.)

```
<body>
<p><img src="images/showdown8.jpg" width="320" height="240"> </p>
<p>Here is some text <span id="testspan">inside a span.</span></p>
</body>
```

Figure 13.12 Wrapping a <span> tag around HTML or text makes the span contents modifiable in JavaScript. It also doesn't innately affect the visual presentation of the text.

7. From the Type of Object drop-down menu, select DIV.

8. From the Named Object drop-down menu, select div "Layer 1".

9. In the first Property drop-down menu, select style.backgroundColor.

10. In the New Value text box, enter #CC0000. Your dialog box should now look something like **Figure 13.10**.

11. Click OK to close the dialog box.

12. In the Behaviors panel, click on the down arrow next to the behavior and select onClick from the drop-down menu.

13. Preview the page in your browser. Click on the image. The layer background should turn red (**Figure 13.11**).

That wasn't too hard, was it? Don't worry, it gets harder!

The next two examples are going to require a little HTML tinkering. We'll be using the <span> tag, which is an arbitrary container for HTML. We call it arbitrary because it's meant as a marker for applying styles and it doesn't do anything by itself, unlike, say, a <p> tag, which adds a blank line of space on the page before and after the tag.

To add a <span> to your page:

1. Type some text onto an HTML page.

2. In Code view, click before the text you want to include in the span, and type <span id="testspan">, and then type </span> after the text you want to include (**Figure 13.12**).

3. Press F5 to refresh the design view. It shouldn't look any different.

Now that your text is enclosed in a span, you can change various properties of it using the Change Property behavior.

To change the size of the text:

1. Add a span of text to your page, as in the previous list.

2. Add an image to your page.

3. Select the image.

4. In the Behaviors panel, click on the + (plus) button and select Change Property from the drop-down menu.
   The Change Property dialog box will appear.

5. In the Type of Object drop-down menu, select SPAN.

6. In the Named Object drop-down, select the named span you added to the page.

7. From the Property drop-down menu, select style.fontSize.

8. In the New Value text box, enter 36 (**Figure 13.13**).

9. Click OK to close the dialog box.

10. In the Behaviors panel, click on the down arrow next to the behavior and select onClick from the drop-down menu.

11. Preview your file in a browser. Click on the image. The text size should change (**Figure 13.14**).

In addition to twiddling the size, color or face of the font in a span, you can also change the actual text inside a span. If you're willing to muck around with the HTML a little bit, you can even use JavaScript to fill in the text.

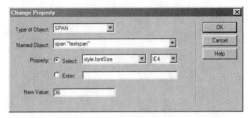

Figure 13.13 As is often the case with test pages, we're choosing obvious formatting changes over sumptuous typography.

Figure 13.14 See?

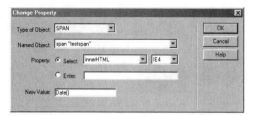

Figure 13.15 You have to jigger the code a little to get the actual date to show up.

Figure 13.16 Consult a good JavaScript reference to see how to format the date the way you want it.

We'll look at how to use Change Property to display the current date and time.

To change the text in a span:

1. Follow Steps 1 through 6 in the previous list.

2. From the Property drop-down menu, select innerHTML.

3. In the New Value text box, enter Date(). Your dialog box should resemble **Figure 13.15.**

4. Click OK to close the dialog box.

5. In the Behaviors panel, click on the down arrow next to the behavior and select onClick from the drop-down menu.

6. Preview the file in your browser and click on the image.

   You'll get little or no reaction. That's clearly *not* what we want, so we need to tweak the file a little.

7. In Code view, find the code that calls the behavior.

   It should be something like
   ```
   onClick="MM_changeProp('test','',
   → 'innerHTML','Date()','SPAN')".
   ```

8. Delete the single quotes that surround Date().

9. Preview the file again in your browser. Now you should get something like **Figure 13.16.**

Creating a Cascading Menu

A behavior that's new to Dreamweaver in MX is the Show Pop-Up Menu behavior. As the name suggests, this behavior produces a menu when users mouse over an image (**Figure 13.17**).

You can create the menu in Dreamweaver, or if you have the full Macromedia Studio MX package, you can create the menu in Fireworks, and export it for use in Dreamweaver.

To create a pop-up menu in Dreamweaver:

1. Create a new HTML page.

2. Add an image to the page. This image will serve as the trigger area for the pop-up menu.

3. Save the file.

   The Show Pop-Up Menu behavior requires that you save the file before you add the behavior.

4. Select the image. In the Behaviors panel, click the + (plus) button and select Show Pop-Up Menu from the drop-down menu.

   The Show Pop-up Menu dialog box will appear (**Figure 13.18**).

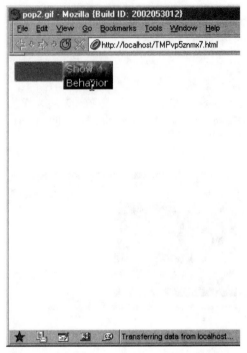

Figure 13.17 The menu pops up when you mouse over the image.

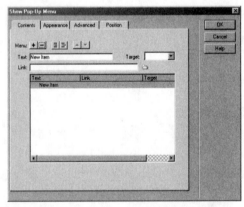

Figure 13.18 The Show Pop-Up menu dialog box is a dense one.

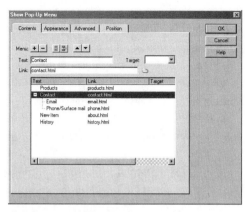

Figure 13.19 You can make the menu cascading by indenting elements...

Figure 13.20 ...which then pop out even further from their parent item.

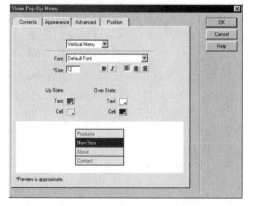

Figure 13.21 The Appearance tab allows you to preview and adjust how your menu will look.

5. In the Text text box, type the, uh, text you want to appear in the first menu item.

6. In the Link file box, type the URL of the file you want to go to when the user selects that menu item.

7. Click the + (plus) button to add the item to the list and prepare to enter a new item.

8. Repeat Steps 5 through 7 for each menu item you want to appear in the pop-up menu.

9. If you want an element to be a submenu selection of the menu (**Figure 13.19**), click the indent menu item button. The items you indent will be a submenu (**Figure 13.20**).

10. When you have added all the items you want the menu to contain, click the Appearance tab of the dialog box. (**Figure 13.21**)

11. From the first drop-down menu, choose Horizontal Menu or Vertical Menu.

continues on next page

CREATING A CASCADING MENU

12. From the next group of menus, specify the look of the text of your menu (**Figure 13.22**).

13. Specify the colors for the up state and the down state of the menu.

The *up state* is what the menu item looks like when the user is not mousing over it. The *down state* is what the menu looks like when the mouse *is* over it.

14. Click the Position tab in the dialog box (**Figure 13.23**).

15. Click whichever of the position buttons corresponds to the location in which you want your menu to appear relative to the image.

16. If you want the menu to stay up even if the user moves the mouse away, uncheck the Hide Menu on onMouseOut event (this is not recommended—it can make the other elements of your page impossible to read or navigate through).

17. Click OK to close the dialog box.

Using the Show Pop-Up Menu behavior creates a file called `mm_menu.js` in the same folder as your HTML file. You need to make sure that that file gets uploaded to your testing server and/or production server (if you've specified one) along with the HTML file, if you want your pop-up menu to work. If your pop-up menu doesn't work on your live site, most likely you haven't uploaded this file.

You can now preview your pop-up menu (**Figure 13.24**).

If you have Fireworks, you can also create a pop-up menu in that program and then export it for use in Dreamweaver. Using Fireworks has the advantage that you can use images instead of text for the menu.

Figure 13.22 You have all the normal font controls.

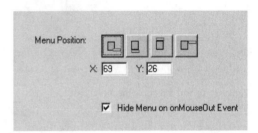

Figure 13.23 The position tab allows you to set where the menu pops out. (We've cropped the Position tab of the Show Pop-Up Menu dialog box here.)

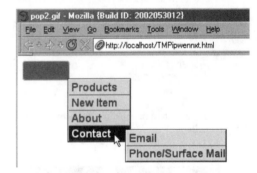

Figure 13.24 Don't overuse these!

CREATING A CASCADING MENU

Figure 13.25
Create the hotspot graphic first.

Figure 13.26
Crop the image, or confusing HTML will result.

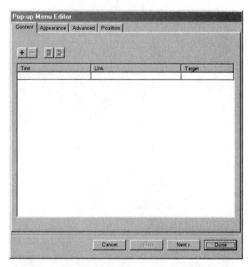

Figure 13.27 The Pop-up Menu Editor in Fireworks is similar but not identical to Dreamweaver's Pop-Up Menu dialog box—capitalization issues aside.

To create a graphical pop-up menu using Fireworks:

1. In Fireworks, create or open the graphic that will serve as the hotspot for your menu. (**Figure 13.25**).

2. Crop the image so that your graphic takes up the whole area (**Figure 13.26**).

   This step is not strictly necessary, but makes the HTML easier to handle later.

3. Select the slice tool ⧄, and select the entire image.

4. From the menu bar, choose Modify > Pop-up Menu, then select Add Pop-up Menu from the submenu that appears.

   The Pop-up Menu Editor dialog box will appear (**Figure 13.27**).

5. Enter the Text and Link location for each of your menu items in the list box.

continues on next page

CREATING A CASCADING MENU

6. Click the Next button to move to the Appearance tab in the dialog box (**Figure 13.28**).

7. Click the Image radio button.

This will switch the display to show image possibilities (**Figure 13.29**).

8. From the drop-down menu at the top of the dialog box, select Vertical Menu or Horizontal Menu.

9. Specify the font, style, size, and alignment you want for the text in the menu.

10. Using the color pickers, select the color you want for your menu text and menu image when in the up (unselected) state.

11. Select the pattern, if any, you want for your menu buttons (**Figure 13.30**).

12. Repeat Steps 10 and 11 for the Down, or selected/moused-over state.

13. Click Done.

The image will now appear in Fireworks with some obscure symbols, indicating that the image, when saved as an HTML file, contains a pop-up menu (**Figure 13.31**).

14. From the Fireworks menu bar, select File > Export to export the HTML file and images to Dreamweaver. (You can also choose other export settings here.)

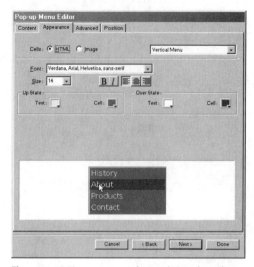

Figure 13.28 Here you can select an image-based pop-up menu.

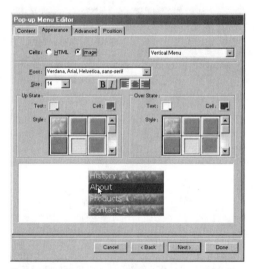

Figure 13.29 Pretty pictures! You can choose lots of different backgrounds and styles for your menu buttons.

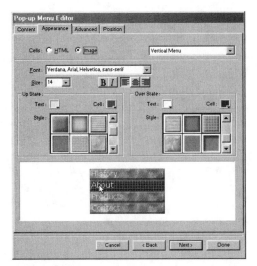

Figure 13.30 The default styles are, in general, chosen for their readability.

Figure 13.31 The weird curved lines indicate that the image triggers a pop-up menu.

15. Choose the location to save your file.

You can also opt to save your images in a subfolder, which is a pretty good idea, because they can clutter things up pretty quickly.

16. Click OK to finish the export.

17. In Dreamweaver, open the HTML file you just created.

You can now preview your menu in your browser, or you can copy and paste the HTML into another file. If you do the latter, make sure to copy the JavaScript references above the body as well.

✔ Tips

■ In the Pop-up Menu Editor dialog box in Fireworks, you can move an item up or down by selecting it and using the Up and Down arrow buttons to move it through the list. You can add items either by using the + (plus) button or by pressing Tab after an existing item.

■ You can add table formatting to your menu items by clicking on the Advanced tab of the Pop-up Menu Editor dialog box in Fireworks. These options are the same as those used to format regular HTML tables.

■ You can also add a delay, hover-activated borders, and shadows to your menu buttons using the Advanced tab.

■ You can add new styles through the Fireworks Style panel. See the Fireworks Help files for more information.

Creating Fancy Rollovers

It's fairly common to have an image change when users mouse over it. Dreamweaver, of course, makes it easy to create this effect with the Swap Image behavior or the command Insert > Interactive Images > Rollover Image. But what if you want to change some text at the same time? You can do that, too, but it takes a little more work.

We'll first look at how to create an effect that changes two images when users mouse over a third image.

To change multiple images on a rollover:

1. Create a new HTML page and save it.

2. Insert an image onto the page.
   This image will be the hotspot for your rollover.

3. Insert two more images onto the page.
   These images will change when users mouse over the first image.

4. In the Property inspector, name the images you just added (**Figure 13.32**).

5. Select the hotspot image.

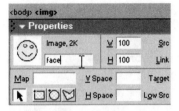

Figure 13.32 Name your images in the Property inspector.

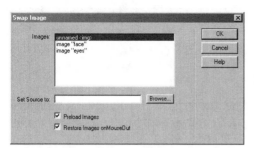

Figure 13.33 The Swap Image dialog box is pretty basic: Select any named image in the Images list box and then click Browse to set a new source for it. You can swap several images at once—the image that triggers this change is the one you had selected when you opened this dialog box.

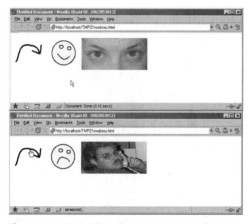

Figure 13.34 Ta-da! The rollovers work...sort of. When we mouse over the arrow, the smiley frowns, and the eyes turn into our coworker, Vlad. If you want Vlad to work elegantly, make sure the image being swapped in is the same size as the one it replaces.

6. In the Behaviors panel, click the + (plus) button and select Swap Image from the drop-down menu.

   The Swap Image dialog box will appear (**Figure 13.33**).

7. In the Images list box, select the name of one of the other two images.

8. In the Set Source To file box, specify the file you want the image to change to.

9. Repeat Steps 7 and 8 for the second target image.

10. Click OK to close the dialog box.

11. Preview the file in your browser.

   The second two images will change when the user mouses over the first one (**Figure 13.34**).

You might have guessed that we're going to use the Change Property behavior we examined earlier to change the text. But this time we'll use the onMouseOver and onMouseOut events to trigger the behavior, instead of the onClick event we used before.

To change text at the same time as you change images:

1. Add some text to the page from the previous example.

2. Surround the text with a **<span>** tag (See *To add a <span> to your page*, earlier in this chapter). Make sure to add an **id** to the **span** tag.

3. Select your hotspot image. In the Behaviors panel, click on the + (plus) button and choose Change Property.

4. In the Change Property dialog box, select SPAN from the Type of Object drop-down menu.

5. In the Named Object drop-down menu, select the named span you added to the page.

6. From the Property drop-down menu, select innerHTML.

7. In the New Value text box, enter the text you want to display when the user mouses over the image.

8. Click OK to close the dialog box.

9. In the Behaviors panel, click the down arrow next to the Change Property behavior and select onMouseOver.

10. Repeat Steps 3 through 6.

11. This time, in the New Value text box, enter the original text.

12. Click OK to close the dialog box.

13. In the Behaviors panel, click the down arrow next to the new Change Property behavior. This time, select onMouseOut from the drop-down menu.

14. Preview the file.

    This time, the text will change with the rollover along with the images (**Figure 13.35**).

For more interesting ways to use rollovers, see Chapter 18, *Toolbars, Tricks and Interactive Design*.

Figure 13.35 The second behavior needs to be triggered on onMouseOut.

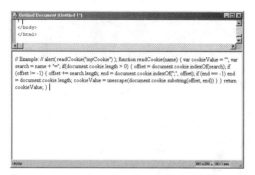

Figure 13.36 You don't want to splatter code all over your page.

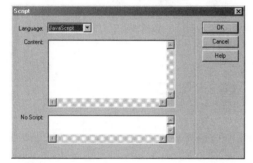

Figure 13.37 We're not using this the way it was intended.

Cookies and Code Snippets

One red flag that many people raise about the Web has always been the use of cookies. They are often cited as potential security or privacy breaches, but many sites still use them. Cookies can be quite useful in helping users remember their login names and in helping sites save personalization information on the user's computer rather than in a centralized database.

In this section, we'll show you how to use cookies, but you'll need to decide for yourself whether they're a good idea for your site.

To write a cookie, you need to use the `readCookie` and `writeCookie` functions that Dreamweaver provides in the Snippets panel.

The Snippets panel is a handy tool containing a fair number of useful JavaScript functions and fragments. They're quite easy to use, with a couple of caveats. You need to be sure to insert code snippets in Code view, and you need to add a `<script>` tag before you insert the snippets themselves.

To add JavaScript snippets to your page:

1. View your page in Code view.

   If you are in Design view, the JavaScript code will be pasted in as text, not code (**Figure 13.36**)—and that won't do anyone any good.

2. From the menu bar, select Insert > Script Objects > Script.

   The Script dialog box will appear (**Figure 13.37**).

3. Click OK.

   What we just did probably seemed pointless, but when you insert a script snippet, Dreamweaver doesn't automatically surround it with a `<script>` tag, so unless you add the tag, the script won't work. We could have manually typed the tag, but we're lazy.

continues on next page

4. In the Snippets panel, expand the JavaScript Folder (**Figure 13.38**).

5. Still in the Snippets panel, expand the folder containing the snippet you wish to insert onto your page.

6. Double-click on the appropriate snippet. The snippet will be added to your page, inside the `script` tag (**Figure 13.39**).

For more information on the Snippets panel, see the *Built-in Tag Writing Shortcuts* section of Chapter 11.

Now, on to cookies. We'll make a page on which the user can select a color, which gets written to a cookie, and then open a new page which gets its background color from that cookie.

To write a cookie:

1. Create a new HTML file.

2. In Code view, click at the very top of the document (**Figure 13.40**).

3. Follow the Steps 1-3 in the previous list to insert a `<script>` tag.

4. From the Cookies folder of the Snippets panel, insert Write Cookie.

5. From the menu bar, select Insert > Form to insert an empty form.

6. From the menu bar, choose Insert > Form Objects > List/Menu.

7. In the Property inspector, click the List Values button.

The List Values dialog box will appear (**Figure 13.41**).

8. Click the + (plus) button to add a new element, and in the Item Label column, type red.

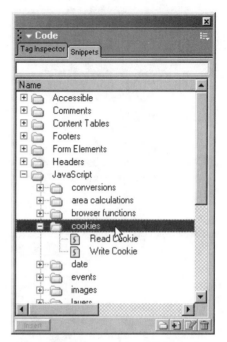

Figure 13.38 You may need to drill down a little to find the snippet you want to insert.

Figure 13.39 Now there's code in the right place.

9. In the Value column, enter red.

10. Repeat Steps 7 and 8 for blue and green.

11. Click OK to close the dialog box.

12. In the Initially Selected list box on the Property inspector, select one of the colors to be the default color (**Figure 13.42**).

13. In the Property inspector, change the name of the menu to colormenu.

14. From the menu bar, choose Insert > Form Objects > Button to insert a button..

15. In the Property inspector, change the button's Label to Thank You.

16. In the Tag selector, select the <form> tag.

17. In the Property inspector, change the Action of the form to page2.html.

18. Select Default from the Property inspector's Method drop-down menu.

19. In Code view, find the HTML code for the button. It will look something like this:

```
<input name="thankyou" type=
→"button" id="thankyou"
→value="Thank You">
```

20. Click in the code right after the value="Thank You" entry, and type the following code:

```
onClick="writeCookie('pagecolor',
→document.forms[0].colormenu.value,
→'1');"
```

It should look like **Figure 13.43**.This line of code writes a cookie called pagecolor, assigns it the value of whatever the user chose in the menu, and sets it to expire in one hour.

21. Save the file as cookie.html.

That's all there is to the cookie-writing file. Now we'll create the file that reads the cookie and sets its background color from it.

Figure 13.40 We'll add the code at the very beginning of the page.

Figure 13.41 Here's where you enter values for a list.

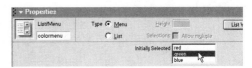

Figure 13.42 You should set a default value for the menu.

```
<input type="submit" name="Submit" value="thank you"
onClick="writeCookie('pagecolor',document.forms[0].colormenu.value,'1');">
form>
```

Figure 13.43 This is the code that calls the code that writes the cookie.

To read a cookie:

1. Open a new HTML file.

2. In Code view, click at the very top of the document.

3. Following the instructions in *To add JavaScript snippets to your page*, earlier in this section, insert the Read Cookie snippet.

4. In Code view, find the opening **<body>** tag.

5. Directly after the **<body>** tag, type the following line of code (**Figure 13.44**):
   ```
   <script language="JavaScript">
   → document.bgColor =
   → readCookie('pagecolor');</script>
   ```

6. In Design view, add some text.

7. Save the file as **page2.html**.

8. Preview **cookie.html** (**Figure 13.45**). Click on the Thank You button. The next page should use the color you chose in the menu as its background color.

```
<body>
<script language="JavaScript">document.bgColor = readCookie('pagecolor');</script>
```

Figure 13.44 Make sure this code is in the <body> section of the page.

Figure 13.45 Here's the color selector page. We won't show you the next page, because it'll just be gray in this book.

Figure 13.46 The JavaScript debugger window.

Debugging Your JavaScript

Dreamweaver includes a JavaScript debugger, which allows you to find problems in your JavaScript code. Even if you're just using the built-in behaviors, there are times when they don't do exactly what you expect, and the debugger can be a valuable tool to find the problem.

To use the JavaScript debugger:

1. Open the page with the JavaScript you want to debug.

2. Select File > Debug in Browser > Netscape (or Internet Explorer). A browser window will open, and a Java Security window will open as well.

3. If you're debugging in Netscape Navigator, click on OK in the debugger warning box that appears, then click on Grant in the Java Security dialog box. If you're using Internet Explorer (Windows only, the debugger doesn't work on Internet Explorer for Macintosh), click on Yes in the Java Security dialog box, then on OK in the debugger warning box that appears.

   The debugger window will appear (**Figure 13.46**), and the browser will stop at the first line of JavaScript code.

4. Click on a line in the code just before you think something is going wrong, and add a breakpoint by clicking the Set/Remove Breakpoint button ◯ or press F7.

5. Click on the Run button ⬇️. The code will start executing, and then stop at the point at which you set the breakpoint.

continues on next page

6. Click the Step Into button 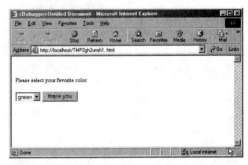 (or press F10). This will step through one line of your code at a time. You can watch what happens in the browser window with each step (**Figure 13.47**).

7. Repeat Step 6 until you find your error or pass the problem area.

Sometimes simply stepping through your code is not enough to figure out what's wrong. You can also watch the values of variables (and even set them) in the debugger window as well.

Figure 13.47 You can watch your code step-by-step.

To watch a variable's value:

1. Follow Steps 1 through 4 above.

2. Highlight the variable that you want to watch.

3. Click on the + (plus) button in the bottom half of the debugger window. The variable will appear in the bottom half of the window.

4. Press Enter (Return)

or

Without highlighting a variable, click on the Plus button and type the variable name. Then press Enter (Return).

5. Click on the Run button. The variable's value will be updated in the bottom half of the debugger window (**Figure 13.48**).

Figure 13.48 The variable's value is updated in the bottom pane of the debugger window.

One of the most useful ways to test any code—including JavaScript—is to set variables to really absurd values. What happens to your life expectancy calculator, for example, when someone claims they were born in 1865? Or what happens when a user clicks on a button 100 times? One way to test these unlikely possibilities is to set the variables in your code directly. The Dreamweaver debugger allows you to do just that.

To set a variable's value:

1. Follow Steps 1 through 3 in the previous list.

2. Click on the line in the code right after the variable gets its initial value. Click on the Set/Remove Breakpoint button.

3. Click on the Run button. This will run the code to the point where the variable has a value already set.

4. In the right column of the variable watch section of the debugger window (Figure 13.46), click on the variable's value. Type in the desired value.

5. Click on the Run button or the Step Into button. This will show you what happens to your page when the variable has the specified value.

✔ Tips

- The JavaScript debugger window works with Internet Explorer for Windows and Netscape version 4.x for Windows. It does not work with Netscape 6 or later or the Macintosh version of Internet Explorer.

- If you use only the built-in behaviors, after you click the Run button, the debugger will not kick in until you actually trigger one of those behaviors.

In the next chapter we'll look at Dreamweaver Templates, which, when used properly, can add coherence and consistency to your Web site.

Using Dreamweaver Templates with XML

Using Dreamweaver templates you can design a page, and then lock some parts of it while making other parts editable. Any number of pages can then be created with the template as a starting point. Updates or changes to the template are automatically reflected in the pages based on the template. You can also use the optional regions and repeating regions seen in Chapter 7 to use dynamic data on pages based on templates.

Template-based pages can also be exported as XML for use in other applications or environments that take XML-tagged documents as input. XML documents created outside Dreamweaver can be imported as the basis for templates.

Templates can take a bit of getting used to, but they are useful tools for repeating design, graphic, and even dynamic elements across many pages in a site. In this chapter we look at getting the most out of using the various kinds of regions to insert content onto already-designed pages. We also take a look at how you can use template syntax and JavaScript to add interactivity.

About .DWT Files and Template Syntax

Dreamweaver template documents use the .DWT extension and are listed in the New Document dialog box (**Figure 14.1**) and the Templates folder in your local site (**Figure 14.2**). When you design a template page, you designate regions of that page as editable. The rest is locked in the Document window, so that when pages are created based on that template, only marked editable regions can be changed.

These regions are marked with XML tags so that you can import data from a database to insert into those regions.

And when you give a coworker the page to edit by hand in the Document window, he or she won't be able to change any locked regions.

If you redesign a template after you've based pages on it, you can easily perform a local update on all pages that use that template.

For instance, if you redesign your site to use a new page background, logo, copyright date, and table width, you simply edit a single file—the template document—and then update all pages based on that template (**Figure 14.3**). After you update the pages, you need to re-upload them to the Web server before your changes will be live.

Template tools

Templates have a category on the Assets panel (**Figure 14.4**), which is part of the Files panel group. To display Templates, select Window > Assets from the menu bar, and then click on the Templates button 📄.

The top half of the Assets panel displays a preview of the template's content, and the bottom half lists the templates available to your local site. (Each local site has its own Templates folder.)

Figure 14.1 You can base a new file on a template in the New Document dialog box. When you click on the Templates tab, the title bar says New from Template, but this is the same New Document dialog box we've been using throughout this book.

Figure 14.2 Templates are stored in the Templates folder in your local site.

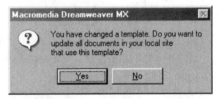

Figure 14.3 You can automatically update all pages based on a template.

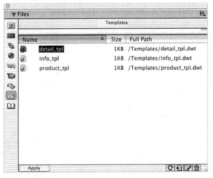

Figure 14.4 Templates have a category all to themselves in the Assets panel.

About template tags

Dreamweaver templates use standard HTML in combination with the DWT flavor of XML.

Table 14.1 lists the XML tags used in templates documents. In documents *based on* templates, the word `Template` is replaced by the word `Instance` in all tags.

Table 14.1

Dreamweaver Template Tags

TAG	PURPOSE
`<!-- TemplateBeginEditable name="..." -->` `<!-- TemplateEndEditable -->`	Editable region. Used on all templates.
`<!-- TemplateParam name="..." type="..." value="..." -->`	Template parameter. Used for writing template expressions, as well as to set conditions for optional regions.
`<!-- TemplateBeginRepeat name="..." -->` `<!-- TemplateEndRepeat -->`	Repeating region.
`<!-- TemplateBeginIf cond="..." -->` `<!--TemplateEndIf-->`	Optional region. You must write a conditional statement for an optional region.
`<!-- TemplateBeginPassthroughIf cond="..." -->` `<!-- TemplateEndPassthroughIf -->`	Used to pass template tags from a parent template to a nested template.
`<!-- TemplateBeginMultipleIf -->` `<!-- TemplateEndMultipleIf -->`	A multiple-condition statement used with optional regions.
`<!-- TemplateBeginPassthroughMultipleIf -->` `<!-- TemplateEndPassthroughMultipleIf -->`	Used when inserting optional regions with multiple conditions with nested templates
`<!-- TemplateBeginIfClause cond="..." -->` `<!-- TemplateEndIfClause -->`	A clause used with a conditional statement.
`<!-- TemplateBeginPassthroughIfClause cond="..." -->` `<!-- TemplateEndPassthroughIfClause -->`	Used to set conditions under which a statement is passed through to a nested template.
`<!-- TemplateExpr expr="..." -->` OR `@@...@@`	Used to insert a template expression.
`<!-- TemplatePassthroughExpr expr="..." -->`	Used when a template expression controls a nested template.
`<!-- TemplateInfo codeOutsideHTMLIsLocked="true" -->`	Insert this tag to lock all scripts that appear outside the `<html>` tag. Set value as false if the application server should be allowed to edit the script.

`<!-- InstanceBegin template="/Templates/templatename.dwt"`
`→ codeOutsideHTMLIsLocked="..." -->`
`<!-- InstanceEnd -->`
	In pages based on a template, defines which template the document references.

About template regions

Previous versions of Dreamweaver used editable regions to define template instances. MX expands on that concept with the following:

- **Editable regions** are containers for content that can be changed on pages based on your template.

- **Repeating regions** are items that will repeat on your page. **Repeating tables** are a subtype of repeating regions. Repeating regions are not themselves editable, but you can insert an editable region within a repeating region or repeating table.

- **Optional regions** are items that are included or hidden in a document based on the results of conditional statements. You must write these statements using template expressions.

- **Editable Tag Attributes** allow you to set one or more attributes of a selected tag as modifiable. This can include the `<body>` tag and can be used to allow modification of text or table formatting.

About template expressions

Dreamweaver templates use a subset of JavaScript called the Template Expression Language. You can define expressions using one of two comment styles:

```
<!-- TemplateExpr: expr = "expresson"-->
```

or

```
@@(expression)@@
```

✔ Tip

- Although it is not reflected in the often excellent Dreamweaver documentation, the parentheses around the expression are required when using the @@ shortcut.

You use expressions in the `.DWT` document, and when you create a page based on the template, Dreamweaver will compute the expression and will display the appropriate value.

You can use an expression to compute or save a value that is then displayed in a document. You can also define if and multiple-if conditional statements using expressions.

You can use most normal JavaScript operators. So you can write an expression like this:

```
@@(firstName+" "+lastName)@@, which
would concatenate two variables.
```

The Template Expression Language supports the following features and operators:

- numeric literals, string literals (double-quote syntax only), boolean literals (`true` or `false`)

- variable reference (see **Table 14.2, Expression Object Model** for the defined variables)

- field reference (the "dot" operator)

- unary operators: +, -, ~, !

- binary operators: +, -, *, /, %, &, |, ^, &&, ||, <, <=, >, >=, ==, !=, <<, >>

- conditional operator: ?:

- parentheses: ()

The following types are used: boolean, floating point, string, and object. The only objects available are those defined in **Table 14.2**.

Dreamweaver templates do not support the use of JavaScript "null" or "undefined" types. Nor do they allow scalar types to be implicitly converted into an object; thus, the expression `"abc".length` would trigger an error, instead of yielding the value 3.

Figure 14.5 The Save As Template dialog box lists templates that already exist.

<<Template>> (overview_tpl.dwt)

Figure 14.6 Templates identify themselves in the title bar.

Creating Templates

The first step is creating the template file itself.

To base a template on an existing file:

1. Open the file you'd like to use as the template for other pages on your site.

2. From the menu bar, select File > Save as Template. The Save As Template dialog box will appear (**Figure 14.5**). Any existing templates will be listed in the Existing Templates list box.

3. If you have more than one local site, select the site the template will reside in from the Site drop-down menu.

4. Type a filename for the template in the Save As dialog box. The .dwt extension will automatically be appended to the file.

5. Click on Save to save the file as a template.

The template will now be displayed in the Document window instead of the original HTML file. You can tell a template by the title bar—it says <<Template>> (**Figure 14.6**).

CREATING TEMPLATES

To create a template from scratch:

1. On the Templates category of the Assets panel, click on the New Template button ⊞. A new Template icon will appear in the Assets panel (**Figure 14.7**).

   or

   On the Templates panel of the Insert toolbar, click on the Make Template button ▤.

2. In the Assets panel, type a name for the new template in place of "Untitled," and press Enter (Return).

3. Still in the Assets panel, double-click the name of the template, or click on the Edit button ✏. A blank Document window will appear. You'll see the name of the template file (*nn*.dwt) displayed in the Document window title bar.

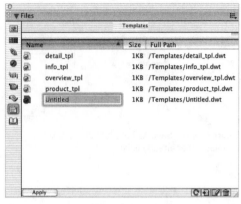

Figure 14.7 New templates show up in the Assets panel.

Using the <head> Tag With Template Files

In pages based on a template, page properties that appear as attributes of the <body> tag are generally not editable, although the page title is. However, you can set any HTML attribute as editable; see *Using editable tag attributes*, later in this chapter.

In previous versions of Dreamweaver, the <head> tag was not at all editable, and all CSS and JavaScript had to be added to the template page and could not be changed on instance pages. (It's still easier to define CSS styles or link to an external style sheet on the template doc itself, in most cases.)

In Dreamweaver MX, the following tag appears within the <head> tag:

```
<!-- TemplateBeginEditable
→ name="head" -->
<!-- TemplateEndEditable -->
```

To make head content editable, set it within that tag. To make *some* head content not editable, set it outside that tag. To lock the <head> entirely (excepting the <title>), remove the `TemplateBeginEditable` comment tag.

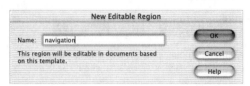

Figure 14.8 You specify options for an editable region in this dialog box.

Figure 14.9 Editable region names are highlighted in the Document window.

Figure 14.10 You can discard template markup.

Setting Editable Regions

For the parts of your page design that you want to be modifiable on every document that is based on your design, use an editable region.

To create a new editable region:

1. Click to place the insertion point where you want the new editable region to appear.

2. From the menu bar, select Insert > Template Objects > Editable Region.

   or

   On the Templates tab of the Insert toolbar, click on the Editable Region button. Either way, the New Editable Region dialog box will appear (**Figure 14.8**).

3. Type a name for the editable region in the text box, using only alphanumeric characters—nothing funny and no brackets.

4. Click on OK to close the New Editable Region dialog box and return to the Document window. The name of the editable region will appear highlighted in the Document window (**Figure 14.9**) in a little box with the name of the editable region on top. You can edit this text, if you like.

✔ Tip

■ For pages based on templates, we will learn what to do with these and other regions in the section *Creating Pages Based on Templates*.

Discarding Template Markup

You can export all your template-based pages to another site minus their XML markup. From the menu bar select Modify > Templates > Export Without Markup. The Export Site Without Template Markup dialog box will appear (**Figure 14.10**). Save your page in the proper folder, and click on OK.

Marking page regions as editable

You can also create a page element and then mark it as editable.

To set an editable region:

1. Type and select an object or some place-holder text, such as "Headline or Image Goes Here" (**Figure 14.11**).

2. From the menu bar, select Insert > Template Objects > Editable Region.

   or

   On the Insert toolbar select the Templates tab, then click on the Editable Region button . The New Editable Region dialog box will appear (Figure 14.8).

3. Type a name for the editable region in the text box. Avoid funky characters, and don't use quotation marks or <angle brackets>.

   Click on OK. The editable region will be boxed in the template's Document window with the name of the editable region on its tab (**Figure 14.12**).

Figure 14.11 It helps to have identifiable placeholder text, so the designer knows what should be in an editable region.

Figure 14.12 The box identifies an editable region.

```
14  <p><!-- TemplateBeginEditable name="SingleBlock" -->
15  Text 1 - Region can consist of only one paragraph or
    block.<br>
16  The user will not be allowed to press Enter to start a new
    block within this region.
17  <!-- TemplateEndEditable --></p>
18
19
20  <!-- TemplateBeginEditable name="MultipleBlocks" -->
21  <p>Text 2 - Block can be expanded to include many
    paragraphs.</p>
22  <!-- TemplateEndEditable -->
```

Figure 14.13 The editable region starting on line 14 exists inside of a <p> tag, so no additional blocks can be created inside that region. The editable region starting on line 20 includes the <p> tag inside the region, so we can do whatever text formatting we like in this region.

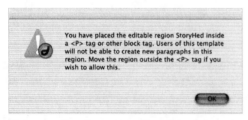

You have placed the editable region StoryHed inside a <P> tag or other block tag. Users of this template will not be able to create new paragraphs in this region. Move the region outside the <P> tag if you wish to allow this.

OK

Figure 14.14 Templates created in earlier versions of Dreamweaver sometimes trigger this dialog box.

```
<p align="left">
<!-- TemplateBeginEditable name="EditRegion7" -->
<font face="Arial, Helvetica, sans-serif">Bottom </font>
<!-- TemplateEndEditable -->
</p>
```

Figure 14.15 Formatting in editable regions can be altered.

```
<p align="left">
<font face="Arial, Helvetica, sans-serif">
<!-- TemplateBeginEditable name="EditRegion7" -->
Bottom
<!-- TemplateEndEditable -->
</font>
```

Figure 14.16 One way to make formatting unalterable is to move the <font> tags outside the editable region...

```
<p align="left" class="storyClose">
<!-- TemplateBeginEditable name="EditRegion7" -->
  Bottom
  <!-- TemplateEndEditable -->
</p>
```

Figure 14.17 ...but a better way is with CSS.

Editable Region Quirks

Marking editable regions is easy for the most part, but there are several variables you must take into account when incorporating text formatting, tables, and layers.

Block formatting

In order to allow text on template pages to be expanded beyond a single paragraph, you must set editable regions outside block tags such as <p>, <blockquote>, <hn>, and so on (**Figure 14.13**). In some templates created with previous versions of Dreamweaver, this wasn't an issue, but if you open these in MX, you may find a dialog box like the one in **Figure 14.14** advising you to move your <p> tags to inside the region tags. Oddly enough, placing an editable region inside the <i> and <b> tags brings up a similar error message.

Text formatting

If you set text formatting in an editable region using HTML tags, those tags can be altered or removed (**Figure 14.15**). In other words, if your region StoryHed is set in the Georgia font, that font face can be changed on template pages.

To make text formatting unalterable on template pages, you have two choices. First, you could, in Code view, move the <font> and other tags to *outside* the region tags (**Figure 14.16**). See *Block formatting*, above, about an error message that may pop up if you do this with some tags.

The better choice is to use CSS. You can redefine entire tags, if you want to make all body text appear in a certain font, for example. For style classes, apply them to an editable region, and the class will be applied to the tag, or the <span> tag will be wrapped around the region (**Figure 14.17**). You can attach a style sheet to a template or you can include CSS formatting inline in the template's head tag.

Tables

You can mark an entire table as editable, and you can mark an entire table row <tr> or a single table cell <td> as editable, but you cannot mark a column or a few cells as an editable region. If you attempt to do so, Dreamweaver will make the table row or the table the content of the editable region.

If you select a cell <td> within a table and set it as editable, that cell and its attributes and contents can be edited.

If you select the *contents* of a cell and set it as editable, the cell's contents will be editable, but the <td> attributes will not be editable.

Layers

If you select a layer <div> and make it editable, all layer attributes and layer content will be editable (**Figure 14.18**).

If you select the *contents* of a layer and make it editable, those contents can be changed but the layer itself cannot be modified—not moved, not resized, no color changes, and so on.

Figure 14.18 You can make layers into editable regions by selecting the <div> tag and marking it as editable.

Figure 14.19 Select the tag whose attributes you wish to make editable in the tag selector.

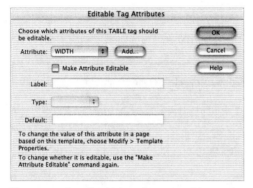

Figure 14.20 Specify which attribute you wish to make editable.

Figure 14.21 Only those attributes already applied to the tag will appear in the menu.

Figure 14.22 You can specify a different attribute here.

Figure 14.23 Click this checkbox in the Editable Tags Attribute dialog box to make the attribute editable.

Setting Editable Tag Attributes

New in Dreamweaver MX, you can choose to make certain tag attributes editable in template pages.

To set a tag attribute as editable:

1. On the template document, click on the object or text you want to edit, and select its tag in the Tag selector (**Figure 14.19**).

2. From the menu bar, select Modify > Templates > Make Attribute Editable. The Editable Tag Attributes dialog box will appear (**Figure 14.20**).

3. Select your attribute from the Attribute drop-down menu (**Figure 14.21**).

   Only those attributes already applied to the tag will appear in the menu; to add another, click on Add. A dialog box will appear (**Figure 14.22**); type your attribute in the text box and click on OK to return to the Editable Tag Attributes dialog box.

4. With your attribute selected in the Attribute drop-down menu, check the Make Attribute Editable checkbox (**Figure 14.23**); more options will appear.

5. Label your attribute something memorable, like sidebarColor or catalogImage.

continues on next page

SETTING EDITABLE TAG ATTRIBUTES

6. Now, from the Type drop-down menu, choose how the attribute can be edited on template pages (**Figure 14.24**):

 ◆ **Text** allows the user to type a value.

 ◆ **URL** allows the user to set a local path for a page, an image, or a media object.

 ◆ **Color** allows the user to use the color picker.

 ◆ **True/False** is used mainly for JavaScript and CSS functions.

 ◆ **Number** limits the entries to numbers, for items such as height or Vspace.

7. Type a default value—which will show up on the page until the value is changed—in the Default text box.

8. Repeat Steps 4-7 for additional attributes.

9. Click on OK to save your changes.

In the Document window for your template file, you'll see in Code view, the formatting for the tag. But in Design view, any visible font formatting will be removed from your text (**Figure 14.25**). On pages based on your template, however (**Figure 14.26**), the default settings will take effect.

In the Property inspector (**Figure 14.27**), you'll see the attributes you originally set replaced by strange-looking code like this: @@(attribute)@@. This is in Dreamweaver's Template Expression Markup Language.

We'll show you how to use editable attributes on Web pages in the section *Creating Pages Based on Templates*.

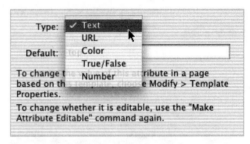

Figure 14.24 Select a type of value for the attribute.

Figure 14.25 In the template, the attributes don't affect the text.

```
<table width="75%" border="1"
  cellpadding="1" cellspacing="1">
```

Figure 14.26 In an instance based on the file, however, they do affect the code.

Figure 14.27 The value for the attribute is represented by a template expression.

Figure 14.28 You can select an already-existing tag to make into a repeating region.

✔ Tips

■ To make an attribute uneditable, follow Steps 1-3, above, and then uncheck the Make Attribute Editable checkbox.

■ Beyond the table and table tags, you can use the editable attribute feature on such tags as <body> (to allow background and link colors to be changed); <img> (to allow source, alignment, and spacing to be changed); <a> (to allow link paths on otherwise uneditable text to be changed), as well as on all sorts of text and font tags, to allow things like color and size to be changed.

Figure 14.29 You can name your repeating region here.

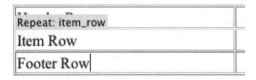

Figure 14.30 The repeating region shows up only once on the template.

Setting Repeating Regions

Setting repeating regions is similar to setting editable regions. You place the repeating region only once, and then on the pages based on that template, you can add instances of that region.

As we saw with editable regions, you can either select some text and then wrap the repeating region around it, or you can insert the region and then edit the text inside it.

To add a repeating region:

1. Click to place the insertion point where you want the repeating region to appear, *or* select text or an object you want to make into a repeating region (**Figure 14.28**).

2. From the menu bar, select Insert > Template Objects > Repeating Region.

   or

   Click the Repeating Region button 🔳 on the Template tab of the Insert toolbar.

   Either way, the New Repeating Region dialog box will appear (**Figure 14.29**).

3. Type a name for your repeating region, and click on OK.

4. The repeating region will appear a single time on your template (**Figure 14.30**).

Unless you want the same text repeated throughout your page, remember to add an editable region inside the repeating region.

To insert an editable region inside the repeating region:

1. Select the text inside the repeating region.

2. From the menu bar, select Insert > Template Objects > Editable Region. The New Editable Region dialog box will appear.

3. Type a name for your editable region, and click on OK.

4. The editable region will appear inside the repeating region (**Figure 14.31**).

✔ Tip

■ You can set a table row as a repeating region, in which case users of the template page will be able to add rows to the table if they need them.

Creating a repeating table

You also have the option of adding to a template a table in which only some areas repeat, such as you might use for a catalog, schedule, or sidebar. For an editable table, you choose which areas you want to be editable. (Other areas may be reserved for header info, blank rows, server-side includes, and so on. See **Figure 14.32**).

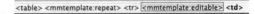

Figure 14.31 To make the copies of the repeating region different, you need to add an editable region inside the repeating region.

Figure 14.32 Usually, you don't want to repeat the first row or so of a table, so it can be a column head.

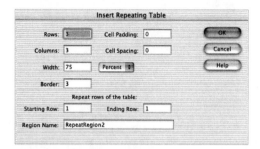

Figure 14.33 Here's where you specify the repeating table options.

Figure 14.34 Repeating tables automatically insert an editable region in each cell.

To insert a repeating table:

1. Open the template on which you want to place the repeating table entry.

2. From the menu bar, select Insert > Template Objects > Repeating Table.

   or

   Click on the Repeating Table button ⊞ on the Templates tab of the Insert toolbar.

   Either way, the Insert Repeating Table dialog box will appear (**Figure 14.33**).

3. The Repeating Table dialog box has two functions: placing the code for the table itself, and designating which areas of the table will be marked as repeating and editable regions.

   In the top half of the dialog box, set the number of columns and rows for your table, as well as any additional table attributes such as border.

4. In the Repeat rows of the table area of the dialog box, set the row at which you want the repeating regions to start and end.

   These numbers should not exceed the total number of columns and rows; you can't stop repeating at Row 7 in a table with 6 rows.

5. In the Region Name text box, type a name for the repeating table region.

6. Click on OK.

The table will appear on your page, including a generically named, blank editable region in each cell you set as repeating (**Figure 14.34**).

✔ Tip

■ Repeating Tables should not be confused with Dynamic Tables, which are a feature of Dreamweaver's data-driven applications tools.

About Optional Template Regions

An optional region, also new in Dreamweaver MX, is a region that may or may not appear on a page, depending on context and whether it's needed. You set template parameters to determine whether the optional region will appear on a page.

You can use this feature to allow the person who creates a page based on your template to include the section if it is appropriate. In an online catalog, for example, some products might have optional accessories, whereas some do not. Fish food does not require any accessories, in general, whereas someone buying an aquarium might want a pump, a filter, or pretty colored gravel.

Although you insert an optional region using a dialog box, you must code the expressions yourself in order for the regions to work in any meaningful way. There is no equivalent of the Behaviors panel for writing these expressions.

Optional regions in templates use a language called Template Expression Language, which is a variant of JavaScript.

✔ Tip

- It's important to remember that template expressions are resolved at design time, not at run time. Which is to say that any template expressions that the page uses will run when you *save* the document based on the template, and not when the server spits out the file for a user request. These are scripts in the template file, but act as static HTML in the pages based on that file.

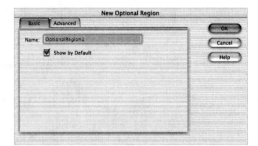

Figure 14.35 This is the simple version of the Optional Region dialog box.

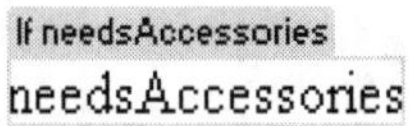

Figure 14.36 The tab for the optional region starts with "If" and includes the name of the region. The region we just inserted won't function until we add conditions for it in the next section.

The idea of an optional region is simple, but its execution is complex enough that you need to understand JavaScript as well as Dreamweaver's template tags, and be comfortable writing your own. You can view a list of template tags and some rudimentary examples of template expression code in Dreamweaver's help files under Working With Multiple Pages > Reference.

To insert an optional region:

1. Open the template on which you want to place the repeating table entry.

2. From the menu bar, select Insert > Template Objects > Optional Region.

   or

   Click on the Optional Region button on the Templates tab of the Insert toolbar. The New Optional Region dialog box will appear **(Figure 14.35)**.

3. In the Name text box, enter the name of the parameter that will control whether the region appears or not.

   It's a good idea to name the region something that will indicate what the region is for. In the above example, we named the region "needsAccessories".

4. Click OK to close the dialog box and add the region to the page **(Figure 14.36)**.

To actually use the optional region, you need to add an editable region inside it. See *Setting Editable Regions*, earlier in this chapter.

Of course, you need to know how to turn the optional region on or off.

ABOUT OPTIONAL TEMPLATE REGIONS

To activate or deactivate an optional region:

1. Open a page based on a template with an optional region.

2. From the menu bar, select Modify > Template Properties.

   The Template Properties dialog box will appear (**Figure 14.37**).

3. Select the parameter that controls the optional region (the one you entered in the Name text box in the New Optional Region dialog box).

   A check box will appear at the bottom of the dialog box (**Figure 14.38**).

4. Check or uncheck the check box to show or hide the optional region.

You can also create multiple optional regions that are all controlled by the same parameter.

To add a second optional region controlled by the same parameter:

1. Open a template with an optional region.

2. From the menu bar, select Insert > Template Objects > Optional Region.

   or

   Click on the Optional Region button 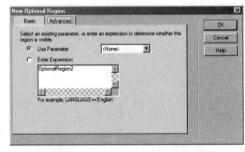 on the Templates tab of the Insert toolbar. The New Optional Region dialog box will appear.

3. Click the Advanced tab of the dialog box. The dialog box will change to reflect your choice (**Figure 14.39**).

4. From the Use Parameter drop-down menu, select the parameter that controls the already-inserted optional region.

5. Click OK to close the dialog box and add the region to the page.

Now that you have an idea of some of the components of templates, let's look at how to create them.

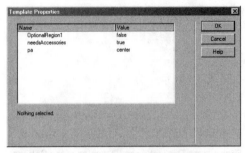

Figure 14.37 The Template Properties dialog box allows you to change the value of variables.

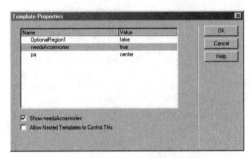

Figure 14.38 The checkboxes reflect the state of the variables.

Figure 14.39 The advanced version of the dialog box allows you to reuse variables or create more complicated conditions.

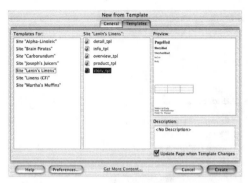

Figure 14.40 In the New Document dialog box, you can base your document on any existing template.

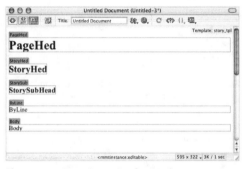

Figure 14.41 A new instance of a template.

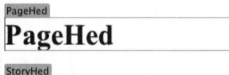

Figure 14.42 Editable regions are marked in blue (although not in this book, obviously), and are marked with the name of the region.

Figure 14.43 On Windows, non-editable regions will show you a "No" sign when you mouse over them in the Document window.

Creating Pages Based on Templates

Once you've got a template with at least one editable region, you can create pages based on that template.

To create a template page:

1. From the menu bar, select File > New. The New Document dialog box will appear.

2. Select the Templates tab. In the Templates For list, select the site you're working with, and all available templates will appear. Select the name of the template on which you want to base your page (**Figure 14.40**).

3. Click Create. The New Document dialog box will close, and a new document window will appear (**Figure 14.41**), that includes the following elements:

   ◆ The formatting of your template, along with any HTML elements or page properties

   ◆ The editable regions of your template, marked in blue boxes with the name of each region on its tab (**Figure 14.42**)

   ◆ Any repeating regions on your template, marked in pale blue boxes.

   Locked regions are not marked but are untouchable. In Windows, this is indicated by a "Don't" sign (**Figure 14.43**).

CREATING PAGES BASED ON TEMPLATES

✔ Tips

- You can also right-click (Ctrl+click) a template icon in the Assets panel and select New From Template from the context menu.

- Basically, any text or objects that are within editable regions can be edited, and any that are not cannot be edited.

- Click within any editable region and edit its content as you would on any other page.

- All editable regions appear at the bottom of the menu Modify > Templates > [region name] (**Figure 14.44**).

- If you want to be able to edit any area of the document, you can detach the page from its template—see the sidebar *Void If Detached.*

Using repeating regions on a page

Repeating regions work pretty much the same as editable regions except for their defining characteristic: They repeat. Repeating region borders on pages based on templates look pretty funny (**Figure 14.45**). Here's how they work:

To repeat a region:

- Click the + (plus) button on the region.

A new region will appear (**Figures 14.46 and 14.47**). If the repeating region is a table row, a new row will appear.

To edit content in a region:

- Click within the repeating region's Editable region box, and add your content (**Figure 14.48**).

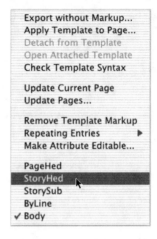

Figure 14.44 Editable regions appear in the Modify > Templates menu.

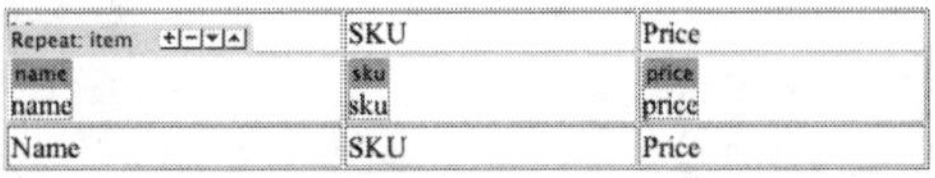

Figure 14.45 The repeating region controls can look confusing on the page.

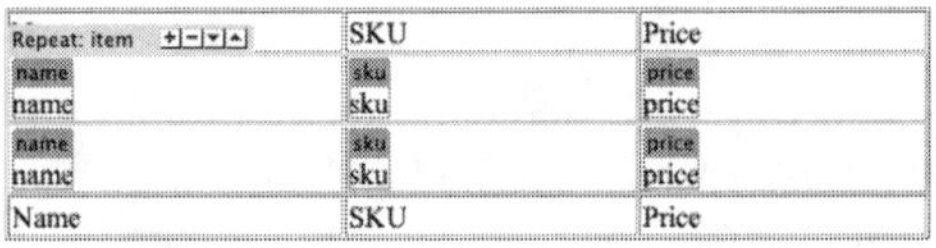

Figure 14.46 Add a new copy of the region by clicking the + (plus) button.

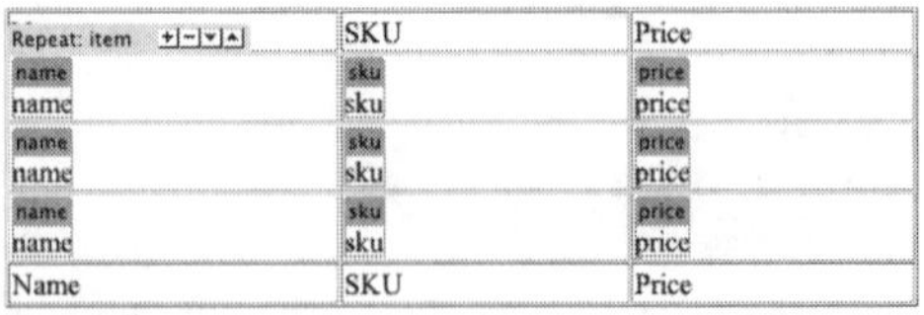

Figure 14.47 You can add as many copies as you want.

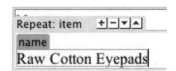

Figure 14.48 You edit content in a repeating region just like anywhere else.

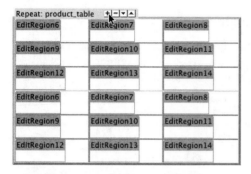

Figure 14.49 Adding rows to repeating tables works just the same way as repeating regions.

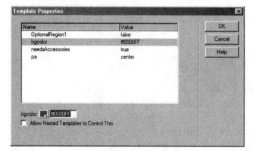

Figure 14.50 You can edit tag attributes you've specified in the Template Properties dialog box.

To subtract a region:

◆ Click the – (minus) button. The region will disappear.

To rearrange regions:

◆ Click on a region, and use the Up and Down arrow keys to change its order in the list.

Using repeating tables

Repeating tables work pretty much the same. You can add content only within editable regions. Click + (plus) to add cells (**Figure 14.49**).

Using editable tag attributes

To edit tag attributes you set as editable, use the Template Properties dialog box.

To edit tag attributes:

1. From the menu bar, select Edit > Template Properties. The Template Properties dialog box will appear (**Figure 14.50**).

2. Make any changes you like to the attributes offered.

3. Click on OK to apply your changes.

Template Troubleshooting

Dreamweaver should verify the syntax of your templates on the fly, but it doesn't always happen. You can find out if your template has any errors, and get the line numbers, by selecting Modify > Templates > Check Template Syntax from the menu bar.

Try these pointers.

◆ If you switch local sites but the Assets panel won't display current templates, click the Refresh button on the Assets panel, or hold down the Shift key while clicking to rebuild your site cache. You may have to quit and restart Dreamweaver.

◆ If you get an error message that a <P> or other block tag is inside the editable region, see *Editable Region Quirks,* earlier in this chapter, and Figure 14.13 in particular. This may not be an error on your part.

◆ If you get an error message that a template references itself, select Modify > Templates > Detach from Template.

◆ If you get an error message that a parameter doesn't exist, two things may have happened. First, you might be trying to insert an optional region without giving it any parameters, or by giving it parameters that seem right but that Dreamweaver doesn't like. Or you may have tried to rename an editable attribute using the dialog box made for that purpose. Instead, you'll have to go into Code view and make sure that the editable attribute names referenced in the body of the document match the ones in the head of the document.

◆ If you rename a template region and then update pages based on that template, sometimes instead of regions or attributes getting renamed sensibly, you'll get the scary-looking Inconsistent Region name dialog box. Follow the instructions in Steps 5-7 of *Attaching an Existing Page to a Template,* and transfer your attributes or region names in turn.

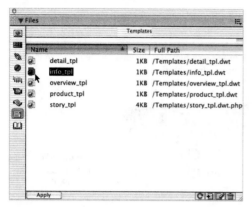

Figure 14.51 You can delete templates from the Assets panel.

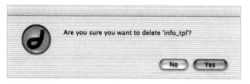

Figure 14.52 Dreamweaver makes sure you really want to delete a template.

Figure 14.53 The New From Template dialog box allows you to specify that a new file you create is not linked to the template...

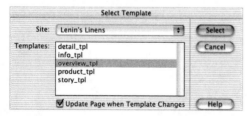

Figure 14.54 ...as does the Select Template dialog box.

Deleting, Renaming, and Editing Templates and Regions

You can update a template at any point in the process.

Editing template documents

Double-click the name of any template file in the Assets panel to open the template and edit it.

When you rename or edit a .dwt file, Dreamweaver will ask you if you want to update all pages based on it. See *Performing Routine Updates*, later in this chapter. If you want to attach pages to a new template, you can rename the file, skip the update, and create a new file with the old template name.

Deleting templates

When it's time to get rid of a template, you can delete it. Just select it in the Assets panel (**Figure 14.51**) and click on the Delete button 🗑. A dialog box will appear asking you if you're sure you want to delete the template (**Figure 14.52**).

References to the deleted template will not be discarded; you'll need to attach affected pages to a new template or remove the code. You can use the Clean Up HTML feature to remove template code from a page.

✔ Tip

■ When you create a new page based on a template, you use the New From Template dialog box (**Figure 14.53**); when you attach a page to a template, you use the Select Template dialog box (**Figure 14.54**). Both these dialog boxes have a checkbox, Update Page When Template Changes. If you deselect this checkbox, the page will look like the template but will not be included in any updates. (This feature did not work in Dreamweaver 4.)

Renaming regions

To rename a template region, select its tab in the Document window, and then type a new name for the region in the Property inspector (**Figure 14.55**).

Removing regions

To unmark a region, first select it. Then, from the menu bar, select Modify > Templates > Remove Template Markup. The region will no longer be editable.

You can also remove selected template tags. In the Tag selector, right-click (Ctrl+click) on the tag and select Remove Tag from the context menu (**Figure 14.56**).

Figure 14.55 Template regions can be renamed in the Property inspector.

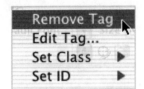

Figure 14.56 You can remove tags with the Tag selector.

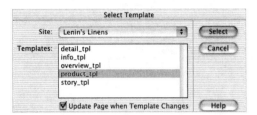

Figure 14.57 You can attach a template to existing pages.

Attaching an Existing Page to a Template

You can attach existing pages to a new template, too. You have to choose a single region to dump all the content into, though, unless the page has similar marked regions.

To attach a page to a template:

1. Open the document to which you want to attach the template. From the menu bar, select Modify > Templates > Apply Template to Page. The Select Template dialog box will appear (**Figure 14.57**).

2. Select the name of the template that you want.

3. To automatically have this page updated when you edit the template, leave the checkbox checked. For more on updating, see *Performing Routine Updates,* later on.

4. Click on Select.

continues on next page

ATTACHING AN EXISTING PAGE TO A TEMPLATE

5. If the document contains content that can't be assigned automatically to an editable region, the Inconsistent Region Names dialog box will appear. (**Figure 14.58**).

Because templates only allow new content to appear in editable regions, you need to select an editable region in which to stick your content. You'll be able to move it from region to region once the page is reopened, but for now, you have to pick one.

 ◆ For region names coming from one template to a different one, select each region name in turn and apply a region name from the current template by selecting the new region from the Move Content to New Region drop-down menu (**Figure 14.59**).

 ◆ For visible content, select Document body and then select a region from the Move Content to New Region drop-down menu.

 ◆ For head content such as scripts and CSS, select doctitle from the menu to transfer those items to the head tag; or Nowhere to discard the head content. (This is a sneaky way to get extra CSS and scripts into a template-based page.)

 ◆ To discard content, select Nowhere from the drop-down menu.

 ◆ To drop all your content into the same region, apply content to one region and then click on Use For All.

6. When all your content is taken care of, click on OK.

7. When the dialog box closes, your content will appear in the region you selected. You can edit your page now.

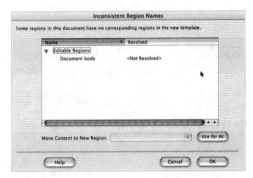

Figure 14.58 This dialog box indicates Dreamweaver can't readily figure out where to put your content.

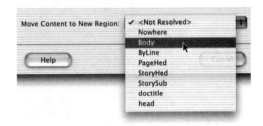

Figure 14.59 You can assign a region to content from a different template.

✔ Tips

 ■ In Step 2, you can create a page that *looks like* your template but isn't attached to the template file. Just deselect the Update Page When Template Changes checkbox.

 ■ If a piece of placeholder text, for example, "HeadingA," matches the name of a template region (in our example, it would also be called "HeadingA"), Dreamweaver will automatically match the placeholder text with the editable region.

 ■ If you've created different versions of a basic design, and you've used the same region names on both template files, you can transfer content from page to page easily. In other words, if the blue template and the orange template use the same region names, you can detach a page from one template and then attach it to the other.

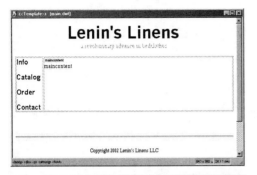

Figure 14.60 Nested templates allow you to have a broad design for your site and specific designs for each section.

Using Nested Templates

In Dreamweaver MX, Macromedia has introduced *nested templates*, which are templates that are based on other templates. One situation in which you would use nested templates is when all the pages of a Web site (for a company, say) have certain elements in common (company logo, copyright information), but sections of the site (each department's portion of the site) are different (**Figure 14.60**). Nested templates are also sometimes called *embedded templates*.

Creating nested templates is pretty simple. Using them, on the other hand, can occasionally be a little more complicated.

To create a nested template:

1. Create a main template. We'll call it Main.dwt (**Figure 14.61**).

2. Create a page based on that template. We'll call it page.html.

3. Save page.html as a template (File > Save As Template), or click the Nested Template button 🗐 on the Templates tab of the Insert toolbar.

   We'll call that second template sub.dwt (**Figure 14.62**), and we can edit it so that it contains different section heads, slightly different layout, and so on. We can add editable regions, too.

4. Now, create a page based on that second template. We'll call it section.html (**Figure 14.63**).

This may seem straightforward, and it pretty much is, but as soon as you try to exert some additional control over which sections are editable and when, the process can get almost as complicated as this sentence.

Keep in mind that all editable regions in a base template (Main.dwt) will appear on all pages based on either the nested template or the base template. In other words, both page.html and section.html will both contain the same editable regions, even if you add the region to Main.dwt after Sub.dwt and section.html have been created.

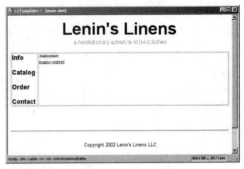

Figure 14.61 The main template contains the overall site design.

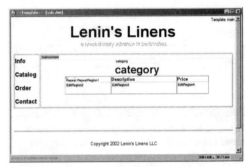

Figure 14.62 The second template contains the section design and is based on the main template.

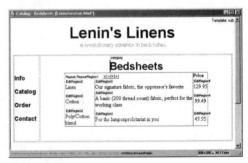

Figure 14.63 The page is based on the second template, but changes to the main template ripple through.

Figure 14.64 Editable regions from the main template pass through to the instance page...

Figure 14.65 ...unless you put an editable region into it.

```
<!-- InstanceBeginEditable name="EditRegion1" -->
This content is editable in both
templates
<!-- InstanceEndEditable -->
```

Figure 14.66 The code for the editable region is highlighted with View > Code.

Basically, any editable regions from the main template will be editable in documents based on the nested template (**Figure 14.64**). There is one exception to this. When you put an editable region into a nested template, the editable region that came originally from the main template is no longer editable in documents based on the nested template (**Figure 14.65**).

In some cases, you might want to make an editable region passed through from a master template uneditable. If you have a main template for your site, for example, and a nested template for each day of the week, the day of the week must be editable in the main template, but you don't want it to be editable in instances of the specific day's template. The template for Friday should always read Friday at the top of the page, for example. Fortunately, there's an easy, if not necessarily obvious, way to lock that region.

To lock an inherited editable region:

1. Open the nested template.

2. Select the editable region you want to lock.

3. From the menu, select View > Code.

   The code for the editable region will be highlighted (**Figure 14.66**).

4. Anywhere between the
   `<!-- InstanceBeginEditable -->` tag
   and the `<!-- InstanceEndEditable -->`
   tag, add the following code:

   `@@(" ")@@`

The region will now be locked in pages based on the nested template.

USING NESTED TEMPLATES

Exporting as XML

You can import and export the editable parts of template-based documents as XML.

Because the editable regions of a Dreamweaver template are all named, you may name them the same things as XML tags you're using (or vice versa—name the tags for the regions). You may then export the content of a template-based file as an XML file, with the editable region names converted into XML tags.

To export editable regions as XML:

1. Open a page based on a template.

2. From the menu bar, select File > Export > Template Data as XML. The Export Template Data as XML dialog box will appear.

3. You may use one of two formats for the exported XML tags (**Figure 14.67**):

   ◆ The Dreamweaver format: `<item name="RegionName"></item>`

   ◆ The editable region = tag name format: `<RegionName></RegionName>`

   Which style you choose depends on whether you want to work with existing HTML tags from either a database or another related XML document.

   Select the radio button for the format you wish to use, then click on OK. Another Export Template Data as XML dialog box will appear, this one looking like a Save As dialog box (**Figure 14.68**).

4. Select the directory in which to save the XML file, and type a name for the file in the File name text box.

5. Click on Save.

You now have an XML file containing the contents of your page, including both XML and HTML tags (**Figure 14.69**). You may edit this file in Dreamweaver's Code inspector or in another text editor.

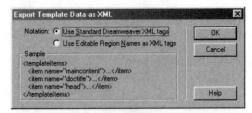

Figure 14.67 Exported XML tags come in two flavors.

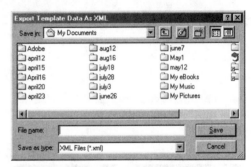

Figure 14.68 You can save your XML anywhere.

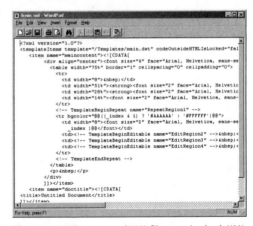

Figure 14.69 The exported XML file contains both XML and HTML tags.

EXPORTING AS XML

Figure 14.70 You can import an XML file into a template.

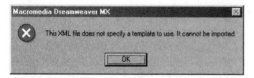

Figure 14.71 You'll get this warning if the XML file does not specify a template.

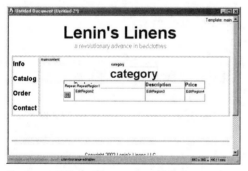

Figure 14.72 You can view a successfully imported XML file in the Document Window, in Design view...

Figure 14.73 ...and Code view.

Importing XML Data

You may also take an XML file you've previously created with Dreamweaver (or with any other program; see *Attention!*, below) and import it to use with a Dreamweaver template. The XML or item tags will become the names of editable regions. You may then add other elements such as page properties, tables, and so on to the file.

To import XML into a template:

1. From the menu bar, select File > Import > XML into Template. The Import XML dialog box will appear (**Figure 14.70**).

2. Select an XML file to use, and click Open. If the XML file does not specify a base Dreamweaver template, a warning dialog box will appear (**Figure 14.71**).

   If this happens, you need to reopen your XML file and specify a template within it.

3. A new, blank HTML window will appear. Dreamweaver will merge the XML file with the template regions, and you can view the result in the Document window (**Figure 14.72**) and the Code inspector (**Figure 14.73**).

✔ Attention!

- This method of importing works best if you first create a Dreamweaver template and export it as XML, using your desired XML tags as the names of editable regions. Failing that, you must include the `<templateItems>` tag and the name of a template within that tag. If you're preparing files from outside Dreamweaver to work with Dreamweaver features, make a copy of a file that Dreamweaver has exported as XML and use that syntax. For more about template tags, see the Help files and select Working with Multiple Pages > Reference.

Performing Routine Updates

After you edit a Dreamweaver template, you can update single pages, selected pages, or entire sites that reference that document. You'll still have to upload the updated pages to your live Web site so they'll reflect your changes.

✔ Tip

- If you rename a template, the Update Files dialog box discussed in this section will appear.

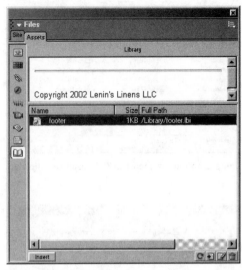

Figure 14.74 Library items appear in the Assets panel.

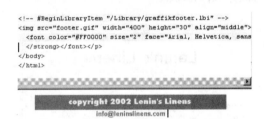

Figure 14.75 Footers are a common use for library items.

About Library Items

Library items, like templates, are updateable throughout a site and use XML tags to define that a library item exists on a page. Also similar to templates, library items are stored in the Library folder of each local site and appear in the Library category of the Assets panel (**Figure 14.74**). Library items are used for material such as footers or toolbars that you want to be able to use and update over many pages. They can be used with templates and are locked on every page that uses them.

One of the most common uses for library items is headers and footers (**Figure 14.75**). Library items and all their vagaries are described in detail in Chapter 17 of the *Dreamweaver MX for Windows and Macintosh Visual QuickStart Guide.*

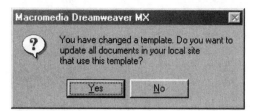

Figure 14.76 When you change a template or a library item, Dreamweaver offers to update the files using it automatically.

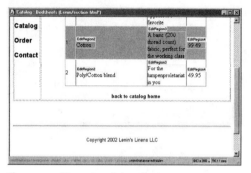

Figure 14.77 You can update a single page.

Updating when you edit

After you save changes to a template or library item, a dialog box will ask you if you want to update your site (**Figure 14.76**). This dialog box lists pages that link to the template or library item you just edited. You can click on Update, or you can postpone your edits.

Updating after you edit

You can update a single page at any time.

To update a single page:

1. Open the page you want to update in the Document window.

2. From the menu bar, select Modify > Templates > Update Current Page.

3. If everything's in order, no dialog box will appear, but the current page will be updated to reflect the newest version of the template (**Figure 14.77**).

Updating sets of pages

You can use the Update dialog box to update both library items and templates. You can update pages that use a particular library item or template, or you can update an entire site.

To update more than one page:

1. You don't need to have any particular page open to update your site. From the menu bar, select Modify > Templates > Update Pages. The Update Pages dialog box will appear (**Figure 14.78**).

2. The Update Pages window lets you update all templates in a local site, or only those pages that reference a specific template.

3. If you're going to search for a specific item, check the box for either library items or for templates (**Figure 14.79**). To update each of these in your site, check both boxes.

   To update an entire local site, select Local Site from the Look In drop-down menu. A menu of your local sites will appear; select the site you want to update (**Figure 14.80**).

   or

   To single out one library item or template and update pages that use it, select Files That Use from the Look In drop-down menu. A menu of your library items and/or templates will appear (**Figure 14.81**).

4. Click on Start. Dreamweaver will scan the selected site's cache, or site index, for references to library items and/or templates.

5. When the update process is complete, a log file will appear, detailing how many files were scanned, which files were updated, and which files, if any, are missing from the Library or Templates folder (**Figure 14.82**).

6. When you're finished perusing this information, you can close the dialog box.

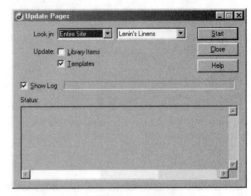

Figure 14.78 The Update Pages dialog box allows you to specify the scope of your updates.

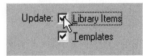

Figure 14.79 You can update templates, library items, or both.

Figure 14.80 You can update any of your local sites.

Figure 14.81 You can update only files based on a specific template or library item.

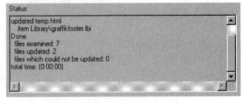

Figure 14.82 The updating process generates a log file.

Using Template Expressions

In Dreamweaver MX, Macromedia has added template expressions, which are a subset of JavaScript, that you can use to automate some of the formatting of your templates.

We'll touch on a couple of examples of how to use this language, but as we mentioned above, the crucial thing to remember about template expressions is that they happen at design time, and not at run time.

Template expressions have access to two objects: the _document object (which refers to the template) and the _repeat object, which refers to a repeating region, and is only available to expressions that occur in a repeating region. **Table 14.2** describes the Expression Object Model in more detail.

Table 14.2

Expression Object Model	
OBJECT	CONTENTS
_document	Contains the document-level template data. There is a field for each parameter in the template, as well as several fields providing built-in information about the document.
_repeat	Only defined for expressions which appear inside a repeating region. Provides built-in information about the region:

	_index	The numerical index (from Ø) of the current entry
	_numRows	The total number of entries in this repeating region
	_isFirst	True if the current entry is the first entry in its repeating region
	_isLast	True if the current entry is the last entry in its repeating region
	_prevRecord	The "_repeat" object for the previous entry. It is an error to access this property for the first entry in the region.
	_nextRecord	The "_repeat" object for the next entry. It is an error to access this property for the last entry in the region.
	_parent	In a nested repeated region, this gives the _repeat object for the enclosing (outer) repeated region. It is an error to access this property outside of a nested repeated region.

Template expressions and optional regions

When you insert an optional region, Dreamweaver writes the template expression for you. It adds a declaration of the variable to the head of the template:

```
<!-- TemplateParam
→ name= "needsAccessories"
→ type = "boolean" value = "false">
```

And it also surrounds the optional region with an if statement:

```
<!-- TemplateBeginIf
→ cond="needsAccessories" -->
<!-- TemplateEndIf -->.
```

This is by far the most common use of the if statement, but you can also do more complex ones, like

```
<!-- TemplateBeginIf cond=
→"needsAccessories && specialOffer" -->
<!-- TemplateEndIf -->
```

or something similar.

Template expressions and repeating regions

Perhaps the best use of template expressions is in a repeating region. You can do some interesting things based on the position of an element in a repeating region, which is contained in the _index property.

The easiest way to see how the _index property works is to show it on the page.

USING TEMPLATE EXPRESSIONS

Figure 14.83 You can automatically generate a row number with a template expression.

Figure 14.84 You can color alternate rows.

To show the _index in a table:

1. Create a template with a repeating table.

2. In the top leftmost table cell that is not an editable region, add the following code: @@(_index)@@.

3. Save the template.

4. Create a new page based on the template.

5. Add several rows to the repeating table.

   The row number (starting with 0) will appear in the leftmost cell of each row (**Figure 14.83**).

✔ Tip

- Because the index of the first row is 0, if you were to use that expression on an actual page, you'd probably want to use @@(_index + 1)@@.

An even more interesting thing you can do with template expressions in a repeating region is to color the backgrounds of table rows in alternating colors.

To alternate table row colors:

1. Create a template with a repeating table that repeats one row.

2. Find the spot in the code where the repeating row appears (usually right at the beginning of the repeating region).

3. In the <tr> tag, add the following code:
   bgcolor="@@((_index & 1) ? '#AAAA
   → AA' : '#FFFFFF')@@"

   The rows will now alternate between white and light gray (**Figure 14.84**).

Template expressions elsewhere

Template expressions are most useful when dealing with optional regions and repeating regions, but you can use them to control many aspects of an instance page, based on a template variable.

For example, if you had a template for your site that used an optional region to show stock prices during the week, but not on the weekend, you could use template expressions to make the day of the week appear in red on the weekend.

If your template variable is workweek, the code in the head of the template would look like this:

```
<!-- TemplateParam name= "workweek"
→ type = "boolean" value = "true">
```

To make the day of the week appear red during the weekend (when workweek is false), you would use the following code:

```
<font color="@@(workweek? '#000000' :
→ '#FF0000')@@">
```

Templates and Dynamic Content

Templates work pretty much as you would expect with dynamic content, with one consideration.

Virtually all of the various languages Dreamweaver uses to provide dynamic content require some code to be inserted before the HTML portion of the page. By default, any code outside the <HTML> tags of a template is editable.

When a instance of the template is first created, it gets whatever text is in the editable regions of the template, including outside the HTML. So when you create an instance of a template with dynamic application code, the instance will have whatever the template did.

Pretty much any time you muck around with dynamic content, you are changing the code outside the HTML. So it's good that the code is editable.

The downside of the code being editable is that if you change the code in the template, the changes are not reflected in the instances of that template. This is because Dreamweaver treats any text that is in an editable area in the template document as placeholder text.

If you want to ensure that any code changes in the template are reflected in the instance documents, add the following code to the head of the template:

```
<!-- TemplateInfo codeOutsideHTMLIsLocked="true" -->.
```

You can synchronize all the instances of the template by adding the above code and saving the template. Dreamweaver will change all the instances to have the same code. You can then change the parameter to false to allow the instances to control the code.

USING HEAD ELEMENTS

The head of an HTML document contains information that is used behind the scenes: by Web browsers, Web servers, CGI scripts, and robots that index the Web for search engines and so on.

The <head> of a document includes the document title, and it can also include scripts and CSS style definitions. In this chapter, we're going to discuss the other tags that are used in the document head to provide information about the document. Informally, these tags are often known as meta tags because the tag for many of them is <meta>. Similar to the anchor tag <a> or the <input> tag used for many different kinds of form fields, the <meta> tag can serve different purposes depending on what attributes it's given.

The kinds of head tags we'll look at in this chapter include keywords, page descriptions, page refresh instructions, base tags, and link tags.

Using these tags, you can provide search engines with information to categorize your page; you can provide structural information to the Web server that stores your pages; and you can make the page do funny things when it loads. In the sidebars in this chapter, you'll find information about making sure that robots do or do not index your page; how to keep a page from being cached by the visitor's browser, and how to create fades and other transition effects using Internet Explorer extensions.

About the Document Head

When you create a new Web page in Dreamweaver, the head of the document looks like this: ⟶

The `<title>` tag is included within the `<head>` tag and its contents are displayed in the title bar of both Dreamweaver and the Web browser.

The second tag is a `<meta>` tag. This particular `<meta>` tag indicates the content type of the document, which for most Web pages is `"text/html"`. The `charset` attribute indicates the language encoding of the page (in this case, Western).

The document head can include other meta tags and document information. The head tag may also include scripts, style sheets, links to such things, and so on.

```
<head>
<title>Untitled Document</title>
→ <meta http-equiv="Content-Type"
→ content="text/html; charset=
→ iso-8859-1">
<head>
```

✔ Tips

- The `<head>` tag isn't used in all Web documents—that is, it's not included in behind-the-scenes files such as XML files, CSS definitions, server-side includes, and Library items, which generally contain only the bare minimum data and don't necessarily have HTML's structural requirements.

- You can set a different `charset` attribute for your page by specifying encoding in the Page Properties dialog box (Modify > Page Properties) or for an entire site in the Fonts category of the Preferences dialog box (Edit > Preferences, or in Mac OS X, Dreamweaver > Preferences).

- Some pages include scripts outside of the document head—either within the `<body>` tag or outside the `<html>` tags.

- XHTML files include some doc-type information outside the `<html>` tags. See *Creating and Complying with XHTML* in Chapter 11.

Kinds of Head Tags

People often refer to all head tags as meta tags because it sort of sums up "all the head tags that aren't the page title." We're going to look at three tags: <meta>, <link>, and <base>.

Meta tags

The word *meta* means "about," and meta tags include data *about* the page they appear on. Standard HTML meta tag types include the following: Keywords, Description, and Refresh. Meta tags do not take a closing tag, and they look like this:

```
<meta name="keywords"
→ content="baseball, mom, apple pie">
```

Most meta tags use the name attribute to declare what kind of meta tag it is; the refresh tags use http-equiv instead. The value of name can be a common one, such as description; a proprietary one, such as documentID, creationdate, or generator; or a custom one for your purposes, such as subversion or blogpage.

The content attribute includes the actual meta data or instructions.

✔ Tip

- In XHTML, the meta tag is "empty" and closes like an empty XML tag: <meta />. See *About XHTML Compliance* in Chapter 11 for more syntax details.

Let's look at each meta name type in turn.

continues on next page

Keywords describe the content of the page and are used by some search engines when filing the page into categories or when building an index of search terms. Including pertinent keywords in your page can help you "float to the top" of the search engine heap. In other words, if you include the keywords `"spelunking"` and `"urban"` in your document head, someone who searches for "urban spelunking" has a good chance of finding your page.

The page **Description** is also often used by search engines, some of which display the page description when they return search results to a user on the Web. Some internal databases use the description data for similar purposes. Use keyword-type words in your description, too. A description like "Twelve-year-old Tommy Frenulum writes weekly reviews of Freeport, Maine's Little League softball games" will help both you and your prospective visitors much more than "I like baseball."

Refresh can be used to reload a page or to send the user to a different URL. This requires no JavaScript; any browser after version 2 supports such actions.

Others: You can also create your own custom meta tags for use with a database, a server, for personal use, or for use with another indexing system. For example, some filtering software relies on `meta` tags that "child-safe" or "pornographic" pages insert on their pages.

Other head content tags

The **Link** tag isn't the same as the clickable links that appear on the page. The URL defined in the `<link>` tag within the document head is used to define a relationship between the current page and another page, whether that be a style sheet, a script, a help file, or what-have-you.

The **Base** is the URL that is the location of the main page in the site. When documents are linked relatively, the Base URL is the one they are considered to be relative to. This is not a meta tag; it is the same `<base>` tag you can use to set base fonts and base targets.

Script and **Style** are used to enclose JavaScript and CSS style definitions, respectively.

And of course **Title** sets the visible page title. You can set the page title in the Document toolbar or in the Page Properties dialog box (Modify > Page Properties).

✔ Tip

- For details about how search engines work, how they index their pages, and some interesting media crit of the whole search-engine thing going back to 1995, visit
  `http://www.searchenginewatch.com/`.

Meta-http tag (content type)

Description tag

Meta tag (other)

Title   Style   Keywords

Script   Meta-http tag (other)   Refresh tag

Figure 15.1 The Head Content toolbar/viewing area. Even blank pages in Dreamweaver will contain two items: one for the page title, and one for the document type.

Viewing Head Content

Dreamweaver includes two tools for managing your head content in the Document window: the Head Content viewing area and the Head tab of the Insert toolbar.

To view head content:

◆ From the Document window menu bar, select View > Head Content. The Head Content toolbar will appear (**Figure 15.1**).

On pages in Design view, the toolbar appears at the top of the Document window. In Split view, the toolbar appears at the top of the Design view pane. In Code view, the toolbar does not appear.

On a new page or a page to which you haven't yet added any additional head content, you will see two icons, one each for the page title and the content type.

To examine head content:

◆ To view the code for a head icon in the Code inspector or Split view, select the icon. The code will be selected (**Figure 15.2**).

◆ To view the properties of an icon in the Property inspector, click on the icon (**Figure 15.3**). (Double-click on it to make the Property inspector appear.)

✔ Tips

■ You may also see head markers for CSS definitions and for scripts.

■ Figure 15.1 labels most of the different icons for reference. **Figure 15.4** shows the Head tab of the Insert toolbar.

Figure 15.2 Select the code for a head tag by selecting the tag's icon.

Figure 15.3 The Property inspector will show you what's in the head tag.

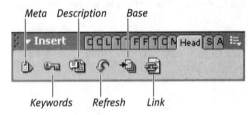

Figure 15.4 The Head tab of the Insert toolbar is a good shortcut for inserting these tags.

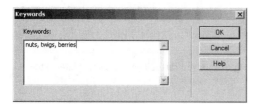

Figure 15.5 Type your keywords in the Keywords dialog box.

Inserting Keywords

Keywords are words that relate to the content on the page, even if the page itself doesn't actually use those words. Keywords are used by some search engines to index pages.

Search engines that use keywords ignore duplicates and many have a limit to how many they will index. So no, it won't do you any good to type "SEX SEX SEX" on your page hawking car wax. If you're curious about what criteria a particular search engine uses, visit the help files for that site.

To insert keywords:

1. From the Document window menu bar, select Insert > Head Tags > Keywords.

   or

   Click the Keywords button 🔑 on the Head tab of the Insert toolbar.

   Either way, the Keywords dialog box will appear (**Figure 15.5**).

2. In the Keywords text box, type a short list of words related to your page. Separate them by commas (although not required, commas make the list more readable).

   These should be relevant words that people might search on. Many indexes use only the first 50 (or fewer) keywords. On the other hand, you may want to include common synonyms or even common misspellings of words that people will search for.

3. When you're finished, click on OK. Dreamweaver will add the Keywords icon 🔑 to the Head Elements toolbar, and the code will look like this:

```
<meta name="keywords"
→ content="Olympia Washington,
→ theater, theatre, musical, rock
→ opera, gothic, trance, Nomy Lamm,
→ The Need, gender, transgender,
→ vampires, globalization,
→ conspiracy theory, corporate
→ America, subversion">
```

INSERTING KEYWORDS

To edit keywords:

1. Click on the Keywords icon  in the Head toolbar. The Property inspector will display Keyword properties (**Figure 15.6**).

2. Make any changes to your keywords, and click elsewhere to apply them.

(Of course, you can also edit your keywords in Code view.)

✔ Tip

■ It's a good idea to view the head content (View > Head Content) for your page while you're working, because Dreamweaver does not safeguard against inserting multiple head tags. If you do insert two keywords tags, for example (**Figure 15.7**), any search engines indexing the page will at best ignore the second tag and at worst penalize you by ignoring both tags.

Figure 15.6 You can edit your keywords later in the Property inspector.

Keywords tag

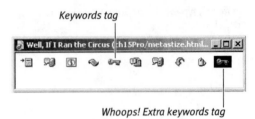

Whoops! Extra keywords tag

Figure 15.7 Some head tags, such as refresh, can be used more than once, but don't duplicate keywords, description, or title tags.

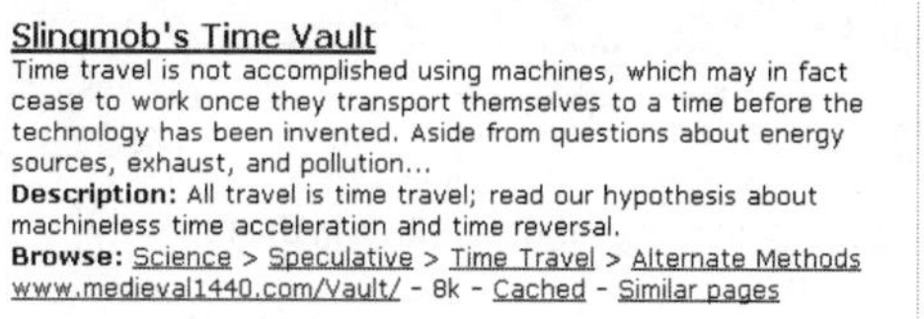

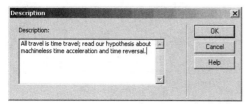

Slingmob's Time Vault
Time travel is not accomplished using machines, which may in fact cease to work once they transport themselves to a time before the technology has been invented. Aside from questions about energy sources, exhaust, and pollution...
Description: All travel is time travel; read our hypothesis about machineless time acceleration and time reversal.
Browse: Science > Speculative > Time Travel > Alternate Methods www.medieval1440.com/Vault/ – 8k – Cached – Similar pages

Figure 15.8 Many search engines, such as Google and Dmoz Open Directory, use descriptions as part of the displayed search results.

Figure 15.9 Type a brief summary of your site in the Description text box.

```
<meta name="description"
→ content="Hanker for a hunk of
→ cheese? Our hand-crafted goat
→ cheddars and soy cottage cheese
→ will really whet your appetite.
→ Visit our store in Montpelier,
→ Vermont, or order yourself or
→ your family a gift from our
→ virtual cheese counter.">
```

Inserting a Page Description

A page description describes the purpose or content of a page. Some search engines display the page title and page description when returning search results (**Figure 15.8**).

To insert a page description:

1. From the Document window menu bar, select Insert > Head Tags > Description.

   or

   Click the Description button on the Head tab of the Insert toolbar.

   Either way, the Description dialog box will appear (**Figure 15.9**).

2. In the Description text box, type a short description of your page, using lots of relevant words that people might search on. Many indexes display only the first 50 words of a description.

   For example, if you're selling something, list the items for sale. If the page is an article or essay, include the first paragraph or write an abstract of the article. If it's for a small business, describe where it is and what it does.

3. When you're finished, click on OK. Dreamweaver will add the Description icon to the Head Elements toolbar, and the code will look like this:

To edit your page description:

◆ Click on the Description icon in the Head toolbar. The Property inspector will display Description properties (**Figure 15.10**). Make any changes to your description that you wish and then click elsewhere to apply your edits.

✔ Tip

■ In some instances, we found that selecting the page description and clicking within the text box in the Property inspector revealed the keywords rather than the page description. If this happens, you can select the Description icon and then edit the description in the Code inspector or Code view.

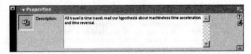

Figure 15.10 Edit your description in the Property inspector.

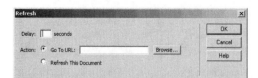

Figure 15.11 In the Refresh dialog box, you can specify just a delay time, in which case the page will refresh every [n] seconds, or you can specify both a delay time and a new page for the browser to fetch without the visitor having to click a link.

Inserting a Refresh Tag

The refresh tag, like other http-equiv tags, mimics server instructions for a page loaded in a browser. The browser responds as if the instruction had been sent by the server.

A refresh tag can reload your page or send the viewer to another page. You often see refresh tags used when a page has moved, to send the visitor to the new, correct URL. You can also use refresh tags with JavaScript, cookies, or CGI scripts to reload the page and make it use, say, a new color, or play a new song.

To insert a refresh tag:

1. From the Document window menu bar, select Insert > Head Tags > Refresh.

   or

   Click the Refresh button on the Head tab of the Insert toolbar.

   Either way, the Refresh dialog box will appear (**Figure 15.11**).

2. In the Delay text box, type the number of seconds after the page has finished loading before the refresh action will occur. Five seconds is often enough to let the user see the current page before the new one loads; use 0 seconds to rush past the initial page.

   If you're going to have a continual refresh—that is, if you're not going to send the user to another page but are going to keep reloading the first page, be sure to set a decent number of seconds before the page reloads. This is how Webcams work—when you request a new document, the page, which has been updated in the last 30 or 60 seconds with a new image, loads and looks brand-new.

continues on next page

INSERTING A REFRESH TAG

3. If the action is to continuously reload the current page, click on the Refresh This Document radio button.

or

If the action is to have the Web browser open a new page (**Figure 15.12**), click on the Go to URL radio button. Then, type (or paste) the URL for the new page, or use the Browse button to open the Select File dialog box and locate a page in your local site.

Note: For this to work on all browsers, you must use a full URL, not a relative one, even if both pages are in the same folder. In other words, if Dreamweaver codes a relative link, type in the full URL instead, starting with `http://`.

4. When you're finished, click on OK. Dreamweaver will add the Refresh icon to the Head Elements toolbar 🔄 , and the code will look like one of the following:

New page: ⟶

Continuous: ⟶

To edit your refresh tag:

1. Click on the Refresh icon in the Head toolbar 🔄 . The Property inspector will display Refresh properties (**Figure 15.13**).

2. Make any changes to the number of seconds or to the URL, and click elsewhere on the Property inspector to apply your changes.

✔ Tips

■ In some instances, we found that selecting the refresh tag and clicking within the text box in the Property inspector cleared all data from the tag or inserted the keywords data instead of the refresh data. Yikes! In this instance, you should edit the tag within the Code inspector or Code view instead of the Property inspector.

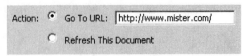

Figure 15.12 It's good practice to specify a full URL for a refresh tag.

Figure 15.13 You can change your refresh in the Property inspector.

```
<meta http-equiv="refresh"
→ content="5;URL=
→ http://www.digitalsf.org/">
```

```
<meta http-equiv="refresh"
→ content="30">
```

■ If you refer two pages with refresh tags to each other, the browser will bounce back and forth between them, forever.

■ Remember that leaving the URL blank will cause a continuous refresh.

More Fun with http-equiv

There are many other `http-equiv` tags, including those used by PICS for page filtering; try these.

`<META HTTP-EQUIV="Window-target" CONTENT="_top">`

On many, but not all, browsers, the `"window-target"` attribute makes a page load in a stand-alone rather than framed page so that the page won't appear locked within someone else's frames.

`<META HTTP-EQUIV="Pragma" CONTENT="no-cache">`

The only valid value for `"Pragma"` is `no-cache` and it keeps the browser from caching a page that should be able to be refreshed often, such as a news page.

`<META HTTP-EQUIV="Expires" CONTENT="Wed, 21 Aug 2003 08:21:57 GMT">`

An expiration date makes sure the browser will retrieve a new version of the page, rather than the cached version, when the user requests it. The expiration date format above is standard.

Table 15.1

Transition effects to use with blendTrans and revealTrans	
Box in	0
Box out	1
Circle in	2
Circle out	3
Wipe up	4
Wipe down	5
Wipe right	6
Wipe left	7
Vertical blinds	8
Horizontal blinds	9
Checkerboard across	10
Checkerboard down	11
Random dissolve	12
Split vertical in	13
Split vertical out	14
Split horizontal in	15
Split horizontal out	16
Strips left down	17
Strips left up	18
Strips right down	19
Strips right up	20
Random bars horizontal	21
Random bars vertical	22
Random	23

PICS and Pans

PICS stands for Platform for Internet Content Selection, and it is the standard for rating the appropriateness of content. Kid-friendly sites and porn peddlers both use PICS tags to indicate a "child-safe" or "adult" rating for a page.

If you have an interest in including these ratings on your pages, you may provide your own ratings or submit your site to a site that will certify your pages as okay for youngsters.

For information about the standard, how it works, and how to format your PICS meta tags, see the PICS Guidelines at http://www.w3.org/PICS/.

INSERTING A REFRESH TAG

Fading Fast: DHTML Page Transitions

Warning: We're about to show you a really cool trick that only works in IE 4 or later. This uses meta tags to activate the "effects" filters built into the Microsoft browsers and control a fade or cut effect when the page loads.

Try this http-equiv trick to create a fade:

```
<META HTTP-EQUIV="Page-Enter" CONTENT="blendTrans(Duration=4.0)">
```

Experiment with a different number of seconds. One that's particularly cool uses 20 seconds with a white page for a weird fade effect that makes the last page disappear. You change the duration by replacing 4.0 in the examples on this page with a different number of seconds.

In addition to duration, you can set a transition method, which looks like this:

```
<META HTTP-EQUIV="Page-Enter" CONTENT="blendTrans(transition=12,duration=4.0)">
```

These transitions, indicated by numbers, are fade-ins in different patterns, which are listed in **Table 15.1** on the previous page. To use a transition, replace the number 12, above, with the transition's code number. In other words, to apply "Wipe up," set it as follows:

```
<META HTTP-EQUIV="Page-Enter" CONTENT="blendTrans(transition=4,duration=4.0)">
```

When you test these in your browser, sometimes you won't see them unless the page is visibly different than the last page you loaded. One way to do this is to change the background color each time you preview a page. Another way is to add JavaScript to the page that has the body tag change the background color onLoad. (These fades look great with random colors—see the next sidebar, *How to Make a Random Fade*.)

Additionally, you can use the transition "revealTrans" instead of "blendTrans" for more dramatic effects.

And finally, you can set either Page-Enter, Page-Exit, Site-Enter, or Site-Exit for "Page-Enter" above. The exit methods let you use effects when the user clicks a link to leave your page.

To view some examples, visit http://www.tarin.com/newtoys/refresh/.

How to Make a Random Fade

You can set a random background color in the browser when the page loads, using a little JavaScript. The fade part of this won't work in browsers other than IE 4 or later (sorry, Netscape), but the random background color will.

1. Insert a fade as described in the sidebar, *Fading Fast: DHTML Page Transitions*. For our example, we're going to use this one:

```
<META HTTP-EQUIV="Page-Enter" CONTENT="revealTrans
→ (transition=4,duration=4.0)">
```

2. In your document head, you can type the following code, or you can skip to Step 3, copy the functions, and paste the functions into the Insert Script dialog box (see *Script Editing Tools* in Chapter 11).

Anyway, that code is:

```
<script language="JavaScript" type="text/JavaScript">
<!--
-->
</script>
```

3. Between the opening and closing comments, insert the code from the following three snippets, in this order:

- JavaScript/Conversions/Base Conversion/Dec To Hex

- JavaScript/Randomizers/Random Number

- JavaScript/Randomizers/Random Background Color

(For more on inserting snippets, see *Using the Snippets Panel* in Chapter 11 and *Cookies and Code Snippets* in Chapter 13.)

Now, when your page loads, the effect will transition in with a random color each time. Try using a meta-refresh to make the page reload itself, and also try using a page-leaving fade at the same time.

INSERTING A REFRESH TAG

Inserting Other Meta Tags

There are any number of meta tags you may need to put on your page. Of course, you can always type them in the Code inspector—or you can use Dreamweaver's tools to help.

To insert a meta tag:

1. From the Document window menu bar, select Insert > Head Tags > Meta.

   or

   Click the Meta button 🗋 on the Head tab of the Insert toolbar.

   Either way, the Meta dialog box will appear (**Figure 15.14**).

2. From the Attribute drop-down menu, select either Name (meta information about the page) or http-equiv (for page transferring attributes; this is what `refresh` uses).

3. In the Value text box, type the kind of meta tag this is. Examples include `Author`, `Language`, `CreationDate`, `Robots`, and so on. There is no list of valid values; these are used differently by different browsers and servers.

4. In the Content text box, type (or paste) the data content of the attribute. For example, you could include PICS rating data, information about the page author, or information for a specific database or search engine.

5. When you're finished, click on OK. Dreamweaver will add the Meta icon 🗋 to the Head Elements toolbar, and the code will look something like one of the following:

Keep in mind that meta name tags for description, keywords, and refresh each have their own dialog box in Dreamweaver.

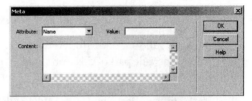

Figure 15.14 You can insert meta tags other than description, keywords, and refresh using this dialog box.

```
<meta name="author"
→ content="Joe Brainard">
<meta name="CreationDate"
→ content="June 2, 2006">
<meta name="language"
→ content="American English">
```

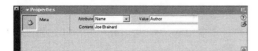

Figure 15.15 Edit your meta tags in the Property inspector.

To edit your meta tags:

1. Click on the Meta icon in the Head toolbar; be sure to select the right one, because each page will include an http-equiv meta tag that designates the language encoding, and pages may contain any number of meta tags. The Property inspector will display Meta properties (**Figure 15.15**).

2. Make any changes to your meta tags, and click on some blank space on the Property inspector to apply your changes.

Pygmalion for Robots

Robots, in Web terms, are little pieces of software that set out on a truffle hunt over the Internet, searching for some kind of data or other. The noble search robot sniffs out Web page addresses, indexes them, follows their links, and stores the result of the search in a database used by a search engine to help people find a page they're looking for. Nefarious robots search Web pages for mailto: links and @ signs, trying to build a giant database of addresses that later get sold on those "millions" spam CDs.

There's not much you can do to protect your pages from being sniffed by a mean robot, other than not printing any e-mail addresses.

Robots that work for the forces of good, however, will follow instructions left in meta tags and will index or not index a page based on what you tell it.

The tag looks like this:

```
<meta name="robots" content="noindex,nofollow">
```

The noindex attribute means, "do not catalog this page." The nofollow attribute says, "don't follow links on this page and try to index them, please."

You can also use the attributes index and follow, but they're not necessary—a robot that finds no instruction will index your page and follow its links.

If you're administrating an entire site, you can also use a robots.txt file to provide instructions; see http://www.robotstxt.org/ for more on this.

Inserting a Base Href

A Base Href tag indicates the location of the central page in the site that relative links are based on. Generally this is the `index.html` page (or other default page) that is the central content page for the entire site. When you insert this tag on different pages throughout a site, each one will indicate its document-relative location to the base page.

To insert a base href:

1. From the Document window menu bar, select Insert > Head Tags > Base, or click the Base button 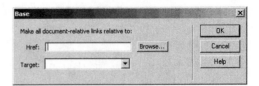 on the Head tab of the Insert toolbar. The Base dialog box will appear (**Figure 15.16**).

2. In the Href text box, type the location of the base target page; or, click on Browse to open the Select File dialog box and choose a file from your local site. In the latter case, Dreamweaver will code the correct document-relative link path for you.

3. The `target` attribute sets a base location in which all the links on the page should open. This can be a frame, a new window, or a JavaScript window. To make all links open in a new window, select `_blank`. To make all links open in the current window, select `_top`.

4. When you're finished, click on OK. Dreamweaver will add the Base icon to the Head Elements toolbar, and the code will look like this:

To edit your Base Href tag:

◆ Click on the Base icon in the Head toolbar. The Property inspector will display Base properties (**Figure 15.17**).

Make any changes to the base page location or the target, and click elsewhere on the Property inspector to apply your changes.

Figure 15.16 When you insert a base tag, you can set a base href, a base target, or both.

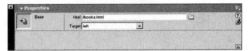

Figure 15.17 Edit your base href and your base target in the Property inspector.

```
<base href="../appendix/index.html"
→ target="_blank">
```

Covering the Bases

You may have seen two other base tags, `base target` and `basefont`.

`Base target` is used mostly for frames, although you can use it on any page in which you want all links to open in a certain window. The tag looks like this:

```
<base target="left">
```

`left` is the name of your frame or window. You can use the `href` attribute in the same base tag as the target attribute, which would look like this:

```
<base href="/" target="left">
```

You also can use specialized targets with this tag. These are as follows:

`_top` Opens links in same window, replacing all framesets

`_parent` Replaces immediate parent frameset with contents of links

`_self` Ensures links opens in same window or same frame

`_blank` Opens links in new browser window

The `basefont` tag is used to set font information for a page. It is being deprecated in favor of CSS, but the tag goes *inside* the `body` tag (you can use it inside the `head` tag, but not in IE4, so go figure) and looks like this:

```
<basefont size="6" face="Arial, Helvetica, sans-serif" color="#339966">
```

Inserting a Link Descriptor

A `<link>` tag does not appear in the body of the page and is therefore not clickable, although browser software or scripts may use the contents of a link tag to interpret the data. Link tags are used to indicate the relationship between the current page and other pages in a series or a set.

Several attributes can be applied to a link, although currently many of them have not been implemented in a browser. The HTML 4.0 Transitional spec has lots of ideas about using the link tag to be able to index, print, or otherwise collate documents.

For instance: ——————————————→

The `rel` attribute describes a relationship between the current page and another document. The `href` attribute describes the location of that other page. You may have seen these attributes used when linking to a style sheet: ——————————————→

Examples of `rel` relationships that appear in the W3C spec include `stylesheet`, `glossary`, `appendix`, `subsection`, `section`, `chapter`, `content`, `index`; and the aforementioned `start`, `prev`, and `next`; as well as `alternate`, `help`, and `bookmark`. You can see the potential here, even if it hasn't been exploited: You could offer a menu of alternate pages, an index, a help site, and so on. You can even create a browser profile that uses new data types, although this too is still nascent. If you want to define more than one `rel`, you separate the contents by spaces: `rel="stylesheet help"`

The counterpart of `rel` is `rev`, which describes a reverse relationship. If your `rel` is bookmark, your bookmark file would include a `rev` pointing to its pages. This is still mostly hypothetical rather than practiced.

```
<TITLE>Part III: In Which Gertrude
→ Loses Her Favorite Neckerchief
→ and Discovers Herself </TITLE>
<link rel="prev" href="partii.html">
<link rel="next" href="partiv.html">
```

```
<link rel="stylesheet"
→ href="../hh.css" type="text/css">
```

The *id* attribute is a unique identifier for your link. You don't need to include this unless your document will be parsed for it by, say, an XML tool. You must include it in XHTML.

The `title` attribute is another new attribute that can be used in all kinds of crazy ways. When dealing with the link tag, it's reserved for style sheet selectors that have not yet been implemented. These would allow the user or the user's software to choose a style sheet based on the equipment being used. As accessibility standards become more widely implemented, these tags will be further refined and examples to learn from will exist (and perhaps these tags will even be included in dialog boxes in Dreamweaver).

✔ Tip

- For more information on the `<link>` tag and how links and anchors work, visit the W3C spec at `http://www.w3.org/`. When you get there, search for "link tag," or browse to Section 12 of the HTML spec.

continues on next page

INSERTING A LINK DESCRIPTOR

To insert a link:

1. From the Document window menu bar, select Insert > Head Tags > Link, or click on the Link button 🔗 on the Head tab of the Insert toolbar. The Link dialog box will appear (**Figure 15.18**).

2. In the Href text box, enter (or paste) the URL for the related page, or use the Browse button to open the Select File dialog box and locate a page in your local site.

3. In the Rel text box, enter the relationship to the linked page.

4. If you have uses for ID, title, or rev, fill in those blanks.

5. When you're finished, click on OK. Dreamweaver will add the Link icon 🔗 to the Head Elements toolbar, and the code will look like this: ————————

To edit your Link tag:

1. Click on the Link icon in the Head toolbar. The Property inspector will display Link properties (**Figure 15.19**).

2. Make any changes to your link properties, and click elsewhere on the Property inspector to apply your changes.

Figure 15.18 A link tag can be used to establish the relationship of documents in a series.

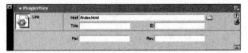

Figure 15.19 Edit your link tag in the Property inspector.

```
<link rel="index"
→ href="../index.rdf"
→ type="text/rdf">
```

Editing Head Elements

After you insert a head element, you can edit its content in the Properties inspector. Click on a head icon in the Document window toolbar, or double-click it to make the Property inspector appear. Editing each type of tag is discussed in the relevant section.

Cookie, Cookie, Cookie, Starts with Meta

Cookies are little markers that Web sites drop onto their visitors' computers that tell them, at the least, that the visitor has been to the site before. Of course, cookies aren't an exact science—the visitor has to be using the same browser on the same computer or the cookie doesn't track them. (In some cases, the user must use the same login name, in addition to the same browser and computer, before a cookie activates.)

There are a few security concerns about cookies—it's very difficult for the user to tell what information the cookie is tracking, or for the user to ensure that the cookie is retrieving only itself and not other private data. On the other hand, cookies are quite useful for remembering login names for sites that require user registration.

One method for setting a cookie—that is, leaving a note in the user's "cookies.txt" file—is to set it with a meta tag. An example tag is the following:

```
<META HTTP-EQUIV="Set-Cookie" CONTENT="cookievalue=xxx;
→ expires=Wednesday, 21-Aug-02 18:21:21 GMT; path=/">
```

Above, xxx is the value of your cookie. The expires attribute, discussed earlier in this chapter, sets the expiration date for the cookie itself. The path is the path you want the cookie to mark; the slash above is for the root page, but you could also set it for a specific page within the site.

See *Cookies and Code Snippets* in Chapter 13 to set a cookie using JavaScript. For more about cookies, on both sides of the debate—including how to use them to track users, editorials and news about privacy concerns, and useful examples—see http://www.cookiecentral.com/.

ACCESSIBILITY: CONSIDERING YOUR AUDIENCE   16

Of course, you want the widest possible audience to visit your Web site—and enjoy the experience. Extending your Web site to reach as many people as possible isn't just a desirable practice—for many Internet users, unless you take pains to include them, they won't be able to experience much of your site at all.

According to statistics from the Census Bureau, one out of every five individuals is disabled in one form or another. These numbers increase as the median age of the population increases. Some of the specific challenges of the disabled include, for example, not being able to view Web content and not being able to type text using a keyboard.

Web accessibility has historically been concerned with making "text only" sites that can be navigable by as many kinds of equipment as possible. However, as the list of alternative browsers continues to expand, many people who thus far have been limited by a disability from accessing the Internet at all are coming online and enjoying it. Today disabled people can access the Web using text-to-speech screen readers, Braille and large-print browsers and refreshing screens, mouth pointers, and specialized keyboards.

Even though the disabled often rely on technological aids to assist them to view Web pages, the effectiveness of these tools is often dictated by how accessible the Web site is. To reach these individuals, you need to think about a few basic principles: making your site navigable, legible, and understandable to as many people as you can, by providing the proper format for your images, media, forms, frames, and tables. Not only is it a recommended best practice, in some situations it's also demanded by law. Many governmental organizations and some public educational facilities are required to follow the accessibility guidelines discussed in this chapter.

Luckily, Dreamweaver includes a variety of tools to help us as developers plan and execute sites that are accessible to as wide a variety of devices as possible. In this chapter we'll illustrate best practices for accessible Web sites and show how Dreamweaver's accessibility controls and reports can help you present your content to the widest possible audience.

Accessibility Considerations

Most mainstream Web browsers, when given any Web page, will know how to load it, because they're all based on the design popularized by Mosaic, extended by Netscape, and universally adopted by software engineers ever since. Generally, you see a toolbar at the top of the browser window, which includes an address bar and buttons for "Back," "Home," and so on. You'll see scrollbars and resize bars with which you can change your window size and view, and you can easily play sounds, click links, and so on. Most browsers display a seamless layout of text, tables, colors, pictures, layers, and other elements. A designer on a media-heavy, slick-looking page may sensitively address questions of color theory, readability, typography, and so on to make a page easy to read in a standard browser window, but most designers have no idea what their page "looks like" to people using other devices. Which leads us to the question of what exactly constitutes "accessible" HTML.

What is accessible HTML?

For our purposes, we'll define *accessible* HTML as code that makes pages available to text-only browsers, thus also rendering the pages available to alternative browsing methods such as text-to-speech, large print and Braille.

HTML at its simplest is used to describe the content and format for Web pages. But the tags and attributes that make sense in graphical browsers, such as the width and background color of tables, may be entirely irrelevant in accessible pages. Making HTML accessible involves setting HTML tag attributes that allow the page to be rendered in a way that can be deciphered and presented by

non-graphical browsers. These settings are interpreted by the browser or viewing device and displayed or read to the user. Most HTML accessibility concerns have to do with images and other multimedia, tables, frames, and forms. In all cases, the user and the user's software need to be able to decide in what order to read the text on the page, how to deal with the objects that aren't text, and how to navigate from one area of a site to another.

Text-only browsers and accessibility standards

As we'll see in this chapter, accessible pages are often all-around easier to navigate and faster to download.

The browsers that present text via many accessible devices are based on popular text-only browsers, such as Lynx. Before there were any accessibility standards per se, it was understood that making your pages accessible to a text-only browser would theoretically make them accessible to text-to-speech, large-print, and Braille readers, because the content on the page would be viewable and readable regardless of the images, media, or constricted design elements.

Text-only browsers were widely used and evangelized during the early days of the Web, first by line-command coders, then by people with slow Internet connections, and then by Web purists who grew quickly weary of pages bloated with dancing kittens and the like. Fans of text-only browsers preferred to retrieve information purely in word form, such as news stories and academic articles, without having to wait for superfluous pictures, such as toolbars and ads, to download.

When users encountered a media file that they did want to download, such as an accompanying photograph or chart, they could, on well-planned sites, read the Alt text description and decide to download the file in either the browser or a helper application. Even people running early versions of Netscape or Internet Explorer often turned off auto-image loading and downloaded only those pictures that were pertinent to the story they were reading.

(You might or might not recall the days when all online images needed to be retrieved separately and opened in a helper program. Even once the graphical Web browser had taken over nearly every Internet capability, most media, including the simplest sound files, still needed to be downloaded separately.)

Many sites bragged back in the old days that they were Lynx-capable, which generally meant the following: They were navigable even if you didn't have images loaded, so that having a navbar made of images wasn't the only way of getting around a site. The images that actually presented content were tagged with Alt attributes so users could determine whether they wanted to download the picture, and vision-impaired users could get a sense of what the picture added to the story. And Lynx-capable sites didn't use media plug-ins that might work only on one kind of browser or computer.

Additionally, early versions of Lynx didn't respond well to tables. It was difficult for text-only browsers to figure out whether the cells in the table were to be read across or down. As for the later innovation of frames, the `<noframes>` tag was included specifically in Netscape's spec so that browsers that were only able to open one document at a time could still access the information on a frames-based site. (A frames-based page consists of a frameset document, plus an additional HTML document for each frame visible in the browser window.)

Section 508 and international Web standards

The World Wide Web Consortium (or W3C for short), the governing body that decides what HTML, among other things, should look and act like, was the first organization to set standards for accessibility. The Web Content Accessibility Guidelines (WCAG) include checklists for compliance, and a three-level priority scale for meeting the guidelines. Section 508 of the United States Federal Rehabilitation Act is based on the WCAG, as are the rules in Canada, the UK, Australia, France, Germany, and elsewhere.

In summary, the U.S. regulations require that all federal electronic and information technologies have an equivalent accessible version available (to potential disabled federal employees and clients), including computers, software, and networks, "used for the creation, conversion, or duplication of data or information." So far what this means for Web developers is that all Web sites provided as work tools to federal employees, and all federal Web sites provided to information-seeking members of the public, must be rendered accessible to many different kinds of devices. The summary of the laws specifically mentions using image Alt tags, providing easy navigation schemes, organizing the information in Web forms, providing alternatives to information contained in animations or multimedia presentations, and using CSS to enhance accessibility.

Some government Web sites, such as the Department of Justice site, provide an online pledge to deliver their content in an alternate format if requested by a user who cannot otherwise access it. (We suspect that in many cases this may just be a long, raw text file that contains pure information and no formatting.)

ACCESSIBILITY CONSIDERATIONS

If you create a Web site for or on behalf of the federal government, you must adhere to these standards in that work. For information about accessibility in other countries, you should look up the Web site for the government agency in charge of administering disability accommodation programs.

Visually impaired users

Visually impaired Internet users can access the Web using one of several tools: text-to-speech browsers or screen readers that read the pages aloud; large-print browsers or printers; or Braille equipment—either refreshable Braille displays or Braille page printers. For users who need to hear the content of the page, the client software needs to be able to interpret the order of the cells in a table, for example, which you can do by using headings. Some typographical conventions may also need re-thinking. To emphasize a block of text, your options include indenting it as a blockquote, setting it in the color red, using the <i> tag for italics, or using the <em> tag for emphasis. The <em> tag is interpreted by alternative browsers as being "read" with emphasis, whereas if you use the <i> tag, the browser may interpret it as a citation or typographical choice and not read the text any differently. As the color red and the blockquote format are typographic formatting, you may choose whether to translate this additional formatting for alternative browsers.

Similarly, users who rely on pages being printed in a different format (such as Braille or large print) can't just tell the browser to print the page at 60 points; the text would simply run off the page. These users need software that can help them format the text on the printed page or on the screen so that it's legible and navigable. The availability of such software may determine how you format your pages in the future.

Other accessibility concerns

Other disability concerns have to do with mobility, motor skills, and other impairments that may prevent the use of standard computer equipment. Users who cannot use a mouse easily or comfortably may still be able to navigate sites by pressing Tab or Enter (Return) on the keyboard. (Try this in your browser, in a page without forms: Pressing Tab will move from link to link, and pressing Enter (Return) will open the highlighted link.) Disabled users may also use assistive devices such as touch screens, mouth pointers, or voice-recognition tools.

Portable devices

Making Web pages accessible to as broad a range of devices as possible may have the added benefit of making them available to wireless devices and personal digital assistants. By using the WAP protocol or the Wireless Markup Language, a flavor of XML, you can make your pages accessible via phone or PDA.

Online Resources

The W3C Web Accessibility Initiative includes how-to guidelines and links to alternative browsers:

`http://www.w3.org/WAI/`

The WCAG checklists are also available here:

`http://www.w3.org/TR/WCAG10/`

The U.S. Section 508 site includes news and product resources as well as rules:

`http://www.section508.gov/`

Macromedia's own guide to accessibility:

`http://www.macromedia.com/macromedia/accessibility`

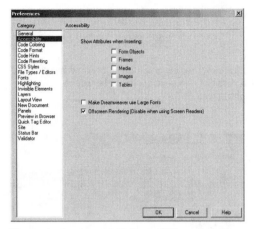

Figure 16.1 Dreamweaver's Accessibility preferences let you toggle on and off the dialog boxes that prompt you for accessibility controls.

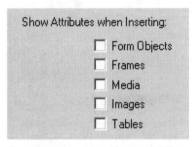

Figure 16.2 You can turn on Accessibility dialog boxes for Form Objects, Frames, Media, Images, and Tables.

Dreamweaver's Accessibility Features

Dreamweaver includes a variety of tools to make authoring accessible pages easier for developers and designers. Dreamweaver includes accessible page templates, several dialog boxes that help you control the format and content of your documents, an accessibility validator, and accessibility reference files.

In order to make the most of these tools, you should activate Dreamweaver's accessibility preferences. You can turn these preferences on and off whenever you like.

Accessibility preferences

To activate the dialog boxes that will prompt you to make your forms, tables, and so on accessible, you turn on accessibility settings in Dreamweaver's preferences. These preference settings allow you to configure Dreamweaver to automatically prompt you for accessibility information.

If you're a developer who uses assistive equipment for a visual disability, you can also turn on Dreamweaver's internal accessibility assistance aids.

To turn on Dreamweaver's accessibility authoring controls:

1. From the menu bar, select Edit > Preferences. The Preferences dialog box will appear.

2. In the Category list, select Accessibility. The dialog box will change to reflect your choice (**Figure 16.1**).

3. To have Dreamweaver prompt you for accessibility settings, check the checkbox for one or more of the following: Form Objects, Frames, Media, Images, and Tables (**Figure 16.2**).

4. Click on OK to close the Preferences dialog box, or continue to the next list to turn on Dreamweaver's own accessibility features.

To turn on Dreamweaver's own accessibility features:

1. Follow Steps 1–2 in the previous list to open the Accessibility preferences.

2. To have Dreamweaver use large fonts for its panels, check the Make Dreamweaver use Large Fonts checkbox (**Figure 16.3**).

3. By default, Dreamweaver renders its pages offscreen—that is, to prevent flicker, the changes in a page are processed backstage, stored in memory, and then drawn onscreen rather than rendering on the fly—this is called *double-buffering*.

   This process may not work well with screen readers. To turn off double-buffering, deselect the Offscreen Rendering checkbox.

4. Click on OK to close the Preferences dialog box. You may get a dialog box advising you of the next step.

5. To make your changes take effect, quit and restart Dreamweaver.

✔ Tip

■ System preferences may overtake preferences you set in Dreamweaver. That is, on Windows machines, if you have your font sizes set as Normal, then large fonts might not be displayed as such in Dreamweaver. To set your Windows system font size, go to the Control Panel (Start > Control Panel) and open the Display dialog box. Click on the Appearance tab, and set your system font size in the Font size drop-down menu (**Figure 16.4**). Depending on your video card, monitor resolution, and version of Windows, you may get warnings telling you the screen won't look as good as you want it to; and you may or may not have to restart your computer to see the changes take effect. Still, after attempting to load large fonts in Dreamweaver, the changes were apparent for only some panels, and not at all for useful tools like the Property inspector.

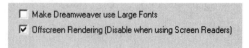

Figure 16.3 You can also turn on Dreamweaver's own accessibility features for viewing large fonts or working with screen readers.

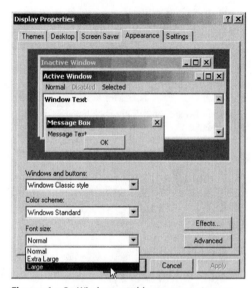

Figure 16.4 On Windows machines, you can turn on large or extra-large fonts to make menus, toolbar components, and dialog box titles easier to read. Windows XP is pictured here.

DREAMWEAVER'S ACCESSIBILITY FEATURES

Figure 16.5 The New Document dialog box includes a Page Designs (Accessible) category.

Figure 16.6 Browse through the list of page designs and view the thumbnail previews.

Figure 16.7 This basic design for a page header and footer includes accessible tables.

`<body.BodyBackgroundColor> <table> <tr> `**`<td.HeaderColor>`**` <h3>`

Figure 16.8 The style names in this page do not include definitions but rather are suggestions for where you might want to use CSS to define fonts or colors.

- Some elements in these page designs are marked with undefined ID or class attributes such as tdColor or bodyBackgroundcolor (**Figure 16.8**). These are placeholder suggestions for using CSS to define text and color attributes so that plain-text readers can see the page regardless of your high-end design. If you leave them alone, nothing will break, but you can also create an external or inline style sheet that includes these suggested attributes. Unfortunately, because they're undefined, these IDs and classes do not show up in the Edit mode of the CSS panel.

Accessible Page Designs

Dreamweaver provides sample templates incorporating standard techniques for accessibility. Pre-built templates can be used as guides or as a base from which to build other accessible pages.

These pages incorporate W3C standards for forms and tables, among other things, which we'll take a closer look at later in this chapter. if you want to learn about accessibility, or if you need to get a site up in a hurry, these are a good starting point.

To start off with a page that uses only accessible tags:

1. From the menu bar, select File > New. The New Document dialog box will appear.

2. In the Category list, select Page Designs (Accessible). A list of page designs will appear in the next list box (**Figure 16.5**).

3. In the Page Designs (Accessible) list box, click on a title to see a preview of the page (**Figure 16.6**).

4. If you find a design you'd like to use or examine more closely, click on Create.

   The New Document dialog box will close and your page will appear in the Document window (**Figure 16.7**).

✔ Tips

- Creating an accessible page from the New Document dialog box does not automatically turn on Dreamweaver's accessibility controls. To do so, see the previous section, particularly the list *To turn on Dreamweaver's accessibility authoring controls.*

ACCESSIBLE PAGE DESIGNS

Using the Accessibility Dialog Boxes

Dreamweaver MX provides a set of accessibility controls that remind and prompt you to add extra tags and attributes to your page to make it more accessible to users with disabilities.

Making Forms Accessible

Forms contain a variety of input elements, like menus, radio buttons, and checkboxes, that can create accessibility problems. A screen reader, for example, would have to tell the user "checkbox1, checkbox2, checkbox3" if a form wasn't properly labeled, and that wouldn't be much help to the user at all.

Dreamweaver's accessibility controls make it easy to do the following: add labels attached to form elements; define access keys and tab order to allow for easier keyboard navigation between form elements; and define tab order between form elements. Section 508 standards specify that labels are required. Access keys and tab index settings are optional.

Once you've turned on your preferences, you will be prompted to provide accessibility controls for all *new* form objects. For existing forms, you'll need to set these options using the Tag Editor dialog box. (See *The Tag Editor* in Chapter 11 for instructions on using this tool.)

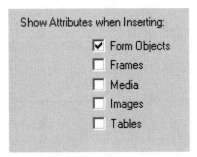

Figure 16.9 Turn on Form Object accessibility controls to get the dialog box in Figure 16.10 whenever you insert a form field.

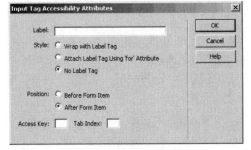

Figure 16.10 For form accessibility, you can control the way form labels are presented, and you can tag each form field with an access key and a tab order.

To make forms more accessible:

1. If you haven't done so already, turn on your Accessibility preferences for Form Objects. See the previous list, *To turn on Dreamweaver's accessibility authoring controls* (**Figure 16.9**).

2. The next time you insert a form element, the Input Tag Accessibility Attributes dialog box will appear (**Figure 16.10**). This same dialog box appears even for form fields that do not use the `input` tag, such as the `select` tag used for lists and menus.

3. **Required:** Type a label in the Label field. This label will be visible; you can control its appearance using CSS or the `font` tag.

4. The Style section of the dialog box lets you control how the label is inserted. (See the Tips at the end of this exercise for more details on these options.)

   Wrap with Label Tag: The label is inserted using the `<label>` tag, which surrounds the `input` or `select` tag and thus tells any device exactly which form field is being described:

   ```
   <label>Label Text
   → <input type="text"
   → name="textfield3">
   </label>
   ```

   Attach Label Tag Using "For" Attribute: This follows the input or select tag with the label tag. The label tag then bears the attribute `for`, with the value of for being the name attribute of the input or select tag, like so:

   ```
   <input type="checkbox"
   → name="checkbox" value="checkbox"
   → id="checkbox">
   <label for="checkbox">Text</label>
   ```

   No Label Tag: Inserts a text label but does not use the label tag.

   continues on next page

MAKING FORMS ACCESSIBLE

5. In the Position area of the dialog box, indicate whether you want the label code to appear Before or After the form object code.

6. To set an access key, type a letter or number that would allow users to access the form element by holding down Alt and pressing that key.

7. To set a tab order for the form object, type a number in the Tab Index text box. Dreamweaver will add the `tabindex` attribute to the form field tag. When the user presses the Tab key, the cursor will move from form element to form element in the order that you specify with the Tab Index attributes.

8. Click on OK to close the Input Tag Accessibility Attributes dialog box and insert your form field.

✔ Tips

- Each time you insert a form field with Form Object Accessibility preferences turned on, you'll get the Input Tag Accessibility Attributes dialog box. If you click Cancel in this dialog box, the form field will be inserted, but without the accessibility safeguards.

- When setting access keys, be sure not to specify a key commonly associated with common browser functions such as F, W, or Q.

- There's no universal language for access keys, so you need to let your users know what yours are. A common technique is to use Cascading Style Sheets (CSS) to underline the appropriate letter in the label so it looks like this:
  L̲ast Name
  or this:
  4̲. Last Name

What's in a Name? How About a Label or an ID?

When using the Input Tag Accessibility Attributes dialog box, Dreamweaver doesn't provide much in the way of naming controls. We'd prefer if Dreamweaver provided a `name` attribute here so that you could define the tag and all its attributes in one spot, but instead Dreamweaver names form fields sequentially and provides no opportunity for controlling the `for` attribute, in this dialog box, either.

For example, take the code in Step 4 of the previous list:

```
<input type="checkbox"
→ name="checkbox"
→ value="checkbox"
→ id="checkbox">
<label for="checkbox">
→ Text</label>
```

If you rename the form field in the Property inspector, from `checkbox` to `sendEmail`, you need then to remember to manually rename the `for` attribute of the label tag, because Dreamweaver won't do that for you. Additionally, if you want to reset the `value` and `id` attributes to be more useful than `checkbox`, you need to do that on your own as well.

If you want to edit tag properties using the Edit Tag dialog box, see *The Tag Editor* in Chapter 11.

Figure 16.11 Here, when we select the label tag, we also select the form field it modifies.

- When choosing the Style for your labels, there are a few things to consider. The first option, Wrap with Label Tag, generates simpler code, but you do have to be sure to keep the label and the form element together if you move them. The best way to ensure that you move them together is to select them by clicking on the `<label>` tag in the Tag selector (**Figure 16.11**) and moving both tags at once.

- The second Style option, Attach Label Tag Using 'for' Attribute, generates more code, but you don't have to worry about the label and the form element being adjacent. You can move them separately without any trouble. This method is not only technically sound, it is the preferred method for accessible forms, because it allows touch-screen or mouth-pointer users to select any part of the text *or* the form field in order to select within the form field.

- To edit tags on pages you've already created, see *The Tag Editor* in Chapter 11. Right-click (Ctrl+click) on the tag in Code view, and use the Edit Tag dialog box to apply accessibility attributes.

MAKING FORMS ACCESSIBLE

Tab order considerations

Setting tab order for forms is a good way to tell an alternative browser how to read a form, particularly if that form is laid out in a table. Without tab order, the browser would have to guess which form object came next on a page like **Figure 16.12**.

You can set the `taborder` attribute for links, as well, so that when the user is tabbing through a form, they can easily navigate through them as though they're part of the form rather than tabbing through the entire form and then tabbing through the links. In **Figure 16.13**, the mailing list link would come first, then its checkbox, and so on.

If you set tab order for any form object, you should set it for all the objects in the form.

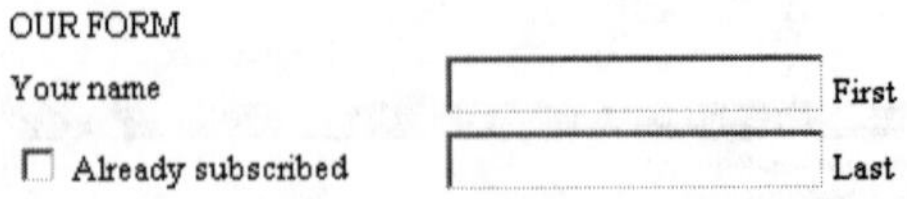

OUR FORM

Your name _____ First

☐ Already subscribed _____ Last

Figure 16.12 In a form like this one, tab order is important. We'd put First as 1, Last as 2, and the checkbox as 3.

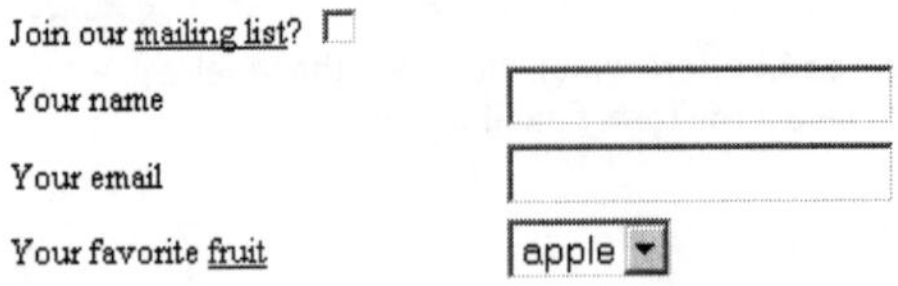

Join our mailing list? ☐

Your name _____

Your email _____

Your favorite fruit [apple ▼]

Figure 16.13 You can set the tab order in a form like this one to include the links as well as the form fields.

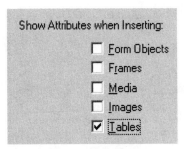

Figure 16.14 Turn on Form Object accessibility controls to get the dialog box in Figure 16.15 whenever you insert a form field.

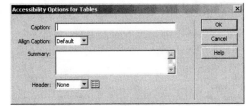

Figure 16.15 Accessibility controls for tables include a table caption, a summary, and header rows or columns.

Making Tables Accessible

You can identify your tables with captions and descriptions to make their contents known before users read the entire thing. In the case of screen readers, the software will read the caption and description aloud before setting off on the table itself.

To use table accessibility controls:

1. If you haven't done so already, turn on your Accessibility preferences for Form Objects. See the list earlier in this chapter, *To turn on Dreamweaver's accessibility authoring controls* (**Figure 16.14**).

2. The next time you insert a table using the Table button on the Insert toolbar or the Insert > Table command, the Accessibility Options for Tables dialog box will appear after you fill out the Insert Table dialog box. (**Figures 16.15**).

3. In the Caption box, type a caption for the table. This caption will appear on the page and will be read by screen readers.

4. From the Align Caption drop-down menu, choose an alignment for the caption: Default, Top, Bottom, Left, or Right. (See the Tips at the end of this exercise.)

5. In the Summary text box, type a description of the contents of the table. Screen readers will read this description, but it will not appear on the page.

continues on next page

MAKING TABLES ACCESSIBLE

6. From the Header drop-down menu, choose whether you want a header row, header column, both, or none. Header rows and columns help screen readers make sense of the table contents (**Figures 16.16** through **16.18**).

- ◆ Select None to skip the headings.
- ◆ Select Column to provide a column that will include a header for each row.
- ◆ Select Row to make the first row in the table include a header for each column.
- ◆ Select Both to define both the first row and the first column as headers.

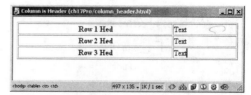

Figure 16.16 Set the header option as Column to make the first column consist of header cells to define each row in the table.

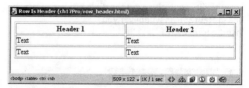

Figure 16.17 Set the header option as Row to make the first row consist of header cells to define each column in the table.

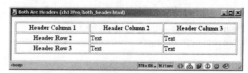

Figure 16.18 Set the header option as Both to make both the first row and the first column consist of header cells to define the content in the table.

Figure 16.19 The caption can appear above or below the table, and is not outlined with a table cell.

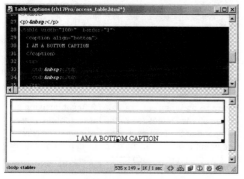

Figure 16.20 When you select the whole table, you also select the caption.

✔ Tips

- Although the caption does not appear in a cell as part of the table layout (**Figure 16.19**), the caption tag does appear within the table tag so that when you select the table, the caption will be included in your selection and will move with the appropriate table code (**Figure 16.20**).

- When setting alignment for a table caption, keep a few things in mind. First, the `align` attribute of the caption tag has been deprecated in HTML 4.0 in favor of using CSS to set any text properties for this tag. Second, the `top` and `bottom` values are the only universally supported attributes for the `caption` tag. They determine whether the caption appears at the top or the bottom of the table. In the HTML spec, `left` and `right` would make the caption itself appear to the left and right of the table. In Internet Explorer, however, captions are aligned at the top or bottom of the table using not `align` but the `valign` attribute, whereas the `align` values of `right` or `left` align the text itself to the right or left of the table cell. IE also supports a `center` attribute for the same reason. To make your alignment work on all browsers, use `top` or `bottom` for the value of the `align` attribute, and align the text itself using CSS.

Making Frames Accessible

Each frame in a frameset is a discrete HTML document. Frames have been around long enough now for most software to be able to load them properly, but not necessarily to know which frame to deal with first or whether a frame is important to the content of a page.

Frames always have a name attribute that you use when targeting links into a particular frame. For accessibility purposes, frames also take a title attribute that can be the same text as a frame name but can instead be meaningful text such as "Table of Contents," "Main Body," "Just a Logo," or "Visit Our Sponsor."

To deal with alternative browsers, add the title attribute to your frames.

1. If you haven't done so already, turn on your Accessibility preferences for Frames. See the list earlier in this chapter, *To turn on Dreamweaver's accessibility authoring controls* (**Figure 16.21**).

2. The next time you create a frameset using one of Dreamweaver's pre-built frames commands (see the Tips on the next page), the Frame Tag Accessibility Attributes dialog box will appear. (**Figure 16.22**).

3. The names for your frames will appear in the Frame drop-down menu. If you're creating a page using Dreamweaver's pre-built frames layouts in the New Document dialog box, these names will make sense (bottomFrame, mainFrame, etc.).

   You can change these names later if you like.

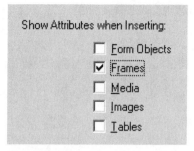

Figure 16.21 Turn on Frames Accessibility controls to get the dialog box in Figure 16.22 whenever you insert a form field.

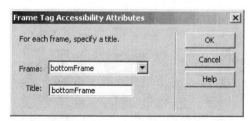

Figure 16.22 When you create a frameset by using a button on the Frames tab of the Insert toolbar, or by using one of the Frameset page designs in the New Document toolbar, this dialog box will prompt you for the title attribute of each frame in the frameset.

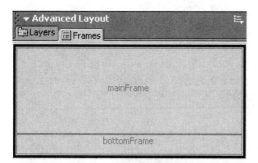

Figure 16.23 Display the frames panel before you create a frameset, and the frame names will appear in it when the Frame Tag Accessibility dialog box is open.

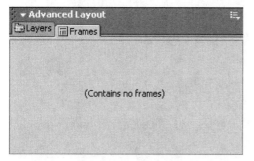

Figure 16.24 Sometimes the Frames panel will not display the names while you're using the Frame Tag Accessibility dialog box.

4. In the Title box, type a name for the frame listed in the Frame drop-down menu. This should be meaningful text, and you can use whatever spaces, capital letters, and so on that you wish.

5. Choose the second frame from the Frame drop-down menu and assign it a name in the Title box.

6. Repeat Step 5 for any additional frames.

7. Click on OK to return to the Document window.

✔ Tips

■ If you create a frame by dragging, the accessibility controls will not be triggered. (You do this by viewing frame borders with the View > Visual Aids > Frame Borders command, and then by holding down the Alt key while dragging a frame border. You create a valid frameset this way, but you do not get prompted with a dialog box. You can add the `title` attribute to a frame on the frameset page by hand.)

■ When you create a frame by clicking a button on the Frames tab of the Insert toolbar, or by selecting a design from the Frameset category of the New Document toolbar, the accessibility dialog box will appear.

■ Frame names are displayed in the Frames panel (**Figure 16.23**; Window > Others > Frames). You need to open this panel *before* creating a frameset page in order to use it to verify the positions of frame names while using the Frame Tag Accessibility dialog box. Occasionally, the Frames panel will appear blank while you are creating a frameset (**Figure 16.24**). You can always double-check the names later, and you can change frame names in the Property inspector at any time as long as you do it before targeting your links.

Alternatives to Images and Media

Images and other kinds of media can be tricky, in terms of conveying their content to visually impaired users. You can't replicate an image in text, much less a multimedia application. The best you can do at this point is to provide a description of the content that users would otherwise miss.

Figure 16.25 Type a text description of your image in the Alt text box in the Property inspector.

Figure 16.26 For non-content images, set a blank Alt attribute so the screen reader will skip them.

Always use Alt text

Some users, like those who access your site with text-only browsers like Lynx or visually impaired users who use screen readers that turn text into speech, will not be able to see the images on your site. For those users you should use the Alt attribute of the <img> tag to provide alternative text in lieu of the image. Alternative text is required by Section 508 standards for images that provide content. (See Tips at the end of the following stepped list.)

To add Alt text to an image:

1. Select the image in the Document window.

2. In the Property inspector, type the alternative text in the Alt text box (**Figure 16.25**). This should be a description of the image.

Figure 16.27 Another useful purpose for Alt text: tool tips. The browser and platform need to have these enabled for them to appear.

✔ Tips

- For images for which you already provide a descriptive caption, you do not need to provide an additional Alt attribute.

- For images such as placeholders, spacers, logos, and other non-content items, you can designate the image as a spacer by giving it an empty Alt attribute, like so :
  `<img src="foo.gif" alt="">`
  In the Property inspector, select the image, and then select `<empty>` from the Alt drop-down menu (**Figure 16.26**). The screen reader or other device will be satisfied that it can safely skip the image.

- Alt text will appear as a tool tip in many standard browsers when the user mouses over the image (**Figure 16.27**).

- You can use an alternate description of any length, but a suggested length depends on who's making the recommendation. Some say stop at 150 characters; others recommend limiting the text to 10 words or 60 characters.

- For images such as buttons on a toolbar, consider two things: First, if you provide text equivalents of the links on the buttons, you can designate these as spacers, because users can navigate your site by other means. Second, if you have a toolbar that appears at the top of every page, screen readers may read the Alt text every time a user goes to a new page, so that the first thing they hear would be "Home, Search, About..." and so on. It might make more sense to provide these as text links at the bottom of the page.

- Image maps present their own difficulties. Don't rely on server-side image maps, in which the destinations of the links are hidden from users until they click. Client-side image maps can be used in some contexts. In any case, for all kinds of smart reasons (including unforeseen problems with your code), you should provide text equivalents of all the link destinations in the image map, either on the same page or on a page called "Text Only Site Map" or some such thing.

Using Dreamweaver's accessibility controls for images

1. If you haven't done so already, turn on your Accessibility preferences for Images. See *To turn on Dreamweaver's accessibility authoring controls* (**Figure 16.28**) earlier in this chapter.

2. The next time you insert an image using Dreamweaver, an Image Tag Accessibility Attributes dialog box will appear (**Figure 16.29**).

3. To provide Alt text for the image, type it in the Alternate Text text box.

4. To provide the URL for a longer description of the image, type it in the Long Description text box, or click on the Browse button to pick out the file in your local site.

5. Click on OK to return to the Document window.

Using Dreamweaver's accessibility controls for media objects

1. If you haven't done so already, turn on your Accessibility preferences for Media. See *To turn on Dreamweaver's accessibility authoring controls* earlier in this chapter (**Figure 16.30**).

2. The next time you insert a media object using Dreamweaver, a dialog box will appear.

   For Flash, Shockwave, and ActiveX, this dialog box will be called Object Tag Accessibility Attributes (**Figure 16.31**) and will allow you to set a Title that describes the media object. You can also provide an access key and a Tab order, but this is really useful only for elements such as Flash Text or Flash buttons that are used in navigation. These elements are not required.

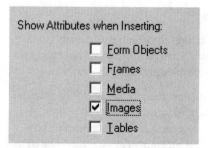

Figure 16.28 Turn on Images Accessibility controls to get the dialog box in Figure 16.29 whenever you insert a form field.

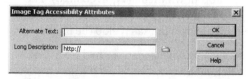

Figure 16.29 When you insert an image, this dialog box will prompt you for the required Alt text and the optional long description.

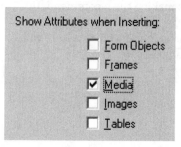

Figure 16.30 Turn on Media Accessibility controls to get one of the dialog boxes in Figures 16.31-32 whenever you insert a form field.

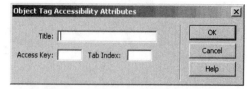

Figure 16.31 When you insert a Flash or Shockwave object, an ActiveX control, or a plug-in that uses the object tag, this dialog box will prompt you to give the media object a title and an optional tab index number and control key. You can also apply the Alt attribute by hand.

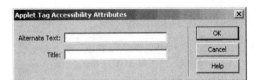

Figure 16.32 When you insert a Java applet, this dialog box will prompt you to give the applet an `Alt` attribute and a title.

For Java, the dialog box will be called Applet Tag Accessibility Attributes (**Figure 16.32**). This allows you to set an Alt text description of the applet and a title for it, if you wish.

For Netscape plug-ins other than Shockwave or Flash, the accessibility attributes may depend on the type of plug-in and the type of browser that interprets it.

3. Click on OK to return to the Document window.

✔ Tips

- You can use the `alt` attribute with the `object` tag for Flash, plug-ins and so on, even though the dialog box doesn't provide for it.

- For multimedia files that provide navigational content, such as links or image maps, be sure to provide a text equivalent of the file.

- You can use an audio-only equivalent of the page if you like. Or, for a movie, you can tell the user, by way of the Alt text or the description of the movie, that the user can play it and enjoy the audio without the video.

- You can use behaviors to provide redirects from media-heavy pages to pages that use only text or only audio. See Chapter 13 for more about behaviors.

Using CSS-2 to Make Pages Useful Across Devices

The CSS-2 spec, which extends the typographic and positioning aspects of cascading style sheets, includes many options for using CSS to make pages accessible. As of this writing, most of these specifications are pure theory, because the devices that may one day implement them don't yet exist.

As a starting guideline for using CSS for accessibility, always define your font sizes in points, or relative sizes such as large and small, instead of pixels. TTY or TTD (text telephone device) screens for the deaf, some of which are also used for Internet communications, can't deal with pixel sizes.

In the future, when more of these devices exist, you will be able to declare media types with styles; detect the type of reader and use the appropriate style sheet; provide page break markers; declare voice type cues; and devise audio presentations that would be read if the browser is a CSS-capable screen reader.

You'll also be able to devise alternate style sheets that would display text in different sizes and layouts depending on the device.

None of these aspects of CSS are supported directly by Dreamweaver except page breaks, which are available in the Extensions category of the Style Definition dialog box. As these have yet to be implemented in any consistent way, it's difficult for us to advise you how to put them on your pages.

To read about the possibilities, visit the spec itself at `http://www.w3.org/TR/REC-CSS2/` and especially see Section 7: Media types; Section 13, Paged Media; and Section 19, Aural Style sheets.

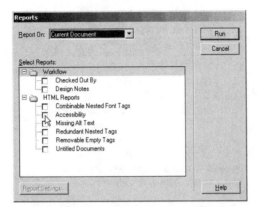

Figure 16.33 Use the Reports dialog box to check for accessibility compliance and missing Alt descriptions of your images.

Figure 16.34 Your results will show up in the Site Reports panel of the Results panel group.

Validating Code & Using Site Reporting

You can validate your pages for accessibility compliance at any point in the development process. Keep in mind that, as with any HTML validation tool, the accessibility checker will turn up errors that aren't really errors just because it can't read your page like a human would to see if it really passes muster.

To run an accessibility check on the current page:

1. Save your page.

2. From the menu bar, select File > Check Page > Check Accessibility

   or

   From the menu bar, select Site > Reports, and in the Reports dialog box, select the Accessibility checkbox (**Figure 16.33**). Then click Run.

   Either way, Dreamweaver will run a check on the current page, and its findings will appear in the Site Reports panel of the Results panel group (**Figure 16.34**).

✔ Tip

- In the Reports dialog box in Figure 16.33, you can also run a report on a page, a site, or a folder, requesting a list of those images that don't have Alt attributes included. See *Browser Profiles* in Chapter 11 for more on using this dialog box. (The Results panel tools work the same way for Browser Profiles, Site Reports, and Target Browser Checks.)

To find out more about an error:

1. Run an accessibility check as described in the preceding list.

2. Click on the description in the Site Reports panel.

3. Click on the Info button 🛈 .

   A full description of the checkpoint and the possible error will appear in the Reference panel of the Code panel group (**Figure 16.35**).

✔ Tips

■ To find out more about following all these rules, see the next section, *Using the Accessibility Reference*.

■ To save your report as XML or HTML or load it in the browser window; or to run a report on an entire folder or site, see *Browser Profiles* in Chapter 11.

Using the Accessibility Reference

The Accessibility Reference included in Dreamweaver includes many of the accessibility checkpoints specified by the W3C, the WCAG, and Section 508.

To use the Accessibility Reference:

See the preceding section to use the Accessibility Reference with site reporting, or follow the steps below:

1. Open the Reference panel (Window > Reference).

2. From the Book drop-down menu, select UseableNet Accessibility Reference.

3. Browse the Rule menu and select a rule to read more about it.

Figure 16.36 shows what the Reference panel includes in its descriptions.

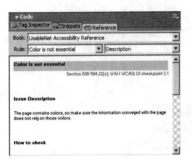

Figure 16.35 You can read a description of the error and how to remedy it in the Reference panel.

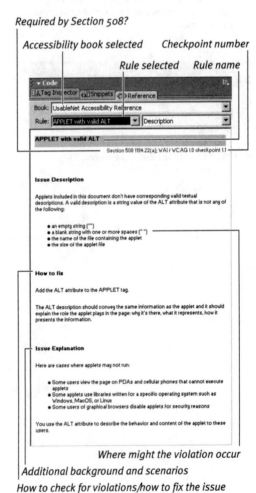

Required by Section 508?

Accessibility book selected   *Checkpoint number*

Rule selected   *Rule name*

Where might the violation occur

Additional background and scenarios

How to check for violations/how to fix the issue

Figure 16.36 The accessibility rules described in the Accessibility Reference can be both helpful and cryptic.

Understanding Compliance Rules

First of all, no one is going to send you to jail for noncompliance with accessibility standards. The standards themselves recommend transitional content—that is, content where you're trying your best to present to as wide an audience as possible, understanding that you may not have gotten around to providing text equivalents of your Flash games.

Secondly, the wording of rules themselves as presented in Dreamweaver can be confounding. Some are presented as positives and some as negatives, so that when you run a check, you may not know whether you've broken a rule or not. "Scripts are accessible" sounds like an affirmation that the scripts on your page are doing just fine, but in fact it's a motto that actually means "Make sure your scripts are accessible."

We covered the basics for forms, frames, tables, images, and media in this chapter. Here are some of the more obscure-sounding rules with some ideas of how to address them.

◆ *Colors are visible* and *Color is not essential.* These both mean that your pages use colors in the text, background, and table elements. Be sure that the colors and backgrounds contrast enough so that the text is readable. If you use CSS to present your colors, the page is probably perfectly readable as black and white without the style sheet loaded.

◆ *Style sheets should not be necessary.* After all the advice given about using CSS to make sure your pages are *more* accessible, the standard makers go and tell us not to rely on CSS. In a truly accessible page, the page shouldn't have to *rely* on CSS to present content. The far-reaching guidelines intend that people using ancient

equipment are able to view your page as well. You can temporarily detach a style sheet from your page, or use design-time style sheets, to make sure the text is still legible and the links still work.

◆ *Skip repetitive links.* You can actually provide a "Skip to Content" button that could be disguised as a placeholder for standard browsers and that lets the user decide not to listen to your toolbar at the top of every page and instead skip straight to the article.

◆ *Avoid causing the screen to flicker* and *GIFs do not cause screen to flicker.* Screen flicker can cause fatigue, and in the worst of cases, seizures for those with photosensitive epilepsy. Animated GIFs or Flash animations with a frame refresh rate between 2 and 55 frames per second may cause unnecessary flicker. Make your animated GIFs faster than 55 FPS, or be sure that they don't change between dark and light at this slow rate. You may get these warnings for any media object on your page.

◆ *Clarify natural language usage* and *Use clear language for site's content.* The latter language note here is a reminder that all users will benefit from using clear, concise grammar and style to get your point across. On the other hand, the first rule, "clarify natural language usage," points to the little-implemented `lang` attribute of various HTML tags. In the future, this attribute might be used for screen readers to assume different accents, although most extant screen readers can read in only one language, generally English. To set this attribute, see *The Tag Editor* section of Chapter 11.

continues on next page

◆ *No auto redirect is used* and *No auto refresh is used.* Accessibility guidelines recommend that you don't use these automatic page-loading controls because users currently don't have control over them. Automatically refreshing a page may disorient a user who isn't sure what's happening, and when a page reloads in a screen reader, the reader begins the page over again. For small screens and old browsers, the problems are similar. These page properties are discussed in Chapter 15. Instead of using auto redirects (which can actually come in handy to point a user's browser to a text-only or media-free page) for pages that present updated content, use cache expiration controls.

◆ *No JavaScript links are used.* If your page includes links that can only be triggered by using JavaScript, make sure you provide equivalent content for browsers that can't handle JavaScript or for user events that can't be triggered by alternative browsers. To make sure your null links can work in as many environments as possible, use "#" for the link instead of "javascript:". Another suggestion is to simultaneously use onKeyPress with onClick or onMouseOver for the user event. See Chapters 13 and 18 for more information.

About WML: The Wireless Markup Language

The wireless markup language, or WML, is a flavor of XML designed to be used by portable devices such as mobile phones and personal digital assistants. Most of these devices in their current form have tiny screens, generally in black and white or a limited number of colors.

WML is technically not an accessibility standard, but it does require that sites consider an alternate presentation of their content. For example, the same Alt text and descriptions used to tag images, forms, and tables, can be used by WAP-compatible devices to decide how to present or describe information. A whole row of buttons marked IMAGE IMAGE IMAGE doesn't do cell-phone users any more good than it does visually impaired users.

As the name implies, WML is a full-fledged language with its own scripting component and controls known as the deck/card elements and the event elements. Although the common WML tags are listed in the Tag Chooser dialog box described in Chapter 11, none of them have definitions. Also, in the Tag Library editor described in Chapter 12, you can add attributes, tags, and formatting to WML tags.

We found a few good resources for developing wireless pages and applications:

◆ The Wireless Developer Network:
http://www.wirelessdevnet.com/

◆ The WML/WAP pages at Web Reference, including some emulators for Windows. Go to http://www.webreference.com and search or browse for WML.

◆ The WAP Forum at Open Mobile Alliance, at
http://www.wapforum.org/

DRAWING TIMELINES

Timelines let you create animations on a Web page without having to use Flash or write the Dynamic HTML code yourself. Timelines animate layers and thus appear to animate any object that's in a layer on the page.

Timelines use JavaScript to control layers (see **Figures 17.1** through **17.4** on the next page). A layer can move, resize, appear, or disappear—and these actions are controlled by a sequence of *animation frames*.

These frames are similar to the idea of frames in films, cartoons, and flipbooks. And if you've made movies with Flash, Director, or Final Cut Pro—or even if you've made an animated GIF—then you've already manipulated frames to create animation. Just like the frames of footage in a movie, each frame can be slightly different from the last, which creates the illusion of movement over time on a 2-D surface. In this case, of course, the 2-D surface is a Web page projected on a computer screen rather than a film projected on a movie screen.

Timelines can look kind of cute, and on the few sites that use them, they provide cool special effects. But can they actually be useful? Well, because certain properties of a layer change (such as visibility, position, stacking order, and size), and because these properties can be triggered by a user event, you could use them to create showy navigation schemes or, in combination with JavaScript, you could even trigger requests for user registration, set cookies, or provide bubble captions to go with a photo gallery or catalog that someone is browsing. But you could do those things using image rollovers or the Change Property or Show-Hide Layer behaviors without creating a timeline. (Those behaviors are covered in Chapter 13.) Because the intrinsic function of timelines is to make these events happen over time, the main use of timelines is for simple animations—and whether animation is useful is a question you'll have to answer for yourself.

✔ Tips

■ Because timelines rely on layers in order to work their magic, they can only be viewed in 4.0 and later browsers.

■ A layer, you may recall, is a container for content that can be positioned anywhere on a page. Layers can also overlap or stack on top of one another, a property called z-index or stacking order. Layers generally use the <div> tag and their other properties include size, visibility, and background color or transparency.

■ If you need a comprehensive guide to inserting and editing layers, see Chapter 14 of the *Macromedia Dreamweaver MX for Windows and Macintosh: Visual QuickStart Guide* by J. Tarin Towers.

Figure 17.1 The magic bus at futurefarmers.com uses a timeline in a JavaScript pop-up window.

Figure 17.2 It moves!

Figure 17.3 It keeps moving until it's off the screen, and then it starts over.

Figure 17.4 One click opens a new little window with a new timeline.

What Timelines Can Do

Timelines can incorporate three types of objects: layers, images, and behaviors.

In this chapter, we're going to rely on a few modules to try to illustrate motion on the page. The layers on this page include a bordered one with an image of a little person in it, and a map.

Layer properties that a timeline can change include the following:

Figure 17.5
The timeline moves the layer from left to right. You can use more complex movements, too.

Figure 17.6 You can use a timeline to show or hide layers. In this case, three layers appear over the background image. You can have this happen over time or you can have a user event trigger the action. The layers can appear all at once or in sequence.

- ◆ **Moving a layer** by changing its X+Y coordinates (on the page or within the parent layer) (**Figure 17.5**).

- ◆ **Showing or hiding a layer** by changing its visibility. You can switch between the three optional states: visible, hidden, or default (**Figure 17.6**).

- ◆ **Changing the stacking order**, or Z-index (**Figure 17.7**).

- ◆ **Resizing a layer** by adjusting its dimensions (**Figure 17.8**).

Figure 17.7 The timeline changes the Z-index of the layers. In the first screen, the layers "person" and "deadend" are stacked behind "map." In the second screen, the map layer has the lowest z-index and is thus stacked behind the other two.

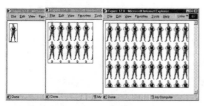

Figure 17.8 The timeline increases the size of the layer. This layer uses a background image that is tiled as the layer expands.

✔ Tip

■ Navigator 4 does not support resizing layers during a timeline.

The only image property that a timeline can change directly is the **image source**. (You cannot change, say, the image size or border.) By swapping the source—that is, by making the image path point to a different image— you can perform image rollovers during a timeline without writing additional JavaScript, or inserting additional behaviors, or asking the user to do anything at all.

Timelines can also **call a behavior** from a particular frame. You can also use a behavior to start, stop, or skip to a particular frame within a timeline. (If you're not familiar with behaviors, they're little interactive JavaScript widgets that you can write using Dreamweaver's tools rather than by hand-coding. These events can be *called*—that is, triggered— by a user event or by another script, which is what the timeline itself is. JavaScript and behaviors are covered in detail in Chapter 13.

The Timelines Panel

The Timelines panel (**Figure 17.9**) is the tool you use to create and modify timelines in Dreamweaver.

To view the Timelines panel:

◆ From the menu bar, select Window > Others > Timelines.

or

Press Alt+F9.

Either way, the Timelines panel will appear in its own panel group at the bottom of the Document window. We show it both docked and undocked in this chapter.

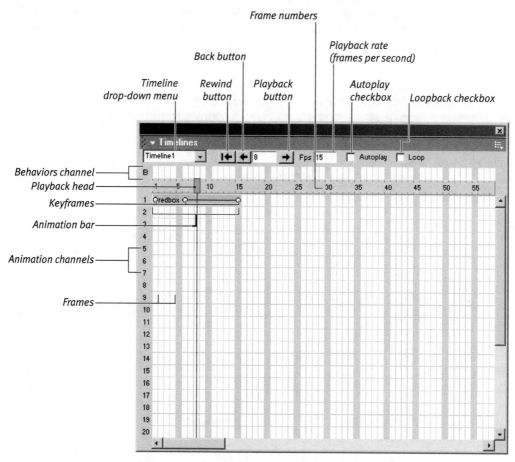

Figure numbers
Playback rate (frames per second)
Back button
Timeline drop-down menu
Rewind button
Playback button
Autoplay checkbox
Loopback checkbox

Behaviors channel
Playback head
Keyframes
Animation bar
Animation channels
Frames

Figure 17.9 The Timelines panel.

Dissecting the Timelines Panel

Each part of the Timelines panel controls a different aspect of a timeline. Some of these elements won't really make much cognitive sense until you see them in operation, but you can use this page as a reference for what things do. Let's start at the top (**Figure 17.10**).

If you include more than one timeline on a page, you can switch between timelines by choosing the timeline name from the **Timeline drop-down menu**.

You can play timelines in the Document window using the Timelines panel's playback controls. The **Rewind button** rewinds the timeline back to the beginning. The **Back button** rewinds one frame at a time; hold it

down to play the timeline backwards. The **Playback button** advances one frame at a time; hold it down to play the entire timeline. The current frame is indicated in the **Frame number** text box.

The **playback rate** is in frames per second (fps). The default is 15 fps; you can set it higher or lower depending on your content.

You can easily add behaviors to control how the animation plays when loaded in the browser. The **Autoplay checkbox** adds a behavior that will make the timeline start as soon as the page finishes loading. The **Loopback checkbox** adds a behavior that will make the timeline play continuously while the page is in the browser.

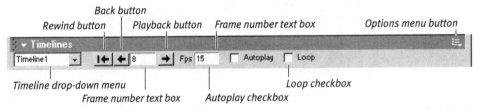

Figure 17.10 The Toolbar on the Timelines panel.

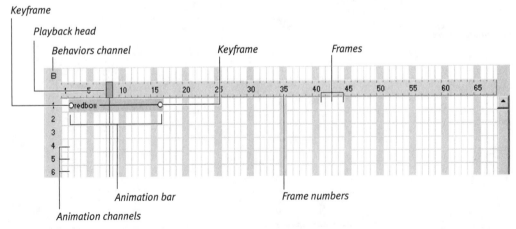

Figure 17.11 The content area of the Timelines panel.

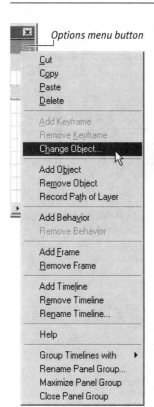

Options menu button

Figure 17.12
The options menu on the Timelines panel offers quick access to timeline commands.

Now we move to the part of the Timelines panel that controls the content (**Figure 17.11**).

Use the **Behaviors channel** to add behaviors that will be called from a certain frame in the timeline.

Each numbered column in the Timelines panel is a **frame**. Each frame is numbered. The **playback head** (the red bar) shows the advance of the playback. As the playback head passes over each frame, the frame number will appear next to the Playback button.

Each numbered row in the Timelines panel is an **animation channel**. Different objects usually use different animation channels.

When an object is added to a timeline, the Timelines panel displays an **animation bar** in that object's animation channel. The little bullets at the beginning and end of the animation bar are **keyframes**. You can add other keyframes in the middle of an animation bar to add actions to the timeline.

✔ Tips

- A *keyframe* is a point on a timeline where something happens. A timeline is comprised entirely of "frames"—like the frames in a movie—and a keyframe, just like in animation or digital video, is an action point. When you set two actions in two keyframes, the animation program—Dreamweaver in this case—creates a smooth flow to get from one point to another. So if in one keyframe King Kong is on the ground, and in another keyframe King Kong is on top of the Empire State Building, in the intervening frames, he'd be ascending the building.

- In Figure 17.10, at the right side of the Timelines panel, you can see an Options menu button. This button pops up a menu of commands (**Figure 17.12**) you can use when editing a timeline.

Adding a Layer to a Timeline

You create a timeline by adding a layer to the Timelines panel. Once you drag or add the layer, Dreamweaver creates a timeline for it and adds the code to the page automatically.

To add a layer to a timeline:

1. Make sure the object you want to animate is in a layer, and that the layer has the size and position that you want it to start with.

2. Select the layer in the Document window (**Figure 17.13**) by selecting its handle or tag.

3. From the menu bar, select Modify > Timeline > Add Object to Timeline.

   or

   Right-click (Ctrl+click) on an animation bar in the Timelines panel, and select Add Object from the context menu.

A new, named animation bar will appear in the Timelines panel (**Figure 17.14**).

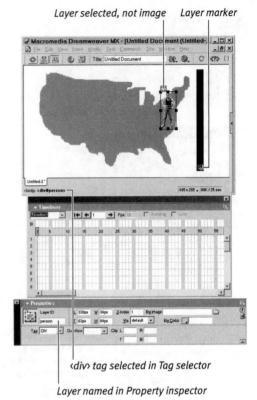

Layer selected, not image   Layer marker

<div> tag selected in Tag selector

Layer named in Property inspector

Figure 17.13 Select the layer in the Document window. Notice that the Timelines panel doesn't have any objects in it yet.

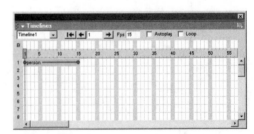

Figure 17.14 When you add the layer to the timeline, an animation bar appears in the first available animation channel.

ADDING A LAYER TO A TIMELINE

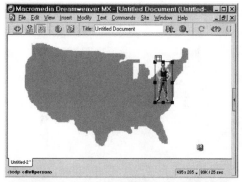

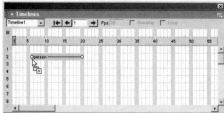

Figure 17.15 Dragging and dropping a layer into the Timelines panel—it lands in the channel and starts at the frame where you drop it.

✔ Tips

- Before you add a layer to a timeline, be sure that you name it in the Property inspector. Named layers are easier to manage than numbered ones.

- You can also have a timeline call image rollovers or another JavaScript behavior. See the sections *Adding an Image Rollover to a Timeline* and *Adding a Behavior to a Timeline* later in this chapter.

- You can also drag a layer onto the Timelines panel to add it to the timeline. Click on the layer and drag it to the location (channel and frame) where you want it to appear (**Figure 17.15**).

Timeline Actions

Timeline actions were briefly described in *What Timelines Can Do* earlier in this chapter. In the next few sections, we're going to go over each action, step by step, starting with moving a layer. As we go through each action a layer can perform, we'll describe the various modifications you can make to a timeline.

Moving a layer

The easiest way to start learning about timelines is to move a layer on the page.

To move a layer using a timeline:

1. Add the layer to the timeline.

2. In the Timelines panel, click on the keyframe bullet at the end of the layer's animation bar (**Figure 17.16**). The playback head (the red bar) will move to that frame.

   The layer will automatically be selected in the Document window.

3. Click on the layer's selection handle and drag it to the position on the page where you want it to end up (**Figure 17.17**).

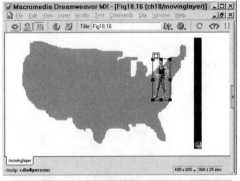

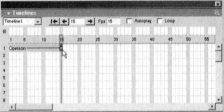

Figure 17.16 Click on the last keyframe bullet in the layer's animation bar to select that frame as well as the layer.

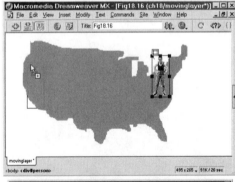

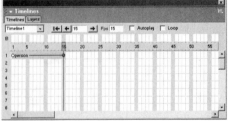

Figure 17.17 With the end keyframe selected, drag the layer to a new location and let go.

Figure 17.18 The Timelines panel will record the new position and draw a line from position 1 (where the layer used to be) to position 2 (where you dropped the layer).

You'll see a line drawn from the layer's old position to its new position (**Figure 17.18**). The line connects the top-left corners of the layer in each position. This is the path the layer will follow.

✔ Tips

■ Notice in Figure 17.17 that we've stacked the Layers panel with the Timelines panel. We can flip back and forth between them easily and save desktop space, and we don't have to keep the side stack of panels open. (By default the Layers panel appears initially on the Advanced Layout panel group.) To move a panel onto or off of another one, click the panel's Options menu button and select Group [Panel] With > [Other Panel Group].

■ Notice also that in Figure 17.17 the layer marker is no longer visible. From the menu bar, we selected View > Visual Aids and unchecked Invisible Elements.

TIMELINE ACTIONS

Recording movement

If you want your layer to travel in a line that isn't straight, you can record its movement.

To record a layer's path:

1. Select the layer by its handle and move it to its starting position.

2. In the Timelines panel, click within the animation frame where you want movement to begin.

3. From the menu bar, select Modify > Timeline > Record Path of Layer.

4. Drag the layer's selection handle along the path you want to use. Loop-de-loops are allowed (**Figure 17.19**). As you drag, dots will mark the path you're drawing.

5. When you let go of the mouse button, the layer's path will be translated into an animation channel (**Figure 17.20**), with keyframes marking specific spots between which the layer travels along its path.

6. Click and hold the Play button [→] to watch the layer retrace the path you drew for it.

✔ Tips

- Recording the path of a layer will add the layer to the timeline, even if it already appears there. To rearrange animation bars, see the next section.

- Occasionally, you may get an error message stating that a layer with the same name is already in the timeline. Click within a different frame and draw your movement again.

Figure 17.19 Using the Record Path of Layer command, we can drag a layer all over the place and the timeline will follow. The little dots represent points that the top-left corner of the layer has graced.

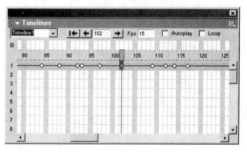

Figure 17.20 After we recorded the path of the layer, the layer appeared as an object in the Timelines panel—with more than 100 frames.

Setting the Playback Rate

The default playback rate for Dreamweaver timelines is 15 frames per second. Macromedia advises not to set this rate much faster; the 15 fps rate is based on optimal performance on the average machine. Setting a faster playback rate might not actually make the animation go faster; although it might do so on your local machine, all the images and layers that you're playing with are stored in your memory cache. You can, however, set a lower rate for slower speeds.

TIMELINE ACTIONS

Figure 17.21 If you've already added this layer to the timeline, Dreamweaver will add a separate animation sequence (with its own beginning and ending keyframes) after the initial sequence.

Figure 17.22 In this case, we haven't added any actions to the initial animation sequence. We can select it and delete it. We can also cut, copy, and paste it, as long as it doesn't overlap another sequence with the same object in it.

Figure 17.23 After deleting the sequence that didn't have any actions in it, we select the sequence that includes the recorded path by clicking on a non-key (unmarked) frame.

Figure 17.24 We drag the sequence to Frame 1 of the timeline. You can also drag sequences to later in the timeline or to other animation channels.

Deleting and moving animation sequences

Recording the path of a layer adds that layer to the timeline. If the layer already appears in the timeline, Dreamweaver will add the layer again later in the same animation channel (**Figure 17.21**). Animation bars cannot overlap.

You can delete or move animation bars. For example, in Figure 17.21, the initial, blank bar remains. We select the bar (**Figure 17.22**) and press Delete to remove it. Then, we select the bar that includes the recorded path (**Figure 17.23**) and drag it to the beginning of the timeline (**Figure 17.24**).

TIMELINE ACTIONS

Playing it back

You can watch the movements you've recorded by playing back the timeline.

To play back a timeline:

1. In the Timelines panel, click on the Rewind button ![rewind] to move the playback head back to the beginning of the timeline.

   or

   Click on Frame 1 in the Timelines panel to move it back (**Figure 17.25**).

2. If the Timelines panel is undocked, move it out of the way in the Document window.

3. In the Timelines panel, click on and hold down the Play button ![play].

You'll see the layer move across the page (**Figure 17.26**).

✔ Tips

- You can click within any frame to see what the page looks like at that point in the timeline.

- You can play and rewind little bits of the timeline with the Rewind, Back, and Play buttons (**Figure 17.27**).

- To fine-tune a point within a timeline, see *About Keyframes*, on the next page.

Previewing in a browser and setting Autoplay

A timeline won't play when previewed in a browser unless you instruct it to do so. If you add the Autoplay behavior, the timeline will play as soon as the page finishes loading.

Just check the Autoplay checkbox on the Timelines panel (**Figure 17.28**), and then preview the page (**Figure 17.29**). For more on controlling timelines, see *Making Timelines Go*, later in this chapter.

TIMELINE ACTIONS

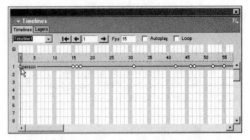

Figure 17.25 Click on Frame 1, or click on the Rewind button to return the timeline to its beginning.

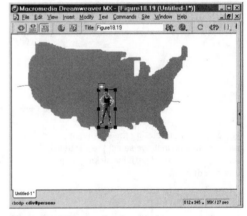

Figure 17.26 The timeline in mid-play.

Figure 17.27 The Rewind, Back, and Play buttons.

Figure 17.28 Click on the Autoplay checkbox to make the timeline play in the browser window.

Preview button

Figure 17.29 Preview your timeline in a 4.0 or later browser.

Playback head   *Current frame number*

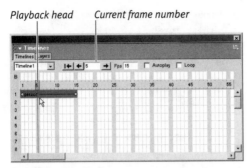

Figure 17.30 Click at the point on the animation bar where you want to add the new keyframe. The playback head will move, and you'll see the frame number in its text box.

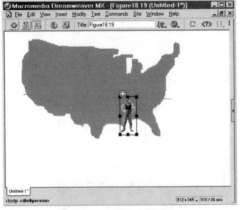

Figure 17.31 Our person goes from Maryland straight to California. We want her to pay a visit to New York City first. We play the timeline and stop at a fairly early point, where we'll add a keyframe.

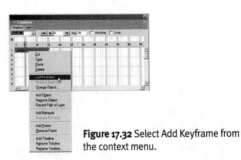

Figure 17.32 Select Add Keyframe from the context menu.

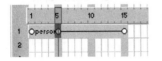

Figure 17.33
A keyframe bullet will appear on the animation bar.

About Keyframes

The Timelines panel tracks the movement of a layer from one point to another, frame by frame, and it paces the movement of an object so that the frame-to-frame transitions are smooth.

If there are only two points in a timeline, the line in which the layer moves must be a straight one. You can add a third point to a timeline to make a layer move in an arc, or you can add points for multiple positions or actions.

You do this by adding keyframes. A *keyframe*, as mentioned earlier in the chapter, is a point on a timeline where something happens. Each animation bar in a timeline includes at least two keyframes: the beginning frame and the end frame.

To add a keyframe:

1. In the Timelines panel, click on the place on the animation bar where you want the new action to happen (**Figure 17.30**), or press the Play button until you reach it (**Figure 17.31**). The playback head will move to the new frame.

2. From the menu bar, select Modify > Timeline > Add Keyframe.

   or

   Right-click (Ctrl+click) on the object's animation bar in the Timelines panel, and select Add Keyframe from the context menu that appears (**Figure 17.32**).

   or

   Press F6.

The Timelines panel will add a keyframe bullet to the animation bar (**Figure 17.33**).

Now you can attach a new position to that keyframe.

To add a new layer position to a keyframe:

1. In the Timelines panel, click on the new keyframe. The layer will become selected automatically (**Figure 17.34**).

2. Move the layer to the position on the page where you want it to be when that keyframe is played (**Figure 17.35**).

The line drawn between the beginning position on the page and the end position on the page will now arc to fit the third point into the movement line (**Figure 17.36**).

Play back the timeline now to see how this movement looks.

Now you know how to change a layer's position, play back a timeline, and add keyframes (and therefore, additional actions) to a timeline. Let's look at some of the other things timelines can do.

✔ Tips

- You can add keyframes and then attach other actions to them, too. We'll do this throughout this chapter.

- How do you detach movements from a layer? What if you make a layer move and then change your mind? First, click on the frame in which the layer is where you want it to be. Then, open the Property inspector and take note of the L(eft) and T(op) measurements. In the Timelines panel, move to the keyframe where the movement changes. In the Property inspector, type the numbers you jotted down in the L and T text boxes. Repeat for any additional keyframes where the layer's position attributes have changed.

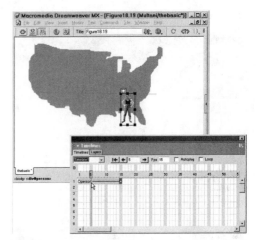

Figure 17.34 Select the keyframe, and the layer will automatically become selected.

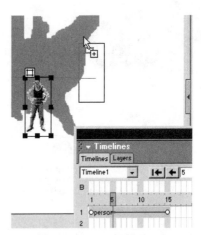

Figure 17.35 With the keyframe selected in the Timelines panel, move the layer to its new location.

Figure 17.36 We fast-forwarded to later in the timeline so you could see the arc drawn by Dreamweaver between the three keyframes.

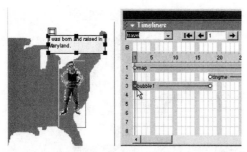

Figure 17.37 First, we add the new layer to the timeline, and put text in it.

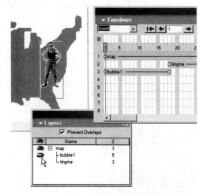

Figure 17.38 Then, we set its initial visibility to hidden on the first keyframe.

Keyframe 5 is selected for "bubble1" layer

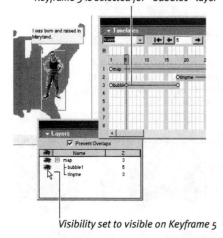

Visibility set to visible on Keyframe 5

Figure 17.39 Finally, we added a new keyframe and set the layer's visibility to visible on the fifth keyframe. When the timeline plays, the second layer will appear on Keyframe 5 after the first layer starts moving.

Showing and Hiding Layers

You can show or hide a layer in a timeline by changing its visibility to visible, hidden, or default.

To show or hide a layer:

1. If the layer is not already added to the timeline, add it.

2. Click on the first keyframe on the layer's animation bar (**Figure 17.37**).

3. Using the Layers panel or the Property inspector, set the layer's visibility to the state you want it to be in when the timeline begins playing (**Figure 17.38**).

4. On the layer's animation bar, add the keyframe where you want the visibility change to occur.

5. With the proper keyframe selected, change the visibility of the layer (**Figure 17.39**).

6. If you want the layer to change visibility again at the end of the timeline, click on the keyframe at the end of the layer's animation bar, and change the layer's visibility.

To change the location of a keyframe:

1. In the Timelines panel, click on the keyframe you want to move.

2. Hold down the mouse button and drag the keyframe bullet to a different frame.

3. Let go of the mouse button.

Voilà! The keyframe has moved.

✔ Tip

■ Images that are in hidden layers are automatically downloaded with the page. This is a good way to preload images for swapping image source. Or skip the source swapping altogether and just show or hide the layers that the new images are in.

Changing the Overlaps

As you know, a layer's Z-index, or stacking order, is what makes layers so layer-like. You can change the way layers overlap during a timeline (**Figure 17.40**) so that layers appear stacked in a different order. If you want Pop on top, you can make him hop.

✔ Tips

- Make sure all the layers have the Z-index you want them to have at their beginning keyframe(s) in the timeline (Figure 17.40).

- Z-index numbers affect the overlap of only those objects that are inside a layer; you can't make a layer hide under an image that isn't in a layer itself.

To change the Z-index of a layer during a timeline:

1. In the Timelines panel, add any keyframes you need to the layer's animation bar.

2. Click on the keyframe that marks the point at which the Z-index will change. The layer will be selected automatically.

3. Using the Layers panel or the Property inspector, change the Z-index number of the layer (**Figure 17.41**).

4. Play back the timeline to watch the layer move over or under another layer on the page (**Figure 17.42**).

Figure 17.40. You can change the Z-index of a layer in the timeline. We set the Z-index in the first frame so that the marble overlaps the elephants.

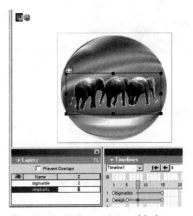

Figure 17.41 At Frame 8, we added a keyframe and changed the Z-index of the elephants layer so that it will surface over the marble.

Figure 17.42 Here are three frames from a timeline. In Frame 1, only the marble is visible. In Frame 5, the elephants appear, and the marble is stacked on top of them. In Frame 8, the elephants' Z-index changes so that they're on top of the marble.

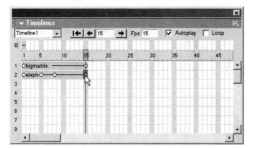

Figure 17.43 Click on the end keyframe and drag it to a new location.

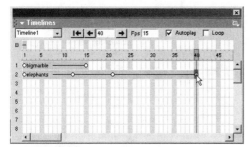

Figure 17.44 We lengthened the animation bar we selected in Figure 17.43. Notice how the keyframes in the middle of the animation bar are spaced out over the new length of the animation bar.

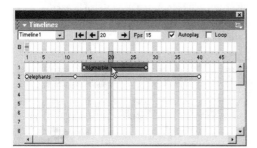

Figure 17.45 We moved the animation bar with the marble in it. It will both start and end later in the timeline now.

Figure 17.46 You can also type a different playback rate in frames per second (FPS) in the Fps text box. Keep in mind that many computers can't process a faster playback rate than 15 FPS.

Changing the Timing

You can change the length and duration of an animation bar if you want an action to start sooner or end later within the timeline.

To move the beginning or end of an animation bar:

1. In the Timelines panel, click on the beginning or ending keyframe on the layer's animation bar (**Figure 17.43**).

2. Drag the keyframe to a new frame number within the animation channel (**Figure 17.44**). You may notice the other elements in the timeline moving around as you drag the keyframe.

3. Play the timeline to see how it looks.

4. Repeat Steps 1 and 2 as needed.

Longer timelines allow for more actions and more gradual movement.

✔ Tips

■ If you drag the end keyframe to lengthen the timeline, any keyframes within the timeline will be spaced out in proportion to their original position, to preserve the gradual arc of the timeline (Figure 17.44).

■ You can also move an entire animation bar to make the action for that layer start at a different time. Click on the middle of the bar (not on a keyframe) to select the whole thing, and drag it to a new location (**Figure 17.45**).

■ To find out how to move an individual keyframe, see *To change the location of a keyframe*, earlier in the chapter.

■ You can also change the frames per second (fps) of a timeline. Type a number *less than* 15 in the Fps text box (**Figure 17.46**). Remember that most computers can't process faster playback speeds.

Changing Layer Dimensions

Besides changing the visibility and Z-index of a layer, you can also use a timeline to change the dimensions of the layer.

✔ Tips

■ Layer size changes work only in Navigator 6 and Internet Explorer 4 and later, and not in Navigator 4.

■ If you want to make a layer shrink in size, remember to change the layer's overflow setting to *hidden* or scroll in the Property inspector; otherwise, the shrinking may not have any effect.

To change the dimensions of a layer using a timeline:

1. In the Timelines panel, click on the keyframe where you want the size change to occur. The layer will become selected automatically (**Figure 17.47**).

2. Change the size of the layer by dragging its handles, or by changing the W(idth) and H(eight) settings in the Property inspector (**Figure 17.48**).

3. Play back the timeline to see how the settings affect the size change.

✔ Tips

■ Because the timeline code makes layer properties change gradually rather than abruptly, the size change will begin a few frames before the set keyframe (**Figure 17.49**).

■ If, instead, you'd like to see an abrupt size change, put two keyframes in adjacent frame numbers. In the first keyframe, we'll call it Frame 8, set the size at its status quo. In Frame 9, then, set the layer's size at its new measurements. The layer will appear to jump into its new size.

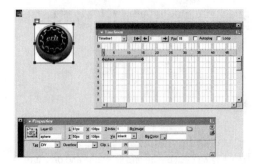

Figure 17.47 We added the layer to the timeline.

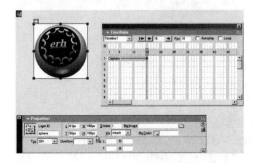

Figure 17.48 We selected the end keyframe and changed the size of the layer. If we click on each individual frame on the animation bar, the Property inspector will display the layer's size in each succeeding frame, leading up to the end frame's dimensions.

Figure 17.49 Three browser windows showing the progression in size from Frame 1 to Frame 8 to Frame 15. We set two sizes: one in Frame 1, and one in Frame 15. With Dreamweaver timelines, these changes happen gradually; for an abrupt change, make the size change happen in two adjacent keyframes.

Adding an Image Rollover to a Timeline

Figure 17.50 In our map timeline, we use two different map images: a green one (the solid map, on top) and a pink speckled one. We use a rollover to make the images switch at a certain point in the timeline.

Figure 17.51 In the example on the next page, these are the two images we'll be using.

Figure 17.52 Name your image before you add it to the timeline.

Figure 17.53 Add the image to the timeline by right-clicking (Ctrl+clicking) on an empty animation channel and selecting Add Object from the context menu.

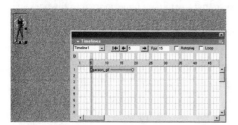

Figure 17.54 Here we are in the Document window. We've just added the image of the person—this time independent of any layers—to the timeline.

You can also add an image rollover to a timeline (**Figures 17.50** and **17.51**). The only available action for images that are *not* in layers is swap source: That is, you can make an image roll over, but you can't make it hide or disappear unless it's in a layer. (In that case, you apply the changes to the layer tag and not the image.)

To add the image rollover to a timeline:

1. Place (or select) the initial, pre-roll image in the Document window.

2. Name the initial image, using the Property inspector (**Figure 17.52**).

3. From the Document window menu bar, select Modify > Timeline > Add Object to Timeline.

   or

   Right-click (Ctrl+click) on an empty animation bar in the Timelines panel, and select Add Object from the context menu that appears (**Figure 17.53**).

A new animation bar will appear in the Timelines panel (**Figure 17.54**).

On the next page, we'll add the rollover.

✔ Tip

■ One way to preload images for source swapping is to place them in a hidden layer on the page. Another is to add the Preload Images behavior to the page. See Chapter 13.

Making the rollover work

Changing an image source with a Timeline is similar to using the Swap Image behavior to create image rollovers, except the rollover will occur as time elapses rather than when triggered by a user event.

To change an image source using a timeline:

1. Add the image to the timeline, as described on the previous page.

2. Add any keyframes you need to the image's animation bar (**Figure 17.55**).

3. Click on the keyframe in which you want the image to roll over.

4. In the Property inspector, change the source of the image to the source of the new image (**Figures 17.56** and **17.57**) by editing the filename in the Src text box, or by clicking on Browse ▢ and selecting a new image.

5. To make the image stay in its second state for the rest of the timeline, select the end keyframe and set the source to be that of Image 2.

   or

   To make the image revert to its original state, add two keyframes, first the end-stop for the source for Image 2, and second, the resetting of the source for Image 1.

Play back the timeline to watch the effect (**Figure 17.58**).

✔ Tips

■ Sometimes, when you change the source of the image, Dreamweaver discards height and width information for both the original and the preloaded image. If you want the images to conform to a certain size, jot down the height and width before you create the rollover, and go back and fix them afterward.

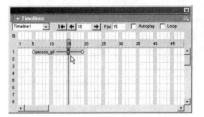

Figure 17.55 We added a keyframe to the image's animation bar; that's the point at which the source will change.

Figure 17.56 The two images, side by side for comparison. With the keyframe selected, change the source in the Property inspector. The image, which we selected with the mouse, shows the rectangular borders of the transparent image.

Figure 17.57 Edit the filename in the Src text box (for example, type person2.gif instead of person.gif), or click on the Browse button to open the Select Image File dialog box and choose a different image.

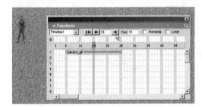

Figure 17.58 When the timeline plays the keyframe, the source changes to the second image. In this case, it's a subtle change of colors from one image to the next so that the person fades more into the background. You can use whatever images you like for the rollover, as long as they're the same size.

■ In previous versions of Dreamweaver, the image's animation bar had to be extended to the end of the timeline to make the source stay swapped. This has been fixed as of Dreamweaver 4 and should function properly in Dreamweaver MX.

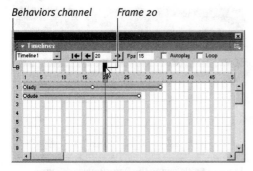

Behaviors channel   Frame 20

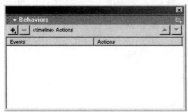

Figure 17.59 We double-clicked on the intersection of the Behaviors channel and Frame 20, and the Behaviors panel appeared. It's empty until you add an action.

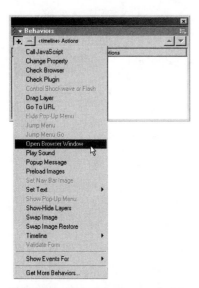

Figure 17.60 On the Behaviors panel, click on the + (plus) button, and choose an action from the pop-up menu.

Adding a Behavior to a Timeline

All the clever behaviors that come with Dreamweaver MX can be added to a timeline. For instance, you can make the timeline execute an animation and then load a new page; you can play a sound at a certain frame in a timeline; or you can use a timeline to start playing a Shockwave movie at a certain frame.

To add a behavior to a timeline frame:

1. In the Timelines panel, click on the frame that will launch the behavior to move the playback head to it.

2. Double-click on the frame number within the Behaviors channel (**Figure 17.59**). The Behaviors panel will appear in the Design group (and of course it can be undocked). The browser version (4.0 and later browsers) will be preset.

3. In the Actions area of the Behaviors panel, click on the + (plus) button 🔘 to pop up the menu of available actions (**Figure 17.60**).

continues on next page

4. Choose the action you want to add. The associated dialog box will appear.

5. Fill out the dialog box and click on OK. The name of the action will appear in the Actions list box (**Figure 17.61**). The event, onFrameNumber, will be added to the Behaviors panel automatically.

The behavior will be added to the timeline. You'll see a little marker at that particular frame in the Behaviors channel.

✔ Tips

■ For details about using JavaScript behaviors in Dreamweaver, see Chapter 13. For a thorough look at behaviors for beginners, see Chapter 16 in the *Dreamweaver MX Visual QuickStart Guide*.

■ You can add a behavior to a frame by moving the playback head to that frame and selecting Modify > Timeline > Add Behavior to Timeline from the menu bar.

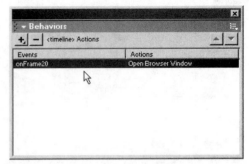

Figure 17.61 We added the Open Browser Window action to Frame 20 of the timeline; when the timeline is played, the window will launch on Frame 20. The event will be added automatically after you finish selecting the action.

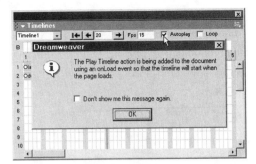

Figure 17.62 When you check the Autoplay checkbox, a dialog box will appear informing you that it's going to add the Autoplay behavior. Once you get the point, you can make this dialog box go away by checking the Don't show me this message again checkbox.

Making Timelines Go

Timelines won't start playing in a browser unless another piece of JavaScript tells them to. There are two ways you can make a timeline start playing, both of which use JavaScript behaviors.

One way is to make the timeline play automatically when the page is finished loading. The other way is to use a behavior, so that a user event such as a click or a mouseover triggers the timeline.

The Autoplay behavior is an onLoad behavior; once the page loads, the animation will begin.

To make a Timeline play automatically:

◆ In the Timelines panel, place a checkmark in the Autoplay checkbox. A dialog box will appear (**Figure 17.62**) letting you know that Dreamweaver will add the Autoplay code.

Simple, yes?

MAKING TIMELINES GO

Behavior Modification

What sort of behaviors could you add to a timeline? The timeline itself offers actions similar to Show/Hide Layer and Rollover Image. Here are some ideas to get you started.

◆ Set Text of Layer, Set Text of Status Bar, Set Text of Text Field, Popup Message: The user sees a message when a certain frame in the timeline passes.

◆ Open Browser Window, Popup Message: During or at the end of the timeline, a window or dialog box opens.

◆ Drag Layer: An animation plays in the timeline, and after it's over, all the layers become draggable.

◆ Play Sound: On a certain frame, a sound plays. For example, when the mouse hits the cat in the head with a hammer, the user hears "Doink!"

◆ Check Browser: When the page loads (onLoad), the user is sent to a page with a timeline if the browser is 4.0 or later, and to a page without the timeline if the browser is 3.0 or earlier. (It would be a nice idea to detect the browser with a timeline frame, but 3.0 browsers may or may not play the timeline properly. If you want to try this, you should test it in the browsers you're targeting.)

Making a Behavior Play a Timeline

You can also make a behavior play a timeline when the user clicks on or mouses over a link or image.

To make a behavior play a timeline:

1. In the Document window, click on the object you want to use to make the timeline play (a, img, input for menu or form button). Make sure you do not have a behavior selected in the Timelines panel, or the behavior will be added to the timeline instead of the link.

2. If a timeline is on your page, the browser version will be preset to 4.0 and Later browsers. To check this, click the + (plus) button, and then select Show Events For > 4.0 and Later Browsers.

3. In the Actions area of the Behaviors panel, click on the + (plus) button.

4. From the menu that appears (**Figure 17.63**), select Timeline > Play Timeline. The Play Timeline dialog box will appear (**Figure 17.64**).

5. If there is more than one timeline on your page, select the timeline you want to use from the Play Timeline drop-down menu.

6. Click on OK to close the Play Timeline dialog box.

7. To specify the user event that triggers the action, click on the arrow button and choose the event (onClick, onMouseOver) from the menu (**Figure 17.65**).

The event will play the timeline when the page is loaded in a browser.

✔ Tip

■ To make a link that can play a timeline and doesn't open a page, the content of the link should be "#".

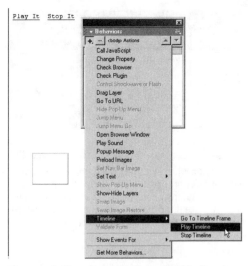

Figure 17.63 We selected the link called Play It and added the Play Timeline action.

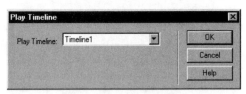

Figure 17.64 We chose Timeline > Play Timeline from the Add Action menu, and now we can select our timeline in the Play Timeline dialog box.

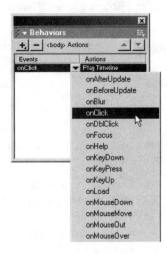

Figure 17.65 After you select the Play Timeline (or other) action, specify the user event by choosing it from the drop-down list.

Figure 17.66 Having selected the Stop It link, we chose Timeline > Stop Timeline from the Add action menu.

Figure 17.67 In the Stop Timeline dialog box, you can choose to stop all timelines or one selected timeline.

Stopping a timeline

You can also make a behavior stop a timeline. This is a quite smart thing to do, especially if you're using the Loop function (we'll get to that in a minute). The browser's Stop button will not stop an in-progress timeline.

To make a behavior stop a timeline:

1. In the Document window, click on the object you want to use to make the timeline stop (a, img, form button).

2. On the Behaviors panel, click on the + (plus) button [+], and from the menu that appears, select Timeline > Stop Timeline (**Figure 17.66**). The Stop Timeline dialog box will appear (**Figure 17.67**).

3. If there is more than one timeline on your page, select the timeline you want to use from the Stop Timeline drop-down menu.

   or

   Select ALL TIMELINES from the drop-down menu.

4. Click on OK to close the Stop Timeline dialog box.

5. Click on the arrow button and select the user event from the drop-down menu (onClick, onMouseOver, and so on).

✔ Tip

- You cannot make the same link (or image) both play and stop a timeline. An event that signals both a Play and a Stop event will only advance the timeline one frame at a time. (If the order is Stop and then Play, it won't stop at all.) We have to admit, though, that this was a great way to get screen captures for this chapter.

Loop and Rewind

Some timelines are so beautiful, you wish they'd go on forever. (Actually, the first 10 or so timelines you make will automatically be that beautiful.) You can make a timeline repeat either indefinitely or a certain number of times by using the Loop feature.

To add the Loop:

◆ In the Timelines panel, place a checkmark in the Loop checkbox. A dialog box will appear, letting you know that Dreamweaver will add the Go To Frame behavior code (**Figure 17.68**).

The Loop behavior uses the Go to Frame action. In case of automatic loop, the timeline reaches the end and returns to frame 1.

To modify the Loop:

1. In the Timelines panel, locate the last frame in the timeline. You'll see a marker in the Behaviors channel in the frame after that.

2. Double-click on the last Behaviors marker (**Figure 17.69**). The Behaviors panel will appear.

3. Double-click on the action Go To Timeline Frame listed in the Actions list box. The Go To Timeline Frame dialog box will appear (**Figure 17.70**).

4. To make the loop pick up at a frame other than Frame 1, type the frame number in the Go to Frame text box.

5. To make the loop continue for a number of times less than infinity, type a number in the Loop text box.

6. Click on OK to close the Go to Timeline Frame text box.

Preview the timeline in a 4.0 or later browser to see if it does what you think it will.

Figure 17.68 Click on the Loop checkbox, and this friendly dialog box will appear to tell you what's up and to which frame number it's adding the behavior. To make it go away, click on the Don't show me this message again checkbox.

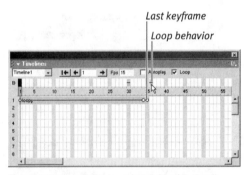

Figure 17.69 The Behaviors channel in this timeline has two behavior markers. The one that follows the last frame is the one to double-click if you want to edit the Loop behavior.

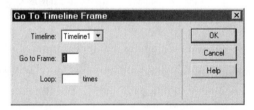

Figure 17.70 The Go To Timeline Frame dialog box controls the Loop behavior.

✔ Tip

■ You can move a behavior to a different frame if you want. Just click on the associated keyframe, if any, and move it to a different frame, and then click on the behavior (as in Figure 17.69) and move it to that same frame.

Figure 17.71 First, select your object. Then, click on the + (plus) button on the Behaviors panel, and select Timeline > Go to Timeline Frame from the menu.

Figure 17.72 In the Go To Timeline Frame dialog box, we specified Frame 45.

Figure 17.73 We added the onClick event and the Go to Timeline Frame action to the "Play the part with the pie" link.

✔ Tip

■ You can add a Go to Timeline Frame behavior within a timeline, too—not just at the end. Just add the behavior to the Behaviors channel within your timeline. Imagine this: On Frame 8, an image appears in a layer. On Frame 14, the Go to Timeline action makes the timeline jump back to Frame 7. With the number of loops set to 3, the timeline would go back to Frame 7 three times to make the image pop up three times before the animation continued to the end.

Jumping to or starting with a specific frame

You can also use the Go to Frame behavior with an object outside the timeline. For instance, you can have a "Play Animation" button, a "Stop Animation" button, and a "Go Back to the Part with the Pie" button. You can use a link or button to begin playing the timeline at any frame.

To add a Go to Frame behavior:

1. In the Document window, click on the object you want to use to make the Timeline jump to a particular frame (a, img, form button).

2. Be sure that you don't have a behavior selected in the Timeline panel; click on any frame without a behavior marked in the Behaviors channel.

3. On the Behaviors panel, click on the + (plus) button ⊞, and from the menu that appears, select Timeline > Go to Timeline Frame (**Figure 17.71**). The Go To Timeline Frame dialog box will appear (**Figure 17.72**).

4. If there is more than one timeline on your page, select the timeline you want to use from the Timeline drop-down menu.

5. Choose the frame to go to (the frame to rewind or fast forward to), and type its number in the Go to Frame text box.

   You cannot set a loop from outside the timeline.

6. Click on OK to close the dialog box.

7. Click on the arrow button and select the user event from the drop-down menu (onClick, onMouseOver, and so on) (**Figure 17.73**).

When the user commits the event, the action will cause the timeline to jump forward or backward to a particular frame.

Adding and Removing Frames

We've already told you how to move the beginning and end of an animation bar, as well as the keyframes. You can also add frames to or remove frames from the middle of a timeline.

To add frames to a Timeline:

1. In the Timelines panel, click on a frame to move the playback head to the place in the Timeline where you want to add a frame (**Figure 17.74**).

2. From the menu bar, select Modify > Timeline > Add Frame.

   or

   Right-click (Ctrl+click) on the object's animation bar in the Timelines panel, and select Add Frame from the context menu that appears (**Figure 17.75**).

The frame will be added to the right of the playback head (**Figure 17.76**).

You can also remove frames from a timeline if you want to shorten the duration of the animation or the space between keyframes.

To remove frames from a Timeline:

1. In the Timelines panel, move the playback head to the place in the timeline from which you want to remove a frame.

2. From the menu bar, select Modify > Timeline > Remove Frame.

   or

   Right-click (Ctrl+click) on the object's animation bar in the Timelines panel, and select Remove Frame from the context menu that appears.

The frame that the playback head is resting on will be removed.

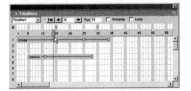

Figure 17.74 We placed the playback head one frame before a behavior on our Timeline.

Figure 17.75 Right-click (Ctrl+click) on the frame, and select Add Frame from the context menu.

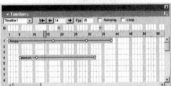

Figure 17.76 We added five new frames between the playback head and the behavior. If we want, we can move the keyframe back five frames by dragging it.

✔ Tips

■ Tinkering with the middle of the timeline by changing the number of frames is easier than moving around all the keyframes, behaviors, and objects.

■ Adding and removing frames from the middle of a timeline will remove any keyframes or behaviors that reside in those frames.

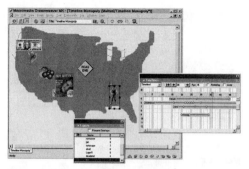

Figure 17.77 The Before Picture: Here's Timeline 1, in mid-play.

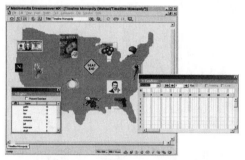

Figure 17.78 The After Picture: We just added Timeline 2. All traces of Timeline 1 are hidden—all the pictures are placed in their original positions, they're all visible, and they've got their original overlap settings.

Figure 17.79 Choose which timeline to work with from the drop-down menu on the Timelines panel.

Using Multiple Timelines

You may want to use more than one timeline if you want more than one animation to be available on the page. You can use the same objects in different timelines, which could then be called by behaviors attached to different links or buttons.

To add a timeline:

◆ From the menu bar, select Modify > Timeline > Add Timeline.

The Timelines panel will reset, hiding the animation bars for the original timeline; additionally, all the indicators of the timeline will disappear from the Document window (**Figures 17.77** and **17.78**).

To toggle between timelines:

◆ In the Timelines panel, select the name of the timeline you want to work with from the Timeline drop-down menu (**Figure 17.79**).

You can have as many timelines as you want.

✔ Tips

■ Each timeline should be fairly simple, or your page will take several days to load and will offer more opportunities to crash browsers around the world.

■ You can have both timelines play simultaneously, or you can have a behavior in a keyframe in the middle or at the end of one timeline call another timeline and have it start playing. Use the Play Timeline behavior, and add it to the first timeline.

Renaming and Deleting Timelines

Tired of flipping between "Timeline 1" and "Timeline 2"? Rename them.

To rename a Timeline:

1. View the timeline you want to rename.

2. From the menu bar, select Modify > Timeline > Rename Timeline. The Rename Timeline dialog box will appear (**Figure 17.80**).

3. Type the new name for your timeline in the Timeline Name text box.

4. Click on OK. The Rename Timeline dialog box will close.

The new name for your timeline will appear in the Timeline drop-down menu in the Timelines panel.

Removing a timeline from a page is easy. Make sure you select the proper timeline—and if you want no timelines, delete each one.

To remove a timeline:

1. In the Timelines inspector, select the name of the timeline you want to remove.

2. Click on the Options menu button on the side of the Timelines panel, and select Remove Timeline from the menu (**Figure 17.81**).

Poof! It's gone.

✔ Tips

■ If you have a timeline with objects and behaviors already added to it, it is a good idea to save a version of the document (File > Save As) before deleting so that you don't lose the entire thing. You might decide that you want to use a version of it later on.

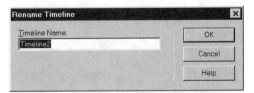

Figure 17.80 Type a new name for the timeline in the Timeline Name text box.

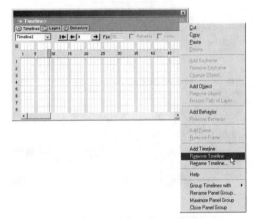

Figure 17.81 Select Remove Timeline from the shortcut menu to remove the timeline code from the page.

■ If you accidentally remove a Timeline, remember the magic word: Undo. Select Edit > Undo from the Document window menu bar, or press Ctrl+Z (Command+Z).

RENAMING AND DELETING TIMELINES

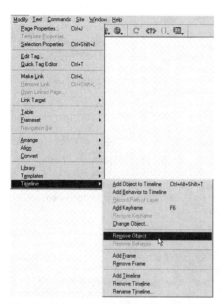

Figure 17.82 To remove an object, select Modify › Timeline › Remove Object. The Timelines panel doesn't even need to be open for this.

Figure 17.83 The Change Object dialog box allows you to transfer an animation channel from one object to another.

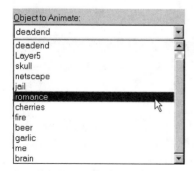

Figure 17.84 To switch which object is animated, select the name of an object from the Object to Animate drop-down menu.

Removing or Changing Objects

You can remove an object from a timeline if you no longer want to include it in the animation, or you might decide that the actions you've set up for a layer are dandy, but that they'd work better for a different layer.

To remove an object from a timeline:

1. In the Timelines panel, click on the animation bar for the object you want to remove from the timeline.

2. Press Backspace (Delete). The object will be removed from the timeline, but it will remain on the page.

✔ Tips

■ You can also select the object in the Document window and then use a menu command to remove it. From the menu bar or from a context menu, select Modify > Timeline > Remove Object (**Figure 17.82**).

■ To remove a behavior from a Timeline, select Modify > Timeline > Remove Behavior from the menu.

To change objects:

1. In the Timelines panel, select the animation bar for the object you want to switch with another object.

2. From the menu bar, select Modify > Timeline > Change Object. The Change Object dialog box will appear (**Figure 17.83**).

3. From the Object to Animate drop-down menu, select an object (**Figure 17.84**).

4. Click on OK to close the Change Object dialog box. The animation bar will now describe the object you selected.

Bringing It All Together

Timelines are quite versatile, although moving objects are difficult to illustrate in print. To wrap up this chapter, we're going to visually dissect a quasi-useful timeline we constructed using almost all timeline capabilities. Follow the figure captions for **Figures 17.85** through **17.93**.

One note about **Figures 17.90** through **17.92**: The Map layer doesn't do anything in the second timeline, but we added it so it would be visible while working. Dreamweaver displays the default image rather than the one that's been swapped in.

✔ Tip

■ To see this timeline in action, pay a visit to www.tarin.com/newtoys/toys.html.

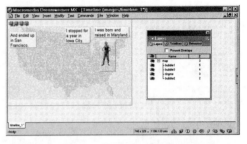

Figure 17.85 Here are the raw materials. The page contains five layers: the map, the person, and three "bubbles." The other layers need to be positioned relative to the map, so they're all nested within the map.

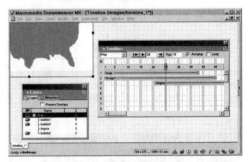

Figure 17.86 Frame 25 of the first timeline, called Map. We want the window to be blank to start. Then the first map is brought in from off screen.

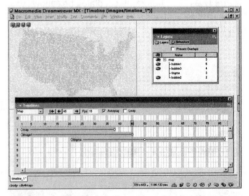

Figure 17.87 Frame 45 of the Map timeline. A few frames after the map layer arrives, the image source changes into a different map (on Frame 45, we changed the source in the Property inspector). This map has a larger file size, but the image had been preloaded in a layer.

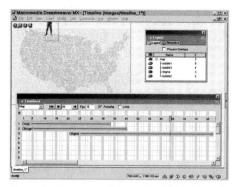

Figure 17.88 Frame 64 of the Map timeline. The person layer ("tinyme") begins to arrive from off screen. Like the map layer, the person was given negative coordinates (L –400px,T –300px) at the start of the timeline.

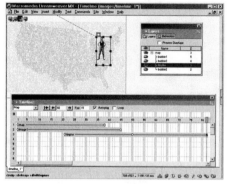

Figure 17.89 Frame 82 of the Map timeline. The person has arrived. A few frames later, in Frame 95, a behavior will play the second timeline, called Travel.

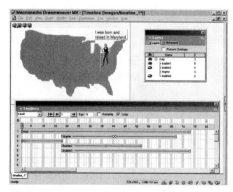

Figure 17.90 In Frame 1 of the Travel timeline, the layer "Bubble 1" appears above the person's head.

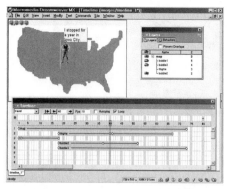

Figure 17.91 Frame 41 of the Travel timeline. The person has moved halfway across the country. Bubble 1 is hidden and Bubble 2 appears. Note that the playback rate is 10 fps rather than 15; this timeline moves more slowly.

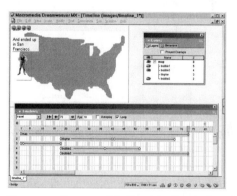

Figure 17.92 Frame 73 of the Travel timeline. At the end of the timeline, the person is all the way across the map. Bubble 2 is hidden, and Bubble 3 appears. We also added a Loop behavior inFrame 80; after a pause, the second timeline will replay.

Figure 17.93 The work in action. We created a link to this timeline in a JavaScript window the same size as the map images.

TOOLBARS, TRICKS, AND INTERACTIVE DESIGN

18

As the Web grows, so does the variety of ways to accomplish any given site-design task. The days of simple HTML and GIF files are long gone. Despite the additional complications for designers, this is actually a good thing. By using gadgets such as pop-up layers and various kinds of responsive rollovers, Web designers can create sites that are more interactive and provide a significantly better user experience.

In this chapter, we look at a number of ways Dreamweaver lets you take advantage of the more advanced interactive elements available to today's designers. We look at Flash Text and Flash buttons, which let you take advantage of the Macromedia Flash engine, without having to learn the Flash application itself. We take a quick look at JavaScript image rollovers, which you can use without knowing any JavaScript. We'll dip our toes into Macromedia Fireworks to look at one way to speed the creation of navigation bars for use on your pages in Dreamweaver. We'll show you how to hide page controls in a layer that pops up when the user mouses over or clicks a button. We'll also look at some examples of how to use interactive elements (forms and navigation bars, in particular) with frames-based pages.

Flash Text

You can use the Macromedia Flash engine to embed Flash Text into your Web page. Flash Text offers three features: You can include non-standard fonts on your page without using an image editing program; you can set custom colors for the text and, if you like, a rollover color; and your Flash Text object can act as a link to another page or file.

To add Flash Text to a page:

1. Create a new page in Dreamweaver and save it

   or

   Open an existing page in Dreamweaver.

   You can add Flash Text only to pages that are already saved, because Dreamweaver needs to know where to put the SWF file that contains the Flash Text.

   Important: For the links in Flash Text to actually work, they must use document-relative links, and the Flash Text SWF files must live *in the same folder* as the page they're on.

2. From the menu bar, select Insert > Interactive Images > Flash Text.

   The Insert Flash Text dialog box will appear (**Figure 18.1**).

3. In the Text text box, type the text you want to appear.

4. From the Font drop-down menu, select the font you wish to use for your text. (Leave the Show Font checkbox checked to get a preview of your formatting.)

5. Specify the size, style, and alignment using the standard controls.

6. Select a color for the text.

   If you want to use a rollover color when the user mouses over the object, pick a different color using the Rollover Color color box (**Figure 18.2**).

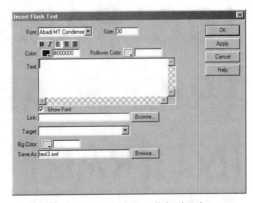

Figure 18.1 The Insert Flash Text dialog box lets you format the text.

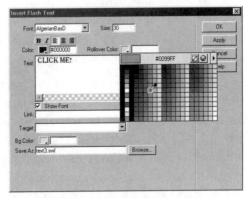

Figure 18.2 If you want the text to react to the mouse, you can add a rollover color.

FLASH TEXT

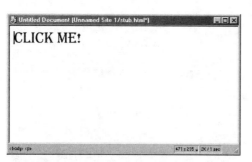

Figure 18.3 The text appears with full formatting in Design view...

Figure 18.4 ...but you need to tell Dreamweaver to play the rollover in the Document window. (It'll be turned on automatically in the browser.)

✔ Tips

■ Flash Text files need to reside in the same folder as the pages that use them. Dreamweaver's documentation implies that you can use site-root relative links with your buttons, but you'll get an error message in the Insert Flash Text dialog box if you try this. We used site-root relative links for the navbar of a new site and discovered the buttons only worked in Internet Explorer 6.0, so we had to redesign the site using image rollovers.

■ If you want pages in several folders to use the same Flash Text files, you could just make copies of the file for each folder. These files are generally less than 2K. If you want to make more sophisticated Flash gadgets that can be accessed from different locations, you'll have to actually use the Macromedia Flash software itself.

■ You can try using full URLs (starting with http://) in your Flash text objects if you want to reuse them across a site.

7. If you want the Flash Text object to be a link, you can specify the destination of the link, and the target frame or window, if any, in the Link text box and Target drop-down menu, respectively.

You should use document-relative links or full URLs here, or one of two things may happen: You'll get an error message telling you not to use site-root relative links; or your link data may be erased from the SWF file when you close the Flash Text dialog box.

8. You can specify a background color for the text in the Bg Color text, if your page is a color other than white. (For an exact match, you can use the eyedropper tool to click on your page background, or anything else on your desktop.)

9. Finally, specify the filename that Dreamweaver assigns to the text, as well as the location, in the Save As text box.

10. Click OK to close the dialog box.

The Flash Text object will appear on the page (**Figure 18.3**).

11. To see the text react to the mouse, in the Property inspector, click on the Play button (**Figure 18.4**).

Be judicious about your use of Flash Text. As in any design, going overboard with a bunch of fonts and twitchiness can make your page look very amateurish.

Flash Buttons

Flash buttons are another example of Macromedia's integration of the Flash engine into Dreamweaver. These are animated buttons that use rollovers. Some of them take the form of Forward and Back arrows and the like, but most of them include blank space to which you can add text.

✔ Tip

■ See the Tips on the previous page for information about where to save these files. And please test all your links before launching a live site using any kind of media for navigation.

To add a Flash button to your page:

1. Create a new page in Dreamweaver and save it.

   or

   Open an existing page.

2. From the menu bar, select Insert > Interactive Images > Flash Button.

   The Insert Flash Button dialog box will appear (**Figure 18.5**).

3. In the Style list box, select the type of button you want.

4. In the Button Text text box, type the text (if any) you want to appear on the button. (Buttons that are arrows and the like obviously don't take text.)

   The amount of text you can add to a button is very limited. Depending on the style of button and the font size you choose, you may be limited to as few as eight characters. If you try to add too much text, you'll get unsatisfactory results (**Figure 18.6**).

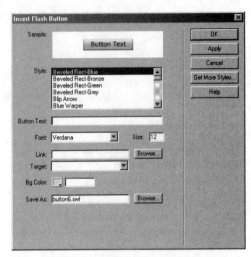

Figure 18.5 The Insert Flash Button dialog box lets you select a style and add text and links.

Figure 18.6 The length of your text is limited to the length of the button.

Figure 18.7 The button appears on the page as you would expect.

Figure 18.8 If you play it, it'll interact with the mouse.

5. Specify the font and size.

6. Specify the link for the button and the target, if any, in the Link text box and Target drop-down menu.

7. If your page is a color other than white, specify the background color for the button to match your page in the Bg Color text box. (You can use the eyedropper tool to click on your page background for an exact match.)

8. Specify the filename for the SWF file in the Save As text box. You can click Browse to locate the proper folder for storage; otherwise, Dreamweaver will save the button in the same folder as the page.

9. Click OK to close the dialog box and add the button to your page.

The button will appear on the page (**Figure 18.7**).

10. On the Property inspector, click the Play button and move the mouse over the button.

The button will do its animation thing (**Figure 18.8**).

As with Flash Text, you should be careful about overusing these buttons. They can easily become overwhelming for visitors to your site.

FLASH BUTTONS

Rollover Images

Another way to add interactivity to your Web page—this time without using the Flash engine—is to use what Dreamweaver calls Rollover Images. (Other folks call them image rollovers.) In these cases, when the user mouses over a button or other image file, that image is replaced by another of the same size. What actually happens is that when the user triggers the rollover, the src attribute of the image file changes and requests that another image in the same site be displayed in its place.

For these gadgets, Dreamweaver uses a couple of JavaScript behaviors to change an image when the user mouses over it. We'll show you the quick way to add them here. For the nitty-gritty on behaviors and how to edit them, see Chapter 13, *JavaScript and Dreamweaver Behaviors*.

To add a Rollover Image to your page:

1. From the menu bar, select Insert > Interactive Images > Rollover Image.

   The Insert Rollover Image dialog box will appear (**Figure 18.9**).

2. In the Image Name text box, name the image something descriptive.

3. In the Original Image text box, specify the image that should appear when the page loads.

4. In the Rollover Image text box, specify the image that should appear when the user mouses over the image.

   It is usually best to use two images that are the same size. If the rollover image is a different size from the original, the browser will scale the image to be the size of the first image, and distortion will result.

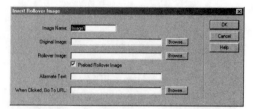

Figure 18.9 Here's where you link your images to each other.

Figure 18.10 You need to preview rollover images in a browser to see them interact.

5. Leave the Preload Rollover Image check-box checked. (This ensures the rollover will happen right away rather than after sending and receiving an HTTP request for the file.)

6. In the Alternate Text text box, specify the text that will appear if the user is using a text-based browser or is otherwise not automatically loading images.

7. In the text box labeled When Clicked, Go To URL, select the page to go to when the user clicks on the image.

The image will now react when the user mouses over it (**Figure 18.10**).

Importing Slices from Fireworks to Use As a Toolbar

Macromedia has worked hard to integrate Fireworks, its Web-oriented image editing program, with Dreamweaver. One example of this is the ability to create a complex image in Fireworks, complete with rollovers, and export it, with code, to Dreamweaver. You can export slices of a single image as separate images that will then display in Dreamweaver aligned as they were in the original image.

One handy use for this is to create a navigation bar, or *navbar*, in Fireworks, and then import it into Dreamweaver. A navbar is a series of buttons that indicate where you are on the site and what other pages you can go to. We'll show you how to create a simple navbar in Fireworks, and how to use Dreamweaver to place it on your page.

The process works slightly differently, depending on whether you're planning on using frames in your Web site design or not, so we'll show you both ways.

For a frames-based site, you need create only one navbar. The navbar would live in its own frame, in, say, the left-hand or topmost frame. The navbar would not need to load with a page section marked by a "down" state because the section doesn't load in the first place until you click on the button for that section.

You can export a simple navbar even for pages without frames, but Fireworks also offers a navbar that loads with the button for a specific section already in the "down" state. So for the "Specials" section, the "Specials" button would already be "pushed in" when the page loads; and the same would go for the other sections in the site. Fireworks can help you export section-by-section navbars with different buttons set in the down state.

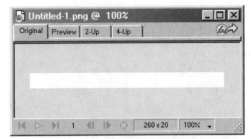

Figure 18.11 Start with a blank Fireworks document.

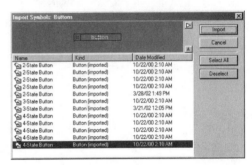

Figure 18.12 A 4-state button includes up, down, over and over-while-down states.

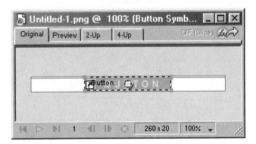

Figure 18.13 The button with Fireworks controls.

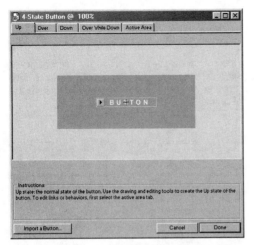

Figure 18.14 There is a separate dialog box for editing the button.

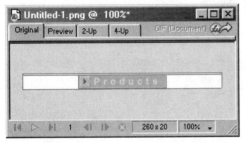

Figure 18.15 You can adjust the text for each button (good thing, too).

Using Fireworks, we'll create and slice our images, turn them into buttons, and export them as images and HTML.

Let's start by creating the images.

To create the images for the navbar:

1. Open Fireworks.

2. Create a new image that is the total size of your toolbar (we used 260 by 20 pixels) (**Figure 18.11**).

3. From Fireworks menu bar, select Edit > Libraries > Buttons.
   The Import Symbols: Buttons dialog box will appear (**Figure 18.12**).

4. From the list, select a 4-state button.

5. Click Import to add it to your image.
   The button will be added to your image (**Figure 18.13**).

6. To change the text of a button, double-click on it.
   The button editor will open (**Figure 18.14**).

7. Double-click on the text of the button.
   The text will be selected and the cursor will change to the text-editing tool.

8. Change the text to indicate what the button is linked to.

9. Click Done to close the dialog box.
   The button text has changed (**Figure 18.15**).

continues on next page

10. In the Property inspector in Fireworks, specify the Web page to which the button should link in the Link text box.

11. **For frames pages only:** In the Target text box, the target for the link should be mainFrame or whatever the appropriate name is for the frame the links should appear in when clicked (**Figure 18.16**).

    When using links on any frames pages, you need to make sure you specify the correct target; otherwise, the link won't work as expected and may either not load at all or load in the wrong frame-navbar. (The rollovers will work, but the links won't.)

12. Repeat Steps 3 through 11 for each button in your navbar.

    You may want to arrange the buttons in a more pleasing fashion (**Figure 18.17**).

Now we're ready to export the images and HTML so we can use them on our pages.

Figure 18.16 We'll be using the default frame name, so set your target as mainFrame to get the links working properly. (You can use other names in future projects, of course.)

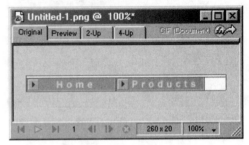

Figure 18.17 You may need to manually line up the buttons.

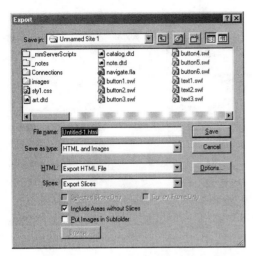

Figure 18.18 The Export dialog box is not a simple one.

To export a single navbar (for sites with frames or that don't need down states marked):

1. From the Fireworks menu bar, select File > Export.

   The Export dialog box will appear (**Figure 18.18**). The huge array of options here allows us to export slices and HTML, which is what we want to do here.

2. Name the HTML file in the File name text box.

3. We recommend you check the Put Images in Subfolder option to save the actual images in a separate folder, such as `images/`. This will save you *drive clutter,* which is a term meaning "where are my images?" With four states for each button, that's a lot of clutter.

4. Click Save to save the HTML and GIF files. Although you can easily update your image paths later on, Fireworks will save the HTML and image files in the same folder.

Now that we have our images, we're ready to use them. Let's look at how to insert a navbar on a page that uses frames. Then, we'll take a look at Fireworks' fancy many-pronged export for pages that use down-state buttons to mark sections.

To put the navbar on a page that uses frames:

1. Back in Dreamweaver, from the menu bar, choose File > New.

   The New Document dialog box will appear (**Figure 18.19**).

2. In the Category list, select Framesets.

3. In the Framesets list, select Fixed Top (**Figure 18.20**).

4. Click Create to create a new frameset.

5. From the File menu, select Save Frameset As, and in the dialog box that appears, save the file in the same folder you saved the navbar file in Step 3 of the previous stepped list.

6. From the Site window, drag the navbar file into the top frame of the frameset (**Figure 18.21**).

   The source for the top frame will now be your navbar.

7. Click within the bottom frame, which will be the file for the first page of your navbar.

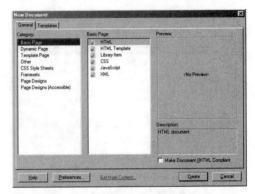

Figure 18.19 The New Document dialog box allows you to choose a category (such as Framesets) for the new document...

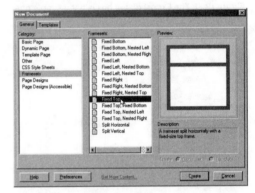

Figure 18.20 ...then allows you to choose an item within that category. These are pre-built framesets that take a lot of the drudgery out of creating frames-based pages.

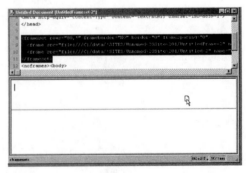

Figure 18.21 You can drag a page into a frameset.

Figure 18.22 The navbar indicates which page you are on.

8. From the Document window menu bar, choose File > Save Frame As. Note that you have to name the file whatever you specified as the link in your navbar.

9. Create a new HTML file for each one of the other buttons in your navbar.

10. In your browser, open the main frameset page.

    Note: In many cases, the image for this page will not highlight properly in the navbar. This appears to be a bug in Macromedia's navbar code.

11. Click one of the navbar links.

    The new page will load in the bottom frame and the button for that page will highlight in the navbar (**Figure 18.22**).

That was an involved process, but it's not anything like how involved it could get without predefined navbar behaviors!

✔ Tip

- If your buttons, when clicked, load in the entire browser window rather than in the correct frame, then your targets aren't set up properly. This may be a Fireworks or Dreamweaver bug, or you might not have typed the names properly. In the Document window, click on each button in the navbar, and verify, one at a time, that the Property inspector's Target text box indicates the exact, correct name of the frame the link should load in. If it doesn't, type the correct name.

Marking a multiple-section site with down-state buttons

If you want to mark the sections in your site with down-state buttons, or if you just don't want to use frames, you can have Fireworks export several versions of the same navbar. We'll show you how to export the navbar into several files, and then we'll talk about what to do with them from there.

To export a navbar for each button:

1. Follow the steps under *To create the images for the navbar* earlier in this section. You don't need to specify a target in Step 11.

2. From the File menu in Fireworks, choose Export to export the HTML and the images.
   The Export dialog box will appear (Figure 18.18).

3. Name the HTML file in the File name text box.

4. Again, we recommend you check the Put Images in Subfolder option to save the actual images in a separate folder, such as images/. That'll help you keep track of the large number of buttons that are about to appear on your hard drive.

5. Click the Options button.
   The HTML Setup dialog box will appear (**Figure 18.23**).

6. Click the Document Specific tab.
   The Document Specific pane of the HTML Setup dialog box will appear (**Figure 18.24**).

7. Click the Multiple Navbar HTML Pages checkbox.
   For a detailed explanation of the naming conventions, see the Fireworks online help. We'll ignore them for now.

8. Click OK to close the HTML Setup dialog box.

9. Click Save to export your images and HTML.

Fireworks will export a separate navbar on a separate HTML file for each state of your toolbar. Assuming you have not changed the image naming defaults, if you saved the file as `navbar.html`, your files would be named `navbar_1.html`, `navbar_2.html`, etc.

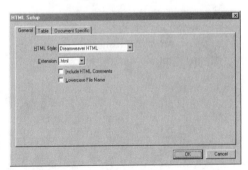

Figure 18.23 Fireworks' Export dialog box is less simple than it first appears!

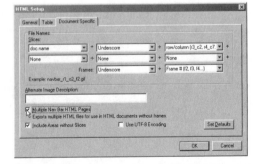

Figure 18.24 You can set options for the current document.

What to do with multiple navbar pages

You've got several options for what to do with these pages. The first thing we recommend doing is making a backup copy of each page, so that if you accidentally overwrite one of them, you won't have to recreate the navbar.

If you do want to edit your navbar, you can do so in Dreamweaver. Select Modify > Navigation bar from the Dreamweaver menu bar, and you'll get a dialog box in which you can change the image source for any of the button states.

The next thing we recommend doing with these new navbar files is renaming them (after you make backups). Therefore, we'd rename, say, `navbar_1.html` to `home_nav.html`, and `navbar_2.html` to `info_nav.html`. That makes the pages much easier to keep track of.

The next thing you do depends on how much you feel like learning yet another new tool at this point.

◆ You can save copies of these pages as templates to reuse over and over again. For example, you can save a template called info.dwt and a template called home.dwt, each of which would include its own version of the navbar. For more on templates, see Chapter 14.

◆ You can select a navbar, including all its JavaScript and images, and add it to Dreamweaver's library. You can add each individual version of the navbar to the library under a different name, so that one is called home_toolbar.lbi, another info_toolbar.lbi, and so on. To add an item to the library, select all the relevant code and select Modify > Library > Add Object to Library. The navbar will appear in the Library category of the Assets panel. You can update the library items if you add or remove buttons, and all the pages that use those navbars will also be updated. See Chapter 14 for an introduction to libraries and instructions on using the Update features.

◆ You can simply keep a blank version of the page and do a Save As each time you want a new page with that navbar on it.

◆ Or, you can cut and paste the navbar onto any page that wants to use it.

Let's look at the cut and paste option in detail, because for both this option and the library item option, you need to know what exactly to select.

For example, if the first button in your navbar is Home and the second is Info, you would do the following things to add the navbar to those two pages.

To paste the navbar into a non-frame page:

1. Open up the home.html page.

2. Open up the navbar_1.html file, or, if you've renamed your files, the home_nav.html page.

3. In the navbar_1 file, select the navbar (**Figure 18.25**).

   If the navbar uses tables, select the entire table. If the navbar buttons are not in a table, make sure you select all the relevant opening and closing a and img tags.

4. Copy the navbar, and paste it into the home.html file.

   The images and their attached code will be added to the home.html file (**Figure 18.26**).

5. Save home.html, and close both files.

6. Open the info.html file.

7. Open the navbar_2.html (or info_nav.html) file.

8. In the navbar_2 file, select the navbar (**Figure 18.27**).

9. Copy the navbar, and paste it into the products.html file. Dreamweaver, in all its demonic brilliance, will automatically paste the relevant JavaScript into the document head.

10. Repeat for each page.

This way obviously requires a lot more management of files, and if you change the structure of your site, you will need to edit each file to update the navbar. That's why, if you have the time or inclination to dig a little deeper into Dreamweaver, using Templates or Library items would be the key here. When something changes, you make the change to the Template file or Library item file, and from there you can update your whole site. Again, see Chapter 14 for more on this.

Figure 18.25 Copy the navbar graphics, including their links...

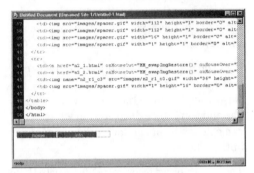

Figure 18.26 ...paste them, and the code comes too!

Figure 18.27 When you build a whole set of navbars instead of just one, you can copy them from page to page, or save multiple copies of the pages.

Other Fireworks Tricks

There are other ways you can use Fireworks to prepare images and HTML for Dreamweaver. Pop-up menus, for example, which we discussed in the *Creating a Cascading Menu* section of Chapter 13, can be created in Fireworks.

You can also insert any Fireworks-created HTML and image combination. From the menu bar, select Insert > Interactive Images > Insert Fireworks HTML.

See the Fireworks documentation for more ideas about what you can do with that application.

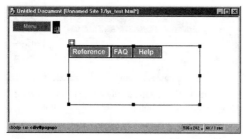

Figure 18.28 You can put in a layer any controls you want to hide.

Figure 18.29 You can hide the layer using the Vis drop-down menu in the Property inspector. (You can also use the eyeball buttons on the Layers panel.)

Pop-Up Layers

When designing a Web site, you might be tempted to give your visitors instant access to every single section and subsection of your site by splattering buttons all over the page. This can be very handy for an advanced Web user who wants instant access to everything, but often confusing for someone unfamiliar with the Web, or even just with your site.

One way to deal with this problem is to hide less-used controls until users specifically ask for them. You can do this by using hidden layers.

Because you can control the visibility of a layer through JavaScript, you can hide the controls until users click a button to call them up. We'll show you how to do this.

To hide controls in a pop-up layer:

1. Create a new HTML page (or open an existing one) in Dreamweaver.

2. From the menu bar, select Insert > Layer to add a layer to the page.

3. Add buttons or a toolbar or whatever controls you want to the layer (**Figure 18.28**).

4. In the Property inspector, name the layer popup.

5. From the Vis (visibility) drop-down menu in the Property inspector, select hidden (**Figure 18.29**). This will keep the layer hidden when the page loads.

continues on next page

POP-UP LAYERS

6. Select a clickable object on the page (such as an image, link, or form button).

7. In the Behaviors panel, click the + (plus) button and select Show/Hide Layer from the drop-down menu that appears.

The Show-Hide Layers dialog box will appear (**Figure 18.30**).

8. Click the Show button to set the layer to show, and click OK to close the dialog box.

9. Click the down arrow in the Events column of the Behaviors panel and select onClick from the drop-down menu that appears.

When you preview the file in a browser, you can pop up the controls by clicking on the object to which you attached the behavior (**Figure 18.31**). If you want, you can add another link to hide the layer.

✔ Tips

■ You can make the Show/Hide Layer behavior be triggered by the onMouseOver event, too.

■ Some objects, like Flash buttons and Flash text, don't live well in layers. You can give it a shot, but the layers don't always stay hidden or retain their size or position settings. For controls in a pop-up layer, you probably want to stick to images and plain old HTML.

Figure 18.30 Here, you specify which layer you want to show (or hide) when the user clicks the link.

Figure 18.31 Clicking on the image pops up the layer.

Figure 18.32 Here is a blank frameset.

Forms and Frames

Occasionally, you'll want to have a form in one frame that triggers an action in another frame. There are a number of ways to do this, but we'll show you the most common way, which uses JavaScript. The purpose of this basic demonstration is to show how targeting works between the form and the frame.

We'll make a simple form in one frame, with one text box and a button. When the page is loaded in the browser, the visitor can type a page name in the text box and click the button. Then, the form will load that file into the other frame. For our purposes, we'll limit the files to the current directory.

Additionally, for simplicity's sake, we'll use only the default names that Dreamweaver assigns for all the form and frame elements.

To change a frame using a form in another frame:

1. From the File menu, select New. The New Document dialog box will appear.

2. From the Category list, select Framesets.

3. From the Framesets list, select Fixed Top.

4. Click Create to create the new frameset (**Figure 18.32**).

5. Click in the top frame. From the menu bar, select Insert > Form.

continues on next page

6. From the menu bar, select Insert > Form Objects > Text Field.

7. From the menu bar, select Insert > Form Objects > Button.

8. Switch to Code view, and locate the code for the button.

9. After the `value="submit"` portion of the code (before the `>`), add the following line of code:

```
onClick="top.mainFrame.location.
→ href='./'+document.form1.
→ textfield.value"
```

The terms `mainFrame`, `form1`, and `textfield` are the default names that Dreamweaver gives to the bottom frame in a fixed top frameset, the first form you add to a page and the first text box you add to a page, respectively.

10. Click within the file and save the file as `getPage.html`.

11. Click in the second frame.

12. Save the frame (yes, it's blank). It doesn't matter what you save it as.

13. Click on a frame border to select the frameset file.

14. From the menu bar, select File > Save Frameset As and give it a name.

15. Open the file in your browser and type the name of a file in the same directory into the text box (**Figure 18.33**).

16. Click on the button, and the file you specified should appear in the bottom frame (**Figure 18.34**).

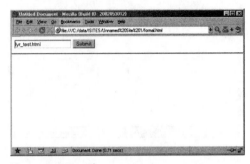

Figure 18.33 Specify a page to open.

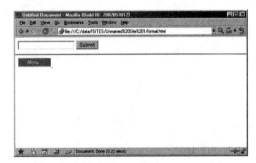

Figure 18.34 The file should appear in the bottom frame.

Other Interactive Gadgets

Dreamweaver provides a number of other interactive gadgets to help you make your site navigable. If your site is database-driven, for example, you should be able to populate a menu on the fly using dynamic text (see Chapter 5, *Dynamic Text and Recordsets*). Chapter 6 goes into more detail about dynamically created forms that can be tailored to a log-in name.

Additionally, Dreamweaver provides a form-based tool called Jump Menus, which is covered in detail in J. Tarin Towers' *Macromedia Dreamweaver MX: Visual QuickStart Guide*. You can provide a list of links in menu form that your visitors can use to jump to popular pages in your site.

In Chapter 13, *JavaScript and Dreamweaver Behaviors*, we touched on the possibilities of rollovers and using JavaScript to control user interaction. There are, however, many more ways to use those tools to make your site more interactive. Any user-driven event, as we've seen with a simple rollover, can make your site seem really high-tech and smart without much effort on your part.

And in Chapters 5 and 11, we not only showed you how to serve visible, text-and-media kind of data dynamically, but how to change the attributes of HTML tags from your database, so that you can change the colors, sizes, and CSS styles of objects on a page so that it responds to your visitors choices.

A final word on interactivity and interface design: A good design always includes breathing room. If you have pop-up layers and jump menus and Flash buttons and rollover images and frames that change other frames, it is very easy to confuse and overwhelm your visitor. Pick one or two methods of interaction and then stick with them.

CUSTOMIZING DREAMWEAVER

19

Dreamweaver is an extremely customizable program. In fact, it's very possible to render the program completely unrecognizable. You can change the toolbars, the menus, the floating panels—pretty much everything but the Macromedia copyright notice.

The key to customizing Dreamweaver is to have a solid understanding of JavaScript and XML. This is because a vast majority of Dreamweaver is written in JavaScript. But although that can have something of a negative effect on the program's performance and stability, it also means that if you know JavaScript, you can customize the program to fit perfectly with the way you work. (Just like Web pages have to wait for all their concomitant parts to load, so does Dreamweaver, which can make for occasional sluggishness and the occasional crash when you try to run conflicting scripts—that is, use conflicting features—at the same time.)

If you aren't familiar with JavaScript, you probably shouldn't read any further in this chapter. Or at least you shouldn't start significantly altering Dreamweaver. It's fairly easy to screw the program up, and much less easy to figure out what you did to break it.

In this chapter, we look at the Dreamweaver JavaScript Application Programming Interface (API), how it's organized, and the ways it lets you poke around the inner workings of Dreamweaver. We show you how to create custom menus and toolbars and how to edit existing ones. And we also show you how to create a new behavior. Finally, we let you in on some of the other ways you can customize Dreamweaver, once you are familiar with the API.

The Dreamweaver JavaScript API

The Dreamweaver JavaScript API is extensively documented in the Extending Dreamweaver Help file, but we'll hit the highlights here.

The API includes a document object model (or DOM) that is very similar to the W3C DOM used by Navigator and Internet Explorer. You can think of the DOM as something like a family tree (albeit a parthenogenetic one—that is, there's often only one parent). In this model, the DOM functions as the founding member, and several generations, or *children*, of the family are contained within it. The second generation includes the Forms and Images branches of the family, among others. These children of the DOM are usually called *nodes*. A third branch would include the attributes of some tags. For example, `name` and `target` are two children of the `a` tag.

The Dreamweaver DOM differs from the W3C DOM in that the Dreamweaver application oversees the relationships between documents. JavaScript sees the application as an object (called `dreamweaver`, or `dw`) that has a number of functions that can pass all sorts of useful information to the API. To get the document that is currently selected in the Dreamweaver document window, for instance, you would make the following call:

`dreamweaver.getDocumentDOM();`

This call returns a reference to a document, which you can then manipulate like any other JavaScript document object.

Enough setup, let's go on and actually change some stuff!

✔ Tip

■ If you want to cut and paste the scripts found in this chapter rather than typing them, you can visit the Web site for this book. See the back cover for our URL.

Customization Basics

In this chapter, we deal with some of the more sophisticated Dreamweaver customizations you can execute. For detailed information on some of the more basic things you can customize in the program, see the *Customizing Dreamweaver* chapter in J. Tarin Towers' *Macromedia Dreamweaver MX: Visual Quickstart Guide*.

The guide covers everything from arranging panels, adding custom objects, and editing menus, to changing keyboard shortcuts.

About Configuring Dreamweaver for Multiuser PCs

In a multiuser environment such as Windows NT, Windows XP, or Mac OS X, you may want to modify the configuration files only for your user name, and not for the entire computer. (Older operating systems such as Mac 9.x and Windows 98, and Windows ME don't use user-configuration folders; they use the application copies for every user and so don't rely on multiple configuration folders.)

In some cases, you may not even have permission to write or change the files in the central configuration folder. In any event, it's probably a wise move, even if you're the only user on your multiuser machine, to make copies into your user folder before working with them. Once you create those files—or Dreamweaver does, unbeknownst to you—Dreamweaver will default to them and those files will override the ones in the program folder.

Dreamweaver will, in fact, automatically make a copy of the main configuration file and copy it to your user folder if you change a keyboard shortcut, for example.

If you are a superuser, you can modify the files in the following location; or, you can copy these files into your user folder:

◆ **PC:** `C:\Macromedia\Dreamweaver MX\Configuration`

◆ **Mac OS X:** `Macintosh HD: Applications: Dreamweaver MX: Configuration`

If you only want to modify files for a single user, you go here instead:

◆ **Windows 2000/XP:** `C:\Documents and Settings\[User Name]\Application Data\Macromedia\Dreamweaver MX\Configuration`

◆ **Windows NT:** `C:\WinNT\profiles\[User Name]\Application Data\Macromedia\ Dreamweaver MX\Configuration`

◆ **Mac OS X:** `Macintosh HD:Users:[User Name]:Library:Application Support: Macromedia:Dreamweaver MX:Configuration`

If you accidentally change something you shouldn't have, or if you get in trouble for "improving" someone else's workspace, you can find backups in the `Configuration-1` folder—but of course you won't need them because you made your own backups for everything, right?

THE DREAMWEAVER JAVASCRIPT API

Creating a Command

Let's look at how to create a simple command that you can call either from a menu or a toolbar. We'll create a simple text-editing function that makes whatever text is selected lowercase.

This command is a slightly modified version of the one found in the Extending Dreamweaver Help file. It's an HTML file comprising two parts: a <head>, where we'll put the JavaScript functions that do the actual work for the command, and a <body>, where we would put a dialog box if the command needed one, which it doesn't.

The command has two functions. The first, called canAcceptCommand(), is what Dreamweaver uses to decide whether the command should be enabled. The second, changeToLowerCase(), does the actual work of changing the text to lower case. (The Dreamweaver DOM contains this command because it's used to format HTML tags in the user preferences and when applying the Commands > Apply Source Formatting option.)

We want the command to be enabled in a menu or toolbar when the user has a document open and has selected some text. So we'll test for those two conditions.

To create the enable/disable function:

1. Open a new HTML file.

2. Delete whatever Dreamweaver put there, and add the following code: ⟶

   This code lets Dreamweaver know it's part of a command file and that we're about to add some JavaScript. Strictly speaking, we don't need the <title>, but if we wanted to add a dialog box later (so the user could choose all upper or all lower case, for example), it would be easier if the dialog box were labeled.

Script 19.1

```
                        script

1    function canAcceptCommand(){
2        var theDOM = dw.getDocumentDOM();
3        if (theDOM == null) return false;
4        var theSel = theDOM.getSelection();
5        var theSelNode =
    ⇢ theDOM.getSelectedNode();
6        var theChildren =
    ⇢ theSelNode.childNodes;
7        return (theSel[0] != theSel[1]
    ⇢ && ((theSelNode.nodeType ==
    ⇢ Node.TEXT_NODE) || (theChildren[0]
    ⇢ != null && theChildren[0].
    ⇢ nodeType == Node.TEXT_NODE)));
8    }
```

```
<!DOCTYPE HTML SYSTEM "-
 ⇢ //Macromedia//DWExtension
 ⇢ layout-engine 5.0//dialog">
<HTML>
<HEAD>
<TITLE>Make Lower Case</TITLE>
<SCRIPT LANGUAGE="javascript">
```

CREATING A COMMAND

3. Type the function you see in **Script 19.1**.

Let's look at the code line by line. In Line 1, we declare the function. Dreamweaver looks in the command file for a function called `canAcceptCommand()` when the user clicks on the menu. If the function returns true, then the command is enabled. If it returns false, then the command should be disabled (grayed out).

In Line 2, we use the special `dw.getDocumentDom()` function, which asks Dreamweaver to give us a reference to whatever document is currently open, or, if there is more than one document open, to give us the one the user is currently editing.

In Line 3, we test to make sure that there is actually a document open. If not, there's obviously no text selected for us to change, so the command should be grayed out.

Once we have a document reference, or DOM, we can use it to find out what's selected, by using the `getSelection()` function on Line 4.

In Line 5, we again use the document object to get the selected node. A *node* is a construct of the DOM, but for our purposes, we can think of it as the set of tags surrounding a place in the document (in this case, the selection).

In Line 6, we get the children of the selected node. We do this because the current node could be a form (which is not a text node), for example, but the form can contain text.

Line 7 does the actual checking. First, it looks to make sure the selection beginning and end are not the same, which would mean there is nothing actually selected. Then, it checks to see if either the current node or its first child exists and is of type `Node.TEXT_NODE` (which means they contain text). If both those things are true, it returns true and the command is enabled. Otherwise, it returns false and the command is disabled.

Now that we've added the code to enable or disable the command when appropriate, let's look at how to use this document to make selected text lowercase.

✔ Tip

■ This function doesn't work perfectly. In some cases, it isn't active when it should be. Rather than take 50 pages of this book explaining the special cases and the ins and outs of the W3C DOM (which is hundreds of pages long), we are simply erring on the side of caution.

To actually change the content of the text:

♦ After the previous function, add the code you see in **Script 19.2**.

We start this function by declaring it in Line 1, and then by getting a reference to the user document in Line 2, just like we did in the previous function.

And like we did in the previous function, we get the selection In Line 3. The selection is an array of two numbers: the number of characters from the beginning of the file that the selection begins, and the number of characters after the beginning of the file that it ends. Note that the number of characters is looking at the code, rather than the text of the file.

In Lines 4 and 5, we also get the `documentElement`. This corresponds to the `<html>` tag in the document. The `docEl.outerHTML` is everything inside the `<HTML>` and `</HTML>` tags, plus those tags themselves. We need to get exactly this because it's what the selection is based on.

In Line 6, we get the actual selected text and assign it to the `selText` variable.

In Line 7, we take all the HTML before the selection, add to it the selected text, smash the selection into lower case, and Dreamweaver takes all the HTML after the selection and replaces all the HTML in the document with it. This has exactly the effect we are looking for, which is that nothing changes except for the text that was selected.

Finally, in Line 8 we set the selection back to what it was originally and then end the function.

In its current state, this second function will never be called. So we need to add the rest of the code to finish up the file. This way Dreamweaver can parse it so that the function actually will be called.

Script 19.2

```
1   function changeToLowerCase() {
2       var theDOM = dw.getDocumentDOM();
3       var theSel = theDOM.getSelection();
4       var theDocEl = theDOM.
          documentElement;
5       var theWholeDoc = theDocEl.outerHTML;
6       var selText = theWholeDoc.
          substring(theSel[0],theSel[1]);
7       theDocEl.outerHTML = theWholeDoc.
          substring(0,theSel[0]) +
          selText.toLowerCase() +
          theWholeDoc.substring(theSel[1]);
8   theDOM.setSelection(theSel[0],
      theSel[1]);
9   }
```

Pasting Code vs. Typing Code

You can find many of the code blocks like the ones we print in this chapter on the companion Web site for this book (`www.peachpit.com/vqp/dreamweaver` MX). That way, you won't have to type everything over again if you don't want to.

```
</SCRIPT>
</HEAD>
<BODY onLoad="changeToLowerCase()">
</BODY>
</HTML>
```

To finish up the file:

◄— **1.** Add the following code to the file:

2. Save the file as make_lower_case.htm.

Let's take a closer look at what we just did. In the first and second lines, we ended the script block that we started at the beginning of this section, as well as the head tag we opened.

In the third line, we start the body section, and add the onLoad() function, which calls the function we declared earlier in the document head.

Because we don't want a dialog box, we leave the body blank in the fourth line, just ending it and the HTML (in the fifth line).

That's all there is to creating a custom command. Next we'll look at how to put it in a menu and then in a toolbar.

CREATING A COMMAND

431

Adding Commands to a Menu

Dreamweaver's menus live in a file called menus.xml. This file is located in what we'll call the Dreamweaver menus folder:

◆ **Windows:** C:\Program Files\ Macromedia\Dreamweaver MX\ Configuration\Menus\

◆ **Macintosh:** Macintosh HD:Applications: Macromedia DreamweaverMX: Configuration:Menus:

Note: if you're running Dreamweaver on a multi-user machine, even if you're the only user, see the sidebar *About Configuring Dreamweaver for Multiuser PCs* to find out the location of your user files and why you should edit those.

The menus.xml file contains all the menus that Dreamweaver uses, keyboard shortcuts assigned to each menu item, and JavaScript code that Dreamweaver uses to determine whether a menu item is enabled or not (**Figure 19.1**).

We won't get into all the details of the tags that menus.xml uses. There is an overview in the *Macromedia Dreamweaver MX: Visual Quickstart Guide*, and there is a file available for download from the Macromedia Dreamweaver Support Center at www.macromedia.com/support/dreamweaver. Search this section for more detail about the menus.xml tags.

To get a sense of how you add commands to a menu, let's add the command we created in the previous section to the Dreamweaver menus. This involves copying the command file into a place where menus.xml can see it, and actually editing the menus.xml file.

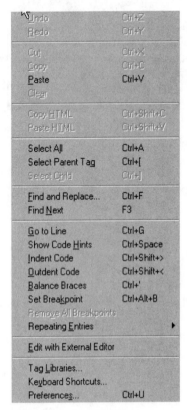

Figure 19.1 Undo and Redo are not enabled. Paste, on the other hand, is.

To add the command to the menu:

1. There is a subdirectory within the Dreamweaver menu folder called MM. This is where most of the command files are located. Copy the `make_lower_case.htm` file into this directory.

2. In the Dreamweaver menus folder, make a backup copy of the `menus.xml` file.

3. *With a program other than Dreamweaver,* open the `menus.xml` file.

   If you try to edit the `menus.xml` file in Dreamweaver, you can crash the program, because it'll be looking for the menus in that file. You can use any text editor that can handle long files. Wordpad for Windows and BBEdit for the Mac are good choices.

4. Because the command changes text, we'll add the command to the end of the Text menu. In your text editor, search for `menu name="_Text"`.

   This will bring you to the very beginning of the Text menu, which is roughly four-fifths of the way down the file.

5. We'll add the command to the very end of the Text menu. Scroll down until you see the `<menuitem name="Chec_k Spelling"` line.

6. After that line, add the following one:
   ```
   <menuitem name="Make _Lower Case"
   → file="Menus/MM/Make_Lower_Case.htm"
   → id="VQP_Make_Lower_Case" />
   ```
   We'll examine this line in detail in a moment.

7. Save the `menus.xml` file.

8. If Dreamweaver is open, close it.

9. Open Dreamweaver.

10. Test the menu item.

    It should be active when there is a document open and text is selected (**Figure 19.2**) and grayed out otherwise (**Figure 19.3**).

Let's look at that line we added in Step 6. The first portion, `<menuitem name="Make _Lower Case"` is the name that will appear in the Text menu. The underscore before the L indicates the menu accelerator key, for Windows users.

The next portion of the line is obviously the file where the command is located. The final portion is where we add a unique ID for the menu command. In XML, when the tag has no contents, it takes a space before the closing slash.

Now that we've seen how to create a menu command, we'll look at how to create a custom toolbar and add the command to it.

Figure 19.2 Here our new command is enabled.

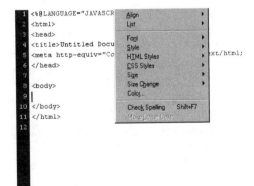

Figure 19.3 Here it is disabled, because we have no text selected.

Creating a Custom Toolbar

Toolbars work similarly to menus, and their commands are compatible with menu commands as well, which is convenient for our purposes, because we can make use of the Make Lower Case command we created in the previous exercise.

We'll be making a toolbar with one button on it. As you might imagine, that button will trigger our command.

But before we start creating the toolbar, we need to make a button for our command. Actually, we need to make two buttons: one for when the command is active, and one "grayed out" button for when the command is disabled.

You can make the buttons in any program you want, but it's best to make them small. They can also be in any image format that Dreamweaver can display (GIF, JPEG, PNG).

For our purposes, we made a couple of .GIF files in Photoshop and named them lower.gif and lower_dis.gif (**Figure 19.4**). We saved them in a VQP directory that we created, the full path of which is

On the Macintosh, that path would be

✔ Tip

■ All the command files and images we're creating could be stored in any folder inside the configuration folder. They're easier to find, though, if you organize them sensibly.

We could create a new toolbar in one of two ways. We could add a toolbar to the toolbars.xml file or we could create a new file for our new toolbar. We'll do the latter, because there's less chance of screwing up the built-in toolbars that way.

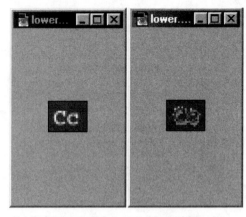

Figure 19.4 Our enabled and disabled buttons.

```
C:\Program Files\Macromedia\
→ Dreamweaver MX\Configuration\
→ Toolbars\Images\VQP\
```

```
Macintosh HD:Applications:
→ Macromedia DreamweaverMX:
→ Configuration:Toolbars:Images:VQP:
```

Script 19.3

```
                    script
1    <?xml version="1.0"?>
2    <!DOCTYPE toolbarset SYSTEM "-//Macro-
     → media//DWExtension toolbar 5.0">
3    <toolbarset>
4    <toolbar id="VQP_toolbar" label="VQP">
5    <button id="VQP_Make_Lower"
     → image="Toolbars/Images/vqp/lower.gif"
     → DisabledImage="Toolbars/Images/vqp/
     → lower_dis.gif" update="onSelChange"
     → tooltip="Make Lower Case"
     → file="Menus/MM/make_lower_case.htm" />
6    </toolbar>
7    </toolbarset>
```

Figure 19.5 Ooh! Our toolbar shows up.

To create a custom toolbar:

1. In a text editor, create a new file.

2. Type the code you see in **Script 19.3**.

3. Save the file as VQP_toolbar.html in the Configuration/Toolbars folder.

4. Close Dreamweaver if it's open, then start the program again.

   Your toolbar will show up (**Figure 19.5**).

Lines 1 and 2 of this code include the toolbar header stuff, which you can just copy into any new toolbar you create.

Line 3, <toolbarset>, tells Dreamweaver that you're going to be defining some toolbars.

Line 4 contains the declaration of a toolbar. Here we give it a unique id, and specify what to call it.

Line 5 contains the complicated part of this code. Here we are defining a control on the toolbar—in this case, a button. As with all the new objects we define, we gave it a unique ID and then specified the enabled and disabled images. We also add a tooltip to help the user know what the little incomprehensible button means. Finally, we specify the file that contains the command code. Sounds easy enough; however, one of the difficult aspects of writing this part of the code lies in figuring out when to check if the button should be active. If you check too often, Dreamweaver will grind to a halt. If you check too rarely, the button will be active when it shouldn't be. In this example, we're checking only when the selection changes.

Lines 6 and 7 are XML cleanup code.

In addition to buttons, you can have color pickers, menus, checkboxes, and many other interface elements in a toolbar. See the Extending Dreamweaver Help file for the full list.

You're probably tired of making things lower case by now. Fortunately for you, we're finished with that command. Next, we'll look at how to create a custom behavior.

CREATING A CUSTOM TOOLBAR

Creating a Custom Behavior

If you know JavaScript and have quite a bit of patience, you can create your own behaviors. The process is a little more involved than creating a custom toolbar or menu, but it can be quite useful when you've finished.

In this section, we'll show you how to create a custom behavior to check that two password fields are the same. This is most useful for user registration pages, where you want to make sure the user has entered the password she thinks she has.

A behavior defined

Like a command, a behavior consists of an HTML file with a mess of JavaScript. Behaviors have a number of required JavaScript functions that interact with the Dreamweaver interface.

At the very minimum, a behavior must insert into the target document a function and an event handler.

Like commands, the HTML document of the behavior contains a form in which the user can specify the parameters for the behavior.

How to create a behavior

We'll walk you through creating a behavior, but you should know a couple of things. Because behaviors are fairly tightly coupled with the Dreamweaver interface, it's relatively easy to crash Dreamweaver while working on them. Therefore, you should create your own behaviors only if you know what you're doing, at least as far as JavaScript goes.

You should also be familiar with the W3C (World Wide Web Consortium) object model, because Dreamweaver is based on it. The DOM documentation is at `http://www.w3.org/TR/REC-DOM-Level-1/`.

Finally, unlike menus, you can work on behaviors within Dreamweaver itself. If your behavior kicks up an error at any time, however, you'll have to quit and restart Dreamweaver to apply it again, even if you have fixed the problem.

Now, on to the coding.

To create the Confirm Password behavior:

1. Open a new HTML document.

2. Delete anything that's in the document, or, if you feel comfortable, edit the stuff so that it looks like what's in Step 3.

3. At the top of the document, type the following code:

   This block mainly identifies to Dreamweaver the kind of document it is, with the exception of the `<title>` tag. The title of the document is what shows up in the Behaviors panel, as well as the title bar in the dialog box.

```
<!DOCTYPE HTML SYSTEM "-
→ //Macromedia//DWExtension
→ layout-engine 5.0//dialog">
<html>
<head>
<title>Confirm Password</title>
<meta http-equiv="Content-Type"
→ content="text/html">
```

4. Add the following line:

   This code is one of Macromedia's helper scripts that lets you dynamically set the options of a drop-down form menu.

```
<SCRIPT
SRC="../../Shared/Common/Scripts/
→ ListControlClass.js">
</SCRIPT>
```

5. Now begin the script block by declaring the one global variable we'll use:

```
<script language="JavaScript">
var theMenu;
```

6. Add the first function:

   This relatively modest function is what does the actual checking of password fields. It just takes two fields and compares them to see if the contents match. If not, it throws up an error message, and then clears the second field and puts the cursor in it.

```
function compareFields(field1,
→ field2) {
  if (field1.value != field2.value) {
  alert("Your password does not match
  → your confirmation");
  field2.value = "";
  field2.setFocus();
  }
}
```

continues on next page

7. Now add the second function: ————————▶

The second function is required for all behaviors. It determines whether the behavior is enabled or disabled (**Figure 19.6**) in the Behaviors panel menu, depending on what's selected and what the document contains. It also specifies the preferred event(s) for the behavior.

In this case, we checked the selected object to make sure it's an element (i.e. a tag). And then we checked to see if it's an <input> tag and if it's a password field. If all those conditions are true, we return onBlur, which is the event handler that makes most sense to use. If all those conditions aren't true, we return false, because we want the behavior to be active only when a password field is selected.

```
function canAcceptBehavior()
  {
  var theDOM = dw.getDocumentDOM();
  var selObj = theDOM.
  → getSelectedNode();
  if (selObj.nodeType ==
  → Node.ELEMENT_NODE && selObj.
  → tagName == "INPUT" && selObj.
  → getAttribute("type").
  → toUpperCase() == "PASSWORD" )
  → return "onBlur";
  return false;
  }
```

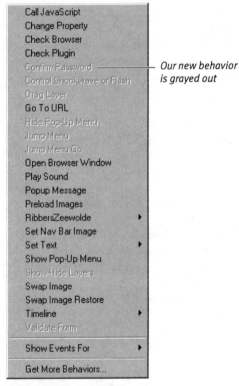

Our new behavior is grayed out

Figure 19.6 Our behavior is disabled because we don't have a password selected.

```
function behaviorFunction()
  {
  return "compareFields";
  }
```

```
function applyBehavior()
  {
  var theDOM = dw.getDocumentDOM();
  var firstField = theMenu.
  → getValue();
  var secondField
  → = dw.getElementRef("NS 4.0",
  → theDOM.getSelectedNode());
  return
"compareFields("+firstField+",
→ "+secondField+")";
  }
```

8. Add the third function:

This is a required utility function for all behaviors. It tells Dreamweaver which function to paste into the top of the document. If you have multiple functions that need to be added, you can return a string that looks something like:

```
return "func1,func2";
```

9. And the fourth:

This is the function that puts the event handler in the document. Note that we build the function call as a string, because that's the way the HTML document and JavaScript expect it. This is another required function.

continues on next page

CREATING A CUSTOM BEHAVIOR

10. Now add the function you see entered in **Script 19.4**.

This is by far the largest function in the behavior, but ironically, all it does is populate the drop-down menu in the behavior dialog box with a list of the password fields in the document. We'll walk through it so that you get a good sense of what it's doing.

The first few lines are variable declarations. One thing to notice is that we are setting the value of the global variable **theMenu** to a **ListControl** object, which references the drop-down control in the HTML form in the behavior's dialog box (it'll come, don't worry!). This allows us to make changes to the drop-down menu dynamically, which are then reflected in the menu.

We are making one potentially faulty assumption here when we set the variable **theForm** to the parent of the selected node: that the selected password field is a child node of the form. This will usually be true, unless the password field is in a table inside a form, for example. We'll leave sorting that thicket out as an exercise for you in your spare time.

Next, in the first **for** loop, we step through all the elements in the form and look to see if they are passwords. Any passwords are converted to JavaScript objects and added to the **passList** array. See the sidebar *DOMinating JavaScript* for some notes on this conversion.

In the second **for** loop, we step through the array we just created and add each element to the **ListControl** object, which adds it to the drop-down menu in the form. Dreamweaver doesn't seem to report the name of the password fields correctly, so we get the name from the JavaScript object name of the element.

Script 19.4

```
     script

1    function populateMenu()
2    {
3      theMenu = new
       → ListControl("firstestField");
4      var theDOM = dw.getDocumentDOM();
5      var selObj =
       → theDOM.getSelectedNode();
6      var theForm = selObj.parentNode;
7      var allElements = theForm.childNodes;
8      var i, tmp;
9      var passList = new Array ();
10     for (i=0;i<allElements.length;i++)
11     {
12         tmp = allElements.item(i);
13         if (tmp.nodeType ==
           → Node.ELEMENT_NODE &&
           → tmp.tagName == "INPUT" &&
           → tmp.getAttribute("type").
           → toUpperCase() == "PASSWORD" )
           → passList.push(dw.getElementRef
           → ("NS 4.0", tmp));
14     }
15     for (i=0;i<passList.length;i++) {
16         tStr = passList[i].toString().
           → split(".");
17         uStr = tStr[tStr.length - 1];
18         theMenu.append(uStr,
           → passList[i].toString());
19     }
20   }
```

```
</script>
</head>
<body>
Please select the field to confirm
→ the selected field against.
<form name="theForm" method="post"
→ action="">
   <select name="firstestField"
   → id="firstestField"
   → onFocus="populateMenu()">
      <option value="x">**no password
      → fields**</option>
   </select>
</form>
</body>
```

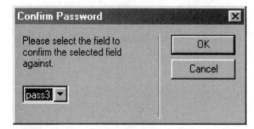

Figure 19.7 Our custom dialog box.

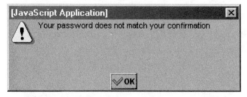

Figure 19.8 Here's what happens when the passwords don't match.

11. Finally, we end the script and actually put the form into the document:

Here we're adding some instruction text, and then we're creating a form with only one item, a <select>, or drop-down menu item. We have assigned the onFocus method to trigger the populateMenu function. Because it's the first control in the form, the firstestField drop-down gets the focus automatically.

We also put a placeholder menu item in, in case something goes wrong.

Note that in addition to the controls we have specified, behavior dialog boxes always contain an OK and a Cancel button.

12. Now you can save the file. Save it as Check Password.htm in the Configuration/ Behaviors/Action folder.

13. Now you can test it! Quit and restart Dreamweaver, then create a form with more than one password field.

14. Select one of the password fields and click the plus (+) button in the Behaviors panel.

15. From the drop-down menu, select Check Password.

The Check Password dialog box will appear (**Figure 19.7**).

16. Select a field to compare it with and click OK to apply the behavior.

17. Test it out! (**Figure 19.8**)

We'll close this chapter by looking at some of the other ways you can customize and extend Dreamweaver.

DOMinating JavaScript

We often talk about the Document Object Model as if it were a JavaScript thing. It's not, exactly, although the way JavaScript sees the various parts of browser and Dreamweaver documents follows the DOM specification pretty closely.

The thing to realize is that when you deal with a node, that's a construct of the DOM and doesn't necessarily correspond to a JavaScript object. Or rather the nodes are JavaScript objects, they're just not necessarily the ones you expect.

The first thing that you'll find useful if you're working on customizing or extending Dreamweaver is to read the W3C DOM specification, which is available on the web at `http://www.w3.org/TR/REC-DOM-Level-1`.

The second useful thing to know about is a Dreamweaver function called `dreamweaver.getElementRef()`. This allows you to convert a DOM node reference into a JavaScript tag object.

With a little bit (OK, maybe a lot) of trial and error, you will get a sense of how the DOM and JavaScript interact.

Other Things We Could Cover If This Book Were 800 Pages Long

As we have discovered, the JavaScript API allows you access to many of the nooks and crannies of Dreamweaver's interface and functionality. We have only scratched the surface in this chapter, however. We'll touch briefly on some of the other ways you could customize the program.

Floating panels

You can roll your own custom panels. So, for example, you could create a panel that lists the node you have selected and its place in the DOM object hierarchy.

Custom reports

You can create custom site reports. This would allow you to, for example, do a word count for Backstreet Boys on your Marketing to Preadolescents web site, or get the average image size for your site. You could even do things like have a report that checks for adherence to specific accessibility standards.

Code Hints

You can change the content of the Code Hints that pop up when you're editing certain kinds of code.

Property inspectors

You can create custom Property inspectors for specific kinds of objects. So if you had a custom mapping plug in, for example, you could create a custom Property inspector to set its properties.

Things in the 1,900 page range

There are too many ways to customize Dreamweaver to even just list here. All the database integration functions are fair game, and you can even change the way Dreamweaver and Fireworks interact.

Check the Extending Dreamweaver Help file for a more complete list of the things you can customize or add.

The Dreamweaver Exchange Web site has a growing collection of additions people have created for Dreamweaver. You can get there by choosing Dreamweaver Exchange from the Help menu in Dreamweaver. Using other people's creations as your basis for learning, you can install the custom panels they've made, adjust them, and get ideas for your own.

OTHER THINGS WE COULD COVER

WORKFLOW & COLLABORATION

We got acquainted with the Site window in the first few chapters of this book—it's a great built-in FTP tool in which you can also manage local files across all your local sites. Dreamweaver MX also offers tools that can better your experience working with coworkers, workgroups, or even just working by yourself over different computers.

Dreamweaver's collaborative features include file check-in and check-out, which is a low-tech way of identifying who is working with which files. You mark the files you're working on with your name and e-mail address, and your coworkers will know not to make changes to a file that someone else is working on.

Design Notes are another nifty feature that helps you track characteristics of specific files or folders. You can mark files as "in progress" or with version numbers, or you can customize Design Notes and flag specific pages with comments. When Design Notes were introduced in their nascent form in Dreamweaver 3, they were difficult to manage, not very flexible, and they carried no visual flag in the Site window, so it was damn nigh impossible to actually use them. Now, they're much more user friendly, and they allow for some innovative site management shortcuts.

Using Design Notes, you can also customize the columns in the site window, so that you can sort files according to, for example, a version number or a file check-out name. Additionally, you can run site reports to find all files carrying specific Design Notes flags.

And finally, we'll show you the basics of setting up Dreamweaver to work with some popular content management or workflow programs, such as RDS, SourceSafe, and WebDAV.

✔ Tips

- To use any of the features in this chapter, you must first define a local site. If you have any sites listed in the Site window, you've already done this (**Figures 20.1** and **20.2**). A local site is a folder designated within the Dreamweaver environment as the one that holds all the in-progress and completed files for a specific Web site. You may also define a remote site, also known as a production server; and a testing server, which is recommended for sites that use an application server.

- To define a local site, see *Defining a Local Site and a Testing Server* in Chapter 2.

- For tips on working with files in the Site window, see *Using the Site Window* and *Local Site 411*, both in Chapter 2.

- To define a remote site, which you need to do in order to upload files to a live site, see *Additional Remote Server Setup* in Chapter 2. You must define a remote site before you can use file check-in and check-out, described in the next section.

- You do not need to use file check-in and check-out in order to upload files. To upload a file, a folder, or a batch of files to a remote site, select the pertinent icons in Local view and click on Put 🔼. To download files from a remote site to your computer, connect to the site, select the files you want, and click on Get 🔽.

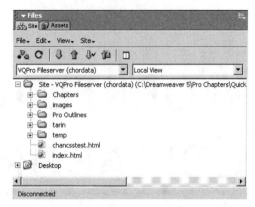

Figure 20.1 The Site window, in local view on a PC. You must define a local site before you can use Dreamweaver's site management tools.

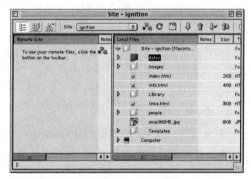

Figure 20.2 On the Mac, the Site window shows Local view on the right and Remote view on the left.

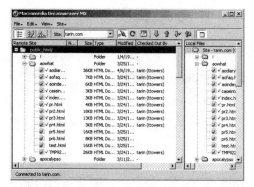

Figure 20.3 The files with checkmarks have been checked out; you can see the check-out names in the Checked Out By column.

Using Names to Check Files In and Out

If several people are collaborating on a site, it might be helpful to know who put which file where, and when they did it. (If there are only one or two of you, you should already know the answer.)

Checking out a file locks it on the remote server and allows you to edit it locally, while a flag appears on it (a red checkmark) that says to others, "Can't Touch This." Checking in a file unlocks it on the remote server, but makes it read-only on your local site so that you don't accidentally edit a file that is not checked out.

Think of it like a library book: When you check out a book, no one else can borrow it until you return it. When someone else checks out a book, you can't check it out yourself. When you or the other person checks the book (or the file, really) back in, anyone can access it.

Checking out a file marks the file with a green checkmark, assigns your username to that file, and locks it in the Dreamweaver Site window. Other team members who use Dreamweaver will not be able to overwrite locked files (files checked out by another person). These files can be overwritten by any other FTP client, however. File check-out in Dreamweaver is a simpler, user-based, and less secure approximation of CVS checkout, a Unix-based tool used in production groups.

Files other people have checked out are marked in the Site window with a red checkmark, and the person's check-out name appears in the Checked Out By column in both the local and remote panes (**Figure 20.3**).

Setting up file check-in

Before you can check files in or out, you must enable that option in the site's definition.

To enable check-in and check-out:

1. From the Site window menu bar, select Site > Edit Sites. The Edit Sites dialog box will appear (**Figure 20.4**).

2. Select the site for which you want to set check-in and check-out options, and click on Edit. The Site Definition dialog box will appear.

   If the Basic tab is selected, click Advanced to show those options. (We don't need to click through a wizard at this stage in the game, do we?)

3. In the Category box at the left, select Remote Info. That panel will move to the front of the dialog box (**Figure 20.5**).

4. To enable check-in and check-out, click that checkbox. More options for file check-in will appear (**Figure 20.6**).

5. If you want to mark all files as checked out when you open them in the Document window, check the Check Out Files When Opening checkbox.

   We suggest unchecking this option until you get used to maneuvering uploads and downloads within Dreamweaver. Otherwise, every time you open a file, it will retrieve it from the remote server, and this may end up being more annoying than helpful. On very clean site setups, however, this may come in handy.

6. Type the name you want others to see when you check out files in the Check Out Name text box. This can be your full name or your username, or it can be a personal designation such as "My Laptop."

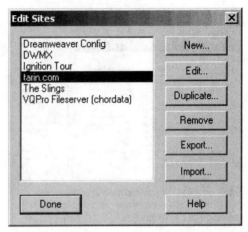

Figure 20.4 Choose which site's check-in preferences to modify in the Edit Sites dialog box.

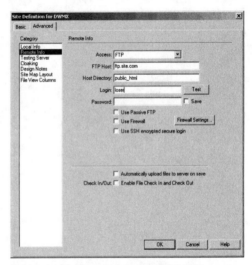

Figure 20.5 The Remote Info panel of the Site Definition dialog box, before file check-in is enabled.

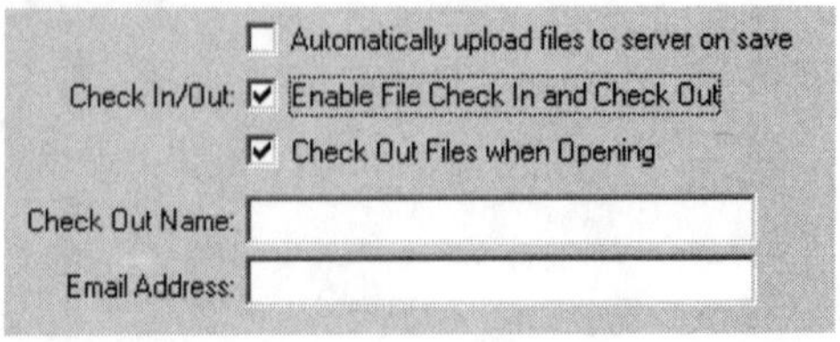

Figure 20.6 Check the Enable File Check In and Check Out checkbox (that's a lot of checks) to show setup information for using this feature with remote files.

Figure 20.7 Check-out names, if they've been entered with e-mail addresses, appear as clickable links in the Site window. The checkout name schlomo appears with the user's name, ttowers@sirius.com, but if the entered e-mail address is different, that e-mail address will appear when the link is clicked.

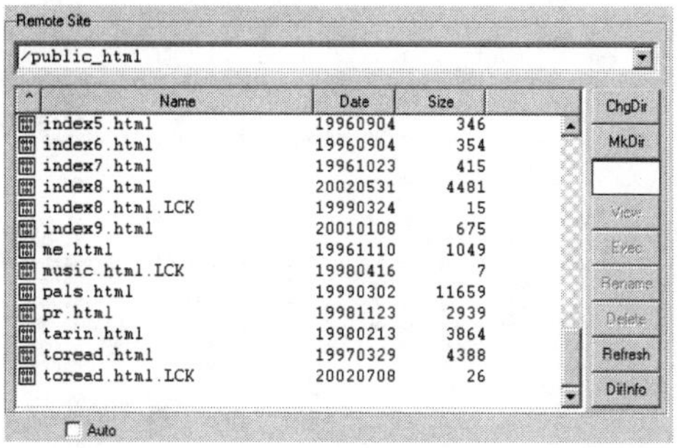

Figure 20.8 You can see the .LCK files if you examine the site with an FTP client other than Dreamweaver's. (This is WS_FTP for Windows.)

About .LCK Files

When you check out a file using Dream-weaver, a lock is placed on the file in the Dreamweaver Site window. This lock is a text file with the .LCK extension. .LCK files are invisible in the Dreamweaver Site window, but you can see them in a different FTP client (**Figure 20.8**).

An .LCK file contains the username of the person who checked it out. This file also shows the date and time of the checkout in the time stamp.

You can see the date and time of a .LCK file in most FTP clients in the date and time column. The .LCK files we examined were only 7 bytes each (there are 1000 bytes in 1 kilobyte), so they aren't going to make you run out of server space any time soon.

7. If you want colleagues to be able to contact you about checked-out files, type your full e-mail address in the Email Address text box. (See Tips, below.)

8. Click on OK. Now, each time you retrieve a file from the remote server, it will be marked as checked out, and each time you upload a file, it will be marked as checked in.

✔ Tips

■ If you decide to access your files from a different computer and find you cannot perform an upload because the files are checked out, you can still upload or download them by using a different FTP client, such as Telnet/CVS, WS_FTP, Fetch, or Cute FTP.

■ Even if you work alone, you might want to use these features. For instance, if you work on two different machines, you can use check-out names such as PC and Mac, or Home and Work, so you'll know where the latest version is hiding.

■ If you're using the Check In/Out feature to prevent others on your team from overwriting each other's work, make sure they are using Dreamweaver to manage their FTP sessions. If they work with another FTP program, however, they will see Dreamweaver's .LCK file listed after the checked-out file. If you let them know what this means, they can open the .LCK file, see the checkout name, and contact you to find out whether they can work on the file.

■ If you use a valid e-mail address in the Site Definition dialog box, your name will appear as a link in the Checked Out By column in the Site window (**Figure 20.7**). Just like with a `mailto:` link in the browser window, other users will be able to click the link and pop open an e-mail message window in their default e-mail client. Your e-mail address will be supplied, and the name of the file will appear in the subject line.

Checking Out Files

When file check-in is enabled, you'll see two new buttons on the Site window (**Figure 20.9**), one for checking in and one for checking out. You can use these just as you do the Get and Put buttons described in the introduction to this chapter—although if you use the same old buttons, files will still be checked in and out with your name.

To check out one remote file:

1. Connect to the appropriate site in the Site window.

2. Select the file in the Remote Site panel (**Figure 20.10**).

3. Click on the Check Out button 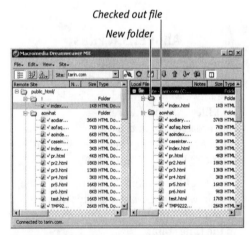.

4. Respond to the Dependent Files dialog box (see Tips, below).

The file (and its folder, if necessary) will be copied to the local site (**Figure 20.11**). To open a file on checkout, see Tips, below.

You may have to refresh the Local site view to see the file (or its folder, if that was freshly created, too).

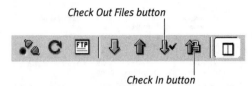

Check Out Files button

Check In button

Figure 20.9 The toolbar on the Site window will include two new buttons after you enable file check-out.

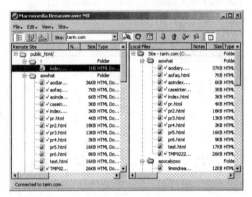

Figure 20.10 Select the file you want to check out in the Remote Site pane.

Checked out file

New folder

Figure 20.11 The file and its folder were both copied to the local site, and the file appears with a green checkmark—indicating you yourself checked it out—in the remote site pane.

✔ Tips

- You can double-click on a remote file in the Site window to open the file in the Document window. Dreamweaver will download the file, but it will not mark the file as checked out. Any changes you make in the Document window will be saved to the local copy, and you'll need to upload (or check in) the page when you're done.

- If you already have a local copy of the file you want to check out, a dialog box will appear asking if you wish to overwrite your local copy (see the upcoming Figures 20.15 and 20.16). Click Yes to download a new copy, or click No and the file will not be transferred.

About Dependent Files

Dependent files include images, JavaScript files, media elements, and CSS documents. When you check out or check in a page (or when you get or put a file without file check-in enabled), you

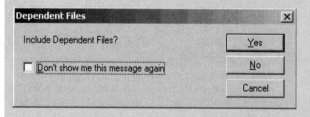

can choose to simultaneously transfer these files in the Dependent Files dialog box by clicking Yes. Click No to upload only your selected files, or Cancel to think about it for a minute. Check the Don't show me this message again checkbox to permanently dismiss this tool.

If you dismiss the dialog box and you decide one day it's useful and you want it back, you can set preferences for it in the Site category of the Preferences dialog box. Once there, you can set separate preferences for dependent files for upload (put) and download (get).

To check out more than one file:

1. Select the files or folders you want to check out in the remote site (**Figure 20.12**).

2. From the Document window menu bar, select File > Check Out (Site > Site Files View > Check Out on the Mac), or click on the Check Out button.

3. Respond to the Dependent Files dialog box.

The files will be transferred to the local site (**Figure 20.13**). The files will get a green checkmark and a .LCK file on the remote server. Your check-out name will appear in the Checked Out By column.

To undo a file check-out:

◆ After checking out the files, select File > Undo Check Out (Site > Site Files View > Undo Check Out) from the Site window menu bar.

If you get a dialog box advising you that files will be overwritten, you can say Yes, No, or Yes or No To All. See Figures 20.15-20.16, next page.

Red checkmarks   Files selected for check-out

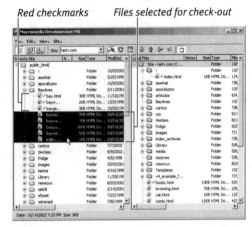

Figure 20.12 This time, we're selecting multiple files. The other files in this folder have been checked out by someone else—if this image were color, you'd see that the checkmarks are red.

Checked out files

Refresh button   New folder

Figure 20.13 After refreshing the site view, the new folder and the files we checked out appear in the local site pane.

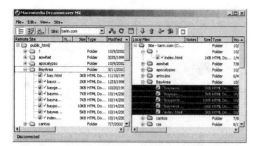

Figure 20.14 We updated the files that were checked out earlier, and now we're going to check them back in.

Figure 20.15 You may get a dialog box like this if you try to overwrite a newer, single file, either when checking in or checking out.

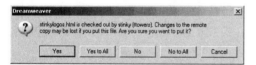

Figure 20.16 You may get a dialog box like this if you try to overwrite a batch of files.

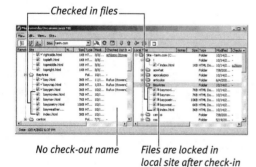

Checked in files

No check-out name *Files are locked in local site after check-in*

Figure 20.17 We checked the files back in, and now there's no name in the Checked Out By column. When files have been checked into the site, they appear locked in the Local pane of the Site window. That's because you're supposed to check out a file before you edit it locally.

Checking In Files

After you've finished working on a file, you can check it back in. That means two things: you're uploading the current version back up to the live site (or the staging server), and you're freeing up the file so others can work on it.

To check in files:

1. In the local site, click to select the files or folders you want to check in (**Figure 20.14**)

2. From the Document window menu bar, select File > Check In (Site > Site Files View > Check In on the Mac). Or, click on the Check In button 🗃.

3. Respond to the Dependent Files dialog box, as well as the overwrite query dialog box in **Figure 20.15** or **20.16**, if one appears.

The file will appear with a locked icon on the local site. The Checked Out status will be removed from the remote server and your name will disappear from the Checked Out By column (**Figure 20.17**).

453

✔ Tips

■ When you check a file back in, it gets locked on your local machine, and a little lock 🔒 will appear instead of a checkmark. That's because Dreamweaver safeguards the file so that you can't work on it unless you check it out first. If you need to work on a locked file you've checked in, and it hasn't changed, and you don't want to bother checking it out again, just unlock it. From the Document window menu bar, select File > Turn Off Read Only (Macintosh: Sites > Site Files View > Turn Off Read only). You can also select Turn Off Read Only from the File Management menu on the Document toolbar.

■ You can also check files in and out while you're working on them, if need be. On the Document toolbar, select Check In or Check Out from the File Management menu (**Figure 20.18**). Files that you check in will be saved automatically before they're put up on the remote site. Remote files that you check out will *overwrite* your work in the Document window. On the other hand, you can also double-click a file in the remote site, examine it in the Document window, and then check it out.

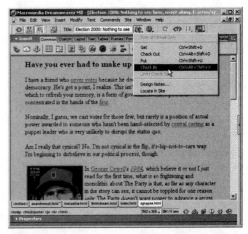

Figure 20.18 You can check in a file while you're working on it, but then it'll lock. You can always select Turn Off Read Only from the same menu to keep working on it.

Figure 20.19
Design Notes let you leave love notes for your Web design team. These files are managed each in their own dialog box, where you can enter status, dates, comments, and other data about a file.

Figure 20.20
Choose your local site in the Edit Sites dialog box. If you haven't set up a local site yet, turn to Chapter 2 for instructions on how to do so.

Figure 20.21
Enable Design Notes by checking the first box in the Design Notes category of the Site Definition dialog box. If you want to share Design Notes and File View Columns, select the Upload Design Notes for Sharing checkbox.

Setting Up Design Notes

Design Notes (**Figure 20.19**) allow you to save workflow information about a file in an attached file—they're discrete XML/text documents. That means you can save non-public information along with a file, rather than saving it as a comment *inside* a file. Using Design Notes, you can flag files that need attention, keep track of who's worked on a file, and store notes regarding just about anything.

In order to use Design Notes, you need to enable the use of them with your local site.

To enable Design Notes:

1. From the Site window menu bar, select Sites > Define Sites. The Define Sites dialog box will appear (**Figure 20.20**).

2. Click on the name of the site for which you want to enable Design Notes.

3. Click on Edit. The Site Definition dialog box will appear.

4. In the Category box at the left, click on Design Notes. That panel of the dialog box will appear (**Figure 20.21**).

5. If the Maintain Design Notes checkbox is checked, leave it alone. If it's unchecked, check the box to enable Design Notes.

6. If everyone in your workgroup is using Dreamweaver to produce a site, you may want to upload Design Notes along with their files. To enable automatic uploading of Design Notes, check the Upload Design Notes for Sharing checkbox.

✔ Tips

- If you're working alone on a project or if your group isn't using Dreamweaver as a team, you should make sure to uncheck the Upload Design Notes for Sharing checkbox, or the server will be cluttered with files useless to everyone but you.

- On the other hand, if you want to keep notes on more than one machine, by all means, share them with yourself.

- To disable Design Notes, follow the steps above and then uncheck the Maintain Design Notes checkbox. See *Turning Off Design Notes* later in this chapter, for details on what this does.

SETTING UP DESIGN NOTES

Extending Design Notes

As we said at the beginning of this chapter, Design Notes have improved greatly since their initial implementation in Dreamweaver 3.

Although you can't use Find and Replace with Design Notes or export only those files that use them, you can run a site report that lists Design Note properties. Site reports and other cleanup tools are covered in Chapter 11.

Fireworks, Macromedia's image editing program, also uses Design Notes. The source files in Fireworks are PNG files; when you export a PNG as a GIF, for example, Fireworks creates a Design Note that lists the name and location of the original PNG file.

If you're a developer, you can use XML and JavaScript to extend Dreamweaver to include a Design Notes inspector or to use a status flag in a Design Note to change tags within a file. You can also write extensions to site reports that search on specific HTML tags as well as on Design Notes. If you're not a developer, check the Macromedia Exchange (Help >Macromedia Exchange) to see if other users have implemented Design Note extensions.

Where Are The Files?

The first time you create a Design Note, Dreamweaver creates a folder called _notes. Unfortunately, there isn't one central folder—Dreamweaver creates a _notes folder for each separate location of each separate file. For instance, if you create a Design Note for a page in the site root folder, and then another note for an image in the /images folder, Dreamweaver creates a _notes folder in each place.

What's more, the _notes folders are not visible using the Site window; to open the folder, you need to use your regular file manager (Windows Explorer or the Finder).

Inside the _notes folder, each Design Note is named for its file, plus an additional extension, .MNO (Macromedia Notes). So if your file is called calendar.html, the Design Note will be called calendar.html.mno.

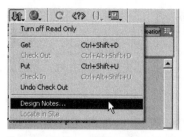

Figure 20.22 Access Design Notes for the current page by selecting Design Notes from the File Management menu on the toolbar.

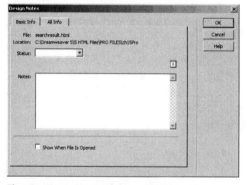

Figure 20.23 Leave notes for yourself or your coworkers in the Design Notes dialog box.

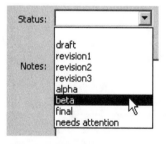

Figure 20.24 Select an option from the status menu. To add a status value that doesn't appear on this menu, see Step 7 and use Status as the Name.

Using Design Notes

A Design Note is basically a hidden text file that stores information about another file. You can use Design Notes not only with Web pages, but also with images, multimedia files, CSS or HTML style sheets, library items, templates, and any other file in your local site.

To create a Design Note:

1. Select the file you want to notate in the Site window, or open it in the Document window. Then, select File > Design Notes from the Site window menu bar or the Document window menu bar.

   You can also select Design Notes from the File Management menu on the toolbar (**Figure 20.22**).

   Either way, the Design Notes dialog box will appear (**Figure 20.23**), displaying the name of the file and its site path/location.

2. The Status drop-down menu allows you to flag a file with the following labels: draft; revision 1, 2, or 3; alpha, beta, or final; or needs attention (**Figure 20.24**). You may select any or none of these.

continues on next page

3. To stamp the current date in the Design Note, click on the Date button above the vertical scrollbar in the Notes text box. Today's date will be printed in the Notes text box.

4. Type any additional notes in the Notes text box.

5. To have Dreamweaver pop open the Design Notes whenever the file is opened, check the Show When File Is Opened box.

6. To add specific notes to be used consistently from file to file, click on the All Info tab to make that panel of the dialog box visible (**Figure 20.25**).

7. To add a new note, click on the + (plus) button. In the Name and Value text boxes, type the information, such as "Project" and "Intranet," "Due" and "[Date]," or "Author" and "vlad" (Figure 20.25).

8. When you're done, click on OK to close the dialog box and save your Design Notes.

✔ Tip

■ You can create file view columns to use with the custom fields you create in Step 7. See *Adding File View Columns,* later in this chapter.

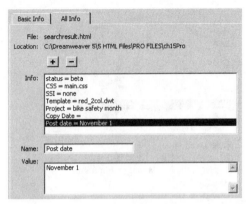

Figure 20.25 Add formatted notes (name=value) in the All Info tab of the Design Notes dialog box. These are some examples of names and values you might find useful.

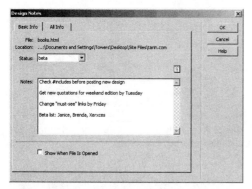

Figure 20.26 The Design Notes dialog box displays information we saved earlier about the progress of the page.

Accessing Design Notes

Opening a Design Note for a Web page or other file is similar to creating one. You open the same Design Notes dialog box, and then you can read and edit the Design Notes.

To open a Design Note:

1. In the Site window, select the file whose Design Notes you want to read.

2. From the Site window menu bar, select File > Design Notes.

   or

   Double-click the Notes icon 💬 next to the filename in the Site window.

   (On Windows machines, you must expand the Site window to view the column for Notes, where you'll see the icon for any files that use them.)

Either way, the Design Notes dialog box will appear (**Figure 20.26**).

You can also open notes for a page in the Document window by selecting Design Notes from the File Management menu on the Document toolbar (see Figure 20.22).

Now you can read, update, or edit the notes.

Cleaning Up Design Notes

After you delete a file, Dreamweaver does not automatically delete its associated Design Notes. You can clean up orphaned Design Notes easily.

To clean up Design Notes:

1. From the Site window menu bar, Sites > Edit Sites. The Edit Sites dialog box will appear.

2. Click on the name of the site for which you want to clean up Design Notes.

3. Click on Edit. The Site Definition dialog box will appear.

4. In the Category box at the left, click on Design Notes. That panel of the dialog box will appear (**Figure 20.27**).

5. Click on the Clean Up button. A dialog box will appear (**Figure 20.28**) asking you if you really want to do that. Click on Yes.

6. Dreamweaver will remove all orphaned Design Notes from the selected site.

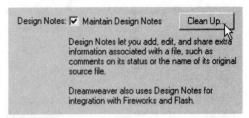

Figure 20.27 A close-up of the Design Notes panel of the Site Definition dialog box.

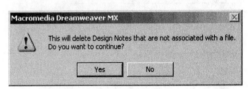

Figure 20.28 After we clicked on Clean Up, this dialog box asked us if we were really sure we wanted to clean up and delete the orphaned files.

Figure 20.29 If you have File View Column sharing enabled, Dreamweaver will warn you that turning off Design Notes will turn off the columns.

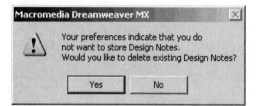

Figure 20.30 You can now choose whether or not to delete all Design Notes after you disable maintaining them.

Turning Off Design Notes

Before you disable Design Notes, keep in mind:

♦ When you disable Design Notes, Dreamweaver can remove notes and _notes folders from your site.

♦ When Design Notes are disabled, you cannot use Personal or Shared File View Columns, and you cannot use any Site Reporting features that include Design Note properties. We cover using both these functions in detail later in this chapter.

To disable and delete all Design Notes:

1. Follow Steps 1–4 in the previous list.

2. Uncheck the Maintain Design Notes checkbox. If you have File View Column Sharing enabled, a dialog box will appear (**Figure 20.29**). Click on OK.

3. Click on OK to close the Site Definition dialog box and save your changes. Another dialog box will appear, asking you if you want to delete Design Notes (**Figure 20.30**). Click on Yes to delete them or No if you want to keep them around.

Modifying Columns in the Site Window

In the Site window in Dreamweaver MX, you can add or remove columns, called *File View Columns*. You can hide columns you don't use, and you can also create columns that are associated with particular Design Notes attributes.

✔ Tip

■ On Windows machines in Dreamweaver MX, the column headers are visible only if you expand/undock the Site window, as seen in the figures in this chapter. When the Site window is docked as a panel, only file and folder names are shown.

To show or hide an existing column:

1. From the Site window menu bar, select Edit Sites. The Edit Sites dialog box will appear.

2. Select the site for which you want to define new columns, and click on Edit. The Site Definition dialog box will appear.

3. In the Category box at left, select File View Columns. That panel of the dialog box will appear (**Figure 20.31**).

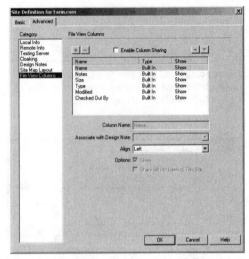

Figure 20.31 The File View Columns panel of the Site Definition dialog box allows you to rearrange and hide columns, as well as add new ones.

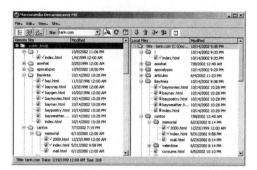

Figure 20.32 Here, we've hidden all but the Name and Modified columns.

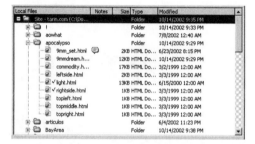

Figure 20.33 This is standard text alignment in the Sites window (local view only, in this figure). To see more or less of what's in a column, you can experiment with rearranging alignment options. Note that the Notes column has Center alignment set, but it still looks like left alignment.

4. Six built-in columns are displayed by default in the Local view of the Site window. These are: Name (filename), Notes (a note icon appears for pages with Design Notes; only shown when Design Notes are enabled), Size (file size), Type (file type, such as HTML or GIF), Modified (date last changes were saved), and Checked Out By (check-out name; only shown when file check-in is enabled).

   To show or hide any of these columns (except Name) or a column you create yourself, check or uncheck the Show checkbox in the options area of the dialog box. **Figure 20.32** shows the Site window with all but the Name and Modified fields hidden.

5. You can also change the alignment of the text in a column. **Figure 20.33** uses default alignment settings. The Name column is set to Left, so that the beginning of the filename shows; the Notes column is set to Center, so that Notes icons are centered in that column; and the File Size column is set to Right, so that the numbers line up with the file size. You can change any of these.

To reorder columns in the Site window:

1. In the File View Columns panel of the Site Definition dialog box, select the name of the column you want to move to the right or left in the Site window.

2. To move the column (**Figure 20.34**), click on the Up arrow to move it to the left or the Down arrow to move it to the right (Figure 20.31).

✔ Tips

- One quirk of Design Notes is that if you set only an option that is matched with a column, you will not see an icon for the Design Note. That is, once you create a "Status" column, a Design Note that carries only information for "Status" will not also get flagged with a little 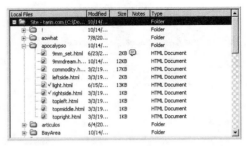 doohickey. Design Notes do get icons if you *type* anything at all in the text boxes. See *Adding File View Columns* for an example of tagging flags in the Site window, including "Status," to specific Design Notes settings.

- After you add personal columns to your site, you can of course rearrange them, show them and hide them, and so on.

Figure 20.34 Here, we've rearranged the standard columns.

MODIFYING COLUMNS IN THE SITE WINDOW

Figure 20.35 Click on the + (plus) button to create a new column in the Sites window.

Figure 20.36 We've added a Status column, in which the labels correspond to status settings in Design Notes on this site.

Figure 20.37 Here we've added a brand-new column called SSI, which corresponds to custom settings we added in the All Info section of Design Notes. SSI, in case you're wondering, refers to server-side includes, and these settings are the name of the include the file uses.

✔ Tip

- In the Associate With Design Note drop-down menu (Figure 20.35), the fields listed include assigned, due, and priority, but these are only suggestions—first off, they don't yet exist until you add them to a Design Note, and second, you can add your own names by typing them in the text box. Other ideas for columns include author names, include or template names, style sheet version names, and weekly or daily site sections. See *Using Design Notes*, earlier in this chapter, to find out how to create these fields and make them available to all Design Note files in your site.

Adding File View Columns

Not only can you show or reorder existing columns, you can add your own columns to the Site window. These columns can display Design Note details, such as the status of a file or other custom fields that you create.

To create a new column in the Site window:

1. Design Notes must be enabled in order for you to add personal or shared columns. See the preceding sections on setting up and creating Design Notes.

2. Follow steps 1–3 under *To show or hide an existing column* earlier in the chapter to display Site View Column details in the Site Definition dialog box.

3. Click on the + (plus) button. A new Personal column called *untitled* will appear (**Figure 20.35**).

4. Type the display name for the column as you want it to appear in the Site window in the Column Name text box.

5. To associate the column with a Design Note field, select it from the Associate With Design Note menu. Not all these fields are already in the Design Notes; see Tip, below. If you have not yet created the field in your Design Notes, you can go ahead and type it in the text box and create it later.

6. To set alignment of the text in the column, select Left, Center, or Right from the Alignment menu.

7. Click on OK to close the Site Definition dialog box and add the column to the Site window.

In **Figure 20.36,** we've added the Status column, which will now display the status we've set for files with Design Notes. In **Figure 20.37**, we've created a new Design Note category called SSI and added a column for it.

Sharing Columns

If you've created a handy column and you want your coworkers or your other machines to be able to use it, you can share the column information.

To share column information:

1. Create a new column, as described above.

2. In the File View Columns category of the Site Definition dialog box, check the Enable Column Sharing checkbox (**Figure 20.38**).

   If you have not previously enabled Design Note sharing in that category of the site definition, a dialog box will appear asking if you wish to do so (**Figure 20.39**). Click on OK.

3. In the File View Columns panel of the Site Definition dialog box, select the column you created.

4. Check the Share With All Users of This Site checkbox. The column Type will change to Shared (**Figure 20.40**).

5. Click on OK to close the Site Definition dialog box and share the column with other users.

The next time your colleagues connect to or refresh their view of the Site window for the selected site, they'll see the new column and the new data (**Figure 20.41**). They can hide this column if they don't want to use it. Keep in mind that anyone can edit or add columns—they can't rearrange the columns in your window, but they can add and rename any Shared column on this site.

✔ Tip

■ You can enable column sharing before you create any columns. In the Design Notes category of the Site Definition dialog box, check the Upload Design Notes for Sharing checkbox.

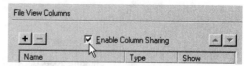

Figure 20.38 Check the Enable Column Sharing checkbox to upload your Design Notes containing file view column information.

Figure 20.39 If you haven't yet enabled uploading of Design Notes and you want to share columns, this dialog box will ask you to turn on that option.

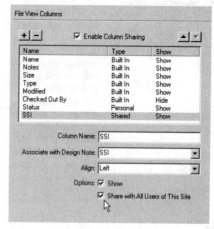

Figure 20.40 When you select the Share With All Users of This Site checkbox, the column type will turn from Personal to Shared, and those columns marked as shared will be uploaded.

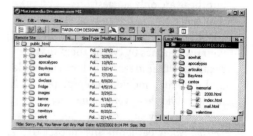

Figure 20.41 Users who share access to this site will see the columns we added, Status and SSI, on both their local and remote site. They can hide the columns if they want to.

Editing personal or shared columns

You can delete a column, rename one, or associate it with a different Design Note field at any time. If this is a shared column, the change will affect all users who share Design Notes on your site.

To edit a column:

1. In the File View Columns panel of the Site Definition dialog box, select the name of the column to edit. You cannot rename or delete a Built In column.

2. To delete the column, click on the - (minus) button.

3. To rename the column, type a new name in the Column Name text box.

4. To associate the column with a different Design Note, select a new note from the Associate With Design Note menu, or type a new name.

Using Site Reports with Design Notes

Site reports, which were described in Chapter 11, allow you to run a check on your site that looks for specific characteristics. The report then gives you a list, in the Results panel group, of all pages in your local site that have the criteria you specified.

In the Site Reports dialog box (Site > Reports) you can run a check for all files that use Design Notes, but you cannot specify other search parameters for Design Notes. You can, however, search only a specific folder for Design Notes.

You can search for a specific check-out name. Check the Checked Out By checkbox, and then click on Report Settings and type the name you're looking for. See Chapter 11 for more on running, saving, and using site reports.

Using Dreamweaver with Content Management

Content management systems, affectionately known as CMS, can be a godsend to large workgroups that are trying to keep track of who touched what file when and whether it's ready for primetime. You must already have these tools installed in order to use them. (We bet you knew that.)

The following systems, which Dreamweaver supports, may not be called CMS in your workplace, but we're placing them under this rubric because they all serve as intermediaries between your local machine and your Web server. Dreamweaver MX supports WebDAV, RDS, and the Visual Source Safe database.

Using WebDAV

WebDAV (pronounced Web Dave) stands for the Web-based Distributed Authoring and Versioning protocol. It's an open standard that's basically an extension of the standard HTTP Web server protocol, and the system allows users to track and edit remote files from their local machines. WebDAV is designed to promote collaboration and accountability.

Many free and commercial products are available for working with WebDAV, including tools for Apache and Microsoft IIS. Once you have WebDAV installed, you (and your colleagues) can mount a WebDAV drive on your desktop as if it were an AppleTalk or local network machine, and then browse and open the files and folders on a remote Web server just as easily as on your own hard drive.

Using WebDAV instead of standard FTP provides stronger security and interoperability features not available with FTP (such as authentication, encryption, proxy support, and caching). Using WebDAV with Dreamweaver shows the contents of the WebDAV drive in the Remote pane of the Site window.

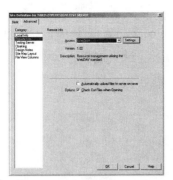

Figure 20.42 Select WebDAV from the Access drop-down menu in the Site Definition dialog box.

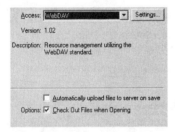

Figure 20.43 A close-up of the options for WebDAV. You can set check-out options like the ones described earlier in this chapter.

Figure 20.44 In the WebDAV Connection dialog box, specify the URL for the Web server that uses WebDAV.

✔ Tips

- To find out more about installing and using WebDAV, visit www.webdav.org.

- Other products offer WebDAV integration, include Adobe Acrobat, Microsoft Office and Internet Explorer, Mac OS X, and content management software such as Vignette and Documentum.

Setting up WebDAV

When you work with WebDAV using Dreamweaver MX, you set up your remote connection so that WebDAV is your remote site, rather than your FTP or local network server.

To set up your remote site info to work with WebDAV:

1. Open the Site Definition dialog box for the appropriate local site.
   If the Basic tab is in front, click on Advanced.

2. In the Category list, select Remote Info.

3. From the Access drop-down menu, select WebDAV. The dialog box will change appearance (**Figure 20.42**).

4. To set up automatic file check-out with Dave, select that checkbox (**Figure 20.43**).

5. Click on Settings. The WebDAV Connection dialog box will appear (**Figure 20.44**).
   The URL may use local server info, but it must include both the protocol and the port number for Dave. An example would be http://staging/WebDAV/home.
   Your username and password must be those you use with that server. Your e-mail address will be attached to your WebDAV check-out name and will appear with your files in the Checked Out By column of the Site window.

6. Click on OK to save your settings, and OK again in the Site Definition dialog box. You're all ready to go. You can use Get, Put, and all the other features as usual, except you're using them with Dave's help.

Using Visual Source Safe Databases with Dreamweaver

Microsoft Visual Source Safe is a version control system for all sorts of code, including HTML, scripts, and images. It's a content-management database that supports file sharing, branching, and merging, makes backups of source code, and prevents more than one user from accessing a piece of code at one time (thereby rendering each other's work either redundant or incomplete). VSS is particularly handy, according to Microsoft, if you're working with chunks of ASP.NET code.

Dreamweaver MX emulates VSS client version 6 and can be used with version 5. Use with the Mac is not supported in MX (see Tip, after the list below).

When you work with VSS using Dreamweaver, you set up your remote site information so that VSS is your remote site, rather than your FTP or local network. The contents of the VSS database will appear as the files and folders in the remote pane of the Site window.

To set up your remote site info to work with VSS:

1. Open the Site Definition dialog box for the appropriate local site, and click on Advanced if the Basic version is showing.

2. In the Category list, select Remote Info.

3. From the Access drop-down menu, select SourceSafe Database. The dialog box will change appearance (**Figure 20.45**).

4. To check-out files from VSS when you open them, select that checkbox (**Figure 20.46**).

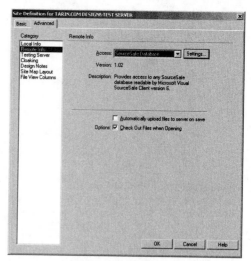

Figure 20.45 Select SourceSafe Database from the Access drop-down menu in the Site Definition dialog box.

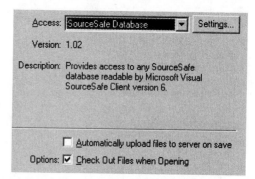

Figure 20.46 A close-up of the options for Visual SourceSafe. You can enable Dreamweaver's file check-out and automatic upload, if you wish.

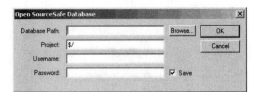

Figure 20.47 In the Open SourceSafe Database dialog box, specify the location of the VSS database file.

5. Click on Settings. The Open SourceSafe Database dialog box will appear (**Figure 20.47**).

6. In the Database Path text box, type the address of the VSS database, or click Browse to select the database file. This file is the `srcsafe.ini` file used to initialize SourceSafe when you connect using the Site window.

7. In the Project text box, type the name of the VSS Project that you want to use as the root folder for your remote site.

8. The username and password you enter must be those you use to log in to VSS. To save your password, select that checkbox.

9. Click on OK to save your settings, and OK again in the Site Definition dialog box.

You're all ready to go. You can use Get, Put, and all the other features as usual, except you're using them on VSS.

✔ Tip for Mac Users

■ Dreamweaver MX no longer directly supports use with Visual SourceSafe on the Macintosh, and Microsoft no longer produces a Mac OS version of SourceSafe. However, it's possible to fudge use of VSS by setting up FTP or Local/Network information to reflect the location of the VSS server rather than the regular Web server—of course, your mileage may vary. To work with VSS on the Mac, you must have the MetroWerks SourceSafe client and ToolServer tools, and you can work with VSS version 5.0, but not 6.0. Visit `www.metrowerks.com` for downloads and information. Dreamweaver 4 supports use of VSS with Mac using the 1.1.0 client.

Using RDS with ColdFusion Server and Dreamweaver

RDS, remote development services, is a protocol used with ColdFusion servers. RDS is similar to WebDAV in that it is based on the HTTP protocol (rather than FTP), and it allows the user remote interaction with the files, folders, and databases on a ColdFusion server.

If you use RDS with Dreamweaver, you work directly with the files on the server, and the files in your local site folder can be considered to be merely locally stored back-up copies of the existing pages you're managing, rather than the files you operate with until you upload.

Additionally, setting up RDS information to work with the ColdFusion server allows you direct access to the ColdFusion server files not only in the Site window but in Dreamweaver's other application server tools, such as the Databases panel.

To set up Dreamweaver to work with RDS:

1. Open the Site Definition dialog box for the appropriate local site, and click on Advanced if the Basic version is showing.

2. In the Category list, select Remote Info.

3. From the Access drop-down menu, select RDS. The dialog box will change appearance (**Figure 20.48**).

4. To check-out files from RDS when you open them, select that checkbox (**Figure 20.49**).

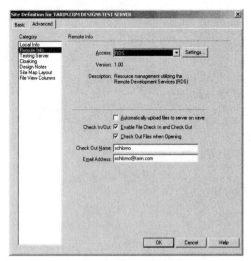

Figure 20.48 Select RDS from the Access drop-down menu in the Site Definition dialog box.

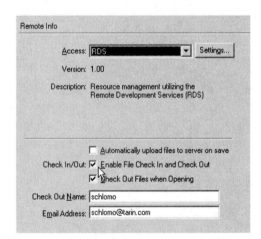

Figure 20.49 A close-up of the options for RDS. You can enable Dreamweaver's file check-out and automatic upload, if you wish.

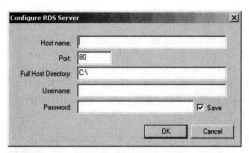

Figure 20.50 In the Configure RDS Server dialog box, specify the host name of the server using RDS, as well as your user information.

5. Click on Settings. The Configure RDS server dialog box will appear (**Figure 20.50**).

6. In the Host name text box, type either the IP number or the URL of the ColdFusion server.

7. In the Port text box, set the port number you communicate with. For HTTP, this port is 80, but check with your administrator if you're not sure.

8. In the Full Host Directory text box, type the full address of the remote root directory that contains your files. An example is c:\server\www\hostdirectory.

9. The username and password information here can be tricky—the options you complete here basically vary based on how the server security is set up.
   - If you have a username and password, go ahead and type them.
   - If you are running ColdFusion server locally, these options may not appear at all; don't worry about it.
   - If you do not have a username, or if you connect using a DSN, you can specify only the server password. If you have neither a username nor a password but connect as part of a "user group" you can try leaving these options blank; otherwise, contact the administrator and have them set up or provide a password for you.

10. Click on OK to save your settings, and OK again in the Site Definition dialog box. You're all ready to go. You can use Get, Put, and all the other features as usual, except you're using them to interact with the ColdFusion server using RDS as the intermediary.

Ye Olde Microsoft RDS

RDS, which in the world of Microsoft stands for remote *data* services, is an interoperability platform originally designed to manage live data in Access or Visual Basic databases by allowing the user to manage the data using forms in a Microsoft Web browser. Like the RDS used with ColdFusion, it's basically just an intermediary way for an administrator to interact with a database.

Microsoft RDS permits interaction with local or remote ODBC database connections and is particularly useful for managing ASP data.

RDS can be considered a precursor to Web services, and it also allows insertion of recordsets onto Web pages by defining the data strings as MIME types, similar to plug-ins (remember ActiveX, anyone?).

Microsoft has deprecated RDS and may remove it from future releases of its Microsoft Data Access Components (MDAC). However, its constituents are big fans, even though the tool is optimized for use with Internet Explorer 4.0 and doesn't work precisely the same way with later versions.

(Those of you who are more familiar with single-user software packages may be surprised to know that people who run servers don't necessarily upgrade every time something new comes down the pike, because if you find something you like in the data-management world, it's generally easier and better to stick with the known-and-liked quantity than to build your systems all over again, unless there's a serious security risk.)

Engineers who have decided to replace RDS components usually do so using a combination of XML Web Services and either ASP.NET server-side controls or the Microsoft SOAP toolkit. Of course, if you wanted to change horses completely, you could commit to ColdFusion and its own, not-too-dissimilar RDS.

INDEX

INDEX